ames, a significant at   women o   1874. D
he first women's rega   tta i   1849   elia
t St. Andrew's.   187   ield creates the sport of modern
ll Saunders defeated Rose   in the first U.S. women's boxing match.   1876—
England Croquet & Lawn Tennis Club holds its first national women's championships a
ale student body.   1887—Softball is introduced as a safer alternative to baseball for
renson introduces basketball to American women at Smith College.   1893—British
founded.   1894—McGill University allows female students to play hockey amongst
Vassar holds the first all-terrain track meet.   1895—   er publishes the
en is held in Berlin.   1896—The first modern Olympics founded by the Baron de
ame is held.   1900—Women's tennis debuts as a part of the second modern Olympics
   1901—*Hockey Field*, the first women's sports magazine is published.   1902—Madge
—Ladies gymnastics debuts as an exhibition sport at the Olympics.   1905—Amanda
b is founded in England.   1910—Annette Kellerman is arrested for swimming in the
even-year-old Sonja Henie competes in the first women's figure-skating event.   1916—
s the first woman elected to the U.S. Congress.   1919—World War I ends with the
20—American women compete in an Olympic swimming competition for the first time
e Feminine International (FSFI), creating venues for women to compete outside of the
923—The Women's Division of the National Amateur Athletic Foundation is founded.
arate Summer Olympics are held in Paris.   1926—Gertrude Erdele breaks the world-
on sponsors the first national basketball championship.   1928—The Olympics in
mnastics competition is held for men.   1929—The stock market crashes, marking the
Gehrig in an exhibition game and soon after is the first woman to sign a contract with a
ams disbands after three strong decades of play.   1932—Babe Didrikson wins six track
ny. She went on to win two golds and a silver in the Olympics.   1934—The first World
ers are invited to compete in the Olympics.   1936—The original American Olympic
a black woman competes.   1937—Tuskegee Institute wins the AAU Nationals in track
esents the Aquacades, showcasing swimming stars Eleanor Holm and Esther Williams.
ics are canceled due to World War II.   1944—The All-American Girls Professional
ssive 5'6.25", Alice Coachman is the first black woman to win an Olympic gold medal.
e Ladies Professional Golf Players' Association (LPGA) is formed, after the Women's
ack champion of Wimbledon.   1952—Baseball commissioner Ford Frick bans women
dual gymnastics competition for women.   1952—Women are invited to ride in dressage
en.   1953—Toni Stone signs a contract with the Indianapolis Clowns, becoming the
essional Baseball League folds after several declining years.   1956—Women are once
.   1960—Wilma Rudolph becomes the first female track and field athlete to win the
ted.   1961—Billie Jean King wins the first of a record twenty Wimbledon victories.
irplane crash on the way to the world championships in Prague.   1963—Betty Friedan
a holdover from the Women's Division, endorses the Olympics for the first time.

Nike
IS A
GODDESS

NIKE IS A GODDESS

The History of Women in Sports

Edited by Lissa Smith

Introduction by Mariah Burton Nelson

ATLANTIC MONTHLY PRESS
New York

Published simultaneously in Canada
Printed in the United States of America

FIRST EDITION

Library of Congress Cataloging-in-Publication Data
Nike is a goddess : the history of women in sports / edited by Lissa
    Smith ; introduction by Mariah Burton Nelson.
        p.   cm.
    ISBN 0-87113-726-7
    1. Sports for women—United States—History.   2. Sports for women—
Social aspects—United States.   3. Women athletes—United States—
History.   I. Smith, Lissa.
GV709.18.U6N55 1998
796'.082'0973—dc21   98-27049
                                                                    CIP

Design by Laura Hammond Hough

Atlantic Monthly Press
841 Broadway
New York, NY 10003

98 99 00 01   10 9 8 7 6 5 4 3 2 1

*For my mother Mary Jane and my father Gilbert
who gracefully coach me through the world;
and to my God-given teammates, Gil, Ramie, and Carrie
who play life's games with such style and soul.*

*For Yo-Yo, who is winning the
toughest of life's games.*

CONTENTS

INTRODUCTION:
WHO WE MIGHT BECOME
Mariah Burton Nelson

The story of women in sports is a personal story, because nothing is more personal than a woman's bone, sinew, sweat, and desire, and a political story, because nothing is more powerful than a woman's struggle to run free. It's the story of women's liberation—not just for those who came before, but for those of us who are here now, stretching and striving and wondering, What might I achieve? What might women achieve together? Through their accomplishments, champion athletes from the past say to any woman or girl who's willing to listen now, "If we can do it, so can you."

The first athlete who said to me "If I can do it, so can you" was Babe Didrikson Zaharias. She died the year I was born but communicated with me through her autobiography, which I discovered when I was in sixth grade. It was the only book in the entire Blue Bell (Pennsylvania) Elementary School library that featured a female athlete, and I read it like a religious text, searching for answers to big questions: How do girls grow strong? How can we win? Where does courage come from?

The year was 1968. I was twelve. I was spending all my free time practicing layups in my driveway so I could make the junior high basketball team the following autumn, but increasingly I was being accosted by grownups who demanded, "When are you going to outgrow this tomboy phase and become a lady?"

Babe Didrikson seemed to be speaking directly to me when she wrote, "Athletics is all I care for. I sleep them, eat them, talk them, and try my level best to do them as they should be done. You must feel that way."

Late in her life, Babe made some concessions to "lady" pressures—girdles, makeup, skirts—but she never relinquished her passion for sports. She validated my competitiveness ("I don't see any point in playing the game if you don't win, do you?" she said) and, through her Olympic track-and-field victories, professional golf career, and myriad other athletic successes, gave me a glimpse of who I might become. Reading her story, I realized I wasn't a tomboy, so I need never stop being one. I was an athlete. A lifelong athlete, just like Babe.

Athletic achievements are concrete, visible, measurable, and culturally valued: obvious, tangible proof of what people can do. Boxer Joe Louis, baseball players Jackie Robinson and Roberto Clemente, runner Jesse Owens: they seemed to succeed not only for themselves, but for all African-Americans, all Hispanics, all people who felt overlooked or discriminated against. Their feats represented key victories over racism, key "wins" in games that were traditionally dominated by white men.

Similarly, female athletes have symbolically surmounted sexism. Back in 1973, Billie Jean King's historic match with Bobby Riggs was televised to a worldwide audience of millions. This was not mere tennis, not just a game or a gamble. This was "The Battle of the Sexes," and at stake, it seemed, was nothing less than the future of women. When King won (6–4, 6–3, 6–3), she didn't win just for herself. She proved to men—and to dubious women—that women can compete with men, and win.

Women's liberation begins with women's bodies. It encompasses such corporeal issues as birth control, sexual harassment, child sexual abuse, pornography, rape, battering, breast cancer, breast enlargement, dieting, cosmetic surgery, abortion, anorexia, bulimia, sexuality . . . and sports. "The repossession by women of our bodies," wrote the poet and author Adrienne Rich in *Of Woman Born*, "will bring far more essential change to human society than the seizing of the means of production by workers."

Female athletes repossess their bodies. Told that they're weak, they develop strength. Told that certain sports are wrong for them, they decide for themselves what's right. Told that their bodies are too dark, big, old, flabby, or wrinkly to be attractive to men, they look at naked women in locker rooms and discover for themselves the beauty of actual women's bodies in all their colors, shapes, and sizes. Told that certain sports make women look "like men," they notice the truth: working out doesn't make them look like men; it makes them look happy. It makes them smile. It makes them radiate health and power. It makes them feel good.

Lunging for a soccer ball, women do not worry if their hair looks attractive. Leaping over a high bar, they do not wish they had bigger breasts. Strapped snugly into a race car, roaring around a track at 220 miles per hour, they do not smile and wave.

While playing sports, women use their bodies to do as they please. If in that process female bodies look unladylike—if they become bruised or bloody or simply unattractive—that seems irrelevant. Women own their bodies. While running to catch a ball, they remember that.

Feminism is also about political power. When they team up, working together toward communal goals regardless of differences in race, class, physical ability, and sexual preference, female athletes create unity through diversity, laying the groundwork for empowering political change. What if women truly trusted other women? What if women became comfortable in female worlds, with female leaders? Women are, after all, the majority. The majority rules, usually.

Feminism is about freedom: the individual and collective liberty to make decisions. Sports have freed women, and continue to free women, from restrictive dress, behaviors, laws, and customs—and from the belief that women can't or shouldn't achieve or compete or win. Sports embody freedom: unrestricted physical expression, travel across great distances, liberated movement. Sports give meaning to the phrase "free time." Athletes find it, use it, and insist on retaining it. Time for sports becomes a time when women free themselves of all the other people and projects they usually tend to. They become the person, the project, who needs care. They take care of themselves.

And feminism is about self-definition. The late poet Audre Lorde warns in *Sister Outsider,* "If we do not define ourselves for ourselves, we will be defined by others—for their use and to our detriment." Susan Faludi writes in *Backlash* that women must "be free to define themselves—instead of having their identity defined for them, time and again, by their culture and their men." Female champions define for themselves what counts as victory, what constitutes defeat, what rules they want to play by, what it means to compete. They redefine what it means to be an athlete, and what it means to be a woman.

Female athletes don't necessarily see it this way. They don't necessarily call themselves feminists. They swim or surf or ski or play rugby because it's fun and challenging, because it feels good, because they like the way it makes them look, because it allows them to eat more without gaining weight, because it gives them energy and confidence and time spent with friends, female or male. Many are ignorant about the women's rights movement. I've heard college students confuse feminism with feminine hygiene.

Some female athletes deliberately dissociate themselves from feminism. They assert that their involvement changes nothing, that they can compete "and still be feminine." These athletes take great pains—and it can hurt—to send reassuring signals to those who would oppose their play: "Don't worry, we're not feminists. We're not a threat to you, or to your ideas of how women should behave. We just want to play ball." It has been a survival strategy.

But the truth is, even when feminism is not an individual's motivating force, it is the result. Regardless of the factors that lead to her involvement, athletic training implicitly challenges patriarchal constraints on a woman's behavior. By reserving time each day for basketball dribbling, or for runs or rides or rows, a woman liberates herself and society. Women's presence in weight rooms and gyms, like women's presence in board rooms and bars, is subtly and insistently changing how society views women, and how women view themselves. Sport alters the balance of power between the sexes. It changes lives. It empowers women, thereby inexorably changing everything.

It all began, in a way, with the invention of a slender, affordable transportation machine called the bicycle. Before Gertrude Ederle swam the English Channel, before Amelia Earhart flew solo across the Atlantic, before women secured the right to vote, before automobiles, and before the modern Olympics, women rode bicycles. In the 1890s, a century ago, about thirty thousand American women owned and rode bicycles.

Many bold women had competed in other sports prior to that. The All-England Croquet and Lawn Tennis Club held its first national women's championship at Wimbledon in 1884. Some women rode horses, golfed, and played badminton in the 1870s and 1880s. Some even boxed and shot guns recreationally. In 1876, for instance, Nell Saunders defeated Rose Harland in the first U.S. women's boxing match. In 1885, Buffalo Bill's Wild West Show featured sharpshooter Annie Oakley.

British women created the Ladies Golf Union in 1893, the All-England Women's Field Hockey Association in 1895, and the Southern Ladies Lacrosse Club in 1905. The first women's sports magazine, *Hockey Field*, emerged in England in 1901.

But the real turning point in women's athletic participation came when the "safety bicycle" replaced the dangerous and difficult "high bicycle" (with the huge front wheel) in 1885. Masses of women in England and the United States eagerly grabbed the handlebars to steer for themselves a new life course. By the "gay nineties," bloomers (designed by Amelia Bloomer in 1849) caught on, as women discarded cumbersome skirts and petticoats in favor of the infinitely more comfortable loose pants. Cheaper and lighter than carriages, bicycles enabled women from all social strata to travel—alone or with male companions. Chaperones, often reluctant to learn to handle the new machines, stayed home, freeing young women and men to explore the countryside or neighboring towns together, alone.

Women raced as early as 1885, when Frankie Nelson won the women's six-day race in Madison Square Garden. An 1899 British novel called *Miss Cayley's Adventures* featured a woman who won a transalpine bicycle race against male competitors. A woman known as Mrs. A.M.C. Allen, while setting a record in 1897 for the most miles (21,026) pedaled in one year, was bitten by a dog but drew her revolver and shot it. She then pedaled another 16 miles before seeking medical treatment.

The political impact of cycling did not go unnoticed. In 1895, nineteen years before women were granted the vote, Elizabeth Cady Stanton wrote, "Many a woman is riding to the suffrage on a bicycle."

That same year, Frances Willard, head of the Women's Christian Temperance Union, wrote an entire book, *A Wheel Within a Wheel,* about the liberating effects of cycling. Having taught herself to ride in her early fifties, Willard was particularly impressed with the ways cycling changed relationships between women and men. She wrote:

> We saw with satisfaction the great advantage in good fellowship and mutual understanding between men and women who take the road together, sharing its hardships and rejoicing in the poetry of motion. . . . We discoursed on the advantage to masculine character of comradeship with women who were as skilled and ingenious in the manipulation of the swift steed as they themselves. We contended that whatever diminishes the sense of superiority in men makes them more manly, brotherly, and pleasant to have about.

Along with the bicycle came basketball, and what cycling did for individual women, and for their relationships with men, basketball did for groups of women, and for their relationships with each other. The first intercollegiate women's basketball game was held in 1896, the same month the first modern, all-male Olympic Games were held in Athens, Greece, and just five years after James Naismith had invented the game, declaring it an ideal sport for women. By the 1920s, most women's colleges, including Mount Holyoke, Smith, Vassar, and Wellesley, fielded teams, and most offered intercollegiate archery, baseball, rowing, tennis, and track as well.

Prominent feminists embraced basketball. Alice Paul, founder of the National Women's Party and author of the Equal Rights Amendment, excelled at the game while at Swarthmore College (class of '02). Charlotte Perkins Gilman (author of *Herland, The Yellow Wallpaper,* and *Women and Economics*) played basketball with her teenage daughter.

Like cyclists, female basketball players perceived the connection between sports and liberation. Senda Berenson, the Smith College professor who introduced basketball to American women in 1892, justified the strenuous game by pointing out that "all fields of labor and all professions are opening their doors" to women, and that therefore women would need "more than ever the physical strength to meet these ever increasing demands."

A writer in Wellesley's 1898 yearbook said of her basketball team, "The grimy and generally disheveled appearance of the players, as they emerge from the fray, fills our athletic souls with pride."

Writer Anne O'Hagen, reflecting on women's participation in all sports in a 1901 issue of *Munsey's Magazine*, wrote, "With the single exception of the improvement of legal status of women, their entrance into the realm of sports is the most cheering thing that has happened to them in the century just past. . . . The revolution means as much psychologically as it did physically."

But not everyone embraced the concept of female athleticism. Some female physical educators and coaches were wary of competitive sports, favoring simple physical fitness instead. In the 1920s, the Women's Division of the National Amateur Athletic Federation maintained that competition would "harm the nervous system, encourage rowdiness, and lead to injury and exploitation." Between about 1920 and 1960, female coaches sponsored athletic events that combined teams from different schools in order to curb competitive tendencies. Seeking to provide opportunities without the pitfalls already evident in men's sports (corruption, commercialism, the pressure to compete when injured, the exclusive focus on victory), they asserted that a young woman's future role as wife and mother was "of far greater importance than any championship she may ever win through competition." They enforced this strict rule: never compete with boys.

Meanwhile, some men—apparently sensing that sports were indeed greasing the wheels of women's liberation—tried desperately to limit women's involvement, refusing women admission to sports clubs, mocking women who competed, and inventing numerous hazards, most gynecological, that might befall athletic women.

Cyclists' saddles, for instance, were said in the early days to induce menstruation and cause contracted vaginas and collapsed uteruses. Further, while appearing to enjoy an innocent, healthful ride, female cyclists might use the upward tilt of the saddle to engage in the "solitary vice" of masturbation.

None of which convinced women to dismount their bikes.

Soon men changed tactics, redefining female athleticism as sexy and romantic, intended not for women's health, enjoyment, or empowerment, but for men's pleasure. In the 1920s, the cover of *Physical Culture* magazine typically featured a young, smiling woman in a semi-athletic, semi-cheesecake pose, the wind blowing her short skirt upward.

Women sometimes colluded in this strategy, peddling their own attractiveness as a way to justify sports participation. Lucille Hill, director of physical education at Wellesley, linked "the delights of athletics" with the "desirability of possessing a strong and beautiful body for both use and ornament." Annette Kellerman, the competitive swimmer whose name became synonymous with tight-fitting, one-piece bathing suits shaped like today's triathlon suits, had her picture taken in poses that set the stage for today's *Sports Illustrated* "swimsuit issue." Even my beloved Babe Didrikson, weary of being denounced by reporters as "boyish," "mannish," a "girl-boy child," "unfeminine," "unpretty," "not-quite female," and a "Muscle Moll" who "cannot compete with other girls in the very ancient and honored sport of mantrapping," eventually adorned herself with hats, dresses, pearls, stockings, girdles, lipstick, perfume, and nail polish in an unabashed bid for acceptance.

It wasn't until the 1960s that female leaders relinquished their focus on fitness ("A sport for every girl, and every girl in a sport") and began openly promoting competitive sports for women. In 1963, the Division for Girls and Women's Sports joined the U.S. Olympic Development Committee in an effort to show teachers how to train Olympians. In 1966, the Commission on Intercollegiate Athletics for Women was founded to govern college games and tournaments. Remarking on these changes, one physical educator proclaimed, "For the first time in my life, competition is no longer a dirty word, and even more important, both teachers and students know it's all right for women to be good in sports and to play to win."

By the early seventies, women were holding decision-making positions that affected not only girls but boys as well. Sylvia Pressley, the hearing officer who in 1973 ruled that Little League must be sexually integrated, explained, "The sooner little boys begin to realize that little girls are equal and that there will be many opportunities for a boy to be bested by a girl, the closer they will be to better mental health."

In the seventies, eighties, and nineties, women's sports opportunities expanded tremendously, mostly because of Title IX, the 1972 federal law that prohibits sex discrimination in federally funded educational institutions. After athletic directors dragged their feet about enforcing the law for the first decade, and after the Supreme Court weakened the law with the Grove City decision in 1984, feminist activists lobbied Congress to pass the 1988 Civil Rights Restoration Act (opposed by the National Collegiate Athletic Association and enacted over President Reagan's veto), which restored Title IX to its full strength.

Many prominent universities still refuse to comply, even when sued by their students, citing myriad reasons for favoring male over female athletes. Some argue that football should be exempt from Title IX considerations because it "makes money for the school." Or that women "deserve" fewer opportunities because their sports are rarely revenue producing. In fact, most women's sports programs do not produce a profit, but 80 percent of football programs lose money too—on average more than $600,000 per year. Besides, the courts—which have never ruled against a Title IX plaintiff—have consistently ruled that financial considerations are irrelevant in Title IX enforcement.

Other college administrators contend that women are less interested in sports than men are—as if any thinking woman would refuse a $10,000 scholarship. In response to such claims, judges have pointed out that interest follows opportunity. In other words, if you build the women's sports program, the women will come.

Men's wrestling and football coaches have lobbied Congress to weaken Title IX, complaining that their programs are being eliminated or reduced to make room for female athletes. Yet the Women's Sports Foundation has noted that since 1980, for every two women's sports programs that have been added, one and a half men's programs have been added. In other words, if administrators had just held the men's programs steady while adding the women's, no men's programs today would need to be cut.

By 1997, despite fierce resistance by athletic administrators, the College Football Association, and wrestling representatives, Title IX had clearly made an indelible mark on the lives of American women. More than 2.4 million girls (one-third of all female students) were playing high school sports, up 800 percent since 1971. In that same time period, college women's sports participation tripled.

Worldwide, women's athletic opportunities also multiplied. In the twenty-four years between the 1972 and the 1996 Olympics, the percentage of female participants rose from 15 to 34. Between 1973 and 1997, women's pro tennis expanded its annual prize money from $1 million to $38 million. Women's Sports Foundation executive director Donna Lopiano summarizes the shift this way: By the 1990s, female athletes had become "not the exception, but the rule."

According to the Sporting Goods Manufacturers Association, as of 1996, 1,155,000 American women were riding a bicycle at least one hundred days each year. Female cyclists around the world now compete in triathlons, mountain bike races, cyclocross, century rides, road races, sprints, and, since 1984, the Olympics.

At the end of the twentieth century, team sports for women have finally gained widespread acceptance. Women's basketball, which debuted in the 1976 Olympics, is now the most popular sport for women in college and high school. The American women's 1996 Olympic basketball team—along with the women's soccer, softball, gymnastics, and synchronized swimming teams—won the gold, capturing the attention and admiration of the American public. In the following year, two women's pro basketball leagues were born, one with the full backing of the National Basketball Association. In 1998, the biggest story of the Nagano Olympics was not fifteen-year-old Tara

Lipinski's figure skating gold, but that women's ice hockey had made its Olympic debut—and that the American women had won again.

Nowadays women also play, sometimes on an equal basis, sports men have tried to reserve for themselves. Girls and women are pinning male opponents to wrestling mats, racing horses and cars and yachts alongside their brothers, and playing pro baseball against men. Almost a thousand girls are playing high school football. Women have pitched in college baseball games and kicked in college football games. Two women are officiating in the NBA. Female sportscasters are anchoring NFL studio shows, announcing pro baseball games, and doing play-by-play for the National Hockey League.

Increasingly, women seem aware that sports are more than games. "When you play, when you win the gold medal, you aren't just playing for yourself, you aren't just winning the medal for yourselves," Representative Patsy Mink, a Hawaii Democrat and a coauthor of Title IX, told the U.S. women's basketball team during their pre-Olympic tour in 1996. "You're winning it for thousands of little girls across the country who want to do what you're doing."

Olympic athletes seemed to agree. Softball player and physician Dot Richardson, who hit two homers en route to her gold, said: "We did it for all the people who played before and are playing now. And for those who are going to play in the future."

Lindsay Davenport, who won the gold medal in tennis, said, "These Olympics, probably more than any before, are showing a lot of little girls it's okay to sweat, it's okay to play hard, it's okay to be an athlete."

Amy Van Dyken, who won four gold medals in swimming, said, "Hopefully we have shown that women can do whatever men can do—and probably do it better. Growing up, we didn't have as many role models as the boys did. Girls need to understand it's cool to be athletic."

At the end of the millennium, it's definitely cool to be athletic. Female athletes know it, and the mainstream culture is catching on. In the *Washington Post*'s annual list of what's "in" and "out," "women playing basketball" was in for 1996. "Women playing hard to get" was out.

Some things have not changed. Discrimination remains the norm. There are still twice as many male as female Olympians. Several countries refuse to allow women to compete in the Olympics at all. Only one Grand Slam tennis event—the U.S. Open—offers women equal prize money. Men are paid more than women for coaching women's teams. Men coach more than half of all women's teams, while women coach fewer than 1 percent of men's teams. And Title IX is still not fully enforced at most colleges and high schools. Men receive two-thirds of all college athletic opportunities, though women constitute more than 50 percent of the student population. At high schools nationwide, the boys often play in the new gyms, or on the new fields, with new lights and new scoreboards and new uniforms, while the girls make do with hand-me-downs and leftovers. In response to frequent lawsuits, high schools and universities are only slowly and begrudgingly coming into compliance with the law.

The media still sometimes interpret female athletes not as powerful or strong, but as charming and seductive and vulnerable. "Strong is sexy!" promise the women's magazines. And "Beauty is power!" A Coca-Cola commercial aired during the 1996 Olympics showed quick images of female athletes interspersed with the words, "Their bodies are so strong and yet so feminine." Athletes have become gorgeous, flirtatious, elegant, angelic, darling.

Ads often pair an action photo of a woman athlete with a shot of her lounging in glamorous evening wear, her face hidden under heavy makeup. Even sports magazines frequently feature models rather than athletes on their covers. Thin, nearly naked women pose passively, smiling, exuding neither strength nor exhilaration. One could get the impression that female athletes, who spend hours each day developing stamina and skill, train not because they love basketball or soccer or swimming or each other—they do it in order to be sexy for men.

Women still buy in. "Athletic girls" still try to prove that they're not unfeminine, meaning not lesbian and not threatening to men. Tennis pro Steffi Graf posed in bikinis for the 1997 *Sports Illustrated* swimsuit issue. In a Sears commercial, Olympic basketball players applied lipstick, painted their toenails, rocked babies, lounged in bed, and posed and danced in their underwear. Center Lisa Leslie said, "Everybody's allowed to be themselves. Me, for example, I'm very feminine."

But the Title IX era—the quarter century since the law's passage in 1972—has been characterized by a cultural shift no less monumental than when thousands of women first stepped out of their cumbersome skirts and onto the seats of those early bicycles. It could again be said that "with the single exception of the improvement of legal status of women, [women's] entrance into the realm of sports is the most cheering thing that has happened to them in the century just past. . . ."

Unfortunately, most of the young female athletes I meet today don't know about Babe and Billie Jean. They don't memorize statistics about Wilma Rudolph or Sonja Henie the way any male fan can tell you what year Reggie Jackson hit three home runs in game six of the World Series. Teaching the history of female athletes is not exactly a high priority for our educational system, for the media, for the publishing world, for the movie industry. Compared to the relentless daily barrage of information about male athletes, news about women's accomplishments is still strangely sketchy and distorted.

So we need books like this one. We need to know about swimmers Esther Williams, Donna de Varona, Janet Evans; tennis players Althea

Gibson, Helen Wills Moody, Martina Navratilova; dogsled racers Libby Riddles and Susan Butcher; golfers Mickey Wright, Nancy Lopez, Beth Daniel; track stars Wyomia Tyus, Evelyn Ashford, and Jackie Joyner-Kersee. These women, and myriad others, have demonstrated clearly and indisputably that women are winners.

We need to know about the politics of sport: that women were not allowed to run the Olympic marathon until 1984; that African-American women could not play in the All-American Girls Baseball League; that for every young woman who receives an athletic scholarship, two men do. Without this information, and more, we can't really know who we are, or where we're going. And without it we can't fully celebrate female strength and female victory.

We need to hear these stories from women. The contributors to this anthology, who are some of the best sportswriters in the nation today, are part of the history of women's sports, part of the story of women's exclusion and insistence and success. According to the Association for Women in Sports Media, less than 10 percent of all sportswriters are women. So even when the media does report on female athletes, the stories are usually filtered through men's eyes. In this book, the stories are all written by women, many of whom have faced in their own careers some of the same discrimination faced by the athletes they're covering. Like the athletes, they have encountered contempt and ridicule as they have pursued their dreams. Like the athletes, they have challenged social stereotypes about how women should behave, and what they should be permitted to do. Like the athletes, they have competed, and won, despite the opposition.

To be our best, female fans need female champions to show us what greatness means. We need female writers to uncover and interpret that greatness. We need to learn about women who succeeded despite the odds, who sprinted past all the people who said "no" and "you shouldn't" and "you can't." We need answers to our big questions: How do women grow strong? How can we win? Where does courage come from?

This book answers those questions.

Track and Field

Somewhere to Run
Kathleen McElroy

Almost anyone can run or jump, but few can make a sport of it, and even fewer command attention because of the speed, height, or distance they achieve in such rudimentary skills. However, the simplicity of track and field belies the tangled history of female participation in the sport. Women began formally competing in track and field about one hundred years ago, with the politics of culture, economics, gender, and race tagging along from the start. In fact, most of the sport's great controversies have not been about particular performances, but debates waged far from the track. However, the most-asked questions still take women's track and field back to its basics: Who runs the fastest, jumps the longest, or throws the farthest? While the answers have changed with every generation causing little fanfare, a handful of women are remembered beyond their victories. They made the world take notice of a sport often ignored, and their stories became the stuff of legends. They were extraordinary women who surmounted the barriers bravely, and with style.

Consider Babe Didrikson, perhaps America's most storied female athlete, who went from jumping over her neighbors' hedges in hardscrabble Beaumont, Texas, to winning three medals and the sports world's attention at the 1932 Olympics. But with all her success came so much notoriety about her mannish looks, her unfeminine behavior, and her cockiness that she would trade in her shorts for frilly blouses and a golf club in hopes of evading the daunting criticism without losing her competitive zeal or her champion's psyche. Less than thirty years later, Wilma Rudolph confronted barriers of a different kind. She overcame her premature birth, polio, and the prejudice directed at her as an African-American from the rural, segregated South before she sprinted to stardom in front of a worldwide audience at the 1960

Olympics. With this hard-won victory, she became the first female African-American superstar and an inspiration to a nation in the throes of the
civil rights era. Two decades later, Jackie Joyner-Kersee, the "First Lady"
of track and field, ignored many of the same problems of race and poverty,
gender and stereotype growing up among the all-too-close street life of
East St. Louis. She learned to jump in a homemade sand pit off her porch
with an enthusiasm and grace that would lead her to six medals in four
Olympics.

The historic cast of characters also includes a couple of dueling French
pioneers, a president of the Girl Scouts, a Dutch "over-the-hill" mother, and
a would-be football coach. These athletes and coaches, and hundreds more
like them, are remembered long after their races have been won, their records
eclipsed, and their careers ended because they mastered the simple skills to
dominate in track and field and went to extreme measures to get themselves
and their athletes allowed on the track.

For men, there have always been opportunities for competitions; leg
races, jumping matches, and throwing bouts are probably as old as human-
ity itself. From the ancient Greek Olympics until the mid-1800s, track and
field mostly consisted of foot races for men (and a few women) at country
fairs and horse-racing meetings, notably in Europe. The first recognizable
men's track and field meet was held at England's Eton College in 1837, with
the first intercollegiate men's meet held in England twenty-seven years later.
As women were discouraged from competitions, often banned from the arena
even as spectators, they created their own occasions to participate in socially
acceptable ways. In 1878, Ada Anderson won $10,000 by walking 2,700 quar-
ter miles in 2,700 quarter hours in a Brooklyn hall. In 1903, 2,500 Parisian
shop girls competed in a twelve-kilometer race; the winner, who finished in
seventy minutes, earned the opportunity to perform in a music hall.

In the 1890s, college women, too, found venues in which to compete
beyond the required "strolling." Physical education gained favor among
American educators, especially at places like the newly formed seven sisters colleges of the Northeast. Their administrations saw exercise as a means
for the growing female upper-class student population to counter the new
stresses of higher education, as well as to create an alternative to the frail
Victorian woman. On November 9, 1895, Vassar staged the first all-female
track meet, at which twenty-two students were scheduled to compete in
five events: the 100-yard dash, the running broad jump, the 120-yard hurdle,
the running high jump, and the 220-yard dash. No men were allowed
among the more than three hundred spectators (although there was a male
referee). Stories in the local *Poughkeepsie Daily* and the *New York Times*
reported the results.

In the following years, other colleges across the country, including coed institutions like the University of Wisconsin, Winthrop, Lake Erie College, and Nebraska, helped pioneer programs and began holding meets for women's intramural or intercollegiate events. They added traditional Olympic events like discus, high jump, and pole vault, as well as contemporary events like baseball and basketball throws.

Not everyone was thrilled with the new athletic model for women. Doctors claimed that girls were impairing their child-bearing abilities; social scientists and journalists wondered if competition damaged the female psyche; moralists decried the public display of women in inappropriate clothing and actions. Worst of all for women's track and field, the second generation of female physical educators held some of those opinions and added criticisms of their own. They did not want a class system in women's sports or the added expense of maintaining such elitist athletic teams. In short, they didn't want women to act like men.

At a 1923 conference headed by the president of the Girl Scouts, Lou Henry Hoover (wife of the future president), the Women's Division of the National Amateur Athletic Federation—which included YMCA officials and college and school educators as well as individuals—began what would be a moderately successful fifty-year mission to downgrade women's competitions. By 1924 many college field days, especially in the East, were turned into play days, during which different schools contributed players to randomly picked teams, with no practices and only minor rewards for winning. The fans stayed home, and no one cheered.

Many of the concerns about the brutish nature of track and field did not filter down to the working classes, where women were not held to the same "feminine" standards as their aristocratic counterparts. The Women's Division's influence could not get through the factory door, where industrial leagues flourished with women's bowling, basketball, softball, and track and field. Sponsored by industries, department stores, insurance companies, railroads, and the like, the leagues were designed to provide recreation, training, and competition for employees. The company line was that they were to boost morale and foster teamwork; the bottom line was to publicize team sponsors or maybe redirect energies that might have been used to form unions. The leagues also offered opportunities for women to make some extra money, often more than their factory jobs paid, and to travel.

Most of the first stars in American women's track and field came from these athletic clubs or industry teams like that of the Prudential Insurance Company in Newark, New Jersey. Behind hurdler Hazel Kirk and basketball thrower Esther Behring, that team won the initial Amateur Athletic Union national championship for women, held in 1923 (the same year the

Women's Division had gotten serious). As a sportswriter noted, the bulk of the early Olympic women's teams would be formed from "girls in factories, girls in offices, girls in shops" and not collegiate women's teams. Women like Jessie Cross, a teenager in New York, would get a job and join a team, too. Cross became one of the "Wanamaker Girls," a track team sponsored by a department store, and traveled to the first Olympics to include women's track and field, the 1928 Amsterdam Games, where she won a silver medal as a member of the 4 × 100-meter team.

Track and field's biggest stage has always been the Olympics, and the Games have always showcased track and field, from the first recorded event in 776 B.C., at which the only athletic competition was a 192-meter race, to the revival of the Olympic Games in 1896, held in Athens, Greece. The modern Games were the brainchild of the French aristocrat Pierre de Fredy, the Baron de Coubertin, and were centered on a belief that sports pursued at their democratic, classical best could end class and geopolitical war. The baron brought back many of the events of ancient Greek competition, along with the tradition of opening and closing ceremonies and the tradition of excluding women.

The women of ancient Greece staged their own competitions, the Hera Games, at which young unmarried girls dressed in robes that bared one breast as they ran their one event, a 160-meter race. Like the women of ancient Greece, women of the early twentieth century held Olympics of their own, designed by Alice Milliat, perhaps the greatest pioneer of women's track and field.

Milliat was a translator by occupation and the head of the Femina Sport, an exclusive sports club founded in France in 1911. In 1917 Femina Sport sponsored the first national championship in women's track and field. Buoyed by the success of these meets, Milliat asked the International Olympic Committee (IOC) to include women's track and field in the 1920 Olympic Games. After being turned down because track and field was deemed inappropriate competition for women, she founded the Federation Sportive Feminine International (FSFI), which created venues for women to compete outside of the IOC jurisdiction. In 1921, the Sporting Club of Monte Carlo staged the first international event for women. Certain that the success of this international meet would ensure sanctioning from the IOC, Milliat applied again. After another rejection for the 1924 Paris Games, the FSFI organized its own Women's Olympic Games in Paris in 1922 with sixty-five women from five countries competing in eleven events with twenty thousand spectators.

The Amateur Athletic Union (AAU) in America agreed to send a U.S. contingent headed by Dr. Harry Stewart, from the Wykeham Rise School for Girls in Washington, Connecticut. Stewart and the AAU worked with the industrial sports leagues and their sponsors, secondary schools, and playground associations to unify the U.S. track scene and come up with a competitive team of women. Stewart used studies he had conducted proving that sports improved women's health to convince the AAU to authorize a team to send to Paris. When the Americans finished second to Great Britain, the women came home to a champion's welcome and mostly positive press coverage. AAU president William Prout told the *New York Herald*, "The girls have become athletes. We can't stop them. We must simply standardize their games."

The IOC was not particularly impressed, however, and it resented any nonauthorized use of the word "olympic." As women were competing in alternate track-and-field competitions worldwide, the IOC urged the International Amateur Athletic Federation (IAAF), which governed track and field, to keep the women under control and negotiate all matters concerning their participation in Olympic competition. In 1924, the IAAF admitted women into the organization in hopes of pacifying them but still kept them from Olympic competition. By 1926, the International Track Federation began negotiations with Milliat. They agreed that in return for recognition of her organization, and women's track and field in general, women would be allowed to compete in the IOC's Olympic Games. Milliat would have to surrender control of women track-and-field competitions to the IAAF, then and still one of the most powerful sports federations, and the women no longer had a say about their own activities. Though the agreement was met with much resistance from both sides, a decision was made to include women's track and field in the 1928 Amsterdam Olympic Games on a trial basis. Five track-and-field events were included: a 100-meter sprint, a 4 x 100-meter relay, an 800-meter run, the discus, and the high jump.

While the female athletes were thrilled by the opportunity to compete in the Olympics, those first Olympians included novices with little formal training or technique. There were several impressive performances, like those of American Jessie Cross and her Wanamaker Girls, who won silver in the sprint relay; American Betty Robinson, who won the 100-meter in 12.2 seconds; Canadian Ethel Catherwood, who won the high jump; Pole Halina Konopacka, who won the discus; and German Lina Radke, who ran the 800-meter in a record time of 2:16.8. Finishing second in the 800-meter race was perhaps the world's first great female all-around athlete, Kinue Hitomi. The Japanese competitor had won two golds in the 1926 Women's Games and was the world-record holder in the 200-meter and the long jump, two events not on the 1928 program. At the 1930 Women's Games, she won four event medals and the gold for top all-around performance. She didn't get a chance to compete at the expanded 1932 women's program, however; she died of tuberculosis at twenty-four.

On the whole, the competitive field was at best uneven, for the track-and-field program in America was still quite young and the stars more a product of raw natural ability than anything. Robinson had been discovered by her coach running to catch a train, and had competed only in four previous races. Catherwood, a young pianist whose fame as the "Saskatoon Lily" was based primarily on her status as a photographers' favorite, was restricted from serious training, as the $3,000 she was awarded by the provincial government had to go toward her piano studies.

The reporters at the 1928 Olympics weren't really prepared either. Seeing women as athletes was a new experience, and women heaving and sweating in public seemed to disarm many. The 800-meter run provided a good example of their reluctance to accept women as serious contenders and became the occasion of the biggest controversy of the 1928 Olympics. A 1000-meter run had been held without incident at the FSFI Women's Olympics a year earlier, but now many sports sections reported with alarm that the female runners were in hysterical collapse at the end of the race. Though eyewitnesses claimed the finishers were no more distressed than the men were at the end of their race, conservatives balked at the images of fallen womanhood and suggested tight restrictions on women's track-and-field Olympic participation. The stewing Women's Division picked up on the furor and used it to support attempts to deemphasize women's track.

In 1929, the IOC voted to remove women's track and field from the 1932 Los Angeles Games. As an alternative, the Women's Division proposed a program that included singing, dancing, and lunching. IAAF members threatened to boycott the men's Olympic program if the women were not included, and a compromise was reached in which 100 meters would be the longest individual women's race in Los Angeles. The women's 800-meter event was not reinstated until the 1960 Rome Games, a race in which the American entrant Pat Daniels Connolly was pushed and fell off the track. Disqualified, she got up and finished the race nevertheless. Though she was filled with disappointment, she was excitedly greeted by the American chaperone, Frances Kaszubski, who exclaimed, "Thank God you got up, oh, thank you. The last time they ran this race and the women didn't finish, they didn't run this race again for over thirty years."

Under the conservative sway of the Women's Division, and wary of bad press, colleges and universities extended little support for women's track and field. American Olympic teams would continue to rely on athletic clubs and industrial leagues to nurture women's track and field. The industrial teams welcomed the publicity their athletes brought during Olympic years and even in off years.

One man especially attuned to the PR potential of sports leagues and their stars was M. J. McCombs, head of the most famous industrial team, the Golden Cyclones, sponsored by the Employers Casualty Company, a Dallas insurance company. In the 1920s, the company had several sports leagues, including basketball, bowling, and baseball. When the IOC sanctioned track and field, McCombs established a women's team. With that venture, he soon created a venue for his best athlete, Babe Didrikson, who would become America's first female track-and-field superstar, competing with the name of his company on the front of her uniform.

Mildred Ella Didriksen was born to Ole and Hannah Didriksen in the summer of 1914 in Port Arthur, Texas, one of a trio of Gulf Coast refinery towns. The Didriksens were poor Norwegian immigrants—the mother an occasional washerwoman, the father a seaman turned cabinetmaker with a salty sailor's tongue that their youngest daughter picked up. The sixth of seven children, the one they called "Baby" or "Babe" was a natural athlete who ruled the gymnasium her father built to keep his children occupied, as well as the Magnolia Elementary playground in Beaumont, Texas. She was among the first to be chosen for school-yard games and had a reputation for beating up boys and anyone else who crossed her. She also picked up her mother's respectable work ethic and family loyalty. By twelve, Babe contributed to the family household fund by picking figs and making potato gunnysacks.

From all accounts Babe had little interest in academics and was mischievous, unfocused, and constantly disruptive in the classroom; she did as much work as was needed to stay eligible to play sports and little more. By the time she started high school, she had already honed her athletic skills. She starred on the tennis, golf, and basketball teams, was a champion swimmer and diver, and could pitch and hit. But she was also a bit of a social outcast and off the playground was scorned by the boys and the Klackers, the top social group for Beaumont High girls.

If any of the derision bothered Didriksen, she never let it show. Perhaps it only sharpened her focus and strengthened her motivation. Many years later she wrote in her autobiography that when she listened to her father read about the 1928 Amsterdam Games she began to plot her course: to be the greatest athlete who ever lived. She thrived on the recognition sports brought her, the attention her athletic successes warranted. William "Tiny" Scurlock, a three-hundred-pound sportswriter in Beaumont, wrote articles about Babe's high school athletic prowess, making her the talk of the town in a state that accepted, even welcomed, women athletes.

Her playing caught the attention of McCombs, who in 1930 offered her $75 a month to become an ECC clerical employee—in reality, to become a pampered basketball player on a winning team. It was a perfect match. Babe quit school, moved to Dallas, and became an All-American forward. She was a sight in her bright, skintight shorts, posing for media shots, talking up the team. In her three years on the basketball team, she led the Cyclones to three Amateur Athletic Union finals and one championship title.

Trying to keep her amused after her first basketball season, McCombs introduced Babe to track and field, a sport in which the Golden Cyclones already had a good team. He taught her basic technique, trained her hard, and stroked her ego with publicity events. Babe put in the hours, but in a ploy that she would repeat throughout her career, she downplayed her training efforts as well as her age. To appear a natural simply made for better copy. She also started spelling her name Didrikson around this same time, perhaps because it looked more American.

Though she continued playing basketball, Didrikson's career as a track-and-field star was solidified in 1930 when she set a world record in the javelin at the AAU meet in Dallas and the next year won the 80-meter hurdles, the broad jump, and the baseball throw at the Amateur Athletic Union Nationals in Jersey City. This was just as well, perhaps, for her larger-than-life ego was alienating her from her Golden Cyclone basketball teammates. Her pouting and prima donna snips and fits made it clear she was not a team player. After she got her first taste of big-time, big-city publicity from the New York newspapers for her track performances, the dimmed limelight she received on the basketball court was not enough.

In hopes of further capitalizing on the publicity Babe was getting, McCombs hit on an idea she had to love: She could be the sole representative from the ECC team at the 1932 Olympic trials. Even though AAU rules limited competitors to three events, he arranged for her to be eligible for eight of the ten on the program. The media loved it, and Babe welcomed the challenge. Her pronouncement to her competitors? "I'm gonna lick you single-handed."

The meet was held in July 1932, in Evanston, Illinois, and Babe did not disappoint. In three hours—other athletes had to wait as events were held up for her—she won six events, setting a U.S. record in the shot put and world records in the baseball throw, javelin, 80-meter hurdles, and broad jump. She tied Jean Shiley for first in the high jump, placed fourth in the discus, and just missed reaching the finals in the 100-meter dash. At meet end, the ECC "team" had won first place with thirty points. Second place went to the Illinois Women's Athletic Club with a total of twenty-two points. Babe later wrote, "It was one of those days in an athlete's life when you know you're just right. You feel you could fly."

The crowd and the press went crazy. One reporter called it "the most amazing series of performances ever accomplished by an individual, male or female, in track and field history." Arthur Daley of *The New York Times* wrote, "Implausible is the adjective which best befits the Babe." But the attention she received wasn't enough. Being the sole competitor for the ECC had been impressive, but she wanted the coming Olympics all to herself, too. Before the Games even started, she would play the harmonica when teammates were being interviewed, stage impromptu competitions for more media attention, even challenge Olympic swimmers to races. In a press account she said, "I came out here to beat everybody in sight, and that is what I am going to do. Sure, I can do everything."

The 1932 Summer Games were in Los Angeles, California, the movie capital of the world, and Babe was to be its star. Hollywood, like sports, became a diversion from the worldwide depression, and such stars as Mary Pickford, Douglas Fairbanks, and Will Rogers were out in force for the Games. All the glamour couldn't hide the impact of economic hard times: With funds from the participating countries dwindling, Olympic participation dropped to 1906 levels and competitors had to scrape up money to compete. To provide the athletes with inexpensive group housing, the tradition of the Olympic Village was initiated. This hospitality, however, was extended only to men; the women stayed at a "downtown" hotel. "Coming home, I traded my train ticket in for a bus fare so I could have some money for souvenirs," said Shiley. But money was hardly an issue for Babe, who had her expenses paid by the Employers Casualty Company.

Olympics rules were not as easy to bend as those at the trials, so Babe could compete in only three events. At the first event, fifty thousand people watched as she threw the javelin 43.68 meters. Though her throw was more of a line drive than the expected arching curve, and the toss tore cartilage in her right shoulder, she won gold. In her second event, the 80-meter hurdles, she took gold in a controversial photo-finish race, beating Evelyne Hall of the Illinois Women's A.C. They crossed the final hurdle at the same time, and they appeared to hit the tape together; Hall bore a welt on her neck from hitting the tape with such force, but Didrikson threw up her arms as if she'd won. While both hurdlers were given an official world-record time of 11.7 seconds, only Babe was given the gold. In the third event, the high jump, Babe faced Shiley, with whom she had tied for first place at the Olympic trials. (She had lost to Shiley as team captain, as well—Lillie Copeland, who later won the gold in the discus, dropped out of the election for captain to ensure that Babe, the third candidate, would not win.) Shiley used the standard scissors kick and went over the high-jump bar legs first, as the women's rules required at the time. Didrikson was using the western roll—as the men were doing, she bragged—in which the head and shoulders trail the body, a style that ultimately cost her the win. The Olympic competition would end as the trials did, with the two women achieving the same new world record—in this case, a height of 5 feet, 5¼ inches—but this time the judges ruled that Didrikson dove in her last jump and awarded the gold to Shiley.

Still, in the aftermath of the games, Babe Didrikson, the twenty-one-year-old "Texas Tornado," was the toast of Hollywood and the nation. She was photographed with Clark Gable, met with Amelia Earhart (who asked her to join one of her flights), and was feted in her hometowns, real and adopted. But despite her performance at the Los Angeles Coliseum, her lively, controversial behavior in social situations, and her typically masculine style of self-promotion, some said she cost track and field style points. It seemed the world wasn't ready for Babe. Sports arenas were still typically male oriented, and Babe threatened the status quo with her short hair and athletic stature. Newspapers attacked her androgynous looks and implied that she wasn't all female, hinting that a woman that much better than others must not be a woman at all. In 1936, Avery Brundage, then the AAU president and later to be the IOC president, remarked, "I am fed up to the ears with women as track and field competitors. Their charms sink to less than zero."

Babe was not alone in facing the scrutinizing eyes of the public. During the 1936 Games in Berlin, Helen Stephens, who won the 100 meters, had to undergo a physical exam to confirm her sex. The examination was requested by the Polish press after she beat Stella Walsh, a Cleveland runner who had won thirty-five national titles, first as an American, then as a Pole after she switched her allegiance in order to continue competing in the 1930s. Beating Walsh was difficult, and any victory over her was headline. Stephens passed the exam; ironically, after Walsh was murdered in a robbery in 1980, her autopsy revealed her to have both female and male sex organs. The only known natural male to participate in a women's event was a German, Herman Ratjen, who said the Nazis forced him to compete in the 1936 Olympic high jump—and he still finished fourth.

Babe's spectacular performance in the 1932 Olympics would be her last in track and field. Soon after, she turned her attention back to basketball, then baseball, and ultimately golf, which became a decade-long interest. She also embarked on a professional career, gave herself a matronly makeover, and wed wrestler and promoter George Zaharias. Still the flamboyant and outspoken athlete of years before, Babe Didrikson Zaharias would make history in yet another sport.

The 1936 Games would be remembered mainly for Nazi propaganda and the way it was punctured by Jesse Owens's gold medals. The Berlin Games also marked the first Olympics in which a black American woman competed. Tidye Pickett and Louise Stokes had been on the 1932 team but were bumped from the 4 × 100-meter race. The two were back on the U.S. team four years later, and Pickett, a product of the Chicago playground leagues, reached the semifinals of the hurdles.

World War II shut down the Olympics in 1940 and 1944, but it didn't stop women from competing. Stella Walsh, the pride of Cleveland, in her mid- and late thirties was still winning AAU and international titles. The 1948 Olympics, in rebuilt London, showcased women athletes changed by a decade of war. Though their performances were exceptional, most women's athletic programs still lacked serious technical training, financial support, and positive public recognition. Despite the impasses, a number of women would stand out during this period: Fanny Blankers-Koen, who came to represent the rebirth of Holland with her four-medal victory in the sprints; French pianist Micheline Ostermeyer, who won the discus and the shot put but lost a concert career; and African-American Alice Coach-man, who got little recognition from segregated America even though she won gold in the high jump.

As an eighteen-year-old, Fanny Blankers had competed in the 1936 Olympics without medaling but considered getting Jesse Owens's autograph the highlight of her experience. By the 1948 Games, she was a thirty-year-old mother of two children and was married to her coach, Jan, twelve years her senior. In those games she matched the achievements of her 1936 idol Owens by winning four gold medals—in the 100-meter, 80-meter hurdles, the sprint relay, and the 200-meter, which was making its Olympic debut as a women's event. She could have won two more medals but was prohibited from competing in the high jump and the long jump, two sports in which she held the world record. Though the opposite of Babe in temperament and femininity, Blankers-Koen received similar criticism from newspapermen, who said she was too old to run and that she should be home caring for her children instead of competing. "I got very many bad letters," she later said. "People writing that I must stay home, that I should not be allowed to run on a track in short trousers."

Ostermeyer, a discus thrower and shot putter from France, faced similar derision because she was a strong competitor in unlikely sports. The social bias in this case cost her a profession as a concert pianist. Before concentrating on music full-time, Ostermeyer had competed internationally in track and field, and with the 1948 Olympics approaching, French officials convinced her to join the team. They asked her to try the discus, though she had competed only once in the event, and the shot put, which was making its Olympic debut for women. After she won both events, as well as a bronze in the high jump, she returned home to her music only to find that critics declared her concert style too "sporty."

The prejudices twenty-four-year-old high jumper Alice Coachman had to contend with were much greater and the barriers set up by the white establishment harder to break through. Despite the achievements of Jesse Owens, and because she was an African-American woman, the race issue weighed heavily on her training and acceptance—Coachman later admitted, "If I had gone to the Games and failed, there wouldn't be anyone to follow my footsteps." As a child in Albany, Georgia, Coachman had wanted to be famous like Shirley Temple and had endured whippings from her traditional father for her tomboyish ways. A track and basketball star at Tuskegee, one of the black institutions to embrace women's athletics, she won ten consecutive national outdoor high-jump titles. In 1946, she was the first African-American selected to be on the All-American team, because she was "quiet, ladylike and reserved." Two years later, however, nine of the twelve women on the Olympic track-and-field team were African-American.

Despite back pains caused by a twisted ovary, Coachman won the high jump at 5 feet, 6¼ inches on her first jump and became the first African-American woman to win a gold medal. Audrey Patterson of Tennessee State had become the first black woman to win any medal when she won the bronze in the 200-meter, though in 1975 a rediscovered photo of the finish showed that Shirley Strickland of Australia should have placed third. An American sweep was expected, but only two medals—those won by Patterson and Coachman—were brought home by the U.S. women's track-and-field team. It has been said that a gold-medal shutout by an overwhelmingly black team might have been disastrous for race relations. But the two medals for African-American athletes were a source of pride for black America and ultimately proved the start-up track programs at black institutions to be legitimate. Unfortunately, off the track, America was still deeply segregated—when Coachman took her gold medal home to a segregated Albany Municipal Auditorium in Georgia, she wasn't even allowed to speak at her own ceremony.

Black men had been Olympic champions since the 1920s, but black women were given little institutional support in sports until the 1930s. Tuskegee Institute, one of the nation's leading black educational institutions, was the first to extend its athletic program to women. Tuskegee was founded in 1881 by Booker T. Washington, with the support of the state legislature, to be a teachers college. By the 1930s, the coed school had developed a women's athletic department under the guidance of the athletic director, Cleveland Abbott. Abbott was the head coach from 1936 to 1955, during which time the Tuskegee Golden Tigers won fourteen national outdoor titles, nine consecutive ones. With black colleges aligned with the AAU instead of the women's division, he showed foresight and determination during a period when women's organizations continued to oppose track and field at white colleges. At Tuskegee, he began to provide the coaching, the support system, and the readiness that are necessary to nurture world-class athletes. In 1937, just four years after he started his program, Tuskegee won the AAU nationals, a milestone for black colleges. As Abbott's model spread to other black institutions, like Tennessee State University, where Abbott's daughter was later the first women's coach, there was a surge of support for black female athletes, as well as a developed structure to assure a long and steady tradition for black women in track and field. As Arthur Ashe wrote in *A Hard Road to Glory*, track and field "was the primary outlet for aspiring black American female athletes." The 1948 Olympics team boasted seven women who attended either Tuskegee, like Coachman, or Tennessee State.

Like Tuskegee, Tennessee State University, a Nashville school, had made a commitment to women's track and field and garnered a brilliant coach, Ed Temple, to develop the program. The school's reputation would attract women like Mae Faggs of New York, and Barbara Jones of Chicago, who both won gold medals at the 1952 Games as members of the U.S. 4 × 100-meter team. At TSU, they became teammates under a young coach who was just embarking on a half century of coaching that would put him in the Track and Field Hall of Fame. Ed Temple produced a hotbed of black athletics and established TSU as the training center for black track-and-field athletes in the coming years.

Ed Temple wanted to be a football or basketball coach, but he took over the women's track team at TSU in 1950 for $150 a month. In 1952, he and the sports information director, Earl Clanton 3rd, nicknamed the TSU women's team the Tigerbelles, a name that would become synonymous with women's Olympics track and field. Temple had strict rules about the behavior of his athletes, insisting on a conservative dress code and ladylike behavior—his motto was "Act like a lady, but run like crazy." He also held them to academic standards of a B average or above and produced an impressive number of scholar-athletes. Temple's most famous pupil, Wilma Rudolph, was the first American woman to win three track-and-field gold medals in a single Olympics. Besides her list of record-breaking performances and stellar victories, Rudolph is important because she came to embody many of the symbols for female athletes and for black Americans: grace, determination, and change in America.

Wilma Rudolph was born in Clarksville, Tennessee, in 1940, eight weeks premature, the twentieth of twenty-two children. By the time she was four she had contracted measles, mumps, and chicken pox and then almost died from pneumonia and scarlet fever. When she recovered, her mother discovered that her left leg had turned in; a doctor explained that in the midst of battling those other diseases Wilma had contracted polio, and he predicted that her partly paralyzed leg would never recover. Determined and hopeful, Mrs. Blanche Rudolph and her daughter sat in the back of the Greyhound bus twice a week for the ride from Clarksville to Nashville for physical therapy at Meharry Medical College, a historically black school that still produces many of the African-American doctors in the United States today. "My mother taught me very early to believe I could achieve any accomplishment I wanted to," she said. "The first was to walk without braces."

In addition to the painful therapy Wilma endured, she also had to cope with staying home rather than playing or attending school. "Being left behind had a terrible effect on me," she wrote in her autobiography, *Wilma.* "I was so lonely, and I felt rejected." Yet she didn't want her family to know; she knew of their faith in God and in her. She made her limp less noticeable, continued the therapy at home, and at seven started school. At ten, Wilma was able to walk without her leg brace, making her first triumphant brace-less walk down the aisle at church one Sunday. Two years later, her mother mailed the brace back to Nashville. Her still skinny little girl didn't need it anymore. "My whole life suddenly changed just as I was ending my sixth-grade year in school," she wrote. "No more brace; I was healthy all over my body for the first time."

After years of watching other kids play basketball, Wilma had developed a well-rounded view of the game. When finally given the chance to start for the Burt High School team as a sophomore guard, she scored thirty-two points in her first game. Then about five-eleven and less than one hundred pounds, Wilma led her team to the state tournament in Nashville, where its second-round loss was viewed by Coach Temple, who was scouting for talent while working the game as a referee. He invited Wilma to his summer track-and-field camp to train.

With Temple's invitation, Rudolph—nicknamed Skeeter because her high school coach said she always buzzed around like a mosquito—started running track for the same reason Babe Didrikson had: as something to do between basketball seasons. "Running at the time was nothing but pure enjoyment for me," she said about her high school career. "I was running without really working." All that changed after a meet at Tuskegee and summer camp at Tennessee State. She lacked the skill and maturity of a serious competitor and was routinely beaten. Still, Temple took her to the 1956 AAU meet in Philadelphia, her first trip north, where she competed in both the junior and senior divisions. She finished second to Faggs, the 1952 veteran from New York, in the 200-meter and ran as a member of the winning relay team. Just as Blankers-Koen remembered Owens, Rudolph would remember the Philadelphia meet for her chance to talk to baseball great Jackie Robinson, who told her she could be the world's fastest runner; he also told her not to let anything, or anybody, keep her from running.

At the Olympic trials in Washington, D.C., a week later, she ran close to Faggs, as the "mother" of the Tigerbelles had instructed her to do, and finished second behind her teammate in the 200 finals. She was a sixteen-year-old girl from Tennessee about to start her junior year in high school. She was also headed to the other side of the world as the youngest member of the 1956 United States Olympic Track team. The 1956 Summer Games in Melbourne, Australia were mired in controversy. The first Olympic boycotts were staged, with the Netherlands, Spain, and Switzerland pulling out over the Russian invasion of Hungary, while Egypt, Iraq, and Lebanon withdrew because of the English-French occupation of the Suez Canal. There would be blood in the water when the Hungarian team, which had left home before the tanks entered Budapest, faced the Soviets in a water-polo match, during which the police had to be called in.

Yet for the American team, and especially for the rural southern girls, Melbourne was an oasis. They were women in what was still considered an unfeminine sport, and they were black in a country that kept them down whenever they left the confines of the black southern track circuit. And most had not done a lot of traveling. "That's when I found out there were two worlds—Mississippi and the rest of the world," said Willye White, a former Tigerbelle who went on to compete in five Olympic Games between 1956 and 1972. "I found out that blacks and whites could eat together, sleep together, play together, do all those things together. . . . Had I not been in the Olympic Games, I could have spent the rest of my life thinking blacks and whites were separate." It was a crucial Games for Rudolph for the same reason. Tom Biracree wrote in his biography of Rudolph in 1988, "For the first time in her life, Rudolph felt that no one cared that she was black. The only judgments made about men and women in the Olympics were determined by stopwatches, time clocks and measuring tapes."

Rudolph's times were not great, and she did not consider her first Olympics a success. When she failed to qualify for the 200-meter finals, she said she felt as if she "had let down everybody back home and the whole United States of America." At sixteen, Wilma believed tiny Clarksville, the Tigerbelles, every black, and every American were depending on her and she hadn't performed well for them. Later that week, when she met the local star of the 1956 Games, Betty Cuthbert, an eighteen-year-old Australian who won three golds in the 100-, the 200-, and the 400-meter relay, her spirits lifted. When Wilma and her three Tiberbelle teammates won the bronze in the sprint relay, she could claim the only medal the American women won in the track events.

Mildred McDaniel won the high jump with a world record, and White won silver in the long jump. Wilma came home to a special ceremony at her high school, which held no classes that day. And remarkably, despite the trip from Melbourne, she played basketball that very night for Clinton Gray, the coach who had named her Skeeter.

Rudolph's fairy-tale career got complicated in the fall of 1958 when she became pregnant by her longtime boyfriend. She was a seventeen-year-old senior in high school planning to run at TSU in the fall. "I was mortified," she later wrote. "We were both innocent about sex, didn't know anything about birth control or about contraceptives, but neither of us ever thought it would result in this." Her religious family understood—with the condition that she never see her boyfriend again—and Coach Temple waived his rule about mothers on his team. Wilma graduated from high school on time and a month later gave birth to a girl, Yolanda, whom she sent to live with one of her sisters in St. Louis.

In the fall, Wilma began college at TSU as she had hoped. Coach Temple, already a strong influence in her life, watched her carefully and trained her hard. She made the Tigerbelles her freshman year and tried to succeed under Temple's conditions, though she had never worked exceedingly hard at school before. With her studies, a campus job, and her child back in Clarksville so Wilma could see more of her, it was difficult to juggle her time. Her sophomore track season was equally beset with distractions and touched by unexpected losses; she eventually had a tonsillectomy that ended a long-running, strength-sapping infection. By the 1960 Olympic trials in Texas, however, she was in top form. She won the 100- meter and set an American record with a win in the 200-meter. She and her Tigerbelle teammates also set a national record in the 4 × 100-meter relay.

Temple was chosen to debut as the U.S. women's track-and-field coach at the 1960 Rome Olympics, and Rudolph, who had missed his guidance in Melbourne, felt more at ease in the competitions. Despite twisting her ankle before the competition began, she repeated the feats of Blankers-Koen and Cuthbert, winning the 100- and the 200-, and, in spite of a bobbled handoff, anchoring the winning sprint relay team of fellow Tigerbelles. But unlike the champions before her, Rudolph won her gold medals while a worldwide television audience watched. Millions read what *Time* magazine reported: "From the moment she first sped down the track in Rome's Olympic Stadium, there was no doubt she was the fastest woman the world had ever seen."

Though there were other media draws there, like Cassius Clay, then a young boxer who fed on the crowds and came away with a gold medal as a light-heavyweight, and an African named Abebe Bikila, who won the marathon running barefoot, Rudolph was the biggest star in Rome that year. Tall and elegant, holding her head high as she crossed the finish line each time, the six foot, one inch, 130-pound formerly crippled girl was an instant international superstar.

The attention she garnered drew nicknames with racial overtones—*la gazella nera,* or the black gazelle, for example—yet her triumphs delighted American blacks, who were in the midst of their epical struggle for equal rights. After a tour through Europe, she finally returned home. With a police escort, she rode through the streets of Clarksville, to "the first integrated event in the history of the town," she later wrote. "The banquet they gave to me that night; it was the first in Clarksville's history that blacks and whites had gathered under the same roof for the same event." A white official who spoke at the banquet noted, "If you want to get good music out of a piano you have to play both the black and white keys." She met Pope John XXIII and President Kennedy and became the first female track-and-field athlete to win the Sullivan Award, annually given to the country's top amateur athlete.

Rudolph retired from track in 1962. "I couldn't top what I did, so I'll be remembered for when I was at my best," she said. She taught at her old elementary school in Clarksville, did some motivational speaking, coached track, and founded the Wilma Rudolph Foundation for children in Indianapolis. "If I left the earth today," she said in 1993, "my greatest moment would be in knowing that I have tried to give something to young people." A month later, she learned she had brain cancer, and a year after that, she died, at the age of fifty-four. At her funeral, Nell Jackson, the first African-American to be named an Olympic coach, said, "Wilma's accomplishments opened up the real door for women in track because of her grace and beauty. People saw her as beauty in motion." One of the mourners, Jackie Joyner Kersee, had read her autobiography in high school. "I sat on my bed and devoured every word. Wilma became my hero that night and has been ever since."

Ed Temple continued to coach the Tigerbelles, and though Temple didn't even have scholarships until 1967, in the course of his forty-three-year career at Tennessee State he produced forty Olympians who won twenty-six medals, seventeen gold. All but one of the forty Olympians he trained earned their undergraduate degrees, twenty-eight got a master's, and six earned a Ph.D. His list of Tigerbelles includes Wyomia Tyus, who was the first Olympian to win consecutive 100-meter races (in 1964 and 1968), and Madeline Manning, the only American woman to win the 800-meter gold (1968). His last great champion was Chandra Cheeseborough, who won two relay gold medals and a silver medal in the 400-meter. In 1984, Cheeseborough replaced Temple as coach of the Tigerbelles.

* * *

Wilma Rudolph's gold-medal performance in the 1960 Olympics was a crowning example of what African-American women could overcome and achieve. She was an exemplary model of the new female athlete. But while the stunning victory and her star reputation led her to the White House and helped ensure later Tigerbelle success, they didn't change the fact that women's track and field was not as organized or widespread as other women's sports such as golf, tennis, or figure skating; they served as reminders of how far women's track and field was from any men's athletic programs. It still lacked the funding, training, and support that individual women's sports and most men's sports received.

For American female athletes, track and field was still not an "appropriate" sport. Society did what it could to control participation in all sports in high schools and colleges across the country. With help from the Division of Girls and Women's Sports (DGWS), a holdover from the Women's Division of the 1930s, competition was discouraged, and championships were kept to a minimum. Private and public high schools rarely had teams, and most colleges were denied programs. Throughout the 1960s, less than 20 percent of the country's universities offered women's intercollegiate competition. Even by the early 1970s, studies show that only 7.4 percent of girls participated in high school athletics.

The AAU was relying on fledgling track clubs in the West, black southern colleges, and municipal organizations for its competitors and future Olympians. The Mayor Daley Youth Foundation in Chicago finished second to Tennessee State in the 1966 AAU nationals. The West Coast clubs were especially noted for nurturing middle-distance runners like Francie Larrieu and Doris Brown, a five-time world champion in cross-country, who might have been bigger stars if the Olympics had run longer races for women.

Colleges came back in the picture in the 1970s. First, the Association for Intercollegiate Athletics for Women was organized in 1971 by female college administrators. The AIAW eventually hosted national championships in nineteen sports, including track and field, and woke up the National Collegiate Athletic Association, the dominant organization in college sports, to the possibilities of the female student athlete.

Women's sports got its greatest legal boost when Congress passed Title IX of the Education Act of 1972. The provision forbids educational institutions that receive federal funding from discriminating—including denying participation or funding—on the basis of sex. Title IX covers the music department as well as the swim team, but its passage particularly meant that universities that spent millions on men's sports and scant thousands on its women would be required to try to balance the scale. By 1981, the average women's collegiate athletic budget had risen to about sixteen percent of what the men's budget was, compared with one percent in 1971.

In January 1981, the NCAA began offering its own championships, and like Madame Milliat's group versus the IAAF in the 1920s, the AIAW and the NCAA could not coexist in peace. In October 1981, the AIAW filed suit against NCAA for antitrust violations. The AIAW folded in June 1982, with many of the large female athletic programs having become NCAA members. The AIAW lawsuit was thrown out in 1984.

The women's track-and-field scene—as well as future champions like Jackie Joyner-Kersee, Gwen Torrence, and Marion Jones—benefited from these changes, but for the athletes during this time of transition, the advocacy came too late. While Rudolph's success increased track and field's profile in the United States, and the Tigerbelles continued to win Olympic golds, it was clear that American women were falling behind what had become the Big Red Machine. Eisenhower and Kennedy both pressed to end the perceived softness of Americans; U.S. Olympic officials also were trying to get more women and better athletes into the program, even though the AAU and USOC were still practically at war with physical education organizations. The headline of a 1963 *Sports Illustrated* article, with a picture of a Russian athlete, asked "Why Can't We Beat This Girl?" American athletes who competed in the 1960s and 1970s against the eastern bloc sports machine and their own slow-moving track hierarchy were seldom seen winning events in the Olympics and world competitions. Virtually shut out of international competition, they brought home few medals and received little recognition. Wyomia Tyus, Edith McGuire, and Madeline Manning were the exceptions; they starred in the 1964 and 1968 Games, showing how remarkable the Tennessee State program was and how weak the rest of the country was in comparison. Manning set an Olympic record in the 800 at the 1968 Olympics, while her countryman Doris Brown, world champion cross-country runner, finished fifth. For the most part, however, American women in those years had to be satisfied with national competitions and hope for a growth in collegiate programs.

Meanwhile, Olympic competition had become more political, and real-world intrusions went from brave statements of black power from the medal stand in 1968 to the devastating Palestinian massacre of eleven Israeli athletes and officials in 1972. Using Olympics dominance as a means of obtaining political prowess, the eastern European program took the international competitions by sweeping margins. Starting with their participation in the 1976 Montreal Games, eastern bloc athletes won forty-four of the forty-nine gold medals awarded to women, and East Germany won six of the nine gold medals in track and field. Their "democratic" sports machine created a long, impressive list of champions, including Iolanda Balas of Romania, who won

140 consecutive high-jump competitions, including two gold medals; East Germans Ruth Fuchs, who won javelin gold in 1972 and 1976, and Renate Stecher, who won 90 consecutive outdoor sprints and the 100-meter gold in 1972; middle-distance runner Tatyana Kazankina of the Soviet Union, who owned world records and won three gold medals; and the Press sisters of the Soviet Union, Tamara and Irina, who won five gold medals and one silver in field events in the 1960 and 1964 Olympics.

One star of the 1976 Games was an eastern European even a Westerner of the time could love: Irena Kirszenstein Szewinska. Born in the Soviet Union of Polish Jewish parents, Kirszenstein competed for Poland in the 1964 Games, winning silvers in the 200-meter and the long jump and a gold in the 4 × 100-meter relay. In Mexico City four years later, she set a world record in winning gold in the 200-meter and also earned a bronze in the 100. In 1972, she won a bronze in the 200. In 1973, she discovered the 400-meter and became a favorite to win in the Montreal Games. She won in world-record time for her seventh medal in her fifth different sport in her fifth Olympics. She tied the women's track-and-field record of Shirley Strickland of Australia (three golds, one silver, three bronzes).

But even though these and other eastern bloc women dominated track and field through the dismantling of communism in the late 1980s, they were rarely in the spotlight—especially in America. While communist pixies on the balance beam were accepted and even idolized, their more muscular countrywomen weren't given the same ink. It was a combination of boycotts, Western bias, unpronounceable names and a clash of cultures, and the suspicion of what the eastern bloc sports machine would do to maintain glory on the athletic front.

In subsequent years, much has been discovered regarding the standard illegal practices permitted in those countries and, as it turns out, some of the concern was legitimate. The two Russian sisters, Tamara and Irina Press, who won medals in field events in the 1960s, disappeared after early sex tests that entailed physical exams were introduced. Chromosome testing, in which cells taken from the inside of the cheek are studied to determine gender, were introduced in 1967, and Ewa Klobukowska of Poland was the first major athlete to fail it despite passing a physical exam. The test is not 100 percent accurate and is in fact dismissed in medical circles and even banned in some countries.

Sex tests affect very few athletes, but drug tests, started at the 1972 Munich Olympics, have become as common and necessary as taping ankles. As athletes and their training have become more sophisticated, so have the drugs used to enhance their performances. The latest steroids or synthetically produced testosterone and other human growth hormones are continually altered to sidestep the newest detector. Women who use steroids to shorten the recovery time needed from high-stress activity to develop more muscle at a faster pace, and have a greater capacity for muscle growth, can use a dose so small that is hard to detect, especially since the drug flushes out of a woman's system much faster than out of a man's. The combination of greater results without greater risk of being caught has completely altered the playing field in women's sports. In 1992, Olga Connolly said that because of the history of drug abuse in field events, "there is no way in the world a woman nowadays can break the record unless she is on steroids. These awful drugs have changed the complexion of track and field."

The East German officials now admit that systematic doping of athletes, with or without their knowledge, was partly responsible for that country's success in the 1970s and 1980s. By the mid-1990s, former athletes were blaming the steroid use for their heart and liver diseases; Heidi Krieger, the 1986 European champion, began a sex change procedure because of the irreversible male characteristics caused by massive doses of testosterone. Eastern Europeans were not the only ones involved. When the USOC ran tests in 1984 and 1985 without threat of sanctions, 50 percent of the athletes tested positive for anabolic steroids.

The eastern European athletes of the 1960s and 1970s were superior athletes, notwithstanding the drug use, and it would take the boycott of seventeen eastern bloc countries at the 1984 Olympics in Los Angeles to create an opening for American women athletes to reclaim their dominance in track and field. With America's boycott of the previous Games in Moscow, athletes like Evelyn Ashford and Valerie Brisco were eager to compete; to do so on their home turf was even better. The 1984 Olympics was to be the sprinters' revival and a dramatic breakthrough for the distance runners.

Women had been officially competing in worldwide marathons for almost twenty years, but until the L.A. Games, the Olympic race was exclusively male (even though women were banned to protect themselves, research now shows that women's bodies are genetically predisposed to excel in longer distances and endurance competitions). Even the Boston Marathon, a racing institution, had always excluded women. In 1967, Kathryn V. Switzer registered as K. V. Switzer in order to get an official number and became the first woman to officially run the Boston Marathon. When it became clear during the race that she was female, people threw food at her and otherwise harassed her, and the race official tried to stop her from running, yelling, "Get the hell out of my race." Even with such distractions, she finished the 26.2-mile race with an impressive time. The first woman ever to receive worldwide fame as a marathon runner is Norway's Grete Waitz, who won the New York Marathon nine times between 1978 and 1988. She was also the silver medalist at this first Olympic marathon in 1984, well behind the gold-medal winner, Joan Benoit Samuelson, a quiet Maine runner who, just seventeen days before the Olympic trials, had arthroscopic surgery on her knee and was running with an injured hamstring.

Joan Benoit was born in 1957 in Maine and discovered distance running as she rehabilitated a broken leg injured in a skiing race. In high school, she was a middle- and long-distance phenomenon, and during her college years at Bowdoin and her graduate years at North Carolina State, she continued competing. Benoit won the first marathon she ever attempted, in Boston in 1979, running two miles before the race to get to the starting line when she got caught in traffic. An immediate star, she continued to run despite being swarmed with endorsements and harassed by publicity, as well as sustaining numerous injuries and surgeries. In 1982, she broke the American record for women, and in 1983 she broke the world record in her second Boston marathon, with a time of 2:22:43. When the marathon was included in the 1984 Olympics, she won the trials despite the recent surgery.

On the morning of the first Olympic women's marathon, she entered the Olympic Coliseum in Los Angeles, injuries and all, well ahead of all other medal contenders. With eighty thousand spectators watching this historic event, she crossed the finish line and won gold in what some called "the greatest individual marathon of all time."

One of the greatest stumbles occurred five days later in another new event, the 3,000-meter race. Mary Decker Slaney, a former running prodigy who at age twenty-six was in the midst of a spectacular comeback, was poised to finally win her first Olympic medal. Everyone was waiting for her showdown with Zola Budd, another running prodigy who had recently broken Slaney's record in the 5,000. A shy eighteen-year-old South African who ran barefoot, Budd had garnered a British passport to bypass her native country's ban from international competition because of its apartheid policies.

About 1,300 meters from the finish, Slaney's foot clipped Budd's ankle. Budd never fell despite being spiked in the heel, but she lost her composure and finished seventh. Slaney stumbled forward then fell off the track, injuring a hip muscle. When she did get up, she blamed Budd for the collision. (Incidentally, the winner was Maricica Puica of Romania.)

The incident marked another bad break for Slaney, perhaps the greatest American runner not to have won an Olympic medal. At twelve, she competed in events ranging from a 440 to a marathon in one week. At fourteen, she was competing internationally. At fifteen, she was winning. The next year, the ailments, injuries, and heartbreaks would start. She missed the 1976 Games; got fit and began setting world records in the middle distances only to miss the 1980 Games because of the U.S. boycott. After another bout with injuries, she became so dominant that she was the first female winner of the Jesse Owens Award, given to the top track-and-field athlete in America. Then came the unforgettable 1984 race.

Slaney did not lose in 1985, again winning at furious record-setting paces, yet when the Olympics rolled around three years later, she finished tenth in the 3,000 and eighth in the 1,500. Foot injuries and an iron deficiency cost her at the 1992 Olympic trials and she did not make it to Seoul.

After making the 1996 U.S. team in the 5,000 in yet another comeback, she learned she had tested positive for having too high a testosterone level; after the Atlanta Games—and yet another on-track disappointment— she convinced American officials that she had done nothing wrong and her level was natural. Slaney turned forty in 1998, yet she is still competing, still drawing crowds, and still considered a top middle-distance runner. And even if she fades soon, she still seems likely to dominate the record books.

The 1984 Olympics was more than races of endurance; the sprinters were dazzling the audiences at the L.A. Games as well. Evelyn Ashford from South Central L.A., who was competing in her second of what would become four Olympics, won the gold medal in the 100-meter and a second as part of the 400-meter relay. Also on this gold medal–winning 400-meter relay team, was another hometown hero, Valerie Brisco. Having already won gold in the 200- and 400-meter sprints, the relay win made her the first woman in twenty-five years to win three gold medals in one Olympics and the only athlete ever to win gold in the 200-meter and the 400-meter at the same Games. Making her Olympic debut, twenty-two-year-old Jackie Joyner began what was to become a twelve-year reign in the women's heptathlon and long jump.

Jackie Joyner-Kersee is America's uncontested track-and-field favorite. Not only has she impressed the world with her six Olympic medals in four Olympic Games, but she has charmed audiences with her gracious nature and competitive spirit despite challenging odds and a modest beginning. Jackie Joyner was born in 1962 on Piggott Avenue, between 14th and 15th Streets, in a not-so-good part of East St. Louis. The seven Joyners—Jackie, her parents, two younger sisters, older brother, and great-grandmother—lived in a small, six-room house in a block of shotgun houses with cement porches. Across the street were a barbershop, a convenience store, a liquor store, and a pool hall that catered to men with names like Squirrel, Slick, and Bubba, the local neighborhood watch, who looked out for the Joyner girls and especially for their brother, Al, a year and a half older than Jackie, who early on was earning money shining shoes for thirty-five cents at the barbershop.

At the Mayor Brown Community Center, Jackie was introduced to the fundamentals of track and field, and at the age of nine, she joined the track team. At ten, she and her sisters began filling potato chip bags with sand from Lincoln Park (a skip away at 15th and Piggott) and depositing the contents in a pile in their front yard. With legs strong from cheerleading and dancing to Jackson Five records, Jackie would leap into her makeshift sand pit from three feet above to practice her form. She was learning to fly. Upon seeing the 1976 Olympics on television, with the performances of Evelyn Ashford, Jackie began to dream of being an Olympic contender.

Taught by her parents that reward and opportunity come with hard work, she immersed herself in athletics, joining the Lincoln High School basketball, volleyball, and track teams while maintaining an impressive grade point average. Nino Fennoy, her coach then, refined her skills and helped her win four consecutive national junior pentathlon championships, the first title when she was only fourteen. Swarmed by college recruiters who were finding support for their growing track programs, she took a scholarship at UCLA to play basketball and run track.

In 1980, at UCLA, Joyner met a young assistant coach who reminded her of Fennoy, a man the others called a terror. Bob Kersee, the son of an American Navy man and a Panamanian woman, would convince her and the college athletic department to concentrate on multi-event track, as well as befriend her when her mother died unexpectedly her freshman year. Jackie was already fast and a good jumper, so Bob worked on her technique, and her brother, Al, taught her to throw and hurdle. In 1982, she chose the heptathlon as her event, and the next year she qualified for the world championships. The seven-event series takes two days, and points are acquired for performance in the 200-meter dash, high jump, long jump, javelin, shot put, 100-meter hurdles, and 800-meter run.

Joyner's first Olympic attempt in the heptathlon, at the 1984 Olympics in Los Angeles, was perhaps her greatest disappointment, even though she finished with the silver. She missed winning gold by only five points, or less than a second in the 800-meter run. When she cried that day, however, it was not for her near miss, but for her brother, Al, who had just won the triple jump. She went on to win the 1986 Goodwill Games in Moscow, becoming the first heptathlete ever to break seven thousand points. She then topped her own record three weeks later at the Olympic Festival in Houston. She received the Jesse Owens Award and the Sullivan Award in 1986. With Jackie as the reigning champ, breaking her own record again and again, the sport grew in interest and participation.

By the 1988 Seoul Olympics, the heptathlon was spotlighted along with its star and her new husband and coach, Bob Kersee. The media praised her outstanding win in the long jump and then her dominance in the heptathlon, in which she again broke her own record and won gold. Yet one post-race news conference centered on comments made by the men's 800-meter silver medalist, Joaquim Cruz of Brazil, who had compared her to a gorilla. Her graceful response: "I never thought I was the prettiest person in the world, but I know that inside I'm beautiful." By the end of the two weeks, attention was centered on her connection to Ben Johnson and the drama surrounding his failed drug test and forced return of the gold medal he won in the 100-meter, as well as her link to Florence Griffith-Joyner, another UCLA track athlete and Bob Kersee protégée, who later became her sister-in-law.

Florence Griffith grew up in L.A. in a deeply religious and very poor family. Like Jackie, she got her start at a local club, the Sugar Ray Robinson Youth Foundation, outrunning even the boys; and in high school she broke all the sprinting and jumping records. She followed her coach, Bob Kersee, from Cal-Northridge to UCLA, training for national championships in sprinting, which she always won. Her first Olympics was the 1984 Games, in which she placed second behind Valerie Brisco, the gold-medal sprinter in the 200-meter. Griffith then essentially retired, taking a day job at a bank and a night job as a nail stylist. It would take Al Joyner, coincidentally Jackie's brother, his love and training assistance, to get her serious again about sprinting. They were married a year before the 1988 Olympics.

Florence Griffith-Joyner, with her six-inch nails and fluorescent uniforms, was reborn as Flo Jo when she burst out of the starting blocks and into the record books, winning the 100 and the 200 at the 1988 United States Olympic Trials in Indianapolis. She was also bursting out of her outfits, mostly one-legged Spandex running suits in candy colors, with a little lace thrown in. "I came here with fourteen outfits," she told the press. Her times, her outfits, and her looks got her on the cover of *Newsweek*, but it was her raw speed at the Seoul Games two months later that backed up her new title as the world's fastest woman. She won three golds, in the 100-meter, 200-meter, and 400-meter relay, and a silver in the 1,600-meter relay, becoming the first American woman in track and field to win four medals in one Olympics.

The sisters-in-law and their respective husband-coaches were the talk of the Olympics, including some negative press when the news media spun a world-class family feud between the Joyners and the Kersees that tried to portray the two women as a "couple of cat-fighting, egomaniacal women." Ever gracious, Jackie said, "I had no reason to envy Florence" and called the reports sexist. Other negative attention suggested that as Griffith-Joyner had gotten training tips from Ben Johnson, her new physique and extraordinary world-record times at the Olympic Trials must be steroid induced, though she denied all charges and passed all tests.

Flo Jo retired in 1989 after the Olympics at the early age of thirty. She designed a line of track clothes, made fitness videos, and was appointed to President Clinton's Council on Physical Fitness and Sports. In 1995, she was elected to the Track and Field Hall of Fame. Jackie continued to compete, gaining endorsements, fame, a foundation back home, an adoring public, and admiring press. When she won the bronze in the long jump and the gold in the heptathlon at the 1992 Olympics in Barcelona, she said she planned to compete through the 1996 Olympics in Atlanta so she would have begun and ended her Olympic career on American soil.

With the Atlanta Olympics approaching, Jackie Joyner-Kersee's competition-worn body wasn't cooperating. She was thirty-four, had torn her Achilles tendon, hamstring, and groin over the years, and was running out of steam. At the Olympic trials, she suffered her first loss in the heptathlon in twelve years. When, in the first event of the 1996 Olympic heptathlon, the hurdles, it was clear that a pull in her right thigh was causing her great pain, Bob Kersee said he had seen enough. Jackie pulled out of the heptathlon. Ghada Shouaa, who would win the competition, gave them both a kiss, President Clinton called, and sports eulogies were recited on television that night and in the newspapers the next day. But Jackie wasn't done. She was still in the long jump; she still wanted to fly.

She calls long jumping her first love. "I care about long jumping the way Maya Angelou cares about her poetry and Whitney Houston cares about her voice," she wrote in her autobiography, *A Kind of Grace*. She considers herself a great competitor, a woman who cares more about effort than outcome, and she wanted to leave the sport with one more great meet. After five of six jumps, she was in sixth place. On her last jump, she let loose a pulled-muscle-be-damned leap that brought a roar from the Olympic Stadium. Though she didn't win the gold or the silver, she had put herself on the podium one last time as the bronze medalist. As she recalls, "They were treating me like a record-breaker and a world-beater, even though I was neither, simply because they knew how hard I tried. Those ovations that night in Atlanta fulfilled and satisfied me more than any others I ever had." For her effort, Joyner-Kersee was given the first Wilma Rudolph Award in 1996, presented by the Women's Sports Foundation to the female athlete who shows courage in competition.

The American athlete most expected to pick up where Joyner-Kersee left off is Marion Jones, who, like Babe, Wilma, and Jackie before her, is a basketball-playing track superstar in waiting. With her win in the 100-meter and the 400-meter relay at the world championships in 1997, coaches think she's the woman who will break Flo Jo's 1988 sprinting records and match Jackie's long-jump achievements. In one of her last competitions, Jackie even pulled Jones aside, saying, "I'd love to come to North Carolina and show you some technique."

The 1996 U.S. Olympic track team had plenty of fresh names and noteworthy firsts in Atlanta. Fatuma Roba was the first female African gold-medal marathoner; Chioma Ajunwa of Nigeria was the first African to win a field event; Ghada Shouaa was the first Syrian, male or female, to win gold in any event; and Marie-José Pérec, a Frenchwoman from Guadaloupe, was the first athlete, male or female, to win consecutive Olympic gold medals in the 400-meter. Her double in the 200 and 400 was not lost in the shadow of Michael Johnson's historic feat in the same two races, and her victories provided an exclamation point to what had been called the Year of the Women. Female track-and-field competitors relish the spotlight they got in Atlanta when the fans embraced their athleticism, and the press documented their triumphs and their disappointments in words that described athletes, not just women. Women were allowed to fall, scream, strain, sweat, cry, show off their abs, and flex their muscles. It was a scene that would have incensed Women's Division members and might have inspired poisoned pen from more than a few 1930s sportswriters. But maybe, at last, the thought of women running, jumping, and throwing doesn't seem all that out of the ordinary. It is quite simple, in fact.

Baseball and Softball

Swinging for the Fences
Amy Ellis Nutt

The year 1876 was as momentous a year as any in American history: 264 men of the U.S. Seventh Cavalry were ambushed and killed at the Battle of the Little Big Horn. Mark Twain published *The Adventures of Tom Sawyer*. And the president of Western Union, William Orton, turned down an offer to acquire Alexander Graham Bell's new telephone, calling it a toy and a "scientific curiosity." In sports, 1876 was equally significant. On February 2 the National League of Professional Base Ball Clubs, the first permanent major league, was founded, designating eight clubs as its charter members.

The great American pastime has been played in one form or another as far back as the Revolutionary War. A direct descendant of the British games of cricket, in which innings and bases are used, and rounders, a children's stick-and-ball game, baseball was called early on by such names as town ball, goal ball, round ball, and base. It was played on New England greens, in southern fields, even at Valley Forge. Men played it on college campuses (except at Princeton, where it was banned in 1787 as "unbecoming gentlemen students"), and in 1824, Bowdoin College student and future poet Henry Wadsworth Longfellow wrote that baseball "communicated such an impulse to our limbs and joints that there is nothing now heard of in our leisure hours, but ball, ball, ball."

Not until 1846, however, were the rules of baseball formalized and the first official game played at Elysian Fields in Hoboken, New Jersey. Alexander Cartwright, president of the New York Knickerbocker Base Ball Club, and his team of twenty-eight men, which included brokers, merchants, salesmen, a doctor, and a photographer, had been playing twice a week in Manhattan for some three years before they finally moved to the more spacious fields of

Hoboken. There, on June 19, 1846, they played their first official, prearranged match, losing to the New York Base Ball Club 23–1.

Thirty years later, and only about ninety miles from Hoboken, the Vassar College Resolutes took the field in high-collared, long-sleeved shirts, ankle-length dresses, high-topped shoes, and identical wide-striped caps. On a warm September afternoon in 1876, behind the Vassar College gates in Poughkeepsie, New York, the Resolutes did what no organized team of women had ever done before: They played baseball.

The uniforms, the equipment, the people who play the game of baseball, all these things change over the years. But not the sights, not the sounds, and not the smells: the shadows tiptoeing across the diamond in the fading summer light, the smack of bat against ball, the fresh scent of green fields. Then and now, this is the story of baseball. The plot changes; the characters come and go. The narrative continues.

One hundred and twenty years ago, only a few dozen women in the United States played organized baseball. Played within the safe confines of all-women's colleges, the games were more about relaxation than competition. Today, thousands of women participate in the great American pastime. From Little League to the semi-pro level, the opportunities for females to play organized baseball have never been greater.

The history of women in baseball can be viewed in terms of three discrete periods. In the early part of this century, dozens of professional barnstorming teams, called Bloomer Girls, toured the country, and sometimes even foreign lands, taking on all comers. Stars of the time included New Englander Lizzie Murphy, who made her living from baseball for nearly two decades, and Alta Weiss, an ace hurler from Ohio. Margaret Nabel, from Staten Island, established herself as the manager and owner of one of the best female teams of the era, the New York Bloomer Girls, in the 1920s. And Amanda Clement made history in 1905 as the first woman umpire.

In the 1940s, when the major leagues were depleted by men going off to serve in World War II, several dozen women were given the opportunity to play professionally as part of the All-American Girls Baseball League. Immortalized in the film *A League of Their Own*, Cincinnatian Dottie Kamenshek became the greatest star of the All-American Girls Professional Baseball League during her nine years as first baseman for the Rockford (Illinois) Peaches in the 1940s and 1950s.

The third, and most recent, era in the history of women in baseball has everything to do with the passing of Title IX legislation in 1972, which mandated that women and girls be given equal opportunity when it comes to athletics. Since then, young girls have played alongside young boys on Little League baseball teams. In fewer numbers, but no less significantly, high school girls have integrated previously all-male teams. And in the late 1980s, Julie

Croteau, a left-handed-hitting first baseman at St. Mary's College in Maryland, became the first woman to play on a men's college team. Croteau would later go on to become one of the original Silver Bullets, the current all-women's professional baseball team.

Nearly as long as the history of women in baseball is the history of women who played softball. First played in 1887, softball was seen as a safer alternative to the faster game of baseball. Over the past 111 years, both men and women have played the game primarily as a recreational and club sport. But for the past half century softball also has been the only diamond sport women could play as a team at the high school and college levels.

Not until 1996 and the gold-medal success of the women's Olympic softball team in Atlanta did the sport of softball, so often regarded as baseball's stepchild, finally receive its due. With the exploits of players like Dot Richardson and Lisa Fernandez, the 1996 U. S. Women's Softball team single-handedly raised the profile of their sport to a new level.

It made sense that a game that was so popular with men—baseball, after all, was played everywhere, in cities and in the most rural towns—would also be popular with women. But in the three decades following that first organized baseball game in Elysian Fields, women still had no venue in which to play organized ball—except in the privacy of their own college campuses, away from the disapproving eyes of men. In 1866, Vassar, an all-women's college, put together two baseball clubs with eight players each. Ten years later, in 1876, the first organized nine-player squad of women played the new national pastime. By 1879, Vassar was fielding seven baseball teams to compete against each other and eventually against other all-women's institutions, such as Smith College, Mount Holyoke, Wellesley, and Barnard. The games were intramural, and the teams represented different classes or dormitories. Played inside the confines of those campuses, women's baseball was allowed to flourish. A letter from Vassar student Annie Glidden in 1866 read, "They are getting up various clubs now for out-of-the-door exercises. They have a floral society, boat clubs and base ball clubs. I belong to the latter, and enjoy it highly, I can assure you."

Shielded as they were from public approbation, these eighteen-, nineteen-, and twenty-one-year-old women played the sport with abandon. If their long dresses were often a hindrance in running and fielding, they were sometimes also a help. The full skirts could easily trap an infield hit, and they offered a modicum of protection when sliding into bases. Minnie Stephens, Smith College class of 1883, wrote to her former classmates years after they had all graduated about a hotly contested game that had taken place in 1880, their sophomore year, that "one vicious batter drove the ball directly into the belt line of her opponent, and had it not been for the rigid steel corset clasp worn in those days, she would have been knocked out completely."

Beyond the walls of their colleges, women's baseball was a rare sight. The fear was that the sport would start catching on with women everywhere, including coed institutions, where it was not as welcome. In 1904, five female students at the University of Pennsylvania joined in a men's baseball game on the campus one afternoon. In little time, according to a local newspaper account, a crowd of cheering students had gathered to watch. "Each play or misplay in which the gentle sex had a part, was applauded long and loud and pandemonium finally broke loose when one of the stalwart co-eds knocked out a two-bagger." It didn't take long for university officials to respond to the excitement. Within days female students were prohibited from playing baseball on the Ivy League campus, and the police were admonished to halt any such activity immediately when it came to their attention.

By the 1920s, nearly two dozen women's colleges fielded intramural baseball teams. Though games were competitive, the intent was probably more social than athletic. Women's sports, prior to this time, centered on individual disciplines—golf, tennis, archery—and so baseball provided for women a rare opportunity for communal activity, in addition to the salubrious benefits of exercise and relaxation. Team sports, however, eventually attracted the attention of a censorious public, including Victorian-minded physical education teachers. Their concern was that team sports encouraged women to do unwomanly things, to be aggressive and to overexert themselves. Sports, they said, should be played by women only as a form of exercise, not as a form of competition, which was the sole province of men.

Even restricted play was no longer acceptable. Educators, newspaper columnists, and politicians all weighed in with their opinions, criticizing the playing of team sports by women. Ironically, Smith College, which had played a significant role in the emergence of women's sports, would forbid baseball and basketball competition. In 1893, fifteen years after baseball began there, Smith was the site of the first organized women's basketball game. Both team sports had maintained major-sport status for several decades after their introduction. Now the college considered baseball and basketball unwomanly, with all the running and the potential for uncontrolled aggression, and a threat to femininity. In 1923, when the National Amateur Athletic Federation proposed that women's college sports become more democratic, more participatory, and less competitive, baseball and basketball gradually disappeared.

The September 9, 1910, edition of the *Nashville* (Tennessee) *Banner* carried this curious headline: "When Father Locates Earl The Bloomer Girls Will Need Another Player." The accompanying news story explained that fourteen-

year-old Earl Mingua had run away from home and was believed to be playing second base on a Bloomer Girls team in nearby Kentucky. Such was the
popularity of the game in the early 1900s as it was being played by dozens of
women's barnstorming baseball teams throughout the country.

When opportunities to play college baseball began to fade for women
at the turn of the century, professional opportunities took their place. In the
1890s and up through the 1920s, "Bloomer" girls teams crisscrossed the country
taking on men's town teams, semi-pro and minor league teams, and occasionally other Bloomer teams. The women played for the sport of it, the
adventure, but also for the money. Longtime *Atlanta Journal and Constitution* sportswriter Furman Bisher maintains that "Bloomergirls" origin rests
with a pioneering suffragette of the time, Amelia Jenks Bloomer, who designed the pantaloons the players wore.

Bloomer Girls teams sprang up in places as far north as Nova Scotia,
as far south as Texas, and in cities like Indianapolis and Cincinnati, Philadelphia, Boston, and New York. These were the years of World War I, when
Americans yearned for anything to take their minds off the terrible things
happening in the trenches of Europe. Bloomer teams traveled across state
and across country to play games, but they also, on rare occasions, traveled
across oceans to play in places as far away as Cuba and Japan. The players
were young, single women who recognized a brief window of opportunity in
their lives in which they could experience the freedom of traveling by themselves and earning their own living. And they made the most of it. Traveling
from town to town by car, rail, or horse and buggy, the Bloomer teams played
exhausting schedules. During one particularly brutal stretch in 1903, the Boston Bloomer Girls played—and won—twenty-eight games in twenty-six
days. During the two-day weekend of July 3–4, they played six games in five
different towns in Oklahoma.

During their existence, the Bloomer teams, which came primarily from
midwestern, southern, and eastern states, achieved a modicum of success
playing against men's teams. Part of that success was no doubt due to the
fact that every Bloomer team included at least one male player, usually a
catcher, and often two or three. The men were called "toppers" because of
the wigs (and sometimes even the skirts) they wore in order to pass as women.
In her book *Women in Baseball*, Gai Ingham Berlage writes, "The manager
of the New England Bloomer Girls was heard once to brag that he had a
player, Clarence Wortham, who made 'as handsome a girl as any boy on the
team.'" A few future major leaguers worked as toppers when they were teenagers, including Hall of Famers Rogers Hornsby and Smoky Joe Wood. It
was good work for a summer. Bloomer Girls teams earned several hundred
dollars for an appearance, which was split among the players and the team's
manager.

Several players for Bloomer Girls teams achieved star status. Among them was Maud Nelson (sometimes misspelled as Nielson in the newspapers of the era), a hard-throwing pitcher and third baseman who began playing in 1897, when she was just sixteen years old. Nelson spent the next four decades doing everything she could to stay involved in the sport. She was a player, a scout, a manager, and an owner. She played for the Chicago Bloomer Girls, the Boston Bloomers, the Star Bloomers of Indianapolis, and the Cherokee Indian Base Ball Club, a Native American men's team from Michigan. Where Nelson grew up is not known, although immigration records of the time indicate that she was born in the Italian Alps in 1881. What is known is that baseball was her life. More often than not, when she was pitching against—and beating—opposing male teams, the headlines the next day credited her with the win.

In 1911, having spent nearly half her young life in baseball, Nelson became owner-manager-scout of the Western Bloomer Girls along with her husband, John Olson, Jr. During the next six years, she trained players, booked opponents, and recruited talent. When her husband died in 1917, she picked up a glove again, at the age of thirty-six, to barnstorm one more time with the Boston Bloomers. She went on to manage a women's team from Chicago and then formed the All Star Ranger Girls in the 1920s. After retiring from baseball for good in the mid-1930s, Nelson and her second husband settled down in Chicago, just a couple of blocks from Wrigley Field. Nelson died in Chicago in February of 1944. Nine months later, Wrigley Field was the site of the first tryouts for the All-American Girls Professional Baseball League.

The most famous of all Bloomer Girls was not a player but a manager and promoter: Margaret Nabel from Staten Island, New York. At the age of twenty-five in 1920, Nabel took over as manager of the New York Bloomer Girls, who barnstormed up and down the East Coast. Nabel's talent for business was clear from the start. She demanded the team's share of the purse before, instead of after, each game they played; demanded that temporary fences be constructed around fields otherwise open to nonpaying spectators; and printed up postcards of the team that were sold to fans at the games. Her baseball prowess also helped the New York team do a brisk business. Games were often sold out, and attendance reached upwards of three thousand spectators. According to legend, the New York Bloomer Girls, whose roster consisted entirely of women from New York's five boroughs, supplemented by one or two players from New Jersey, never lost a game against another Bloomer team in their twenty-five-year history.

With the rise of some of major league baseball's greatest talent in the early 1900s—players like Ty Cobb, Tris Speaker, and Walter "Big Train" Johnson—barnstorming Bloomer Girls teams started to lose their appeal. In addition, the advent of radio suddenly made major league games accessible to millions of Americans. As the 1920s wore on, there was less and less public clamor for baseball played by women. By 1930 the last of the Bloomer Girls had folded up their tents and put away their gloves. After three freewheeling decades, the golden age of women's baseball was over.

With the depression in the 1930s and the Second World War in the 1940s, recreational pursuits like baseball took a backseat to much more serious concerns. Women were needed to keep homes together and homefires burning, so there was little chance for women's baseball teams to stay afloat. Nonetheless, a number of individual women played significant roles on men's baseball teams in the first half of the twentieth century. One of them was Amanda Clement.

Around 1908, at a baseball tournament in the upper Midwest, the crowd booed fiercely, boisterously objecting when the umpires for the game came out onto the field. The officials were stymied. The fans weren't calling for a player; they were calling for an umpire who wasn't even supposed to be there. One of the managers tried to reason with the crowd, explaining that another umpire had already been paid for the game in advance, and suggesting that the fans couldn't possibly expect the two teams to bring in another umpire, at considerable cost, when a perfectly good one was right there. But the crowd refused to back down, demanding to see what the newspapers of the era called the "World's Champion Umpire." They took up a collection to raise the fee necessary to pay for the umpire they wanted—"the best preserver of the peace in the whole northwest." That "preserver of the peace" was also known as the "only lady umpire in the world." Then the fans took up another collection to hire a driver to pick up Amanda Clement.

Amanda Clement didn't set out to be a "lady in blue." In 1905, at the age of only seventeen, Clement, whose family lived in Hudson, South Dakota, accompanied her older brother, Hank, to a semi-pro game in Hawarden, Iowa, where he was scheduled to pitch. When the umpire for the amateur game that preceded Hank's failed to show, Amanda's brother suggested to the teams that they allow his little sister to call balls and strikes. Whether Hank's offer was meant in jest is not known. What is known is that Clement called such a good game that the players in the game to follow asked her to stay on to officiate for them. Thus was baseball history made—and a career accidentally born.

In the first few decades of the twentieth century, baseball umpires did not have an easy life; they were subject to verbal abuse and physical attack, on rare occasions, even leading to death. In the early 1900s games had a sole officiator who stood directly behind the pitcher. Neither spectators nor press spared their criticism. From all appearances, however, Amanda Clement, at nearly six feet tall with an athletic build, was spared such abuse. Male players as well as the primarily male fans clearly felt inhibited in the female umpire's presence. She was commanding and competent in her white starched shirt, blue skirt, and cap, calling plays even in the outfield.

Clement, in fact, thought that this might be the solution to the increasingly uncivil game of baseball. Still a teenager, she was quoted in a 1906 edition of the *Cincinnati Enquirer*, suggesting, "The only objection that is found in this day to baseball is rowdyism. In spite of fines and rules and all, ball players will scrap with the umpire. . . . Do you suppose any ball player in the country would step up to a good-looking girl and say to her, 'You color-blind, pickle-brained, cross-eyed idiot, if you don't stop throwing the soup into me I'll distribute your features all over your countenance!' Of course he wouldn't."

Clement officiated semi-professional baseball from 1906 until 1911, earning enough money to put herself through Yankton College in Yankton, South Dakota. She was paid an average of twenty dollars a game and was in high demand, often recommended to officiate the most significant games in the Midwest. After graduating from college, she pursued a career as a physical education instructor and coach, making occasional appearances as an umpire and also as a basketball referee. When she died in 1971 she had not umpired a professional baseball game in more than forty years.

No woman has ever officiated a baseball game at the major league level, but several, such as Bernice Gera and Christine Wren in the 1970s and Pam Postema in the 1980s, have had abbreviated careers in the minor leagues. The glass ceiling in professional baseball, for both players and officials, has been exceedingly difficult to break through.

Among the handful of notable women in the early 1900s who stood out as individuals playing on men's teams, Alta Weiss and Jackie Mitchell were two of the more heralded. As pitchers Weiss and Mitchell were marquee players, and their teams depended on their novelty to draw big crowds. If it was true that women made good pitchers for publicity reasons, it was also true that women were able to contribute more to a men's team in that role. Good pitching has always involved finesse more than sheer power, and players like Weiss and Mitchell spent a great deal of time perfecting their craft.

An Ohioan, Weiss made her professional debut at age seventeen on September 2, 1907, as a pitcher with the semi-pro Vermillion (Ohio) Independents. The "Girl Wonder," as she was dubbed by the *Vermillion News*, gave up only five hits and one run in five innings of play. Such was the public clamor that for Weiss's second mound appearance less than a week later, extra trains had to be run from Cleveland out to Vermillion to accommodate the overflow of fans.

Weiss's father, a doctor, bought a controlling interest in the Independents at the end of the 1907 season, renaming them the Weiss All-Stars. Alta's career lasted fifteen years, partly because she was the centerpiece of a barnstorming team, and partly because she played only during the summers. She wasn't a gimmick, however. Decades before women trained for sports, Weiss practiced during the off-season in her own home-built gymnasium. She perfected a major leaguer's repertoire of pitches, including a curve, a sinker, and a knuckleball. She also admitted once to knowing how to throw a spitball. One of the first female professional baseball players, Weiss was also one of the first dual-career women. From 1915 until her retirement from baseball in 1922, when she wasn't throwing curves and knucklers to her summer opponents, she was practicing medicine.

In 1917, women still could not vote, could not own property, and could not initiate a divorce. But Lizzie Murphy earned a living as a professional baseball player. Murphy was one of six children born to an Irish millworker father and a French-Canadian mother, and playing baseball was the only thing she ever wanted to do. As a nineteen-year-old, Lizzie was listed in the Warren, Rhode Island, directory simply as "Elizabeth Murphy, ball player." As an amateur, she played on local men's teams, and she boasted to a sportswriter at the time that she had never been struck out.

At only five feet, six inches, Murphy, who was later known as the "Queen of Baseball," was not a particularly powerful player, but she supplemented her skills with her own unusual brand of strength conditioning: beating rugs and chopping wood. She was an accomplished athlete—she played soccer and ice hockey and was an excellent swimmer and runner. In 1911 she was offered money by a men's semi-professional baseball team in Warren. The contract called for a payment of five dollars a game and a share of the pot that was passed around among the fans. After her first game, however, she was refused payment by the team's manager. Instead, the eighty-five dollars collected was distributed among the other players, as well as the promoter and manager. Before the next game, first baseman Murphy refused to board the team bus to Newport until the manager promised to hold to his side of their original bargain. Faced with the possibility of a mutinous crowd in Newport if the team showed up without their star female attraction, the Warren manager agreed. For the next seventeen years, "Spike" Murphy, as she was known to her fans and to her diamond colleagues, made her living from baseball.

Murphy's first professional team was the Providence Independents, but she spent most of her career with Ed Carr's All-Stars of Boston. Playing upwards of one hundred games during the summer, the All-Stars traveled throughout New England and eastern Canada. Once, during a game against a French-speaking Canadian team, Murphy, who spoke French fluently, overheard the first base coach relaying base-stealing instructions to the runner on first base. Murphy was able to signal her team's catcher with the information, and during the game five opposing runners were thrown out.

In the summer of 1922, Murphy was invited to play first base for a team of American League and New England All-Stars in a charity game against the Boston Red Sox. The other All-Stars, smelling a promotional gimmick, were not particularly thrilled to have a woman take the field with them in Fenway Park. Murphy came into the game in the fourth inning and took her position at first base. When the All-Stars' third baseman fielded a ground ball, he held the ball a moment before firing it, off target, toward Murphy. When she caught it cleanly, the third baseman walked over to the pitcher and nodded in Murphy's direction, signaling his approval of the twenty-eight-year-old female pro. Murphy's appearance in Fenway marked the first time in history that a woman played for a major league team in an exhibition game. (A dozen years later, Babe Didrikson would become the second.)

After retiring from baseball in 1935 at age forty-one, Murphy married briefly, then worked for the next three decades as a factory worker in a spinning mill, and later quahogging and clamming along the shores of her beloved Rhode Island.

Virne Beatrice "Jackie" Mitchell weighed less than five pounds when she was born in Chattanooga in 1915. Under her doctor-father's tutelage, she learned to play baseball at an early age and played in amateur games as a teenager, once even striking out nine men. In March of 1931, she sharpened her pitching skills at a baseball camp in Atlanta run by former major leaguer Kid Elberfeld. Just a couple of weeks later Joe Engel, a former pitcher with the Washington Senators and then owner of the Double-A Chattanooga (Tennessee) Lookouts, offered Mitchell a minor league contract, which she signed, the first woman in baseball history to do so.

On a damp, cool April afternoon in 1931, the Lookouts hosted the major league New York Yankees in an exhibition game. The game had been postponed a day because of rain, so the field was still damp and the footing treacherous. It would not be a problem for the Lookouts with Jackie Mitchell on the mound. Mitchell came in for the Lookouts with two outs in the top of the first inning, a run in, and a man on first. The Yankees greatest home run hitter, Babe Ruth, walked to the plate, tipped his hat to the seventeen-year-old southpaw, and dug in. Ruth swung at the first pitch and caught nothing but air. The count went to two balls and a strike before Ruth swung at another sinker and missed again. With a full count, Ruth took the next pitch right down the middle for a called third strike. The Sultan of Swat had been struck out by a teenage girl.

Although Engel had a penchant for Barnum-like publicity stunts—he once staged an "elephant hunt" at Lookout Stadium in Chattanooga—Mitchell did not view herself in those terms. She had been playing baseball for most of her young life and had even received instruction from Brooklyn Dodger pitcher Dazzy Vance. A day before the scheduled start of the Lookout-Yankee game, the *Chattanooga News* reported that several major leaguers who had recently attended Elberfeld's camp thought Mitchell was "one of the most puzzling southpaws" they had ever faced. Mitchell admitted years later that being only seventeen years old at the time probably helped her. She was simply too young to feel intimidated.

After Ruth was retired by Mitchell in that April 1931 exhibition game, he gave the batter's box dirt a kick, chewed out the umpire for a moment, then threw his bat down and returned to the visitor's bench. Meanwhile, the 130-pound teenager waited on the mound for the next batter. Two-hundred-pound clean-up hitter Lou Gehrig, who would lead the American League that year with 46 home runs and 184 runs batted in, stepped in against Mitchell: three pitches, three swings, three strikes. The sellout crowd of some four thousand stood and cheered wildly. The girl from Chattanooga had just struck out the best hitting tandem in the history of baseball.

When Gehrig walked back to the bench, he just smiled and shook his head. Tony Lazzeri, the best second baseman in baseball, was the third batter to face Mitchell. After fouling off the first pitch, Lazzeri kept his bat on his shoulder for the next four and earned a walk. Lookout manager Bert Niehoff then lifted his young southpaw, although Mitchell wanted nothing more than to keep pitching.

As it turned out, major league baseball wanted nothing more of Mitchell. The game was covered by dozens of magazines, newspapers, and wire services and also was filmed by Universal Newsreel, to be played over and over in theaters across the country. Within days of the exhibition game, baseball commissioner Kenesaw Mountain Landis voided Mitchell's contract with the Chattanooga Lookouts on the grounds that professional baseball was too strenuous a game to be played by women. Twenty-one years later, when a second woman was signed to a minor league contract, this time with the Class B Harrisburg Senators, baseball decided it needed to do more. On June 21, 1952, baseball commissioner Ford Frick banned women from that moment on from playing either minor or major league baseball.

As the legend of Mitchell's prowess against Murderer's Row took hold in the public imagination, so did controversy. Was Mitchell the real deal? Certainly, she could pitch. She'd proven that in amateur games before the Yankee exhibition—including games played against men—when she had barnstormed around the country. But the question persists: Did Ruth and Gehrig just play along with what Lookout owner Engel had clearly engineered as a promotional stunt? Over the past twenty years, a number of experts have viewed the film of the game, and most feel the answer to that question remains difficult to determine. Mitchell was a southpaw, whose main pitch, which she'd practiced for long hours, was a sinker. It is not impossible to imagine that both Ruth and Gehrig, both left-handers, were taken by surprise by the movement that Mitchell was able to put on the ball. And Lazzeri's taking four pitches after fouling off the first may have been his way of bailing out of a difficult situation and refusing to be embarrassed by the girl. Certainly, Mitchell, until her death in 1987 at the age of seventy-three, maintained that her fanning of Ruth and Gehrig was not a stunt on their part. She claimed that the only instruction given to the Yankee hitters about how to handle her pitches was not to hit the ball directly back at the young girl.

Whether or not Jackie Mitchell can be credited with one of the most sensational pitching performances in baseball history will long be questioned. What is not in question is that the professional career of the first woman to sign a minor league contract lasted only two-thirds of an inning. It was a momentous two-thirds.

Some baseball players are drawn to the limelight more than others. Players like Ruth, of course, or Mickey Mantle or Ken Griffey, Jr. Mildred "Babe" Didrikson was one of these. Baseball was certainly not Didrikson's best sport, but as perhaps the greatest all-around female athlete in history, she could excel at any sport, given the chance. Didrikson was also a tireless self-promoter and probably the first female athlete to capitalize on the attention of the media. After achieving renown at the 1932 Los Angeles Olympics, where she won two gold medals, Babe was faced with returning to her working-class hometown of Beaumont, Texas. Two years earlier she'd graduated from Beaumont High School, where she'd starred in track and basketball, and her option was either to go home and become a stenographer, or to take advantage of her newfound fame. The choice was an easy one. Because there were no professional sports for women to pursue, Babe's opportunities were limited, but the public was always willing to put up money to see something novel, and a woman athlete in the first half of the twentieth century was certainly that.

The first offer to come in after the Olympics was from promoter Ray Doan, who signed the female star to a $1,000-a-month basketball contract as the centerpiece of the barnstorming Babe Didrikson's All-Americans. It was a sweet deal for Babe, who was earning one hundred times more than the average, working-class female. But it was a difficult life: constantly on the road, traveling by car from one small town to another, and playing at least one game, often two or three, every day. At the end of the basketball season, Babe received offers from several major league clubs to make pitching appearances during spring training games in Florida. Willing to take on any athletic test, she relished the chance to put her skills on the line against the best. Appearing with the Cleveland Indians against their minor league club in the spring of 1934, Babe pitched two innings and allowed no runs. But when she appeared with the St. Louis Cardinals against the Philadelphia Athletics, Jimmie Foxx took her deep. Of Foxx's home run, Didrikson later said: "I gave him my high, hard one . . . and he knocked it into the next county."

Despite her physical gifts—Babe reportedly once threw a baseball 313 feet from center field to home plate—the truth is that she was only an average pitcher against men. When spring training was over, she was hired to play with the famed House of David barnstorming baseball team. The House of David consisted, in its original form, of members of a Michigan religious sect who were distinguished mostly by their long, flowing beards. Appearing again as a pitcher, Babe played at least some part of more than two hundred games between April and October of 1934. One of her House of David teammates, Emory Olive, reportedly said of Babe, after she appeared with the team, that she wasn't "all that good a pitcher . . . but she could hit pretty good." And, as anyone who had seen her at the L. A. Olympics knew, she could run, too.

Unfortunately for Babe, baseball allowed her only a limited role. But it also allowed her a way to capitalize on her early accomplishments and offered her a bridge to her next career, as a professional golfer.

Women weren't alone in trying to break down the barriers that prevented them from playing organized baseball. African-Americans played baseball as early as the antebellum period, but the first records of black teams date to the years just after the Civil War. When the National League was established in 1876, there was no written policy regarding the inclusion of blacks. There was, however, a "gentlemen's agreement" among club owners that no blacks would be hired. But in small major league cities, places like Worcester, Massachusetts, and Stillwater, Minnesota, and Toledo, Ohio, talent was often scarce. It was in such cities that some six dozen black baseball players found a chance to play professionally on white baseball teams. By the early twentieth century, major league baseball officially banned blacks, preventing them—

until Jackie Robinson stepped up to the plate in 1947—from playing on anything but all-black teams.

The force behind what would become the Negro National League was Rube Foster. In 1920 he established the National Association of Professional Baseball Clubs, which included some of the finest teams—black or white—in baseball history, teams like the Kansas City Monarchs, the Pittsburgh Crawfords, and the Homestead Grays. Ironically, it was integration that killed the Negro Leagues in the mid-1950s. By that time nearly two dozen black players were in the majors. The Negro Leagues, which were increasingly being raided for their talent, resorted to gimmicks to revive sagging attendance. Onto this confused stage wandered Marcenia "Toni" Stone. Stone, who grew up in Minneapolis, signed a contract in 1953 to play second base with the Indianapolis Clowns, thus becoming the first woman to play professionally in the Negro Leagues. Stone's hiring clearly had more to do with showmanship and novelty than with simple ball playing. She was a female player on an otherwise all-male team, and the Clowns paid her handsomely ($12,000) to bring fans to the ballpark. Already past her prime when she signed at age thirty-two with the Clowns, she was a solid, if unexceptional, ballplayer. She fielded her position with speed and agility, playing in 53 of the Clowns' 175 games in her first season but batting an underwhelming .243.

The most memorable moment of Stone's Negro League career came on Easter Sunday in 1953, when she got the only base hit off the great hurler Satchel Paige in an exhibition game in Omaha, Nebraska. The following year, she was sold to the Monarchs and replaced by two more women—Connie Morgan, an infielder, and Mamie "Peanut" Johnson, a pitcher. By 1960, the careers of all three players were essentially over. And by 1963 the greatest Negro League team of all—the Kansas City Monarchs—ceased touring.

In the 1940s, with the outbreak of World War II, major league baseball was forced to be resourceful. Not only was the public otherwise engaged, so were many of baseball's men. Players such as Joe DiMaggio, Bob Feller, and Ted Williams left their teams to join the armed forces. Without many of baseball's marquee players, attendance plummeted, and owners were left trying to figure out how to stay in the black. Enter Philip K. Wrigley, owner of the Chicago Cubs. In 1943 Wrigley proposed, then founded, what became the All American Girls Professional Baseball League.

Wrigley's solution was to form four charter teams, each with fifteen players, to launch the 1943 AAGPBL inaugural season. He sent out thirty major league scouts, who traveled throughout the United States and Canada looking for the best female baseball talent they could find. Hundreds of girls and women, ranging in age from fifteen to thirty, were asked to run, throw, and hit, and the best—some 250 women—were invited by Wrigley to Chicago. Many of them had learned their craft first as softball players. With the rain pouring down, a final group of 75 were put through their paces under the protection of the Wrigley Field stands for the final tryout of the All-American Girls teams. When the season started a few weeks later, 60 women from a dozen different states had been assigned to four teams: the Rockford Peaches, the Racine (Wisconsin) Belles, the Kenosha (Michigan) Comets, and the South Bend (Indiana) Blue Sox. A shrewd businessman, Wrigley placed his teams in small towns that had no major league franchises to compete against. Wrigley's teams also were close enough in distance that they didn't need to travel overnight to get to games.

Of all the fine athletes who played for the league, the best may have been Rockford first baseman Dottie Kamenshek, who at five-six and 135 pounds was so good a defensive player that Wally Pipp, the New York Yankee who replaced Lou Gehrig at first base, remarked once to a reporter: "[Kamenshek] is the fanciest-fielding first baseman I've ever seen, man or woman." Kamenshek was only seventeen years old when she left her Cincinnati home to try out for the league, an age requiring her mother to sign a parental release—which years later she admitted she signed believing that her daughter would never make it into the league.

Known for her splits when stretching to make a catch at first, Kammie, as she was called, would practice her footwork with her bedroom pillow. "I threw the pillow on the floor in front of a full-length mirror," she once said, "and pretended it was first base. You try to make yourself as long as possible. I practiced shifting my feet [and] I stayed flexible year-round." A punch hitter, Kammie could hit to all fields and drive the ball when she needed to. In 1946, she won the first of two consecutive AAGPBL batting titles with a .316 average. In 1951, her ninth and final season, she batted an all-time high of .345. So renowned were Kammie's skills that she was offered a contract by a men's minor league club in Ft. Lauderdale. She declined the offer—the AAGPBL would not have allowed her to break her commitment to them in any case—because she feared the Ft. Lauderdale club was looking for a promotional gimmick. If Kammie was anything, she was the consummate professional: a player dedicated to her craft, a lover of the history of the game, and a practitioner of its finer points nonpareil.

By the time she retired from the Rockford Peaches in January of 1952, Kamenshek had racked up a number of honors in addition to her two batting titles: She was a seven-time all-star and had the highest career batting average (.292) of all longtime league players. But most important to Kamenshek was the chance to experience something she knew few women would ever get to experience. Baseball, she said, gave her "the courage to go on" to even bigger personal accomplishments: a college degree from

Marquette University at the age of thirty-two and a longtime career as a physical therapist, eventually becoming chief of the Los Angeles Crippled Children's Services Department.

Over the first few years of the AAGPBL Wrigley improved the brand of game the women in the league played by first introducing base stealing, then lengthening the distance between the bases and changing from a small softball to a slightly larger than regular baseball. With more running and a ball that traveled farther, Wrigley managed to maximize the action for the fans. And the fans loved it. Beginning with a meager total league attendance of 200,000 in its first season, the AAGPBL reached its peak in 1945, when the league had ten teams and close to 1,000,000 in attendance. In 1945, the Fort Wayne Daisies, the league's first expansion team, averaged 1,500 fans—three times the crowd size of the local men's semi-pro team.

Although the women played an exhausting 108-game schedule during the summer—sometimes playing back-to-back doubleheaders in different cities—they were well recompensed. Salaries ranged from about $60 a week up to $180 a week, compared to the average female factory worker's wage of about $40 per week. Sophia Kurys, who recorded 1,114 stolen bases in her eight seasons of professional baseball—seven with the Racine Belles—received as much as $375 a week at the height of her career.

For those salaries, the women of the league had to do more than just play baseball—they had to look good doing it. The women were taught about makeup, how to dress, and how to act in public. They were given coaching in speech and posture. They were also required to wear dresses and makeup in public. And they had curfews. Each team had a female chaperone who monitored the girls' behavior—which included no smoking or drinking—and alerted the teams' owners of any infractions. Usually, fines were levied, but suspension from the team was not out of the question.

On the field the women wore belted tunics; they were also required to have shoulder-length hair and to wear makeup at all times. Publicity photos of the time showed women in their baseball uniforms looking at themselves in their compact mirrors and applying lipstick. Wrigley wanted the fans coming to the parks to see good baseball, but he also knew that good-looking women playing baseball was good insurance. The more than six hundred women who played with the AAGPBL during its twelve-year existence said that the uniforms were the hardest thing to take. Since sliding was an important part of the game, the women's bare legs took a constant beating. The most common injury was bruising, but broken legs and ankles, bad backs, and strained knees were not infrequent.

The women of the All American League saw themselves as performing a patriotic duty; they visited hospitals, raised war bonds, and performed wherever and whenever they were asked to. But without question, they saw their playing days as a chance to experience the world and get paid for doing something they truly loved—playing baseball.

When the league finally folded in 1954 after several declining years, it was for a number of reasons, including competition not only from the major leagues, but also from new forms of mass entertainment, chief among them television. No doubt postwar mores, in which women were back in the home and men were out working in the world again, also contributed significantly.

In the years between the demise of the All-American Girls Professional Baseball League and the enaction of Title IX, women again took up the game of softball in large numbers. Girls had always been excluded from Little League, right from the league's inception in 1939. The baseball organization for boys ages eight to twelve, Little League includes hundreds of community teams in all fifty states and in thirty countries. But young girls had only softball to turn to for organized competition. Described by some as the death knell of women's participation in baseball, and by others as the last link women had to the great American pastime, softball had actually been played in the United States since the end of the nineteenth century. It wasn't until 1933, though, that the American Softball Association made the term *softball* official. It was in the 1920s and 1930s that the sport truly took hold. One reason for the popularity of the game during this period was that physical education instructors at colleges and in community recreational programs throughout the country wanted to deemphasize sports in which the physical demands were seen as too much for women. With its larger ball, softball was a slower game than baseball—even "fast-pitch"—making it the perfect alternative. In short order, high schools and colleges adopted softball as a more appropriate recreational sport than baseball for their female students to play. And there was a clear carryover from school to community teams.

In a tradition that continues today, many factories and businesses during the 1920s organized sports teams, including basketball, bowling, and softball, as a way of solidifying company spirit. In the years between the 1930s and the 1970s, when women were still locked out of baseball—except for those in the AAGPBL—the most significant competitive opportunitities for women were in industrial softball leagues. Public works programs in the 1930s and 1940s, which resulted in the building of hundreds of community ballparks, helped to push softball to new levels of popularity in the 1950s and 1960s. One of the most famous company-sponsored teams was located on the East Coast, though the Midwest was a softball hotbed during the middle of the century. The Raybestos Brakettes of Stratford, Connecticut, won twenty-five Women's Fast-Pitch National titles from 1942 to 1973 and helped to develop the sport not only in this country but around the world. The Raybestos were one of the first women's softball teams from the United States to participate in the Asian Games, the Pan American Games, and, in 1965, the first Women's World Fast-Pitch Tournament in Melbourne, Australia.

When softball reached the peak of its popularity in 1940, there were half a million men's and women's teams in the United States, and nearly a third of the country was coming out to watch those games. Before television brought the game of baseball into millions of living rooms, softball, as it was played by local amateur and company teams on sandlots and in parks across the country, was a more popular game than its hardball counterpart. In high schools and colleges, softball had been the main outlet for women since the unofficial banning of baseball from women's campuses in the 1930s. Excluded from Little League, many young girls did continue to play baseball on sandlots across the country. In cities and in rural communities, in particular, young girls still played catch or pickup games with their brothers' friends, just for the love of the game, and just as they had been doing for more than half a century.

When Title IX became law in 1972, requiring females to be given the same chances as males to play sports, women's participation in both softball and baseball changed dramatically. Women's athletic programs, including softball, got a sudden infusion of money and support. More schools developed softball programs, and more schools participated in softball competitions and championships. Women's teams were able to travel and to pay for equipment, uniforms, and coaching. The level of play inevitably got better, too. Collegiate softball powerhouses were established in California at San Jose State University and Fresno State. And for the first time NCAA championships in softball became fiercely competitive contests.

Within a year of the passage of Title IX, lawsuits were filed on behalf of young girls who wanted to play organized baseball, and Little League was forced to change its charter. For the first time it was official: girls could now join boys on their own Little League fields of dreams. Today, more girls than ever before play baseball on sandlots, in public parks, and under the lights of municipal stadiums. Though girls still represent a tiny portion of the total number of Little Leaguers—about one girl per league—they have pitched no-hitters, won regional Pitch-Hit-Run Championships, and played on teams in the Little League World Series. Many girls still opt to play softball to be among their female peers, but the skills learned in Little League have allowed a few girls to play at higher levels: as members of otherwise all-male high school, college, and even semi-pro teams.

One of these women was Julie Croteau. Croteau, a first baseman, gained fame in 1989 as the first woman to play on a men's NCAA baseball team, at St. Mary's College in Maryland. She first played baseball as a six-year-old and was a .300 hitter when she played on a Little League team a decade after the passing of Title IX. She also went on to play Babe Ruth League baseball, the next step after Little League; she attended baseball clinics and practiced her sport tirelessly. Nonetheless, she was cut from her Virginia high school junior varsity boys baseball team—unfairly, Croteau believed, because she'd already played semi-pro ball in Fredericksburg in the summers. When she got to St. Mary's in 1989, she played first base on a men's team for the Division III school. She started a majority of the games and maintained a .250 batting average over her first college season. Her experiences were very mixed, however. Opposing coaches, even some of her fellow players, made derogatory comments about her playing. In the spring of her junior year at St. Mary's, she left the team and college because of the sexual harassment. What she wasn't ready to leave, though, was baseball itself.

Since Croteau's bold attempt to play on a men's baseball team at the college level, only a handful of women have sought to follow suit. Instead, all-women's baseball teams experienced a mild renaissance in the 1980s and 1990s. A former Atlanta Braves executive, Bob Hope, tried to form an all-women's team in 1984. Hope intended his team, the Sun Sox, to play in the Class A Florida State League. With the support of Hank Aaron and the coaching of several former major league players, the Sun Sox, whose roster had to be filled out by a half dozen experienced men, worked out for several months. Finally, though, their franchise application was denied.

Another women's team was put together a decade later by the Coor's Brewing Company. At major league baseball's 1993 team meeting, it was announced that an all-female baseball team, the Colorado Silver Bullets, would be sanctioned to play in the short-season, men's Double A Northern League. Tryouts were held at several locations throughout the country in February and March of 1993. A team of twenty-four women, out of several thousand who participated in the various two-day tryouts, was selected to start play in the spring of 1994. The soon-to-be Hall of Fame pitcher Phil Niekro was hired to manage the team. With less than two months of training, the team began its regular minor league season. After an opening-day 19–0 loss, the Bullets' coaching staff reassessed the team's schedule and decided that the Bullets should play primarily college and semi-pro teams. The Bullets finished their first season with just 6 wins out of 36. In 1997—which turned out to be their fourth and last season because Coors dropped its sponsorship—the Bullets ended up with their first winning record, posting 23 wins against 22 losses.

With the passing of one team, however, four rose up to take its place. In the summer of 1997, four new women's baseball teams, two from California, one from Arizona, and one from Chicago, began play in a new independent league. In the summer of 1998, two more were added, in New Jersey and in Buffalo, and one team from California moved to Orlando.

While some women continue to try to break down the gender barriers in baseball, either as individuals on men's teams or as players on all-women's teams, many women participate in softball as the sport of their choice. If softball needed to have its public image burnished, it couldn't have picked a better venue than the 1996 Olympics in Atlanta, where it was a medal sport for the first time. For three decades prior to the Atlanta Games, Don Porter, president of the International Softball Federation, had attempted to get softball included as an Olympic sport. The first real shot at achieving Olympic status came in 1968, but the head of the International Olympic Committee, Avery Brundage, basically dumped cold water on the idea: Brundage just didn't see softball as being an international sport. At least not yet. In the United States, the American Softball Association registered 20,000 teams in 1965. By 1991, the ASA had registered 275,000 teams; the sport was being played in eighty countries; and international championships were being held on an annual basis. After years of intense lobbying of the International Olympic Committee, Porter got the thumbs-up from new IOC head, Juan Antonio Samaranch, at an IOC meeting in Birmingham, England, in 1991. Softball would be included in the 1996 Summer Games as a medal sport for women.

At the Atlanta Games, the women's softball event was dominated by the United States team, which eventually won the gold medal against such softball powers as China and Australia. Eight of the fifteen American team members happened to be from California, a state that accounts for the nation's top collegiate teams. The 1996 Olympics marked a watershed for the sport of softball. Though it was being played by high school girls and boys, as well as working women and men in summer leagues all across the country, softball's popularity had always been as an amateur game and recreational activity. With an Olympic team stocked with skilled, aggressive players such as hard-hitting shortstop Dot Richardson and flame-thrower Lisa Fernandez, softball was suddenly seen in all its athleticism. To get an idea of just how good the U.S. women's softball team in Atlanta was, one need only look at the pitching statistics: Of the five female hurlers, four had ERAs under 1.00.

Lisa Fernandez, who played key roles as both a starter and a reliever, as well as third baseman, was the cream of an already select crop. The daughter of Cuban immigrants, Fernandez was once told by a coach that her arms were too short to play softball. Intense and exuberant, she wasted no time in proving at least that coach wrong. At UCLA she compiled a stunning 93–7 pitching record, batted .382 during her four years there, and still holds records in a plethora of categories, including hits (287), runs scored (1,420), and no-hitters (11).

At the Olympics, Fernandez put on a show. In nine starts she pitched twenty-one total innings and struck out a team-leading thirty-one batters. Her 0.33 ERA was second only to that of Christa Williams, who wasn't scored on in 9.2 innings of pitching. And Fernandez's .393 batting average certainly didn't hurt. Appropriately, it was Fernandez who was called on to get the final four outs against China in the gold-medal game. The best closer in the game, she blew pitches past three of the next four hitters for strikeouts and wasted no time in securing the first Olympic championship in softball for the U.S. team. Four months later, the International Olympic Committee voted to keep women's softball on the schedule for the 2000 Olympics in Sydney.

In freckles and braces, Dot Richardson arrived on the softball scene at the tender age of thirteen as the youngest player in history to earn a spot on the roster of a women's semi-pro team in Orlando, Florida. A shortstop, Richardson went on to earn All-American honors at UCLA four years in a row and was named the NCAA Softball Player of the Decade for the 1980s. A veritable vacuum at short, Richardson may be the finest woman to ever field the position. With the soft hands of the orthopedic surgeon she actually is, Richardson has won eight gold medals with the national squad, including three Pan American Games and two World Championships, but none greater than the 1996 Olympics.

In that Olympic gold-medal game against China, Richardson stroked a key two-RBI home run in the third inning. The opposite-field blast into the bleachers at soldout Golden Park proved decisive as the team went on to take the gold by a 3–1 margin. As the peripatetic shortstop, who finished the Olympics with three home runs and a total of seven RBIs, rounded the bases after her Ruthian blast, her eyes grew wide in seeming disbelief. By the time she reached second base, she knew, her arms stretched heavenward, that the moment was truly hers. The greatest infielder in softball history had delivered the biggest hit in softball history. It was one for the ages.

Although softball is firmly entrenched on the college level as an all-women's sport, only a few women today are playing collegiate baseball. Only Californian Ila Borders, a pitcher, is playing professionally on an all-men's team in the Independent Northwest League. If a woman is to someday make it into the minor, or even major, leagues, many believe it will be as a pitcher. The discrepancy in upper-body strength between men and women would seem to make it impossible for anyone but a truly exceptional woman to make it professionally as a hitter. But since technique is just as important as power when it comes to pitching, someone like the left-handed hurler Borders may be the one to finally break one of baseball's last gender barriers.

In the fall of 1995, Julie Croteau, the first woman to play in an NCAA college baseball game, became the first woman to coach a men's NCAA Division I baseball team when she joined the baseball staff of the University of Massachusetts as an instructor. In 1997, she became the Associate Director of Game Development for Major League Baseball. When Croteau returned to school to earn her master's degree in exercise and sports physiology, it was fittingly, at Smith College, where one hundred years ago women first played the game among themselves. When she did, a century of women in baseball had come full circle.

In the meantime, girls continue to play Little League baseball, and greater numbers than ever before are participating in high school and college softball programs. Whether a young girl can play Little League is no longer a matter for the courts. It's her decision. The size of the ball, the composition of the bat, the sex of the batter—none of these things really matter. Only the game does.

Somewhere right now, on a patch of green grass, under a high sun or a halo of stadium lights, a team is taking the field to play baseball. And on that team is at least one girl, her hair tucked under her cap or flowing down her back; dressed in shorts or in baseball pants; wearing sneakers or spikes. And like everyone else, she'll pound her glove; take a few grounders; maybe smooth the infield dirt with her shoes or stretch her legs in the outfield grass.

And then, like thousands of girls have done before her, she'll play some ball.

Tennis

$\mathcal{N}$et Profits

Grace Lichtenstein

The worst thing about tennis is that it looks so easy to play and is actually so tough. The best thing is that women can play as well as men and are often more entertaining. And the very best thing is that you don't have to be big to play it well. When I was a little girl, I didn't know how tough a game it was. What I did know was that girls as short as I was—and men, too—seemed to have a wonderful time smacking fuzzy balls over a net. I wanted to imitate them.

My first tennis idol was my father, barely five feet tall, who was fast on his feet and fiendishly tricky in his placements. My next idol was also a little squirt off the public courts. Her name was Billie Jean Moffitt King. She dazzled me because from the first time I saw her at Forest Hills, she played with such furious energy it seemed as if the game had been created for short, bespectacled, bubbly tomboys. She also talked as good a game as she played, often at the same time. The other women players were mostly circumspect, well-behaved young ladies; Billie Jean behaved like a show-off and a rebel. The others projected themselves in black and white; BJ came through in living color— a Lucille Ball in tennis sneakers, an Elvis in a Perry Como sport. Tennis might still have been locked into its old upper-crust origins back then, but Billie Jean brought a rock 'n' roll attitude to it. She proved time and again that while tennis might have begun among the nineteenth-century British aristocracy, its most important champions have been decidedly female and emphatically not British. King not only won admittance to the Hall of Fame; she almost single-handedly altered the nature of sports forever, creating a viable future for active girls and women in every sport.

This plucky daughter of a Long Beach, California, fireman holds the most titles in tennis's most prestigious tournament, Wimbledon, along with the distinction of being responsible for tennis's preeminence in women's sports

today. A five-foot, four-and-a-half-inch, fireplug with the net game of someone twice her size and a personality to match, King was the catalyst for change.
She helped drag the tennis establishment into the professional ranks, fought
and won the battle for equal pay for female players, founded the Women's
Tennis Association, helped create team tennis, established the first major
women's sports magazine, and set the course for the nonprofit Women's
Sports Foundation, which honors and encourages female competitors in all
sports. In addition, in 1973 she demolished Bobby Riggs in the "Battle of the
Sexes," the most hyped, most watched, most debated match in tennis history. Not surprisingly, scandal and controversy swirled around her long career, which spanned the 1960s and 1970s.

However, well before BJK and after, women's tennis has projected a
uniquely high profile in the international spotlight. In large measure it is
because of two grand rivalries a half century apart, and a terrible stabbing
that derailed a third. The first rivalry pitted a flamboyant Frenchwoman,
Suzanne Lenglen, against an impassive American, Helen Wills Moody, in
the golden age of sport—the 1920s—even though they met on court exactly
once. The second rivalry, fought throughout the 1980s, featured Chris Evert,
a cool Florida baseliner adored by men and women alike as the all-American ideal, against Czech-born Martina Navratilova, an emotional serve-and-
volley specialist who brought a new level of athleticism to the game. As
different off court as they were on, the two forged a legendary competition
and, in the process, proved that great rivals can also be close friends.

In the 1990s, women's tennis was en route to an intriguing new pairing—Steffi Graf of Germany and Monica Seles, originally of Yugoslavia, two
remarkably hard hitters who took full advantage of the latest power-laden
racquet technology. Graf, despite injuries and family crises, is still a contender
for the title of "greatest ever." But her story could have been vastly different
had the two-fisted Seles been allowed to grunt her way to the top. Virtually
unstoppable by 1991, she was the top-ranked player in April 1993 when a
deranged German spectator plunged a knife into her back during a changeover
in a match in Hamburg. It took more than two years for Seles to return to
competition, and she has never been the same carefree, confident athlete she
was in her glory days. Meanwhile, the next generation, including Martina
Hingis of Switzerland, and Venus and Serena Williams of the United States,
promise to bring even more power, not to mention variety, to women's tennis in the new millennium.

Women have been playing tennis for over 125 years, on the highest competitive level as well as for fun. Although in the Middle Ages the French upper
classes played something vaguely resembling tennis, *jeu de paume* was an in-

door game with players using their palms rather than racquets. (This version of the game lives on as "court tennis.") According to one historian at the United States Tennis Association, the first known reference to a woman wielding her *paume* was in 1427; Lady Margot of France was regarded as top drawer at it.

An Englishman, Major Walter Clopton Wingfield, is credited with inventing the sport almost as we know it today. In 1873, he simplified the rules of the game, fancied back then by British aristocrats who batted the ball around with clumsy racquets. He moved it onto an hourglass-shaped outdoor court with a high net and patented it under the name Sphairistike. Lawn tennis, which translated easily onto the clipped grass of croquet, the most popular outdoor game of the time, caught on quickly. In 1874 an American woman from Staten Island, Mary Ewing Outerbridge, is said to have brought the equipment back home with her from Bermuda, and soon Americans were whacking a ball on grass courts throughout the United States. Tennis historians continue to argue about the possibly more influential role of one James Dwight, a Boston physician who brought an imported set of equipment to an estate in Nahant, Massachusetts, in 1874. Moreover, there is yet another contender for the title of "mother" of American tennis, Ella Wilkins Bailey. The wife of an army officer stationed at Camp Apache, near Tucson, Ella reportedly introduced tennis to the outpost, then part of Arizona territory, earlier the same year. Whether it was Outerbridge, Dwight, or Bailey who introduced it, the game became a favorite of physically active American women. Today, women make up 58 percent, or 120,000, of the participants in the United States Tennis Association's various recreational leagues.

The ultimate arena was Wimbledon, where the first women's championships began in 1884, seven years after the start of the men's competition. So did the tradition of teen phenoms, with a nineteen-year-old Maud Watson beating her elder sister, Lilian, 6–8, 6–3, 6–3 in the finals. Wimbledon was the first of the four most widely recognized major tournaments, the other three being the French, the United States, and the Australian championships. In 1887, the first U.S. women's nationals were played outside Philadelphia at the Philadelphia Cricket Club. Ellen Hansell was crowned United States title holder when she beat Laura Knight by a score of 6–1, 6–0. (The United States Open is the contemporary offspring of the Nationals.) The game hardly resembled a great athletic contest in those Victorian times. Women found it hard to dash around on the grass in what was then considered correct attire: long skirts and blouses, under which were corsets and petticoats.

Women's tennis was a part of the second modern Olympics, in 1900. But in 1924 the sport was eliminated as an Olympic event because of a dispute over the distinction between amateurs and professionals. The argument over professionalism was to bedevil women's tennis, as it did men's, for decades. (It was not until the 1988 Seoul Games that tennis returned to the Olympics, with Steffi Graf, on her way to a Grand Slam—victories in the Australian, French, Wimbledon, and United States Opens in a single calendar year—beating Gabriela Sabatini of Argentina for the gold medal.)

The extreme youth of some modern players has been a source of concern in recent times, but in fact, the earliest years of women's tennis were often ruled by teenagers. The English-born, California-bred May Sutton was eighteen when she captured the U.S. singles title, nineteen when she won the first of two Wimbledon singles titles. Britain's Charlotte "Lottie" Dod, a five-time Wimbledon singles victor, became the youngest champion ever when she won her first title at the age of fifteen years, ten months. There apparently were no comments or concerns back then that her athletic prowess might pose problems for her physical development, her psyche, her schooling, or her parents.

It took a French player with a hot temper, daringly short skirts, and a lethal net game to elevate women's tennis into the domain of sporting myth. Many still consider Suzanne Lenglen (1899–1938) to have been the greatest female player ever, period.

Born in Paris, she was the Wimbledon singles champion every year except one from 1919 to 1925, as well as its biggest box office draw. And what a field day the press had with this unconventionally stylish, utterly Gallic dynamo! Allison Danzig of the *New York Times* (dean of American tennis writers until his retirement in 1967) described her: "In the days of ground-length tennis dresses, Suzanne Rachel Flore Lenglen played at Wimbledon with her dress cut just above the calf. She wept openly during matches, pouted, sipped brandy between sets. Some called her shocking and indecent, but she was merely ahead of her time, and she brought France the greatest global sports renown it had ever known. . . . She had brought the glamour of the stage and the ballet to the court, and queues formed at tennis clubs where before there had been indifference. She had emancipated the female player from layers of starched clothing and set the short hair style as well. During her career she won eighty-one singles titles (seven without the loss of a game!), seventy-three doubles and eight mixed. She had brought the game of tennis into a new era."

Lenglen was schooled in tennis by her father, Charles. Given her stocky build, prominent nose, irregular teeth, and dark circles beneath her eyes, she was, as the peerless sportswriter Grantland Rice wrote, anything but a classic "female beauty." "But she was beautiful as an athlete," Rice continued, "when the flaming color she wore began to move around—a red or orange lightness blown by the wind." She was acrobatic on court, stylish away from it. "She dressed divinely and her ugliness became almost an asset," wrote Paul Gallico. "Lenglen wore ermine and partied on champagne, she traveled by chauffeured limo and private rail car, and she knew everyone who ever wrote a memoir about the Lost Generation," Franz Lidz wrote in *Sports Illustrated*. Even more intriguing were her occasional conniptions. Lidz called her "a baseline Zelda Fitzgerald who succumbed routinely to fits of depression and hysteria." Smoking, drinking, stoking her flagging strength during changeovers with brandy-soaked sugar cubes tossed to her by Daddy, Lenglen was a French flapper perfectly in tune with the Roaring Twenties.

Lenglen won her first tournament at the age of twelve and her first major victory, the World Hard Court (clay) championship three years later. With an all-court game that included keen anticipation, great footwork, speed, control, and marvelous net instincts, she was the first complete player in the women's ranks. From 1919, when she won her first Wimbledon singles title 10–8, 4–6, 9–7 in a thrillingly long battle against Britain's Dorothea Douglass Chambers, herself a seven-time title holder, through 1925, she did not lose a single match at the premier event in the sport, although illness forced her to withdraw after the quarterfinals in 1924.

Nonetheless, both in her prime and after, observers rarely limited their comments to Lenglen's shot-making skills. Beyond sport, she was the first female superstar, a grand personality whose clothes, romances, and quirks were discussed endlessly by admirers on both sides of the Atlantic. In an era known for its remarkable athletes, she was as well known as Babe Ruth, Red Grange, and Jack Dempsey. Just as Yankee Stadium was the House That Ruth Built, the modern Wimbledon was the Palace That Suzanne Built; she drew such crowds that the All-England Club was expanded in 1922 to accommodate them. Hemingway made a reference to her in *The Sun Also Rises*. She counted kings and queens among her fans. And in 1938, when she died at the age of thirty-nine of pernicious anemia, she was given a state funeral at Notre Dame and awarded a posthumous Legion of Honor.

There could not have been a greater contrast than that presented by Helen Wills, six years younger than Lenglen. Born in Centreville, California, in 1905; tutored by her father, a surgeon; she was right-handed, as was Lenglen—and the resemblance ended there. Her dark hair and beautiful face were framed by her trademark, a white eyeshade. She was nicknamed "Little Miss Poker Face" for her composed on-court temperament, long before the world was introduced to Chris Evert. She intimidated rivals with her steely concentration; she beat them with strong serves and ground strokes more powerful than any woman before her. The American public caught up with Wills when, at the age of seventeen, she won the U.S. Nationals in 1923. Surely, if anyone could knock La Grande Dame Suzanne off her perch, it would be this strong yet demure American ingenue. When Wills set sail for Europe in 1925 to meet Lenglen at last, in a Cannes tournament, the stage was set for a tennis version of *All About Eve.*

In fact, it turned out to be the most ballyhooed match in the sport. Played almost fifty years before King vs. Riggs, with no money on the line, without benefit of television or women's lib, before a crowd of maybe four thousand people, Lenglen vs. Wills was gripping global drama. In the words of Larry Englemann, their authoritative dual biographer, "This was an international incident. This was history. And millions of people wanted to be part of it. . . . Men and women who could not tell you the difference between a game and a set were now offering to risk cash on this match." Declared Ferdinand Tuohy, it was just "a simple game of tennis, yet a game which made continents stand still." Only Al Laney, the estimable tennis writer for the *New York* and *International Herald Tribune,* writing in 1968 without the benefit of twenty-twenty foresight, underestimated the lust of the world's spectators for a properly hyped tennis match between two colorful racketeers: "Never again in the history of sport," Laney opined, "was such an event allowed to go on under such ridiculous and fantastic conditions. It probably could have filled Yankee Stadium. . . ."

The match took place February 16, 1926, at the Carlton Club, a six-court facility in Cannes. Lenglen was revered on the Riviera, and both the locale and the surface—clay—were ideal for her. Fans, many of whom had come by train from Paris, jammed the rickety bleachers, some of which were still being put up a few hours before the start of the contest. Onlookers who could not get into the club paid owners of nearby villas to watch from their upper windows and roofs.

Lenglen, then at the peak of her game, captured the first set handily, 6–3. But Wills could sense the Frenchwoman tiring. Revived by sips of iced cognac on changeovers, Lenglen held on to win the second set, but only after a false finish—and resulting pandemonium—when a spectator cried "Out!" on a Wills shot at match point, with Lenglen leading 6–5. The umpire, a Wimbledon veteran, restored order, and Lenglen, while losing the game, managed to eke out an 8–6 victory. Later, Wills wrote that Lenglen had lived up to her reputation: "She accomplished and carried to their ideal completion strategic plans which other players try but cannot always consistently finish." Nevertheless, she wrote, "I found her balls not unusually difficult to hit, nor did they carry as much speed as the balls of several other of the leading women players. . . . But her balls kept coming back, coming back, and each time to a spot on the court which was a little more difficult to get to."

Most accounts of the spectacle fail to mention that the two women met a second time in that Cannes tournament, in the doubles finals. Playing with Didi Vlasto, Lenglen prevailed again, but Wills, paired with Helen Contostavlos, kept the match close. The Frenchwomen won 6–4, 8–6. Despite her dominance, Lenglen was said to be shaken by the American girl's power and persistence. Wills looked forward to future meetings. They never happened. Wills was stricken with appendicitis before the French championships that year, where Lenglen won the singles title, and then Lenglen turned pro following a tempest over her lateness for a match at Wimbledon. However, the Lenglen-Wills match sparked an upsurge of interest in tennis worldwide, and especially in recreational tennis throughout the United States. Its growth would continue for decades.

Wills was just beginning her rise into the pantheon of tennis when she played Lenglen. Moreover, there was another outcome to their historic meeting. At the end, spectators surrounded the winner, leaving Wills standing all alone on the court. "I began to feel rather overcome," she wrote. "Then suddenly a young man whom I had met a few days before vaulted over the balustrade from the grandstand . . . and came over to me. He said, 'You played awfully well.'" The admirer was Frederick S. Moody. Soon they were secretly engaged. They married in 1929.

Wills went on to become so overpowering, mentally and physically, that from 1927 to 1932 she did not lose one set anywhere in singles. Her record by the end of her career was four French singles titles, seven U.S. Nationals, eight Wimbledons, plus a slew of doubles titles. She divorced Moody, married and divorced Aidan Roark, and in her long retirement wrote several books, but she kept such a low profile that another great California player, Alice Marble, called her the Greta Garbo of tennis. Nevertheless, several years before her death, she confided to Englemann that she would have come out of retirement for just one reason: to compete against Suzanne Lenglen at the most exalted venue on the planet, Wimbledon. "You should have seen her," the regal old woman said wistfully of her charismatic rival. "Words can hardly describe Suzanne. She was really very special . . . so slender. And so lovely."

In the years just before and after World War II, no player or rivalry caught the public imagination in quite the same way, although there were many great champions. They included Alice Marble (1913–90), the first woman who was said to possess a "big" game that resembled that of her male contemporaries more than that of her female opponents. Helen Jacobs, "the other Helen," (1908–97), was the closest thing to Wills's nemesis. Jacobs, who was also from northern California, lost eight times to Wills until the 1933 U.S. Championships. There, Jacobs prevailed when Wills, behind 3–0 in the third set, defaulted because of back pain. Pauline Betz (1919–) was known for her speed and won the Forest Hills title four times between 1942 and 1946. Louise Brough (1923–) used a great volley to help her capture thirteen Wimbledon titles in singles, doubles, and mixed. She and Margaret Osborne duPont (1918–) were the best doubles team until Navratilova and Pam Shriver. For a few shining years in the early 1950s, Maureen "Little Mo" Connolly (1934–69) was the dominant player, a Southern Californian who in 1953 became the first woman to win the Grand Slam. (The nickname referred not to her height, a smallish five-foot-four, but to her howitzer-like ground strokes; "Big Mo" was the battleship *Missouri*.) Her career was cut short in 1954 when she was hit by a truck as she rode her horse.

The era of explosive power—and integration—arrived with Althea Gibson (1927–). Before Gibson, world-class tennis was a segregated sport. Blacks were not even permitted to enter such tournaments as the Nationals. In 1950 Gibson, whose patron, Dr. Walter Johnson of Lynchburg, Virginia, later helped Arthur Ashe break the color barrier in men's tennis, became the first African-American to play at Forest Hills (which had no black members), as well as the first black champion of Wimbledon. Tennis was segregated by class and by status as well as by race until the late 1960s. Recreational tennis was largely reserved for the country-club crowd, and "pro" tennis was anathema; the powers that be decreed tennis to be an amateur sport. The top players at events such as Wimbledon and Forest Hills were paid secretly, under the table, while maintaining their amateur status. The ones who openly accepted money—Lenglen was one of the first, but then great players such as Rod Laver and Ken Rosewall also barnstormed on pro tours—were refused entry into the major events until 1968. So the game that held its own in sports' golden age languished in the first years of the television age.

It didn't help that the 1950s rewarded conformity, patronized the "feminine mystique," and stigmatized female athleticism. It was permissible for girls to dash around, roughhouse with the boys, and climb trees until puberty. Once those breasts started filling out their sweatshirts, though, most girls were taught that being an athlete was strictly for boys. Oh, it was all right to root for the home team, better than all right to be a cheerleader or a dancer or even a figure skater. But not a shortstop.

Billie Jean Moffitt (1943–) was luckier than most girls of her generation, in addition to being far more athletically gifted. She grew up in Southern California, where playing in the outdoors was a bit more acceptable than it was in the East. Her parents, not happy that she wanted to be either a baseball or a football player, at least gave her three sports alternatives: swimming, golf, or tennis. "What's tennis?" she asked.

Golf was slow, and she wasn't much of a swimmer, so she began taking tennis lessons from a public court pro. A plump, nearsighted bundle of enthusiasm, she didn't exactly look the part. Nor did she dress it until the age of twelve, in 1955, when she was not allowed to appear in a tournament photograph because she was wearing shorts instead of a dress. But by 1960, having secured a dress, more lessons, and a killer backhand volley, she was ranked number four in the United States. The next year, she won what was to be the first of a record twenty Wimbledon victories—the women's doubles crown, with Karen Hantze. An American sportswriter covering Wimbledon for a Boston newspaper was so pleased at their defeat of Australians Margaret Smith and Jan Lehane that he waited "like a stagedoor Johnnie" outside the club, "hoping to congratulate them before one of the imposing limousines chartered for the players rushed them off to the winners' ball." There was not a limo in sight and they were broke, two Cinderellas, once again without the proper dress for the occasion. Bud Collins treated the two American kids to a celebratory pasta dinner.

Billie Jean's first taste of Centre Court at Wimbledon whetted her appetite for more. Despite the snobbism of the All England Club, she loved the way tennis was worshipped at Wimbledon and the way tennis players were treated. "Right away, I had a wonderful feeling. I knew this was the place I wanted to play a lot," she said. She was never intimidated by it, as so many players have been. The next year, she knocked off top-seed Margaret Smith (1942–), the first Australian woman to dominate the world circuit, in the first round of the singles, while repeating her doubles title win. Smith got revenge in 1963, beating Billie Jean in straight sets in the finals. Knowing she needed help to improve her strokes and stamina, Billie Jean dropped out of Los Angeles State College in 1964 at the urging of her fiancé, law student Larry King, and accepted a trip to Australia (paid for by an Aussie tennis patron) to take private lessons from Mervyn Rose, a former Davis Cupper. He ran the extra pounds off her, shortened her swing, and schooled her in "percentage tennis," or on-court thinking.

Billie Jean rose quickly in the international ranks—to number four in 1965 and number one in 1966, her breakthrough year, in which BJ, now Mrs. King, defeated Smith in the semis and second-seeded Maria Bueno of Brazil in the finals for her first Wimbledon singles championship. By the 1967 season she was nearly unbeatable in the majors, sweeping the Wimbledon and U.S. National singles and doubles titles, the latter with a new (and even shorter) doubles partner, Rosemary Casals (1948–). (An outspoken Californian who was a leader of the "let's turn pro" contingent, Rosie won 112 pro doubles titles, putting her second on the all-time list behind Martina Navratilova.)

The more titles she captured, the more outspoken BJ became. Asked for an interview for the women's pages of a newspaper, she exploded: "That's the trouble with this sport. We've got to get it off the society pages and onto the sports pages!" Annoyed at the private clubs that were often the venues for tournaments, she declared tennis had to get "away from the club atmosphere and into the public places, the parks, arenas like Madison Square Garden." The game got little respect from the American public, she lamented, because "people think of tennis as a sissy sport." When the opportunity arose in 1968 to break out of the "shamateur" ranks—where the biggest names were paid under the table by promoters to appear at their tournaments—and join a pro tour, Billie Jean was the first woman to climb aboard. The move toward professionalism by both male and female players proved irresistible, and the tennis powers finally accepted both amateurs and pros into major tournaments that year for the first time.

Then, in 1970, Billie Jean led what was to become an all-out revolt against inequality.

Prize money was now being offered above board, yet ironically, in those first years of the "open" era, the amount allotted for women was being cut back everywhere. The situation was most egregious at a tournament in her home state, the Pacific Southwest Open, held in Los Angeles and run by the legendary Jack Kramer. First prize for the men was $12,500; the entire women's prize money totaled just $7,500, with no payments for any women below quarterfinalists. Billie Jean had tried to coax women into fighting for more "expense" money as early as 1964, without any luck. "Now, the situation was different," she wrote in her autobiography. "It wasn't just a little per diem dough on the line, it was the livelihoods of a lot of women." She and Rosie Casals convinced seven leading players to join them in a boycott of the Pacific Southwest. The nine mutineers played several weeks later in their own Houston tournament, quickly organized by Gladys Heldman, publisher of *World Tennis* magazine, and sponsored by Philip Morris, whose board chairman, Joe Culligan, was a friend of Heldman's. The defiant ones were promptly suspended by the U.S. Lawn Tennis Association (USLTA) for participating in an unsanctioned event. Ultimately, of course, their cause was successful—the Virginia Slims all-women's pro circuit was up and running by 1971. (The USLTA battled back by organizing a rival circuit.) For the rest of her playing days, long past the time when it was politically correct, Billie Jean voiced support for the cigarette manufacturer, in gratitude for helping women gain a measure of independence, as well as equal pay.

King ruled as the queen of tennis, off the court as well as on, in the late 1960s and early 1970s. She had already established Wimbledon as her castle in 1966, 1967, and 1968 with a three-peat in the singles. She added the doubles in 1965, playing with Maria Bueno, and then got into a habit of collecting

Big W doubles trophies with Rosie Casals, winning the first of their titles there in 1967. That year, perhaps her finest, she collected the trifecta—singles, doubles, mixed—at both Wimbledon and Forest Hills. The next year she added the Australian singles title, then Wimbledon. In 1971, the proudly professional King filled her pockets with prize money, becoming the first woman athlete to win more than $100,000 (in her case, $117,000) in a single season. In 1972, she scattered the seeds at the French, Wimbledon, and U.S. Opens, beating free spirit Evonne Goolagong (1951–   ), a loose-limbed Australian of aboriginal heritage who won Wimbledon in 1971 and 1980, at the European legs of the Grand Slam, then dispatching another Aussie, Kerry Melville, at Forest Hills.

At the time, as the winds of women's liberation began toppling sexist myths everywhere, Billie Jean was the perfect jock politician. Her political point of view was unassailable, her tennis sensational, and her public persona dynamic. She was an upbeat, hoydenish gladiator who could always be counted on for a great quote. She chattered to herself on court, and the joy she took from playing well was evident. How refreshing she seemed, after the reserve of Mo Connolly, Margaret Smith Court, and so many other women on the international tennis scene. They were B-52s; Billie Jean was a Spitfire.

Despite her missionary work, Billie Jean was not universally liked by the female players. Some thought she was a showboat. Others were not thrilled about her insistence on organizing a players' union. Still others whispered about her lifestyle, as her relationship with Larry grew distant (although he was still her husband, her agent, and a promoter of women's tournaments as well) and she began to share her life on the road with her female hairdresser. Besides, she had the annoying habit of hailing new blood on tour, then beating the pulp out of every newcomer in her path.

Winning was clearly her drug of choice. And she was about to get involved in a stunt that would crown her career. She had decided to avenge the 1973 "Mother's Day massacre"—Margaret Smith Court's humiliating defeat in an exhibition match against fifty-five-year-old Bobby Riggs, a former champion turned court hustler—by agreeing to play Riggs in the Houston Astrodome in September of 1973. A $100,000 winner-take-all purse and gender bragging rights would be on the line. A prime-time national network television audience would be watching. The "Battle of the Sexes" was a ridiculous, glorious circus of a tennis match that catapulted Billie Jean into the forefront of feminism and gave tennis its greatest worldwide exposure since the Wills-Lenglen match so many years before.

Today, twenty-five years later, it is hard to imagine the country, not to mention the world, getting so worked up about a silly showdown between a male has-been and a female wonder woman. But 50 million TV viewers tuned in to see it. Husbands fought with wives over it. Newspapers editorialized about it. Bets were made, articles were written about King's nerves and Riggs's braggadocio, and writers chased phantom notions about the meaning of it all. But this was not a test of tennis supremacy. It was a test of a female superstar's mental toughness and her ability to carry through a vision.

Billie Jean King passed with flying colors. On the final point in the Astrodome, the scoreboard flashed 6–4, 6–3, 6–3, and Billie Jean flung her racquet toward the rafters. She not only won the hyped exhibition, she seized the moment. While the world debated the significance of her victory, she used her aggrandized fame to promote ideas that live on today. Thanks in part to her victory, women's tennis solidified its place as a premier pro event; the Women's Tennis Association that she founded became a viable negotiating unit; and her magazine (originally known as *WomenSports*, now a part of Conde Nast's *Women's Sports & Fitness*), which advocated the value of all kinds of sports for women, was well received. Perhaps her most important legacy will be the Women's Sports Foundation, the cornerstone for huge gains in the acceptance of women as athletes worthy of the same admiration as their male counterparts. With its leadership, its annual awards dinner, its pioneering research on all phases of women and sports, and its support of Title IX, the foundation has helped to guarantee girls a chance to play in just about any game they choose.

If Billie Jean had lost, would it have changed anything? Doubtful. She had a tougher time maintaining her equilibrium once the Astrodome spectacle was history. She was thirty years old and had creaky knees with surgical stitch marks tattooed all over them. She soldiered on, winning the U.S. Open in 1974 and Wimbledon in 1975, but she was no longer an overpowering force. Nevertheless, she displayed remarkable resilience, beating pros half her age into her fortieth year. In the twilight of a magnificent career at the All-England Club (and with a major assist from doubles partner Martina Navratilova), she captured her twentieth Wimbledon title, a record that still stands. She will never be voted the greatest female player, but at least one partisan, Bud Collins, believes she is more important than that. He says she is "possibly the most influential player in popularizing professional tennis in the United States."

By 1975, Billie Jean King no longer topped the world rankings. However, in proselytizing on behalf of women's tennis rights, she gained a crucial convert: the woman who eclipsed her as number one in the standings and in the hearts of tennis lovers, Chris Evert (1954–   ).

At first, the new kid on the block was cool toward "the old lady," as King referred to herself, and vice versa. Billie Jean felt that Chris, who burst onto the scene as a sixteen-year-old amateur in 1971, was reaping the rewards of equal pay and professional status that others had fought for. Meanwhile, Chris at first believed that Billie Jean was divisive: the youngster was the key player to stay with the USLTA circuit when the Virginia Slims tour was competing with it. Nevertheless, like everyone else who cared about tennis, Billie Jean could see the game's future in the blond "ice dolly" with the ferocious two-handed backhand. In 1974, a few months after she had beaten Chris in her first Wimbledon final, Billie Jean invited her to play doubles. In forsaking her successful partnership with Rosie Casals, Billie Jean said it was because Chris's steady ground strokes would better complement her own aggressive volleying and make a more balanced team. Perhaps Billie Jean also wanted to get to know her—and to propagandize the shy, apolitical Evert on the subject of feminism.

Whatever the reason, they clicked. At nineteen, Evert was just beginning to wriggle out of a tight, conservative family cocoon. She had been brought up by her parents as a good Catholic girl. She was so busy playing Wimbledon in 1973 that she missed her graduation ceremonies at St. Thomas Aquinas High School in Fort Lauderdale, Florida, but she had attended school regularly, unlike the vast majority of players who achieved tennis success in their early teens. She did not turn pro until her eighteenth birthday. Her father, Jimmy, a coach on the public courts, trained her to be both a champion and a conformer. By nature, she was shy, and, as a middle child with an older brother and three younger siblings, she saw herself as a natural peacemaker, so going along with the tennis establishment was not an uncomfortable position for her. Colette Evert accompanied her daughter on her travels and was one of the first mothers to play chaperone on the pro tour. Chris was thus insulated from her older rivals, and they, in turn, were jealous of her success and her audience appeal.

Despite what some felt was her machinelike style of play, Chris Evert was never an automaton. She told interviewers, truthfully, that her extraordinary power of concentration and her cool demeanor were necessary on court, since she had to work so hard to beat those with more natural talent. In her early years on the circuit, her most formidable opponent was Evonne Goolagong, whose insouciant gracefulness Chris admired. "I marveled at how well she glided to the ball, and how naturally she moved," Evert wrote in her autobiography about the first time she saw Goolagong play. "I felt even more mechanical because everything she did was instinctive, with feel and touch."

To Chris, the extroverted Billie Jean King seemed like someone from another planet. On the other hand, she appreciated the fact that Billie Jean never said a negative word about the almost immediate popularity among fans that Chris gained as a teenager. The two were on competing tours in 1971, so they met only at the big championships. A number of players snubbed Evert completely in the locker room, but King kept on insisting that the kid was "good for women's tennis," and she meant it. As they strode onto the grass for their semifinal match at Forest Hills against each other, Billie Jean told Chris, "You're on the crest of a wave, so enjoy it while you can," and then polished her off in straight sets 6–3, 6–2, with a grim visage that nearly matched Chris's. Later, Billie Jean explained that if she had lost to this amateur upstart, it might have spelled disaster for female pros and their hard-fought war for recognition.

When they began to practice and play doubles together in 1974, Billie Jean saw in Chris an intelligence and an aptitude for leadership that others (maybe even Chris) had not yet recognized. Chris saw in Billie Jean a softer side that the public and the other pros rarely glimpsed. Chris Evert's capacity for friendship with people who hold a different view of the world is one of her most estimable traits.

Chris won Wimbledon in that pivotal year, 1974, and it was doubly delicious because the winner of the men's title, Jimmy Connors, was her beau. If ever a pair seemed mismatched, it was the brash Connors and the introverted Evert. The outside world was just beginning to discover how surprising their favorite tennis princess could be. (Interestingly, as a bachelor Jimmy Evert had dated Gloria Connors, Jimmy's mom and mentor.) Chris and Jimbo soon recognized they were too young to make a permanent commitment and called off the wedding they had planned.

Chris had an appetite for knowledge, sophistication, and new ideas that helped sustain her during a long, often lonely career at the pinnacle of tennis. Her ability to grow as a person, not just as an athlete, set her apart from most of the top-seeded tennis stars. Chris Evert would live through an ill-advised first marriage, get a divorce, build up her body through weight training, reign as the president of the Women's Tennis Association, stay among the top-ranked five women for seventeen years, take up skiing, and become an incisive television commentator. As a leader among female athletes with a developing openness, "Miss American Pie" matured into a complex person who was a pleasure to watch, in tennis and in life.

The consistency of Chris's ground strokes, especially her two-handed backhand, made her nearly unbeatable on clay courts. But never has a player so capitalized on what was not an overpowering set of innate gifts. As new players challenged her supremacy—first Goolagong, then Tracy Austin (another American baseliner, who was probably the most sensational young teen ever until injuries stifled her career), then Navratilova—Chris simply raised the bar. She was not fast, she was not terribly strong, she was not a great volleyer, and she did not have a big serve. Yet her list of Grand Slam singles titles covers every surface and every major opponent among her contemporaries: two Australian, seven French, three Wimbledon, six U.S. Opens. In 1985 and 1986 against her greatest rival, Martina Navratilova (1956–   ), in the finals of the French Open, she put an exclamation point on their long competition with two thrilling three-set victories. Though some tagged Evert's game as boring, she was all the more exciting for her psychological resolve. Indeed, she set the standard.

For years the great "secret" inside tennis was that off the court, Chrissie was anything but prissy. Asked about this late in her career, she set the record straight: "I'm not as Goody Two-shoes as people think. They think I am squeaky clean. I'm a normal woman. I've dated a lot of guys, I've had a few drinks, I've told dirty jokes, I've cursed, I've been rude to my parents," she declared. If there was anything abnormal, it was the desire to win, a desire that burned in the silent glares with which she intimidated linespeople, in the refusal to give in to an opponent even when she was playing badly, as she did in a memorable three-set comeback against Laura Golarsa in the quarterfinals at Wimbledon in 1989. Her readiness for new adventures surely paved the way for her friendship with Martina Navratilova. At first, the two were not even rivals, much less pals.

Navratilova, born in Czechoslovakia in 1956, lived a dramatic life, starting with her defection from communist-ruled Czechoslovakia as a teenager, and including liaisons with several lesbian celebrities, plus a nasty split and battle over assets with longtime lover Judy Nelson. Brought up by a mother and stepfather who were both tennis players and skiers, Martina showed an early aptitude for both. She was brought into the international spotlight by the bureaucrats of the communist Czechoslovakian sports world, who entered her in U.S. tournaments starting in 1973. At first, all she did was get fat on American junk food. But her talent—speed, a big left-handed serve and volley style, a great overhead smash—put the rest of the tennis establishment on notice. As she discovered how far tennis could take her, Martina began to feel stifled by the Czech authorities. In 1975, at age nineteen, she defected during the tournament at Forest Hills, knowing she might never be able to return to her homeland. Still, in the next few years, her game began to come together. She won the first of her Wimbledon singles titles in 1978, beating Evert in three sets, then, her face buried in a towel, cried with joy. Here at last was the anti-Evert—an emotional, exhilarating, all-court star, tennis observers declared.

Navratilova was befriended by some savvy companions, including golfer Sandra Haynie, author Rita Mae Brown, and basketball player Nancy

Lieberman, who introduced her to, among other things, a weight-training regimen, a careful diet, and a merciless conditioning program. A sleek new Navratilova emerged, and she was nearly unstoppable. Evert decided that the only way to stop her was to work as hard as she had. "I never would have stayed in the game as long as I did if I hadn't had Martina to challenge me and keep things interesting," Chris said. Martina forced Chris to build up her strength and drop a few pounds in the gym. On court, according to Chris, "she made me take more chances, going for the bigger serve, coming to the net."

Their head-to-head rivalry began in Akron in 1978 and lasted an amazing eighty matches. Chris won most of the early ones, Martina most of the middle ones, and they traded victories toward the end. They grew to be pals, although their friendship hit the skids for a time when Lieberman convinced Martina that she had to hate her chief opponent. They knew they were good for one another and for tennis itself. The purses got bigger, the crowds more involved, the longer the two opposites went at one another. In Chris, Martina saw the ultimate American gal; in Martina, Chris saw the ultimate rebel. And surely they became close because there was no one else who knew what it felt like to be so far ahead of everyone in their sport. After Evert retired, she revealed that the two had "spent a lot of emotional Sundays in locker rooms, and whether I won or she won, the one comforted the other. There's a lot of caring between us." How fitting, then, that it was Martina who one winter invited a despondent Chris to Aspen, where she met former world-class skier Andy Mill, the man who would become her second husband and father of her children.

At the height of her powers in 1983 and 1984, Martina—who was only an inch or so taller than Chris at five feet, seven and a half inches (compared to Steffi Graf, five-nine; and Monica Seles, five–ten and a half)—seemed like a giant to those who faced her on the other side of the net. Her sinuous muscles rippling with every shot, she reeled off one streak of seventy-four straight singles victories, all the while piling up doubles trophies with Pam Shriver. (The pair, whom many experts consider the best ever in doubles, achieved a doubles Grand Slam in 1984.) From 1982 into 1987, Martina was ranked number one in the world for 150 weeks. Steffi Graf broke Martina's record in 1987 and subsequently bested it; Graf was number one for 186 consecutive weeks.

By being super fit, she avoided injuries that hampered many of the top players, but it was her wicked left-handed serve, her swift net approaches, her acrobatic overheads, and her net play that brought ooos and aaahs from spectators. On a more personal note, she became a dedicated American citizen. She was a steadfast member of American teams in the Federation (later just plain Fed) Cup, the women's equivalent of Davis Cup play, in which teams from various nations compete each year. Her triumphant return to Czechoslovakia came in 1986, when she led the American Fed Cup team to victory over a strong Czechoslovak team in Prague. (After their pro careers were over, both Navratilova and King worked with younger players as captains of the American Fed Cup team.) Martina's combination of longevity and versatility made her, in the minds of many, the most complete female player in history.

Navratilova contributed as much to the gay rights movement as she did to tennis. In the 1950s, truly fierce athleticism was equated with lesbianism. Three decades later, when Billie Jean King's palimony story broke, gay rights was barely on the radar of public awareness, much less acceptance. The palimony suit was brought out when Martina's relationship with Judy Nelson, with whom she lived openly in the late 1980s and early 1990s, ended unhappily. Nelson sued Navratilova in Texas for what she said was her share of their assets—fifty percent—even though they were not married and Texas is not a community property state. They reached an out-of-court settlement and the terms were kept confidential. In 1998, most gay athletes, especially women on the pro tennis and golf circuits, remain in the closet because they can count on losing millions of dollars in product endorsements if they make their sexual preference known. Navratilova accepted the one controversial role that Billie Jean refused to acknowledge: spokeswoman for athletes who are out of the closet and proud. She not only acknowledged that she was a lesbian, she campaigned on behalf of gay issues.

What she got in return was a big vocal following among gay and liberal straight fans alike. As Evert recalled, "She revolutionized the game; she brought a fresh new honesty. She's never been afraid to speak out or say what she really thinks, and she always wore her heart on her sleeve." Martina got her share of nasty notes, catcalls, and bashing from the Christian Right, even from as far away as Australia, where Margaret Smith Court, a militant Christian, denounced her sexual preference. Only a handful of athletes, male or female, have dared to take a stand of such candor at the height of their careers. As more gay stars come out, they will have Martina to thank for paving the way.

As Martina and Chris began to slow down, their spot at the top of the tennis ladder was claimed by Steffi Graf (1969–) of Germany, a right-hander whose thundering forehand and formidable serve are complemented by her speed. In 1986 at sixteen years old she proved that she was ready to challenge the top players by beating Evert on one of Evert's favorite surfaces, Har-tru clay, a "green clay" synthetic surface, in the final of one of Evert's favorite tournaments, the Family Circle Cup (Evert won it eight times). The very next year, Steffi won her first major title, the French, beating Navratilova in three sets, in the midst of piling up eleven singles titles. The year after that, 1988, she became the first woman to capture the Grand Slam since Margaret Smith Court in 1970; in between Wimbledon and the U.S. Open, she also took home the Olympic gold medal. Writers dubbed the combination of Grand Slam and Olympic victories that year the "Golden Slam."

Even as Graf began to collect trophy after trophy, mere numbers could not convey how devastating a power she had become. The old wooden racquets had given way to new, lighter, larger ones made of composite materials including graphite. Beginning with Graf, the better-conditioned players pounded opponents at a pace unknown just a few years earlier—and they did not have to come to the net to finish points. Tracy Austin has noted Graf's dominance succinctly: "Steffi Graf has two of the biggest weapons in the game with her forehand and serve. She is also the fastest player in the game. But the biggest reason Steffi is so great is her ability to win the big points in the big matches. Even with all her injuries, her sheer desire and ability to get the job done under pressure has pulled her through so many matches and won her many titles."

Injuries (back, knee, calf, foot) did dog Graf. However, more damaging were the scandals that began to engulf her father, Peter, who was her manager in her early years as a pro. In 1990, tabloids around the world feasted on allegations about Peter Graf's involvement with a woman who allegedly bore his child. Then came the German tax authorities, who investigated, indicted, and jailed Peter Graf on charges of tax evasion.

Throughout these travails, the tennis court became Steffi Graf's refuge. Until knee surgery sidelined her for much of the 1997 season, she was ranked number one for eight out of ten years, having snatched that ranking from Navratilova at the end of 1987. At the start of the 1990s, with Navratilova's playing days coming to a close (she retired from singles in 1994), Graf discovered a new, younger, even harder-hitting opponent: Monica Seles.

Born in 1973 of Serbo-Hungarian parentage, Seles was first schooled by her father, Karolj, who had a physical education background but originally did not know anything about tennis. His son, Zoltan, eight years older than Monica, first caught the tennis bug when he saw Bjorn Borg play on television. However, it was Zoltan's kid sister who really was taken by the game. When Monica reached the age of twelve, the entire Seles family moved to Florida so Monica, clearly a budding star, could attend Nick Bollettieri's famous academy. In 1989, at fifteen, in only her second tournament as a pro, she announced her arrival by beating Chris Evert in the finals of a tournament in Houston. Her potential was immediately evident; she was a left-hander who pounded two-handed shots off both wings, sending the ball at incredible angles deep into corners, and she was still growing.

Seles brought a giggly personality and a variety of hairdos and hair colors to the game, along with a trademark two-note grunt that she sounded as she exhaled on every shot. She began aiming at Graf's supremacy by halting her sixty-six-match winning streak in a tournament in Berlin in 1990. Graf was so furious at losing that back in the locker room, in front of Seles, she slammed her racquet against a wall, gouging a huge hole. Theirs began to grow into a full-fledged rivalry when Monica followed up with a victory over Graf in the French Open later that year. It didn't help that Graf was perceived by the public as cold, while Seles won over fans with her chatterbox teen spirit; she spoke openly of being the tennis version of Madonna. By 1991, with Seles only eighteen, both women were in Madonna's league in terms of money; they both made *Forbes* magazine's list of wealthiest athletes.

Even though the stars grew stronger, richer, and younger, women's tennis in the 1990s was wracked by high crimes and misdemeanors. Jennifer Capriati (1976–   ) of Florida was perceived as the next challenger to Graf and Seles when she burst on the scene as a fourteen-year-old with pulverizing ground strokes in the first year of the decade. Despite beating Graf to win the Olympics gold medal in Barcelona in 1992, Capriati was turning into a sullen, discontented player, and her eventual arrest on marijuana charges ended an awfully quick rise. (Capriati returned to the pro circuit in 1996 but struggled to regain her old form.) Even more disturbing was the spectacle of Jim Pierce, the embodiment of everything that was wrong in tennis parents. The father of rising star Mary Pierce (1975–   ), he became so abusive to his daughter and to her opponents, on court and off, that he was eventually banished from the women's tour.

The worst blow, however, was the 1993 stabbing of Monica Seles. She was nineteen years old and ranked number one in the world. Her great rival, Graf, had demolished her in the Wimbledon final a year earlier, but Monica had won the French. At the start of 1993, Monica and Steffi had gone three gloriously long sets at the Australian Open final before Seles prevailed. Then, in April came the attack, at a tournament in Hamburg. Monica was seated on a changeover with her back to spectators in her quarterfinal match against Magdalena Maleeva, when Guenther Parche, who claimed to be a Graf fan bent on returning Steffi to the number-one ranking, appeared in the stands behind her and drove a nine-inch knife into her back, narrowly missing her spine.

Seles screamed. Her brother jumped out of the stands and rushed to her, along with match officials. She was taken to a hospital in shock. One of the few visitors allowed was Steffi Graf. As she approached Monica's hospital bed, both players began to cry. "I looked up at her, this woman who never showed emotion, and watched the tears fall," Seles later wrote. "It was such a weird moment—two athletes staring into each other's eyes and crying." Afterward, Seles was outraged twice—first when she learned that the tournament was proceeding, although she and others thought it should have been stopped after the stabbing; second when she heard that Graf, along with all the other top players on the tour except Gabriela Sabatini, had voted *against* freezing Seles's top ranking while she recuperated.

Her wound healed, but her psyche would not. She had nightmares and needed extensive psychological counseling before she could approach a tennis court and its crowds again. She finally returned in 1995, first in an exhibition match with Martina Navratilova (an idea put forward by Navratilova herself), then in that summer's Canadian Open. Seles was able to reenter the tour with a ranking of number one, shared with the year's actual top-ranked player, Steffi Graf. The idea for ranking Seles where she had been at the time of the attack came also from Navratilova, then president of the Women's Tennis Association.

Seles had left the game in 1993 a giddy, nineteen-year-old girl who seemed to be on target to become one of the great ones. By 1997, she was the oldest twenty-four-year-old athlete I had ever seen, occasionally brilliant (she won the Australian Open in 1996), plagued by nagging injuries, struggling with her weight and her conditioning, still trying to shrug off the demons from the stabbing. And then came another blow: Her father was diagnosed with stomach cancer. Monica curtailed her schedule to spend time with him.

One bright spot in these nasty nineties has been the ascent of Martina the Second—Czech-born Martina Hingis (1980–   ), who became the youngest top-ranked player in the world in 1997 at the age of sixteen. Named for her mother's idol and coached by her mother as well, Hingis, now a Swiss citizen, is an apparently well-adjusted, happy, cocky, little rascal. At five-foot-six, she marked the return of the little squirt to women's tennis superstardom. Her prospective rivals include the hobbled Graf and the scarred Seles. But they also include some intriguing new faces—two of them African-American. Venus and Serena Williams are teenaged sisters, originally from California, who have stormed to the forefront of the game without playing the junior circuit, one of many unusual decisions made by their father, Richard. Venus, a surprise finalist at the 1997 U.S. Open at the age of seventeen, is six-foot-two, with a huge serve, an all-court game, and an in-your-face attitude. Her sister, a year younger, has vowed in public that she, not Venus, will be the greatest.

Many tennis fans expect that the reign of Martina the Second will be just as filled with high drama as that of Martina the First. Beyond that, long-time followers of women's tennis hope that as the young, incredibly wealthy international stars get older, they will demonstrate the charisma of Lenglen, the candor of Navratilova, the character of Evert, the leadership of King, and the courage of Seles. If they do, women's tennis will continue as one of the most uplifting and entertaining sports on the planet.

Golf

$\mathcal{S}$elling Their Game
Melanie Hauser

Just who invented the game of golf is a question for the ages. No one can pinpoint a time or place other than to say it was a splendid gift the Scots bestowed upon us sometime around the fifteenth century. The first written records of the sport document an attempt by the Scottish Parliament in 1457 to outlaw the game—for interfering with archery practice. Yet golf survived and soon gained powerful advocates among royalty, who not only enjoyed the game but also had abundant land on which to play.

Golf was then, as it is now, a compelling game of precision and strategy brilliantly tucked inside an afternoon stroll along the seaside, across a pasture, or today over the immaculately manicured lawns of expertly designed eighteen-hole courses. There has always been an elegance to the game, seen in the grace of a perfectly executed swing or the flight of the ball. Beyond its apparent simplicity, however, lies the kind of athletic complexity that can take years to master. And yet, there is little rough and tumble to it. Instead of running and sweating and out-muscling opponents, it is a game of concentration, coordination, and poise. Golf was said to be a "gentleman's game," but it was also the perfect sport for a gentle woman, which is why women have always been interested in and allowed to play the sport.

Mary Queen of Scots was seen in 1567, not long after the death of her husband, Darnley, playing away in the fields of Seton. Women played for prizes as early as 1810, and the first Ladies Golf Club was founded at St. Andrews, known as the cradle of golf, in 1867. In those early days, it was a sport in which women could compete as easily as men. There were no barriers in place, other than professionally, and those fell in the 1930s when women left the amateur ranks and began to play for pay and teach professionally. As long as their competitions weren't serious, they found themselves as welcome as the men.

It took until July 1997 for women's competitive golf to steal the show. In fact, women's golf never had it so great as it did the week in North Plains, Oregon, as the best players in the women's game teed up in the 1997 U.S. Women's Open at Pumpkin Ridge Country Club. More often than not, the women's tournaments each week are an "oh-by-the-way, so-and-so's winning" afterthought to the men's games. But for once the women were the top story.

The mountainous backdrop, the presence of the media, the outpouring of fans all played into the excitement of the tournament. But it was the 1997 Open lineup, their profiles and personalities, and the surprises that occurred over the course of the tournament that brought things to a boil. Annika Sorenstam, two-time Player of the Year and the undisputed best player in the game at the time, seemed destined to make history by taking her third consecutive Open. To the surprise of the golf world, this woman, who had won one out of every four tournaments she entered in the last year, whose focus seemed unshakable, caved under the pressure of the biggest women's golf tournament of the year, opening with a 77—nine shots higher than expected, nine shots behind the leaders—ultimately too far behind to make the thirty-six-hole cut. It was her worst round of golf that year.

Sorenstam's exit gave way to an even more compelling drama involving American favorite Nancy Lopez, the gracious forty-something legend with an unforgettable smile, who was making her twenty-first attempt at the one major championship title that had eluded her since her rookie season in 1978. Just about everyone was rooting for her as she battled eventual winner Allison Nicholas of England in the final 18 holes and came up short in an Open for the fourth time in her storied career. Just what happened to her game, even she couldn't explain.

But the point isn't what Lopez didn't do or Nicholas did do, how Sorenstam choked or others succeeded; it is rather what the golf world did. It did something it had never done before. It watched. And not only golf fans, but the world—the tournament was the top story on sports pages and on national television.

The Ladies Professional Golf Association has been around for nearly four decades, and moments like those have been few and far between. Not since Babe Didrikson Zaharias, the most charismatic player in golf history, had the characters been as dynamic, the copy as compelling, the story as engaging. This was the tournament the pioneers of women's golf had been waiting for. Selling the women's game has never been easy. In the first half of the century, amateurs outnumbered pros a zillion to one. A woman who loved the game could spend her time playing leisurely country club golf. A talented woman from a well-to-do family who loved to compete had her choice of amateur events—both national and international—year-round. But a pro had to sell herself, then hope someone would be sold on sponsoring a tournament so she could play.

Those early players were amazing, and we're not just talking about Babe, though, of course, she was the one everyone turned out to see in the 1940s. Something else and something more, her talent and showmanship had been the catalyst for the early LPGA Tour. But back when Babe coaxed Peggy Kirk Bell, an outstanding amateur who would become one of the most influential women in golf, onto the women's tour, there were only about five players or so who could win with regularity. They were tough and brave, not afraid to stand up on the first tee and remind everyone that they, too, were out there to do a job. Just like the men. Most had careers, not families. Most got along on small incomes, sharing cross-country rides and hotel rooms and playing for tournament purses smaller than the first-place prize money on the men's tour.

As the competition increased in the late 1950s and early 1960s, the trio of Kathy Whitworth, Mickey Wright, and Betsy Rawls showed how well the game could be played. Those three Hall of Famers won a combined 225 tournaments during their careers. For Wright and Rawls, the game had come easy. For Whitworth, who would go on to win more tournaments (88) than any other male or female golfer, the game was a test of perseverance and patience. Just like the growth of women's golf.

When Lopez breezed onto the scene in the late 1970s, Title IX was a half decade old, and the pool of top players had grown to fifteen or twenty (the men, meanwhile, had forty or fifty top players). It was Lopez, though, who stood above the rest. She was the one the women's game had been waiting for—the superstar with the total package, the player who would define the women's tour.

Today, any of fifty players—maybe more—from many different countries have a better than average chance to win. That is not to say that the growing pains aren't still there. While many country clubs are still trying to keep Saturday morning tee times and voting memberships away from women, the LPGA players are fighting the battle for financial equality. Or at least major improvement. And, while today's women have a higher profile than those who started the tour, they face the same challenges—sponsors, marketing, and image. They're still searching for their niche in the game and a few more charismatic players like Lopez and Zaharias who can take them there.

Gaze at the faded black-and-white photos of the Babe in the 1940s, and you wonder how she'd fit in today. Would she be another Tiger Woods? You wonder what she would think of the game, the players, and the strides. Then again, you don't. There's only one thing the irrepressible Babe would be thinking—that she could beat 'em all.

The way most folks have it figured, there wasn't anything Babe Didrikson Zaharias couldn't do. She was the first female sports hero, an athlete who could tug on Superman's cape, spit into the wind, and still win going away. She could do anything a man could do—and sometimes she did it better— and didn't mind in the least taking those bows. Or letting a few bawdy jokes roll off her tongue.

At a time when women were expected to be soft and feminine, Babe was loud and proud. A big-boned woman (five-six, 150 pounds plus), she had a hawk nose, thin lips, and a broad-backed, boyish look, but she commanded attention when she walked into a room. She could play a crowd as well, if not better, than she could play whatever game was at hand. She wasn't just an athlete, but rather a unique combination of talent, image, personality, and showmanship. Oh, she could do the pearls-and-dress routine with the best of them away from athletics, but when she was competing, she was tough.

Babe dazzled the world with a pair of gold medals (high hurdles and javelin) and a silver (high jump) in the 1932 Los Angeles Olympics, but that was just a start. By the time she turned her full attention to golf, she was a one-woman sports show. She had played basketball, pitched in exhibition baseball, shot billiards, punted in football, and excelled in just about every sport she tried. She also played a mean harmonica, took a turn in vaudeville, cut a record, and played herself in some cameo appearances on the silver screen.

But her true love was golf. She loved the game, she loved the people, and she loved the competition. People loved to watch her play. It was a match made on fairways and greens across the country—and from the pockets of promoters who couldn't resist the chance to watch the solidly built Babe threaten to loosen her girdle and bust one down the fairway. Of course, she didn't wear a girdle, but this was showbiz—did that matter?

Babe was a character. She would reach out and touch businessmen for money and tournaments from the relative comfort of her hotel rooms. You can see her now, feet propped up, leaning back, telling someone's secretary that she didn't care how busy Mr. So-and-So was. This was Babe calling. "I'd be in the room," says Peggy Bell, one of Zaharias's closest friends, "and she'd be saying, 'Hey, Bill. How about putting on a tournament? Sure, I'll be there. Just put up about $2,500 and we'll have a tournament.'" Bell chuckles. "They'd do it for her. People just think it happened. Babe made it happen."

Babe never met a deal she couldn't swing or a story she couldn't either embellish or use. Take that alleged first round of golf she played with legendary sportswriter Grantland Rice and three of his almost as legendary peers at Brentwood Country Club in Los Angeles not long after those sensational 1932 Games. Twenty-one and single at the time, she led people to believe it was her first round, when it was really the round that turned her full attention to golf. It was eighteen holes of stories and fun with borrowed clubs. And yes, Babe outdrove the guys off the first tee, hitting her tee shot 240 yards down the middle of the fairway. She also raced one of them down the eighteenth fairway to tire him out and ensure that she and partner Rice would win the competition.

Rice later wrote in a syndicated newspaper column, "If Miss Didrikson would take up golf seriously, she would be a world beater in no time." Babe read the column, knew he was right, and did nothing to dissuade people from believing that that round with Rice was her first round of golf. Only much later did she admit the truth. Babe had taken up the game as a teenager in Texas and played on Beaumont High's 1929 golf team.

But it didn't matter. No one held it against her. That was just Babe.

Babe wasn't the first great woman golfer, of course. In fact, there was a string of greats from both sides of the Atlantic. Faded photographs and daguerreotypes of early clubs and matches show women in fitted white blouses and long flowing skirts, their hair swept up under broad-brimmed hats. Society allowed women to play at a leisurely pace and applauded amateurs like America's Curtis sisters, Margaret and Harriet, for whom the amateur event first played in 1932 that pitted teams from the United States and Great Britain against each other is named; six-time U.S. Amateur champ Glenna Collett Vare, who was known for her hard hitting and was honored by the LPGA when it named the annual scoring title, the Vare Trophy, after her; and six-time British women's champ Joyce Wethered, later known as Lady Heathcott Amory, whose grip and swing were enviable, and who played with the legendary men's great Bobby Jones, also an amateur, at his East Lake Course in Atlanta.

Nor was Babe the best player to come along. The professionals who came along in the 1930s were great players before she even took the game seriously. There was feisty, curly-haired Patty Berg, who became famous for her clinics. Betty Jameson, another Texan, was one of the game's first glamour girls. Louise Suggs was a pseudo Ben Hogan—a precise but quiet player. Later, Betsy Rawls, a Phi Beta Kappa in physics who played golf at the University of Texas, arrived on the scene with an incredible short game (cour-

tesy of legendary teacher Harvey Penick) and a focus that won her fifty-five
tournaments. And no one had a better swing or all-around game than the
fabulously talented Mickey Wright.

But, right from the start, Babe was the era's brightest star and undeni-
ably the golfer who brought the women's game into the spotlight. She stole
the show—as a pro, then an amateur, then again as a pro. She won the second tournament she ever played in—the 1935 Texas Women's Amateur—
but her amateur status in golf was called into question because she was a
professional in other sports. The USGA ruled against her, so she took to
traveling and doing clinics with the incomparable squire Gene Sarazen, whose
double-eagle at the fifteenth hole during the 1935 Masters elevated the status of that event.

During that stretch of time, Babe met and married professional wrestler and promoter George Zaharias. They met when the two played in the
1938 Los Angeles Open—yes, she played in a men's event—and both missed
the cut. They clicked and were married later that year. From then on, he
helped direct her career and, thus, women's golf—a sport he thought should
be run and promoted much like wrestling. He was, by most accounts, a loving husband and a controlling one. He promoted her as hard as she had promoted herself.

In 1940, she applied for reinstatement as an amateur and received it
following the obligatory three-year waiting period. As with all professional
sports, women's golf played an abbreviated schedule during World War II.
Some players enlisted in the armed services, but Babe kept playing in tournaments, some of which benefited the armed services charities and put her
in the company of stars like Bing Crosby and Bob Hope.

By 1946 World War II was over, and Babe went on a tear. She won
thirteen tournaments in a row before losing in the first round of the Women's
U.S. Open, then picked herself back up and kept on winning until she turned
pro once again in August 1947.

By that time, the first attempt at an organized women's tour—the
Women's Professional Golf Association—was on life support. The precur-
sor to the LPGA, chartered in 1951, was founded in 1944, but the members
couldn't agree on things. As Betty Hicks, the WPGA's first president, once
wrote, the association "was conceived in wrath, born into poverty and perished in a family squabble." With Hope Seignious, the daughter of a cotton broker who invested her father's money in the tour, and Ellen Griffin,
who went on to become one of the top women instructors, Hicks set the
wheels in motion for women's professional golf. She set up a winter tour
in Florida and published a short-lived magazine. Unfortunately, neither
the magazine nor her idea of a tour was successful, as there was no solid

funding base, a lack of communication between officers, and too much politics.

But the WPGA laid the groundwork for the formation of the LPGA, and in May 1949 the Ladies Professional Golf Players' Association was formed. Babe, who had broken new ground once more when she hired former PGA Tour official Fred Corcoran to manage her career in 1947, won the first tournament—the $3,500 Eastern Open—by thirteen shots and took home $1,000. A year later, the LPGPA dropped a word from its name, and the LPGA was founded, with Babe, Berg, Jameson, and Suggs among its founding members. Corcoran was chosen to run the organization.

Back in the early days, traveling the women's circuit was like cutting a slice from a Katherine Hepburn or Bette Davis movie: elegant pleated slacks, tweed skirts, sweater sets, convertibles, delightful stories, tough-but-tender women, and a trail of cigarette smoke. Sometimes they'd drive until they found a golf course. One story has Babe stopping on the steps of a church with a gang of players one Sunday morning asking if she could smoke inside.

They drove because no one could afford to fly commercial, plus the flights never went where the women played. Bell, one of the most respected golf instructors in the country and the owner of Pine Needles Resort in North Carolina, had her pilot's license and a single-engine Cessna 170 (Hicks was the tour's other pilot), and she would fly from tournament to tournament. It made being on the road much easier and more fun every time Babe hitched a ride.

"We'd take off, and George would drive the Cadillac," Bell recounts. "She would say, 'I'm going with Peg. See ya tomorrow.'"

Anything Babe wanted, companies and sponsors gave her, so Bell begged her to learn to fly, the idea being that a plane would soon follow. Bell had her eyes on a Beech Bonanza, which cruised 40 miles per hour faster than her Cessna and cost twice as much. "I told her, 'Just tell them you're learning, and I'll fly the thing,'" Bell chuckles. Babe did solo and began to collect hours, but she never finished the requirements.

Still, there wasn't much Babe couldn't get. One day, she saw a woman's Rolex watch in a New York jewelry store and decided she wanted one. So she grabbed a telephone book and looked up the address. "She walked into the offices and said, 'Hi, I'd like to see the president,'" Bell says. "The lady said, 'Do you have an appointment?' 'No, just tell him Babe Zaharias is here.' In about a second he was in the waiting room. She told him she had to have one of those [watches]. He said, 'Sure. We'll go to Toots Shor's for lunch, and we'll have the press there. Then we'll go out and play Winged Foot.' And Babe said, 'And I need one for George too.' She figured if she was going to

Toots Shor's for lunch and play with the president, he was going to give her two watches."

No one could play and talk a better game simultaneously. When she wasn't drumming up money and tournaments, she was convincing women to come join the party. "She said, 'We're going to go all over the world with this game. I'm telling you,'" Bell recalls.

Babe was Title IX decades before its birth. She had the vision years before tennis star Billie Jean King, a toned-down Babe, if you will, made it work on the courts. Maybe it was growing up playing every sport she could play. Maybe it was her talent and that first burst of stardom at the Olympics. Whatever it was, she was women's golf. And she took that straight to the bank.

At a time when most of the other top women players were taking in $25 a clinic plus mileage, Babe was getting about $1,000 per exhibition, the same fee as Ben Hogan and Sam Snead. No other woman could have demanded that kind of cash, let alone receive it. They still can't. But it wasn't why they played golf. Babe could have made more money just playing those extra events, but she wanted to play tournaments. So did the other players of that day. They didn't worry about the money. They just wanted to be part of the traveling golf sorority that packed two or more into a room to save money, lived out of the trunks of their cars, and had a fabulous time competing.

There's never been anyone else quite like Babe and likely never will be. She could say things to shock people with utter delight, as Hepburn and Davis did on the screen. She could play any sport at a high level and make everyone stand up and notice. She was the first female multisport star and the first woman to win at the formerly all-men's game of self-promotion. She could have starred in any sport, but golf was what she chose because, she said, it put her with nice people.

Babe won thirty-one times and collected $66,237 before her LPGA career was cut short by the cancer that claimed her life in 1956. She had had warning signs of physical problems as early as 1948, but she didn't pay attention until 1953, when, after her second victory of the year, she was diagnosed with cancer. She was determined to live and to play again, so after doctors performed a colostomy, she looked at it matter-of-factly. It was time to face it and deal with it.

In one of the great all-time comebacks in sport, Babe, colostomy bag and all, won five events in 1954, including her third U.S. Women's Open. But in October of that year, the cancer returned. She continued to play— and won three events in 1955—before her skills declined so much she was forced off the tour.

She spent her last months in Galveston, Texas, and she literally wasted away, from what some estimated as near 170 pounds to under 100. When she died September 27, 1956, a bit of the LPGA died with her. Although Rawls was emerging as one of the next stars and Wright was debuting, no one could provide the charisma Babe brought to the game. The tour went into a tail-spin. Suddenly, it wasn't as much fun to watch the game, even if Wright did have one of the most fabulous swings in history.

Kathy Whitworth had seen exactly two professional tournaments in her life. Since winning a pair of New Mexico State Amateur titles, she had also played a few exhibitions with Mickey Wright and Betsy Rawls, a pair of bona fide LPGA stars—Wright, the quiet one with the marvelous swing; Rawls, the Phi Beta Kappa and short-game whiz who spent time on those long road trips reading books like *The History of Civilization* by Will Durant. In 1958, Wright and Rawls were golf's future. And they knew from those exhibitions what this gawky eighteen-year-old from the New Mexico–Texas border had and what she lacked.

So when Whitworth showed up in Augusta, Georgia, for the Title-holder's Championship, at the time one of the LPGA's majors, Wright and Rawls were stunned. Wright, in fact, simply blurted out, "What in the world are you doing here?" No caddie wanted to carry Whitworth's plaid bag, which came from her father's hardware store in Jal, New Mexico. Not many play-ers even knew her name, and she wasn't about to tell any of them much about herself. And lord, did her game need work—so much so that she finished close to the bottom at that tournament and went on to survive a horrendous rookie season in 1959, the same year Wright won ten tournaments.

Four decades later, Whitworth, Wright, and Rawls all rank among the best ever to play the game. But ironically it is Whitworth who owns the one record no one may ever break—her eighty-eight LPGA victories is a record for both men and women. Snead won eighty-four on the men's side; Wright won eighty-two in her twenty-six-year career. Whitworth won her eighty-eight in three decades, the first coming in 1962, the last in 1985. She rose from awkward teenager to Hall of Famer, winning the money title eight times, Player of the Year seven. She won seven Vare Trophies for the lowest scor-ing average and six major titles, two of them at the Titleholders. The only tournament she couldn't win was the U.S. Women's Open.

If Babe was the catalyst for women's golf, Whitworth was the testa-ment to perseverance and longevity. She spent much of her career in the shadows of Wright and Rawls and wouldn't have had it any other way. She wasn't one for spotlights. She was a shy, gentle woman whose first set of clubs were hand-me-downs from her deceased grandfather. She learned to play on a dusty little nine-hole course and didn't mind playing by herself. She wasn't gregarious or funny or gorgeous. She was dedicated. The only thing

colorful about Whitworth in those days was her Texas drawl and those expressions like "I'm fixin' to" and "I reckon." She wanted to play the game
just inside the ropes. She was a good old Texas girl. She was honest and tough
and talented, and Harvey Penick, who also schooled PGA Tour stars Ben
Crenshaw and Tom Kite, helped to smooth away the rough edges.

Whitworth picked up the game at fifteen, when Wright and Rawls were
tearing up the circuit. Rawls was the more outgoing one of the pair; Wright
was the game's soft-spoken darling. Every shot Wright hit was so impressive that she took the game to another plateau and brought back to the LPGA
tour the media attention lacking since Babe's death. Rawls was a rare combination of warmth and intellect, spiced with a smooth swing. Growing up
in Texas, she didn't pick up the game until she was seventeen, when she also
went to Penick for instruction.

So complex is the golf swing that Rawls once asked Penick not to throw
too much at her because she couldn't absorb it all. Penick figured if this Phi
Beta Kappa in physics—she didn't consider playing golf as a pro until after
her graduation—couldn't handle it, what chance did an average student have
of hearing everything at once? He never taught more than one thing at a time
after that.

Rawls was tough, but Wright was the one to beat. Wright, who grew
up in South Carolina, was the total golfer—a shot maker, a thinker, a blend
of grace and power. She was so good, she often would hit great shots by accident. Her classic swing, dancing eyes, and winning ways made her a crowd
favorite; her demeanor softened the persistent perception that women golfers were too masculine. She didn't make people forget Babe, but she did make
the game fun again.

Wright was an amateur when she met Babe and was appalled by her
language, her showmanship, and her demeanor. She cringed when she saw
Babe take her slip off—on the course. "When I got to know Babe," Wright
said in *The LPGA: The Unauthorized Version,* "I realized she was having her
fun in public and that really she was very sensitive and quite a nice person. I
had respect for her, and she really made the women's tour. But she was the
complete opposite of me."

While the sportswriters were attempting to disarm Wright and understand Rawls's mind and wondering if that pair had a lock on the U.S.
Women's Open (from 1951 to 1963 they combined to win eight of the thirteen titles), Whitworth was making slow progress. The girl who had needed
six months to clear her first $30 cashed her first winner's check in 1962 in
Baltimore, dropped fifty pounds from her five-nine frame, and won eight
tournaments the following season. But the lanky Texan's game went south
in 1964. During the San Antonio event, her first pro, Hardy Loudermilk
told her it was because she had gotten the big head. Whitworth was "de-

stroyed," but she soon realized it was one of the grandest lessons she'd ever learn.

Once her career took off, she rose to the top quickly. But the true test wasn't in getting there, but rather was in staying there. Whitworth won in San Antonio and set the stage for a magnificent run. In the next five years, she dominated. She won forty-two tournaments, closed the decade with fifty-three wins, and started an eight-year streak.

Slowly things were changing. Those lazy days of driving cross-country were gone, replaced by flights between tour stops. The friendships that were forged from long drives and their pulling together just to make it were on their way out. The glamorous looks of the forties and fifties had given way to the sixties pop revolution. It was not uncommon to see the mod look, as it was called—bright orange flowers or wild paisley prints—on golf's version of miniskirts on the fairways. And the pros who once had their hands in everything from public relations to tournament pairings had turned over day-to-day management and operations of the rapidly growing LPGA tour to a commissioner.

In less than a decade, the LPGA had gone from a fledgling tournament run by the women players to a thriving business. The tour began to search for better quality, long-term sponsors, shortened some events from seventy-two to fifty-four holes (from four to three days), lobbied for courtesy cars, and went after insurance and retirement programs. Lenny Wirtz, who became commissioner in 1961, didn't just run the LPGA, he marketed it, increasing purses and coaxing networks to broadcast LPGA events. The first expanded coverage of a women's event was at the 1965 Women's Open, won by the outspoken six-foot-three Carol Mann, who went on to become a Hall of Famer, an advocate for women's sports, and president of the Women's Sports Foundation.

The game was beginning to solidify in the 1960s, but the cast of players was in transition. Wright was playing, but sparingly; a condition known as Morton's neuroma in her foot had become too painful for the greatest talent in the game to play. Berg had retired to her clinics, Suggs had just plain retired, Rawls was only a few years away from retiring, and a new breed of young golfers was on its way up.

Whitworth, however, remained a constant. Oh, she might fiddle a bit with her bouffant, sprayed-in-place hairstyle, but not much else. Once Penick got her to stand taller when she stood over the ball, she could make the full shoulder turn so necessary to a good swing and started hitting the ball straighter. That taken care of, all she needed to do was tweak things here and there. She always had a fabulous short game and may well have made more long putts out there than anyone else in the game, which was probably why she was still winning in the eighties.

"Harvey changed the whole game for me," she says. "He gave me the knowledge of the game and the swing. Harvey kept telling me, 'You have to have your own swing, not somebody else's.'"

In 1975 the LPGA took a sharp turn. So did Whitworth. Just three years after an explosive rules scandal involving type-A personality Jane Blalock, who was accused of consistently moving her ball when marking it on the green, the women hired Ray Volpe as the LPGA's commissioner. Carol Mann, then president of the LPGA, was mostly responsible for the hiring of the former vice president of marketing for the National Hockey League—a man who helped take the tour from a twenty-one-event schedule with a purse of $435,000 in 1971 to a thirty-eight-tournament package and a purse of $4.5 million a decade later.

Volpe came along at a time when the LPGA was cash-poor from the Blalock battle and poised to grow from the implementation of Title IX. Women were stepping out and up, and women's sports were taking on a new look. Women's collegiate golf, thanks to the likes of Tulsa University's Lopez and Beth Daniel and Betsy King, of Furman University in Greenville, South Carolina, was getting attention.

Volpe immediately cashed in on tour sex symbols Laura Baugh and Jan Stephenson (the latter had a cheesecake poster out complete with cleavage and her skirt blown up). Both women were perennial stars of the LPGA annual *Fairway* magazine in which players posed in yearly themes—anything from swimsuits to evening gowns to renditions of glamour-girl movie stars. Later, Volpe, who took advantage of an alliance with powerful Colgate executive David Foster, hit the jackpot marketing Lopez's combination of girl-next-door innocence and talent.

Whitworth wasn't part of that marketing plan. She was too plain, too black-and-white for Volpe's schemes. He needed technicolor. The women were still hustling up sponsors and tournaments; the men were having them dropped at their doorstep. All Whitworth did for the tour was play. By the close of 1973, she was exhausted and fighting herself. Did she want to play or didn't she? It had never been a question before. Her answer was to pull back, gear down. But she kept on winning.

In the late 1970s, Whitworth went through a depression so deep she almost walked away from the game. She was winning but not at the same warp-speed rate. And by 1979—her first winless season since 1961—she was ready to quit. "It got to where I hated to go out to the golf course," she told *Golf* magazine. "There was a panic and a fear. I didn't know where the ball was going or whether I'd even hit it. To have that fear after playing so well is horrible."

She fought that off, bouncing back to win once again in 1981. With every win, her legend grew. She didn't pack people in like Babe or Wright, but did she ever win. And break barriers. She was the first player to make $1 million, and in May 1983 she won the Lady Michelob outside of Atlanta to break the record she shared with Wright of eighty-two wins. In 1984 she won three times and bested Sam Snead's mark of eighty-four wins.

By that point in her career, JoAnne Carner and Pat Bradley were established, and young players like Lopez, King, and Patty Sheehan were on the rise. They grabbed the spotlight, and Whitworth was all too happy to step to the side. It didn't matter where she stood. She kept winning.

There had never been any question she would break Wright's mark. During her quest for that record win, Wright sent her a letter that said, in part, "I would think if your sights are set way at 90 or even 100, they [other players] might not bother you. I would want to set a record of my own that no one would touch and I would think 90 wins would do it." Wright's predicted safe record was just two shy of Whitworth's final total. No one, not even the incredibly talented Tiger Woods, the first man of color to win the prestigious Masters tournament, will ever touch eighty-eight.

Even after that eighty-eighth win—at the United Virginia Bank Classic in 1985—Whitworth remained active in the game. She cut her schedule back and served her fourth separate stint as LPGA president in 1989, helping guide the organization through difficult times. When Volpe left, straitlaced John Laupheimer took over as commissioner and moved the LPGA headquarters to Houston. Whitworth liked Laupheimer, a former USGA official; he brought organization, stability, and steady, slow growth, but he was too low-key for many of the sponsors. Although he raised purses to $12.4 million (roughly $2 million less than the Senior PGA Tour was playing for), he didn't have the dynamic presence and deal-maker attitude the LPGA needed to match strides with the suddenly booming—and sponsor-happy—Senior Tour.

Sponsors were dropping out, and the LPGA's Mazda Hall of Fame Classic, created as the LPGA's answer to the glitzy PGA Tour's Players Championship, lasted only two years. Sponsorship was a problem, and so was the date and site—it was played in Houston on the always oppressively hot Fourth of July weekend. When Laupheimer left, the LPGA hired former liquor company executive Bill Blue. Blue, who had a marketing background, was miscast from the start, and his two-year stint (1988–90) as commissioner was a tough time for the tour and for Whitworth, who still served as the organization's president. Morale was low. No one was happier than Whitworth when Charles Mechem replaced Blue in 1990.

Whitworth announced her retirement that same year, and with her went the last bit of those early days. She had commanded respect on the course and, unlike many of her peers, had never been demanding or controversial. She definitely wasn't flamboyant. Yet if anyone could bring perspective to the growth of the LPGA and its struggle for respect after the 1950s, it was

Whitworth. In many ways, they had faced the same problems—both were plain vanilla in a world that wanted raspberry-blueberry swirl, instant success, charismatic stars, and a lot of flash.

Whitworth was none of the above. She was a blue-collar American dream come true, a self-made kid from New Mexico who made a living playing golf and left a legacy of winning. When asked one time how she wanted to be remembered, her answer was simple and self effacing. She thought that if people would just remember her at all, that would be more than enough.

At the conclusion of the women's professional golf tournament that won the world's attention, Nancy Lopez stood behind the eighteenth green biting her lip and staring at the ground. She didn't know what to say. Or do. As another tear rolled over the red rims of her eyes, she reached up and brushed it aside. She forced a smile. As the NBC production truck put her on hold, she shook her head in an attempt to compose herself. All she wanted to do was cry. It was July 13, 1997, the day she was supposed to finally win the U.S. Women's Open; the afternoon at Pumpkin Ridge Country Club in North Plains, Oregon, when the most popular woman in the sport was given yet another chance to erase two decades of frustration; the day she dug deeper than ever before in an effort to put an exclamation point on her sparkling career.

"I've been wanting to win this for a long time," Lopez said softly as the tears fell. "I really thought this was my chance." No matter what she did, tiny Allison Nicholas had one-upped her. No matter how badly she wanted the 1997 Open, it belonged to a knee-high-to-a-grasshopper Englishwoman who stood barely five feet tall.

Never before had any woman shot four rounds in the 60s in an Open. But Lopez did and lost. Few, if any, had put such pressure on an opponent in the opening holes, but, despite birdying three of the first four holes, Lopez didn't pick up a shot. Even when she flew a sand wedge into the fourth green and stopped it twelve inches from the cup for a birdie, Nicholas one-hopped her approach and shot into the cup for an eagle.

"When she hit it in the hole," Lopez says, "I didn't know what to say."

Four runner-up finishes at U.S. Opens. "Does that equal one first?" Lopez chuckles. If Babe created the LPGA Tour and Whitworth defined its perseverance, Nancy Lopez gave it grace and perfection. After years of grumbling over whether the women were too tomboyish, too sexy, or just a bunch of feminists trying to play a men's game, Lopez stepped onto center stage. Nancy with the laughing eyes, they called her. Nancy with the dazzling smile. Nancy with the million-dollar game.

The daughter of an automobile body shop owner and mechanic, she was born in Torrance, California, in 1957 and grew up in Roswell, New Mexico, which, until Lopez hit the big time, was best known for its extra-terrestrial sightings. Her father, Domingo, told her mother, Marina, that their daughter couldn't wash dishes because those hands were meant only for golf. At age nine, she won her first Pee Wee tournament—by 110 shots—and never looked back.

Lopez entered the 1975 Women's Open as an amateur and finished tied for second. After two All-American years at Tulsa University and an incredible amateur career, she turned pro in 1977, and the women's game would never be the same. A wife, a mother, a Hall of Famer, a player and old-fashioned girl who became a household name as much for who she was as for how many tournaments she won, she was the queen to Arnold Palmer's king. The incredible Palmer brought the men's game into its prime as the conservative fifties were giving way to the turbulent sixties. Two decades later, it was impossible to ignore the comparisons.

Like Palmer, Lopez had a less than picture-perfect swing—hers starts with an unusual wrist cock (Carol Mann once described it as "a collection of corrected mistakes"), his finishes with a loop—but boy did it work. She was honest and always knew the right things to say. She simply substituted that engaging smile for Palmer's wink, and the galleries and sponsors belonged to her. Arnie had his army of fans; Nancy her navy. She was the one the LPGA, which was struggling for a star, had been waiting for.

In the late 1970s, the tour needed the help, too. Despite Volpe's marketing efforts, there wasn't one charismatic figure to draw people to the sport. Players like Carol Mann, JoAnne Carner, and Whitworth had their fans, while Baugh and Stephenson provided the sex appeal. But Lopez? She become a universal draw. Who could forget that *Sports Illustrated* cover of her laughing? The woman who grew up in a modest home in Roswell touched something in everyone. And she won. Five tournaments in a row and nine over all as a rookie. At twenty, she was the first player—man or woman—to be Rookie of the Year and Player of the Year in the same season. She won the Vare Trophy, for low scoring average, as well.

An instant star, Lopez was swept up in a daily hurricane of demands: press rooms, television cameras, photo shoots for magazines, appearances on network morning shows, and $12,500-a-day corporate outings. To America, she was the LPGA tour, and that came with a price. While other players had time to enjoy each other, the pace set Lopez apart from the rest of the players and kept her head spinning.

The late 1970s were a time when the young guns like Lopez, Sheehan, Pat Bradley, Betsy King, Amy Alcott, and Beth Daniel still remembered the past. There was a respect for the veteran players—from Wright through quiet Texan Judy Rankin—who had shaped women's golf. Suddenly, Lopez was being put on an even higher pedestal. "Lots of times in my first or second year, I basically didn't know a lot of players," she says. "I never spent much time with them. I'd play, go to the press room, practice, and by then everyone was gone. I won so many tournaments that even when I didn't win, the press wanted to talk to me. It did get to be a little aggravating. I wanted to say, 'Gosh, don't you want to talk to who's winning?'"

Through everything—public and private—Lopez remained composed and confident. Her mother had died unexpectedly after an appendectomy just before she joined the tour. And when she won her first tournament, the Bent Tree Classic in Sarasota, Lopez, with tears streaming down her face, dedicated the win to her mom. Then, in 1979, she married handsome sportscaster Tim Melton, whom she had met at the Lady Keystone Open in Hershey, Pennsylvania, when he interviewed her. The marriage didn't survive; they were divorced in 1982, and later that year she married former baseball star Ray Knight, a friend of Melton's who was playing for the Houston Astros.

Much about Lopez besides her professional career was public. Her love life. The birth of all three of her daughters. Her ongoing battle with her weight. She tackled every subject with a refreshing honesty that was hard to ignore. This was a woman after everyone's heart. Superstar career. Kids. Loving, all-star husband. No other female golfer—or athlete—had managed to have it all, let alone juggle it with such flair.

By the time she was twenty-six, she had two daughters and had won twenty-six tournaments. And when she won her thirty-fifth tournament in 1987—in Sarasota, the site of her first LPGA win—she became the youngest player ever to qualify for the ultra-rigid LPGA Hall of Fame. Qualifications for the Hall—the single toughest one to enter in sports—are thirty victories, including two different major titles, or thirty-five wins and one major. And there's one more. You have to be an LPGA member for ten years. Lopez had the victories six months short of a decade and had to wait.

When she became a mother, she had expected things to slow down, but they didn't. Every tournament wanted her in its field, and saying no was hard because tournament organizers were offended when she didn't play. But after the birth of her second daughter, she pulled back. Since then, she's played twenty or more events in a year only three times. During that first decade, she shared the spotlight with Daniel and Bradley—who won three of the four major tournaments in 1986—and, ironically, Carner. It was the outgoing Carner, known affectionately as Big Momma, whom Lopez had loved to watch during her younger years. Carner, née Gunderson, could have been the best amateur ever; instead, she chose to turn pro and played her way into the Hall of Fame. "She just always had a character inside her," Lopez says. "You could see the excitement. When she was playing well, you could see it. When she wasn't, you couldn't tell. And she just loved to have fun."

The consistency of Lopez, King, Daniel, and Bradley held the LPGA together in the late 1980s. The tour struggled in the latter part of Laupheimer's tenure as commissioner and barely stayed afloat under Blue. But when Mechem took the reins in 1990, things began to turn around. He immediately gained the respect of sponsors and players and understood the impact of women's trends and issues. Hillary Clinton was on her way to the White House. Title IX was turning out excellent athletes. Women were everywhere from boardrooms to Capitol Hill.

The tour grew in the early nineties, but it wasn't without turmoil. The Hall of Fame came under fire for being too tough. LPGA events were still a tough sell to sponsors. The question of lesbianism on tour, which had been whispered about for decades and called an "image problem," came to the forefront. CBS broadcaster Ben Wright caused a furor during the week of the 1995 LPGA Championship when he was quoted as saying, "Let's face facts here. Lesbians in the sport hurt women's golf." He also insulted Laura Davies by saying she was "built like a tank." The LPGA sent Lopez into the tower to smooth over the statements on the air with Wright, but it didn't work. In 1996 Wright was removed from CBS's golf team. Later that year Muffin Spencer-Devlin became the first player to admit publicly that she was a lesbian, doing so in *Sports Illustrated.*

In the nineties, the tour took on an international look with Annika Sorenstam from Sweden, Karrie Webb from Australia, Laura Davies from Great Britain, and Liselotte Neumann from Sweden. But Lopez—and her popularity—was still the constant. At the start of the 1996 season, she got serious about getting in shape—she had had her third daughter in 1991—and dropped forty pounds. Knight, at the time the manager for the Cincinnati Reds, had urged her to get in shape and get serious again. He'd always encouraged her to play because, he said, she had a talent she couldn't waste. She sharpened her game, too. And when she won the rain-shortened 1997 Chik-Fil-A for her first victory in three years, it was like she had never left.

When she got into contention at the 1997 Open, when she was playing the most important round of her life again, the world was pulling for her. The shots were there. So was the focus. And the putting stroke. The only thing that wasn't there was the Open title. Yet she stood there with that smile on her face that afternoon in 1997 and said she had finally learned how to play an Open. She cut herself open with another loss and let the world in. She showed us, once again, it was okay to be vulnerable. The idea of Lopez never winning an Open? It's easier to swallow that Sam Snead and Whitworth never won the Open than to think Lopez will go through her unparalleled career without one. Lopez, after all, is women's golf.

As 1998 opened, Lopez became the first female player to have her own division of a golf company. Babe and Berg and Wright had club sets named after them, but Lopez has NancyLopezGolf [sic], a division of Arnold Palmer Golf. The timing was impeccable and the pairing with Palmer a natural. Golf was booming, and Lopez was still one of the top players twenty years after her debut. She wasn't just putting her name on clubs, either. She jumped in to oversee the line, which provides everything from clubs to gloves, umbrellas, and bags. The venture became the first line to cater strictly to women, which is the fastest-growing market in the game.

"People keep asking me why hasn't it happened before?" Lopez says. "The time wasn't right. Now it is. For me to be with Arnold Palmer—there have been so many comparisons—is so right. I want to do something for women's golf. This was one area where it was really lacking."

At forty-one, Lopez shows no signs of retiring. She played in sixteen tournaments in 1997 and finished ninth on the money list. And while she'll never match Whitworth's eighty-eight wins, she'll likely get at least fifty. She says she simply wants to be known as one of the best who ever played the game. And one of the nicest.

To America she'll always be Nancy with the laughing eyes and dazzling smile, the woman who electrified the game and made us want to watch, the heart, soul, and face of women's golf.

The great male golfers always had someone to push them. Ben Hogan had Byron Nelson and Sam Snead. Palmer had Gary Player, then Jack Nicklaus. Nicklaus had Tom Watson. As the millennium nears, the women have finally found a dynamic duo—Annika Sorenstam has Karrie Webb. One is Swedish, the other Australian. One spent her honeymoon winning a tournament; the other was the first rookie—male or female—to top the $1 million mark in a season. Both want to stake a claim to a spotlight as bright as the one Lopez still owns, but there's a field full of kids from all over the world trying to stop them.

Although non-American players have been competing on the LPGA tour since its inception, never before have they been such a dominant force. Heading into 1998, international players had won five money titles in a row and six of the previous eight Rookie of the Year awards. Sweden is being applauded for a junior program that churns out athletes who go on to become American collegians at an astounding rate. The Solheim Cup, a Ryder Cup–style competition pitting LPGA players against players from the European women's tour, has been introduced, with the Americans winning the first two, in 1994 and 1996.

Laura Davies burst onto the LPGA scene in 1988 with a powerful game—and a swashbuckling attitude—that made heads spin. The five-foot-ten, powerfully built Brit plays hard and seldom slows down. She bets on everything from dogs to roulette, drives fast cars—and race cars—and has a play-with-the-big-boys kind of game. By the end of 1997, she had won fifteen times, including three major tournaments (the Open she won before joining the tour isn't counted in her total) and four consecutive years at the Standard Register Ping tournament (1994–97). That same season, Liselotte Neumann, a gritty Swede, jumped into the fray by winning the 1988 Open and edging Davies for Rookie of the Year.

In 1996–97, Sorenstam was the most dominant player in the game, winning more often than Tiger Woods. She won fourteen times in that two-year span, eleven times in sixteen months, and seven times overall (six official events) in 1997. She had fourteen top-three finishes and sixteen top tens, set a single-season earnings record of $1,236,789, and was Player of the Year. Sorenstam is known as "the baby-faced assassin," but when she tried for that third consecutive Open title in 1997 (Willie Anderson remains the only player to have done that, his coming in 1903–05), the pressure made her miss the cut. While other players watch videotapes or work on the range, the Swede has all her stats loaded into her laptop, and she spends hours poring over and crunching scoring averages and other statistics. They tell the story.

Webb is more like her countryman Greg Norman. She missed passing the $1 million mark for a second season by a mere $12,394, but she still won three times, finished out of the top ten only three times all season, didn't miss a cut, and walked away with the Vare Trophy. And it was only her second full season.

Now more than ever before, women are able to make a good living playing golf. There are lucrative endorsements and big purses. There are a few characters on tour, but Lopez, mother of three, is still the biggest draw. And there is exposure—on network and cable television. Lopez says there needs to be more. "You have to be seen to be popular," she says. Adds Bell, "I can remember late in my years out there when we were going on television, and that was unbelievable. Now they've got a Golf Channel. They have 'em on TV every week. The women are on a lot now. Sports have boomed, and golf is the boomingest."

Women's golf at the beginner's and the country club levels is booming faster than any other segment of the game. Women's leagues are being formed in every city, and female executives are finding they too can play eighteen and do business at the same time. Male executives have been doing that for years. Yet the growth curve for women's professional golf is painfully slow.

The tour started with a group of women who played for the love of it. Now it's big business, handling everything from sponsors to insurance to traveling child care. With more babies on tour every year, the women now have the Smucker's Child Development Center, which travels with the tour, providing day care and some elementary education. And, as in society as a whole, there's been an upturn in husbands and partners taking on a new role for their golfing women, either caddying for players or simply becoming Mr. Moms.

Those are easy changes. The search for sponsors, network television contracts, and respect remain tough. There has even been talk about the possibility of merging with the PGA Tour, since the men have a surplus of potential sponsors, the women a dearth. In 1998, the scheduling formula revolved around those television contracts and sponsor dollars, but women are playing in front of mostly cable and some network audiences for $32 million in total purses. The men, on the other hand, are playing for $94 million in total purses, and all but a handful of events are on major networks.

When Lopez came on tour in the late 1970s, prize money was creeping up from $1.5 million to $6.4 million. Her first year she made $189,183. It felt like a million. Twenty years later, only two women (Sorenstam and Webb) have cleared $1 million in a season, and they've each done it only once. Eighteen men cleared that mark on the PGA Tour in 1997, seven on the Senior PGA Tour, and three men—Tiger Woods and seniors Hale Irwin and Jim Colbert—won over $2 million each. As for winner's purses, in 1997, U.S. Open champ Ernie Els pocketed $465,000; U.S. Women's Open champ Nicholas earned $232,500. Soaring ratings and a sweet new television contract negotiated in late 1997 will ensure that the PGA Tour fields will be playing for an average of $3 million a week in the near future. The women are struggling to get their purses, which average about $700,000, closer to the $1 million mark.

Whether it's the good old boys thinking the women can't play, the sponsors ducking out, the wrong men holding the commissioner's job—it has become one of the toughest such jobs in America—scheduling problems, or the whispers about players' lifestyles, the LPGA can't totally shake the negatives. Even when Lopez was smiling her way across country and into the Hall of Fame in less than a decade, people were saying, "After Lopez, who cares?" Lopez and Zaharias were unique. Their charisma drew fans to the game. Men were intrigued by Babe; women alternately intimidated and motivated. Lopez is an incredible talent who seemed more like everyone's daughter, sister, or girlfriend. Sorenstam and Webb are more like Whitworth, who win tournaments, not hearts.

The influx of foreign players, in particular those from Sweden, is pushing competition to a higher level. So are the strong collegiate programs that are hitting their stride some twenty-five years after Title IX was implemented. But talent isn't everything. Charisma counts a lot, too.

The phenomenal, game-changing Tiger Woods aside, the PGA Tour continues to come up with rising stars that capture the attention of television audiences. Women's golf doesn't. A handful of players—Lopez, Sorenstam, Webb, and Davies among them—make the headlines, while the remainder have to be content to cash checks. A half dozen or more Lopezes are needed if the women want to stop having to sell the LPGA and start being bought.

Canoeing, Kayaking, Rowing, and Sailing

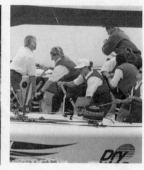

Women on the Water
Anna Seaton Huntington

Women have made their lives aboard and around boats for thousands of years. Since before Christ, people all over the world have relied on boats for simple transportation, hunting, fishing, and migrating. As long as men have been exploring by sail, making war at sea, and earning a living aboard fishing ships and merchant vessels, their wives and daughters have been accompanying them. In the hulls of the most primitive dugout canoes, below the decks of warships, and in the cabins of the most sophisticated sailing vessels, women have borne and raised families, tended to the needs of everyday life, and conducted business.

Boating's long history is far more practical than recreational. There is evidence of boat races in prehistoric China and Egypt, and it is easy to imagine that people have sparred on the water for as long as they have put boats in it, but only in the last century has boating become as much a form of sport as commerce. For women, access to boating sports is even newer. While there are records of women racing in boats as many as five hundred years ago, only in the last quarter century have women begun to make a place for themselves at the highest levels of competition in canoeing, kayaking, rowing, and sailing.

Canoes are boats in their oldest and simplest forms. Human-paddled canoes constructed from local materials to be flat-bottomed and tapered at both ends can be found in many cultures near navigable water. It is fitting that the first official women's regatta on record took place in Venice in 1493 in a type of canoe that was the standard mode of transportation in the city at the time. In honor of a visiting dignitary, fifty peasant girls wearing short linen skirts competed in a boat race that was more spectacle than sport. The race was so popular with spectators that it overshadowed the men's regatta that followed and became an annual event.

If the earliest boats, canoes, were propelled by paddles held entirely in the paddler's hands, rowing boats developed as a close cousin. Two thousand years ago, the Greeks mounted their paddles onto the gunwales, or upper side edges, of their boats. The paddles, now oars, would then pivot in oarlocks attached to the gunwales. The oarlocks act as a fulcrum and provide mechanical advantage. The rower faces backward and pulls against the support and leverage of the oarlock. Rowing boats over the centuries have been used for everything from fishing to Viking exploration to helping build the Roman empire. There were rowing boats as long as 150 feet, powered by fifty indentured rowers at once, and there were much smaller boats equipped just for one person.

The sport of rowing flourished in America and Europe in the nineteenth century, and two categories within the sport evolved. Sweep rowing, in which each person pulls one oar, includes eights, fours, and pairs. Sculling, where each rower pulls two oars, includes quads, doubles, and singles. Rowing boats are also called shells, and sculling boats are often referred to as sculls. For the sake of speed and competition, boat designers developed technological improvements during the nineteenth century. Riggers, or stiff metal frameworks attached to the side of the boat and mounted with an oarlock, positioned the fulcrum outside the boat and allowed rowing boats to become narrower. In fact, modern racing, single sculls, constructed of lightweight fiberglass and carbon fiber, are thirty feet long and as little as ten inches wide. Sliding seats were the other major development. Moving seats meant that rowers could add leg power to the arm and back swing of their strokes, employing all major muscle groups to move the boat and significantly increasing speed.

The overwhelming physicality of rowing probably insured that it was solely a male domain in the past. The sport is not for the feint of heart. While rowing in the long, slender boats appears serene from the shore, it is among the Olympic sports that demand the greatest level of fitness. In the course of a hard practice, people wring the sweat out of their shirts. Ribs are regularly broken by the strain of overdeveloped back and shoulder muscles. And at 2,000 meters, or roughly a mile and a half, races are like six- or seven-minute lactic-acid endurance tests. They leave people twisted in cramps, gasping for air, vomiting, and swearing they'll never do it again. Not a ladylike image, and not an endeavor acceptable for women until fairly recently.

Women's collegiate rowing began at Wellesley at the turn of the century. But for seventy-five years, intramural races were as much beauty contests—emphasizing grace and form—as they were tests of strength and skill.

Women's intercollegiate rowing did not get started full force in this country until the 1970s, and women's Olympic rowing began in the same period.

Rowing excluded women for most of its competitive history, but sailing wins the prize for the oldest of the old-boys' clubs. From the really old-timers like Leif Eriksson and Christopher Columbus to more modern-day heroes like Arctic explorer Ernest Shackelton and America's Cup skipper John Bertrand, the face of yachting's history is distinctly male. From the smallest of dinghies to the grandest of yachts, there is an overwhelming tradition of men at the helm of boats powered by wind. Even at the end of the twentieth century, an old-world order still prevails in most yacht clubs. Habits are slowly changing, but to a surprising extent, women in yacht clubs are still organizing charity balls and fashion shows, and men are still standing at the helm.

Even so, through the centuries, sailors have had to contend with an irrepressible feminine presence at sea. Boats have long been female: "She's a beaut." And, in the belief that a naked woman calms the sea, bows have been adorned with elaborate figures of women in various stages of undress. It's women actually *sailing* on boats that has been objectionable. In a realm laden with superstition, women on boats have been considered bad luck, like starting a journey on a Friday or sighting an albatross. The history of yachting reflects the myth that women are bad luck as well as the drawbacks of being female in a man's world. Women don't play a prominent role.

But seafaring history includes a significant feminine subtext that has given way to a coming of age for women in the sport over the last two decades. Far more women than ever before are sailing recreationally and competitively, and only a handful of significant firsts in yachting remain for women to accomplish. Deep in history are antecedents to today's extraordinary sailing stars like Dawn Riley, Tracy Edwards, and Isabelle Autissier, who have all forged paths for women into the upper reaches of the sport.

Cleopatra, of course, had her barge. It was Queen Isabella, ruling Spain with an iron fist, who sent Columbus on his way to the New World. Queen Elizabeth I oversaw the British Navy at its most powerful—through the pivotal defeat of the mighty Spanish Armada in 1588. And, though Charles II is traditionally credited with bringing the first real sporting yacht to England— *Mary*, in 1661—Queen Elizabeth preceded him by more than sixty years with a small sailing vessel oddly named *Rat of Wight*.

Records of aristocratic women involved with boats, particularly sailing boats, exist through history. Much of the history of more common women on boats, particularly the oldest crafts—canoes and kayaks—is left to our imagination. Beyond the facts and legend of Sacajawea and a few other mentions, we are left to guess who the female precursors were to the women racing aboard canoes and kayaks in the Olympics today.

* * *

Given that canoes provided transportation, subsistence, and pleasure even from the beginning of civilization, we can be relatively certain that women have a long historical familiarity with the crafts. Simple, but not necessarily crude, canoes are a nearly ubiquitous feature of groups of people living near water, salt or fresh. In the Pacific Northwest and in parts of the Amazon where there is an abundance of giant trees, native people carved enormous thirty- to fifty-person dugout canoes from the trunks of whole trees. The boats could be quite fast, powered by so many paddlers, and were used for everything from fishing and hunting to making war. Polynesian cultures added outriggers and sails to their dugouts to make them faster and more sturdy for ocean going. In Arctic regions, such as Alaska and Greenland, where there are few trees, people devised more complicated skin-on-bone canoes. The boats were so seaworthy and responsive they could be used for hunting everything from seals to whales. Native people in the North American interior developed a unique form of canoe made from a wooden frame covered with birch bark. The lightweight, agile boats were perfect for navigating rivers and portaging. European explorers and fur traders adopted the birch-bark canoe, and it became an important tool in their expansion westward.

The beginning of recreational canoeing can be traced directly to an Englishman, John MacGregor, in the middle of the nineteenth century. A man with a penchant for boat design and exploration, he developed a craft based on the Eskimo kayak, which he called *Rob Roy*. He took the boat on long journeys over the rivers and lakes of Europe, lecturing and writing about his travels as he went. His tales attracted a following, and soon there were many other canoes in England based on his design, a kayak design that is still referred to as a Rob Roy.

Canoes are the larger category under which kayaks fall. While all kayaks are canoes, not all canoes are kayaks. Paddlers in kayaks sit with their legs stretched out in front of them, and canoeists generally paddle from a kneeling position. Most canoes are open hulled; kayaks have covered decks. And canoe paddles are typically single bladed, while kayak paddles are double bladed.

MacGregor founded the Royal Canoe Club in 1866 to promote his fledgling sport, and a few years later its three hundred members were spreading the pleasures of canoeing through Europe and North America. It wasn't long before canoe clubs and regattas were springing up throughout Europe and the United States, and design variations were developed for different conditions and bodies of water. The first "modern" canoe race for women was held in Berlin in 1895. By the 1920s, an international governing body was formed to oversee the sport, the Internationella Represenatantskapet för

Kanotidrott (IRK). And in 1936, after years of cajoling by the IRK, canoeing events for men appeared on the Olympic program in Berlin.

Twelve years later, a women's kayaking event debuted at the Olympics, the first women's boating event at the Games. The women's single (K1W) was first held at the 1948 Games, long before women's rowing or sailing appeared on the Olympic program. Since its debut, three canoe/kayak events have been added for women, bringing the women's total number of events to four versus the men's twelve. The pair (K2W) and the four (K4W) are, like the K1W, pure power events held over 500 meters on flat water in kayaks. At race pace, flat-water paddlers take about 120 strokes, or rapid thrusts of their blades through the water, per minute. The flat-water races are all-out sprints that typically last about two minutes. They require extraordinary upper-body strength and balance and allow for not a moment's pause or wobble.

In 1992 a slalom event, also known as white-water canoeing, was added for women. The first such men's Olympic event was held in 1972. The event is staged on a gated, churning white-water obstacle course that inevitably leaves the paddler soaked and cold. Much as in a slalom ski race, the paddler must employ her strength, courage, and agility to navigate the quickest, safest route within the rules. And, as in ski racing, wipeouts and injuries are not uncommon. Each competitor runs the course twice, with the best run, as determined by time and penalty points, counting.

Competitive paddling, particularly among women, has always had a more established popularity in European countries, particularly those of eastern Europe, than in the United States. On the men's side, only five medals were won by U.S. boats from 1936 until Greg Barton of Michigan rose to prominence in 1988. A handful of qualified women paddled competitively in the United States in the early years of the sport's Olympic history, but it wasn't until twelve years after women's canoeing and kayaking events appeared in the Olympics that the United States fielded a women's team.

Glorianne Perrier went to the Rome Olympics in 1960 as a naturally talented but very green paddler in the single. Two other U.S. women, Mary Ann DuChai and Diane Jerome, raced in the K2W. With just one year of experience under her belt, Perrier was notably wobbly on the water and chose to race in a wider, more stable kayak than her competitors. Competitive paddling requires an athlete to be at once nimble and powerfully aggressive. It is not uncommon for newcomers in the sport to flip their boats repeatedly, before they've even applied any pressure to their paddles. Even experienced paddlers occasionally go over. So Perrier's choosing the broader boat was reasonable—she might not even have made it down the race course in a narrower one. But the relatively tubby craft put her at such a disadvantage she didn't come close to making the finals. The K2W did not make it past the preliminary rounds, either.

From this meager beginning, U.S. women kayakers went back to the Olympics in 1964 and surprised the paddling world. Perrier, thirty-five years old, teamed up with Francine Fox, twenty years her junior and more technically gifted, to win the silver in the K2W. Marcia Jones, a competitive swimmer turned kayaker, won the bronze in the K1W. Their success brought attention to the sport in this country and helped draw more women into competitive canoeing.

Jones, who dominated U.S. women's kayaking in her day, returned to the Olympics in 1968 and raced in both the K1W and the K2W, and she competed for the last time in the 1972 Games. But she did not win another medal. As Perrier's and Jones's competitive careers were drawing to a close, they worked as enthusiastic coaches and promoters of their sport. They brought along a new generation of paddlers and produced eight Olympians between them, male and female, including the double gold medalist Greg Barton.

After a long dry spell for Americans at the Olympics, Dana Chladek won the bronze in the K1W slalom event when it made its first Olympic appearance in 1992. The daughter of two-time Czechoslovakian world champion kayakers, Stan and Ema Chladek, then came back from a torn rotator cuff muscle and a ranking of ninth in the world to win the silver medal in Atlanta in 1996.

Olympic medals are rare in canoe and kayak events in this country—and that much more impressive—because the sport has been slow to grow here. It is nearly unheard of as a high school or collegiate sport, so there is no established feeder system to the Olympic level. The sport is not easily accessible. Most paddlers take it up after they happen to come into contact with someone from its very small community. Interestingly, canoe racing is equally popular among men and women. U.S. Canoe and Kayak, which governs the racing side of the sport, estimates that 40 percent of its sixteen hundred members are women.

Much more widespread in the United States—but by no means a national pastime—is the sport of rowing. Rowing's relative popularity here is probably due to its long tradition in England. The Royal Henley Regatta, first held on the Thames in 1839, is among the best-known boat races in the world. The Doggett's Coat and Badge rowing race, first staged on the Thames in 1715, is one of the oldest continuous sporting events in the world.

In the United States, professional rowing, generally in singles, enjoyed a brief heyday in the late nineteenth century. A man could earn up to $6,000 for winning one race. The high stakes led to gambling and corruption, and, as a professional sport, rowing fell from popularity by the turn of the century. At the collegiate level, however, it has a long and thriving tradition. The first-ever intercollegiate sporting event, the Harvard-Yale boat race, was held for the first time in 1852 and continues as a hearty rivalry today. High schools and universities from California to Kansas to Tennessee field rowing teams, and thousands of rowers also compete at the master's level. In all, USRowing, which oversees the sport, estimates that there are 100,000 active competitive rowers in the country.

Wellesley College is credited with starting the first women's collegiate rowing team in 1875. The Wellesley faculty and administration had a policy that "frowned on intramural games, and adamantly opposed interscholastic sports," according to a contemporary report, reflecting the widely held view of women's collegiate sports at the time. Rowing was vigorously promoted at Wellesley not as a competitive opportunity, but as a means to grace and good posture for women. The college held an annual regatta, Float Night, in which contestants, who sang in chorus as they rowed, were judged on appearance and form rather than speed.

As late as 1963, the results of Wellesley's intramural crew races were determined by a point system based in part on technical judging. It wasn't until 1966, nearly one hundred years after women had first rowed on Wellesley's Lake Waban, that women from the neighboring Massachusetts Institute of Technology issued the Wellesley crew a challenge, and they raced to win, not to look pretty. By the early 1970s, women's collegiate rowing was becoming well established on the East and West coasts. The first Ivy League Women's Rowing Championships were held in 1973 and continue twenty-five years later. Women's collegiate national championships have been held since 1981 and received official NCAA status in 1998.

One woman, Ernestine Bayer, is notable as a very important driving force behind the development of women's competitive rowing in this country. Now in her nineties, Bayer still rows, still competes, and still remembers a world in which "rowing was a man's sport, and nobody questioned it."

For years in the early part of this century, Bayer sat on the porch of the Pennsylvania Barge Club boathouse in Philadelphia in the afternoons after work. The pretty, petite young woman watched as her husband and other men from the club shoved off the dock to row on the Schuylkill River. At the time, Philadelphia was home to the heart of competitive rowing in the United States. The clubs along the city's famous Boathouse Row had produced many Olympic rowers. Bayer's husband, Ernest, had won a silver medal at the Amsterdam Olympics in 1928. It was the Vesper boat club that won the premier event, the men's eight, the first time rowing appeared in the Olympics, in 1900. But just as women were barred from rowing in the Olympics, they were unwelcome on the docks of the clubs along the Schuylkill. They gathered there to socialize and to watch the men, but not to row.

One day in 1938, after nearly a decade of watching the men challenge and enjoy themselves in the beautiful, glossy wooden boats on the tree-lined river, Bayer asked her husband why women didn't row.

Ernest responded with finality, "Well, women *don't* row."

"But," probed Ernestine, "*why* don't they row?"

"Women don't row," he said, "and furthermore, they have nowhere to row."

Unconvinced, and spurred by her husband's "inadequate" reasoning, Bayer set out to find a place for women along Boathouse Row. She discovered a well-kept skating club, complete with locker rooms, that was not in use. An officer at the bank where she worked introduced her to the skating club's president. Soon Bayer and a group of women she had recruited, mostly girlfriends of rowers, were renting the club for $40 per month. Although she didn't realize it at the time, Bayer's newly created Philadelphia Girls Rowing Club (PGRC) would be the seed from which women's competitive rowing would grow in this country.

After Bayer founded PGRC, which still exists sixty years later, her husband agreed, with the help of a friend, to teach the women to row. They borrowed a training barge from the University of Pennsylvania, and, at the age of twenty-nine, Bayer got her first taste of the addictive pleasures and challenges of pulling hard on an oar handle. The women's efforts were not appreciated by most of the male rowers on the Schuylkill. "Members of my husband's club asked him why he permitted me to row," says Bayer. "The men from Undine [a Boathouse Row club] refused to speak to any of us. And there were two nurses who joined the club for two weeks and then came to me and said, 'We have to quit. Our boyfriends don't like it.'"

Nonetheless, when the July 4 regatta rolled around later that summer of 1938, members of PGRC decided they were ready to hold their first race. The competition was staged in doubles, or two-person sculling boats, and there were three PGRC entries. That initial PGRC race did not mark the first time women rowed against each other in the United States, but it may have been the first time women rowed with abandon to find out who could cross the finish line first.

Bayer counts her victory in the first-ever women's race on the Schuylkill with partner Jeanette Waetjen Hoover as among her finest moments on the water. But it wasn't until nearly fifty years later, in December 1984, that she experienced what she described as the best row of her life. Along with the women's eight that had just won a gold medal at the Los Angeles Olympics as a direct result of Bayer's early efforts on behalf of women's rowing, she was being inducted into the Rowing Hall of Fame in Philadelphia. At the dinner following the ceremony, the members of the eight invited Bayer, then seventy-six years old, to go out with them for a spin on the Schuylkill.

"After we had rowed upriver for a while, I raised my hand and asked the coxswain if we could take a ten," remembers Bayer. She wanted to feel the sensation of ten fully uncorked power strokes. What could women who had been raised on equal opportunity, and who'd had the chance to train at the sport's highest level, do in a boat? The coxswain, steering in the stern, called for a ten.

"When we finished, I raised my hand again and said, 'Now, can we *really* take a ten?' They were holding back because of me. Well, they did it that time, and I nearly fell out of my seat," says Bayer. From a distance, eights seem to glide smoothly and gracefully over the water with bodies and oars moving perfectly in sync. But, when a boat is at race pace and people are pushing themselves hard, the ride feels more like a bronco bust than a ballet. The crew rowed back to the dock, and Bayer stroked along with the team. Sliding back and forth on her seat in the bow of the boat and looking ahead at all those powerful, muscular women who had reached perfection in the form of an Olympic gold medal, she cried and cried.

Organized women's rowing on the West Coast predated Bayer's efforts in Philadelphia, but like rowing at Wellesley, West Coast women's rowing remained tame for many decades. Four teenage girls who enjoyed rowing in and exploring San Diego Bay in a four-oared dinghy formed ZLAC in 1892. The girls, Zulette Lamb and Lena, Agnes, and Caroline Polhamus, used their first initials to name the club, which exists today.

With the acquisition of equipment and a clubhouse, ZLAC attracted a large membership, and eventually it developed a sort of country club culture. Women joined the club more for its social distinction than its rowing opportunities. Until the mid-1960s, when Lake Merritt Rowing Club in Oakland challenged ZLAC to its first race, the club was first and foremost a social organization—holding ladies' teas, lunches, bridge parties, and fashion shows. Not long after its first race, ZLAC began accepting men into its membership, and it soon emerged as a rowing powerhouse on the West Coast.

Ernestine Bayer started out with a different mission from the organizers of ZLAC. From the moment she opened the doors of the Philadelphia Girls Rowing Club, she was focused on developing competitive rowing for women. She taught hundreds of girls and women to row at PGRC and did her best to nurture racing opportunities for women. But she was ahead of her time, and progress came much too slowly for her taste. "Eventually, the men let us hold races in their regattas, but the women took a long time to get determined about rowing hard," Bayer says. "Some of us loved racing from the beginning, but others felt it wasn't ladylike."

It wasn't until 1956, when Bayer was forty-seven years old, that a chance to race outside of the club arose. She raced with a group of younger teammates in the sixth seat (known as the "engine room" because it is where the strongest rower usually sits) of the PGRC eight that faced off against Florida Southern University at Lakeland, Florida. They lost by a foot. To the frustration of Bayer and other members of PGRC, that race did not lead immediately to more. By the early 1960s women's racing was just getting off the ground with fewer than twenty women's teams, collegiate and otherwise, across the country.

So it was with great prescience that a young PGRC member, Joanne Iverson, wrote a column for the annual yearbook in 1962 that went out to all the members of the National Association of Amateur Oarsmen. The NAAO was rowing's national governing body at the time, made up of "a bunch of old, stuffy men who didn't want to see anything change," according to Iverson. Nonetheless, the NAAO published the twenty-year-old's column, in which she predicted that women's rowing would spread throughout the United States, and that U.S. women would eventually become a power in international rowing.

Iverson recalls being inspired to write the column out of her love for the sport. "Things were really changing then," says Iverson, who went on to become the first coach of the University of Pennsylvania women's crew in 1968. "Women at PGRC were starting to be proud of having calluses on their hands. I would go to a party and be dancing with guys who would say, 'My God, your back is like a rock,' and I loved it."

Iverson's column turned out to be pivotal in the history of women's rowing. Ted Nash, then coach of Lake Washington's women's crew in Seattle and later a pillar of the Philadelphia rowing community, read the column and called Iverson to tell her he was enthusiastic about her ideas. They discussed the fact that because the NAAO was more intent on holding back women's rowing than seeing it flourish, in order for Iverson's predictions to come true, women's rowing needed its own governing body. With Ed Lickess of the Lake Merritt Rowing Club in Oakland, Iverson and Nash founded the National Women's Rowing Association. The NWRA would oversee women's rowing and be registered under the NAAO. Many years later, in 1986, the two organizations melded into the United States Rowing Association, or USRowing.

The NWRA's first priority was to develop racing opportunities for women in the United States. In 1966, the organization held the first women's nationals in Seattle, Washington. The nationals included events for all different sweep and sculling boats and were open to clubs and college teams.

PGRC (with Ernestine Bayer's daughter, Tina, aboard) walked away with the trophy for the premier event, the elite eight.

International competition was next on the NWRA's agenda. The pinnacle of international racing for women was the European Championship Regatta, which had been held since 1954. The NWRA set its sites on entering that race. "We knew that if women's rowing was ever going to get into the Olympics, the United States had to be a part of the European championships. We were the one major country missing from the event," says Iverson. Several European countries—Germany, Denmark, Norway, and Poland—had had women's rowing clubs since the turn of the century, and as a result competition for women had developed more readily in Europe. Many men and women in the United States were skeptical that a boat of American women could race respectably at the European championships. When the NWRA lobbied the NAAO to approve an entry, they flatly refused.

Ernestine Bayer made an end run around the NAAO by coming up with a Billie Jean King–Bobby Riggs–type event at the St. Catherine's regatta in Ontario in 1967. She arranged for the PGRC national champion eight to sprint against a boat full of men who were former Olympians and national champions at the otherwise all-male event. Bayer, coaching the women, proved her point when the women crossed the finish line ahead of the men, and her boat received a formal invitation to the European championships in Vichy, France. At the championships later that summer, the eight finished sixth in the finals, and the door to international competition was finally open to women in the United States.

Several years later, in 1972, when the International Olympic Committee, the all-powerful Olympic governing body, decided to include women's rowing events in the Olympics, rowing in this country underwent fundamental changes. Funding from the United States Olympic Committee (USOC), uniforms, and the cachet of an Olympic medal were now available to women as well as men. Six women's rowing events first appeared at the Montreal Games in 1976, opening up more than sixty Olympic medals to women and making rowing the second largest contingent behind track and field.

The Olympic allure, combined with the passage of Title IX, which came in 1972 as well, fueled exponential growth in women's rowing in this country over the next decade. In 1972 there were fewer than five hundred women rowing competitively in this country. Ten years later, the NWRA was overseeing more than one hundred member organizations with thousands of women on their rosters.

Title IX, legislation that mandates equal funding and opportunity for men and women in federally funded institutions, gave women political clout to fight for equity in high school and collegiate athletics. In many ways it is only now, at the turn of the century, more than twenty-five years after the legislation passed, that Title IX has grown teeth. This was evidenced most spectacularly in the form of a Supreme Court decision against Brown University—which had cut a women's varsity sport in the mid-nineties—and paved the way for true equity in athletic departments because when the students won the case against Brown it set a precedent for punitive damages. Rowing has been instrumental in the process. A rowing program brings an average of fifty-two women into athletic departments, helping to counterbalance the huge rosters of men's football. Over the past four years, more than thirty varsity women's rowing programs—many with healthy budgets for scholarships, travel, and equipment—have been started in such diverse locations as the universities of Virginia, Michigan, Massachusetts, and Iowa.

From the beginning, female rowers were not shy about making use of Title IX. At Yale University in 1976, led by team captain Chris Ernst, the women's crew marched into the athletic director's office and took off their clothes. They stood naked in front of a shocked athletic director with the words "Title IX" written across their chests and backs to deliver the message that they were fed up with the university's little-sister treatment. Embarrassed by the media attention they caused, the school added a women's wing onto the boathouse. The women's crew would no longer have to sit sweaty and cold on the bus after practice, waiting for the men to finish showering so they could make the long drive back to campus.

The summer before leading her crew into the A.D.'s office, Ernst had been a member of one of the feistiest, if more ragtag, women's national team eights ever assembled. The crew was so incongruous by size and age and background that observers held low expectations for their performance at the world championships in Nottingham, England. As women's rowing has long been dominated by eastern European countries, the members of the 1975 American eight seemed to be the only ones who weren't surprised when they finished second behind the East Germans, ahead of the Romanians.

Ernst in the bow was the smallest at five-four, not a logical bet for someone who would have an extraordinary career as a national team rower that encompassed nearly fifteen years and several gold medals. At the other end of the boat sat another rowing legend-to-be, six-foot-one Carie Graves, a University of Wisconsin graduate, member of many national teams, and eventually a key member of the 1984 gold-medal eight. Nearly two hundred pounds of muscle, with a big personality to match, Graves had a reputation as one of the most powerful women ever to pick up an oar, which lives on. Thirty-five-year-old Gail Cromwell was the oldest member of the crew. A mover and shaker, she had been president of the NWRA (while competing as an elite-level rower) when the decision to add women's events to the Olympic program was made. Anita DeFrantz, a law student at the University of

Pennsylvania at the time—and the most powerful woman in amateur sports today—also earned a spot on the national rowing team that summer.

DeFrantz is the first woman ever elected to the vice presidency of the International Olympic Committee (IOC) and is widely regarded as next in line to succeed seventy-six-year-old Juan Antonio Samaranch as president of the IOC. Now forty-five, she has served the United States Olympic Committee since she was elected by her teammates as an athlete representative in 1976.

DeFrantz is African-American and a descendant of slaves, the great-great granddaughter of a Louisiana plantation owner and one of his female servants. She was born in Philadelphia and grew up in Indianapolis. She comes from a family with a tradition of community involvement; her grandfather was a leader in the early YMCA movement. She started rowing at Connecticut College, where her five-eleven stature caught the coach's eye, and when the decision to include women's rowing in the Olympics came down, she set her sights on Montreal.

Training, going to law school, and working nights at police headquarters interviewing defendants, DeFrantz made the 1976 Olympic team and won a bronze medal in the eight. Not fully satisfied, she decided to shoot for a gold medal in 1980. And with that decision, unbeknownst to her, her career in the politics of amateur sports began. The year she had her heart set on winning an Olympic gold medal, President Jimmy Carter made the unprecedented decision that the United States would boycott the Moscow Games in protest of the Soviet Union's invasion of Afghanistan.

"When the boycott was announced, we were all dumbfounded," says Jan Harville, a 1980 Olympic teammate of DeFrantz's, now coach of the seven-time national champion University of Washington women's crew. "Anita mobilized us. Anita had always been a leader, and she led all of us, not just the rowing team, but the whole Olympic team, in a fight against the boycott. She was courageous and outspoken. She testified in front of Congress. She never backed down."

DeFrantz was one of the few Olympic athletes who broke out of the exhausting intensity of constant training to actively protest the boycott. "I knew I had to fight the boycott precisely because of all the hard work I had done to get where I was," says DeFrantz. "Because of my involvement with the USOC, and my work on the Amateur Sports Act of 1978, I knew the president didn't have the authority to tell the USOC, or the Olympic team, what to do. I knew it was wrong."

DeFrantz led her rowing teammates in a letter-writing campaign. Nearly every week, she traveled from Princeton, New Jersey, where she was training, to Washington, D.C., to lobby against the boycott. She testified to the Senate Foreign Relations Committee. Eventually, she filed a lawsuit against the USOC, which was later dismissed, in an effort to force the governing body to follow its charter of sending athletes to the Games.

The American public stood behind their president, however, not their Olympic team. DeFrantz, having given many newspaper and television interviews, was the target of angry phone calls and received boxes of hate mail. She was audited by the IRS. Passing by a Secret Service agent accompanying the vice president's wife on a visit to the Princeton campus, DeFrantz was shocked to be greeted with, "Hello, Anita."

"It was difficult, dealing with all of that on top of training, and my rowing certainly suffered," says DeFrantz. "The biggest challenge was trying to get the American people to understand the global importance of the Olympic Games, and that it was far more important for us to be there than for us not to go."

By the spring of 1980, the door to the Olympics was closed to U.S. athletes, and DeFrantz's competitive career ended on a bitter, but noble, note. Led by DeFrantz, the women's rowing team had been by far the most organized and outspoken group of Olympians opposing the boycott. For her unwavering loyalty to the Olympic spirit, she was awarded the Bronze Medal of the Olympic Order by the IOC. She observed with some irony that she was the only U.S. athlete to receive a medal that summer.

Her fight against the boycott caught the attention of Peter Ueberroth, the chief organizer of the 1984 Los Angeles Games, and he hired her as a vice president to the Los Angeles Games Committee in 1984. Two years later, she was elected to a position within the very clubby and very male IOC, and she has worked ever since to improve opportunities for women in the Olympics.

DeFrantz has played a key role in pushing substantially more women's sports—like soccer, softball, and hockey—onto the Olympic program. She also has spearheaded efforts to increase female leadership in sports internationally. With the proportion of female competitors at the 1996 Olympics well over 30 percent, she says, "The IOC has come close to finishing the work of making sure women are equally represented on the playing fields of the Olympics." She cites her own Olympic experience. When she won a bronze medal in 1976, the rowing races were half the distance of men's, women's uniforms were nearly all Nadia-sized, and male and female athletes stayed in separate Olympic Villages. Twenty years later, men and women row the same distance, uniforms fit, and, thanks in large part to DeFrantz's efforts through the IOC, everyone eats and sleeps in the same village.

Rowing at the elite, international level is a very different experience for women now than it was for the pioneers of DeFrantz's generation. For the most part, women are given equitable treatment to men. Through the USOC and the United States Rowing Association they are fairly well supported financially and are provided top-of-the-line coaching and equipment. They are free to spend their energy on training, not tending to politics and scratching out a living.

The support has paid off. U.S. women rowers have begun to establish themselves as a force in international rowing, bringing home eight Olympic medals since 1984, a haul commensurate with the men's. And female rowers have continued the tradition of excellence off the water that started with Ernestine Bayer's extraordinary commitment to building competitive rowing for women. Women balancing careers as medical doctors, investment bankers, scientific researchers, and coaches have represented the United States at the world championships and the Olympic Games. In 1992 rowing claimed the only Olympic team member of Mensa, an organization of brainiacs with IQs in the top 2 percent of the population—Karen Kraft, who won a silver in the pair.

The privilege of increased support has brought with it a demand for greater commitment. Many of the women who want to make the Olympic rowing team must now move to training centers where they train three times a day and have little time for anything else. "It's a different set of challenges than we faced," says DeFrantz. "The guys nailed our locker room door shut, we got hand-me-down equipment, I drank Kool-Aid in the morning instead of orange juice to save money." DeFrantz is quick to add that she has no regrets or bitterness about the rough road she traveled. "I made the choice to row because I loved it. I hope I haven't finished giving to the sport that's given me so much."

Sailor Lynn Jewell-Shore, who, along with partner Alison Jolly, won the first women's Olympic sailing event in 1988, could almost be speaking to Anita DeFrantz when she talks about how grateful she is to the generation of women who came before her for creating racing opportunities. The history of competitive sailing and rowing are somewhat similar, particularly where women are concerned. Both sports began to thrive in their modern incarnations in the mid-nineteenth century in England and America. And, partly because of the traditions accumulated over the years, both sports have opened to women only in the last generation. "They had it rough, they made the inroads for us, and we owe them a lot of gratitude," says Jewell-Shore of the sailing women who twenty years ago had to fight just to set foot on boats, and whose only competitive opportunities were against fields of men.

The invention of sailboats as a means of transportation came after the development of rowing boats, although the earliest sailboats actually relied on a combination of rowing and sailing. Sailing boats today can travel into the wind by making a zigzag tacking pattern in which the bow is pointed at an angle to the wind. But the first sailing boats could travel only in the same direction the wind was blowing. Their sails were simply pieces of cloth suspended between two upright posts, often paddles or oars. When the sails bellowed with the wind, the boat moved forward. When the wind wasn't blowing in the direction the sailors wanted to move, however, they took down their sails and pushed out their oars.

This limitation was overcome by reconfiguring the sail. With a sail attached to a vertical mast and a horizontal boom, it is possible to create an airfoil in the leading edge of the sail. Air rushes around the curved forward surface of the sail, creates a vacuum, and pulls the boat forward. A keel or centerboard protruding from the bottom of the boat into the water provides stability and minimizes sideways slippage.

A boat cannot travel *directly* into the wind. A bow held dead into the wind brings a sailboat to a standstill. If a sailor's destination is upwind, she points her bow at an angle to the wind and travels at an angle to her destination. At a given point she tacks, or brings her bow through the wind, so that the wind is now coming from the other side of her boat. Using lines attached to the sails at one end and winches at the other, she brings her sail or sails to the other side of the boat. Once again, she is traveling at an angle to her destination, but on the opposite side. (The right side of a boat is the starboard side; the left side is the port side. When the wind is coming from the starboard side, a boat is on a starboard tack; when the wind is from the port side, the boat is on a port tack.) The boat travels a z-shaped course toward the goal, with the goal as a rough midpoint.

Upwind sailing was an important key to opening up the world to exploration and travel; it allowed people to harness the power of the wind to go just about anywhere by water. Another developmental leap came in the seventeenth century when the Dutch invented speedy, agile *jaghtschips* to protect their cargo ships from piracy as they traveled between colonies and the homeland. While the word *yacht* can refer to either a racing or a cruising boat, or even to a large motor boat, the jaghtschips were precursors to today's racing boats. They were fast, maneuverable, and fun to sail.

Soon after the development of jaghtschips, women began to surface in records of seafaring history. There are eighteenth-century accounts of female pirates. And throughout the nineteenth century, hundreds of wives of whaling and merchant ship captains defied superstition and, in some cases, laws, in order to make their lives aboard their husbands' ships. Usually, they sailed as the sole woman, rather than endlessly pacing the widow's walks at home. At the time, the women were known as "kittle cargo," the ships that carried them, "henfrigates."

The women referred to themselves more favorably as "sister sailors." Their journals and letters reveal women well acquainted with the perils of an ocean storm, the slap of a wave in the face, and the mechanics of a sailboat. They sewed, baked, washed clothes, read, and bore and tutored children aboard ship on voyages that often took them to ports all over the world and lasted as long as five years. All this in an era when there were nearly ten yards of cloth to a skirt, and respectable women wore corsets, and sometimes hoops, crinolines, bustles, and bonnets.

In many cases the sister sailors were daughters of sea captains and had been raised at sea. For them, it must have seemed the natural choice to accompany one's husband rather than be separated for months or years.

Perhaps equally important, going to sea also offered a rare chance for adventure in a woman's life in the nineteenth century. It always has. If through time the sea has represented for men a challenge for heroics, it has represented much more for women an opportunity to simply escape entrenched lives on land.

In 1876, aristocratic Lady Annie Brassy became one of a handful of extraordinary women to break from nineteenth-century tradition and embrace the life of an adventurer when she set sail for a year with no goal in mind other than travel. She described details of the journey with her husband in *Around the World in the Yacht "Sunbeam," Our Home on the Ocean for Eleven Months*. Brassy may have been the first woman to sail around the world for the thrill of it, but she does not portray herself as a hero or a conqueror; she focuses on the freedom of her journey.

One of the most dramatic historical examples of a woman liberated by life at sea is that of Mary Ann Patten. Mary's father was a sea captain. In 1853, at the age of sixteen, she married another captain, twenty-nine-year-old Joshua Patten, in Boston, Massachusetts. Patten was a relatively young but experienced captain who had assumed command of the clipper ship *Neptune's Car* shortly before their marriage. Almost immediately after they were married, the couple set out on Patten's first assignment at his new post, a year-long, around-the-world voyage. To pass the time during the trip, Mary made a hobby of learning navigation, a technical skill requiring literacy and mathematics possessed by few sailors.

At 216 feet and 1,616 tons, *Neptune's Car* was one of the biggest and fastest clipper ships ever constructed. Clippers, narrow and with literally miles of sail, were built for speed, not comfort. Their original purpose was to carry eager customers as quickly as possible from the East Coast to the California gold fields by way of Cape Horn at the tip of South America. By 1854, when Patten took over *Neptune's Car*, gold-rush fever was waning, and clippers were being used more as cargo than passenger ships.

Nonetheless, competition among the ships' backers and captains remained fierce. They often advertised eighty-day trips for the fifteen thousand miles from New York to San Francisco, but in actuality, the voyage rarely took fewer than one hundred days. (In fact, the fastest trip on record was eighty-nine days by *Flying Cloud* in 1851, a record that was only recently broken—with a woman at the helm.) The bitter Antarctic climate and often treacherous wintry seas around Cape Horn make the trip unpredictable. Navigation is complicated and often hazardous because the frigid winds drive shore ice and icebergs out to sea.

On July 1, 1856, *Neptune's Car* set out from New York to deliver valuable cargo to San Francisco. Mary Ann Patten was the only woman aboard. Before departure, her husband, Captain Patten, planned a friendly race with an acquaintance, Captain Horatio Gardner, aboard *Intrepid,* another clipper leaving New York at the same time and also bound for San Francisco.

Almost from the start, the ships faced strong headwinds and towering seas. The weather only grew more savage as they made their way south. Another clipper, *Rapid,* had left New York a month ahead but had to turn back after ten of the twenty-four crew members were swept overboard in the icy seas.

The extreme conditions must have added to Captain Patten's fury when he discovered his first mate asleep on his watch. Perhaps because of the premium on speed and the difficult working conditions, clippers had a reputation for attracting crews of rough and irascible sailors. Patten gave the officer a warning but soon afterward found him impeding the boat's progress by reefing, or shortening, the sails when the orders were for full speed ahead. The captain removed the first mate from duty and placed him under arrest.

A few days later, Patten developed headaches and began to become confused, the first symptoms of what is referred to in accounts of the story as "brain fever." His second mate was illiterate and had no knowledge of navigation, which meant Patten had had to assume the duties of two men. He was working around the clock, with only catnaps for breaks.

As the ship approached Cape Horn, Patten was sailing in hurricane-like conditions. Eventually, exhausted and weakened by illness, he had no choice but to retire to his bunk, incoherent.

Incredibly, Mary Ann Patten—who had been on and around boats her whole life and undoubtedly had a greater understanding of sailing than anyone suspected—then calmly stepped up to fill her husband's shoes. According to a journalist's account at the time, she was a "slender New England girl, scarcely 20 years old . . . of medium height with lustrous eyes and very pleasing features." Also, probably unknown to Mary when she embarked, she was pregnant. But as *Neptune's Car* beat into the teeth of a storm around Cape Horn, when instinct would have guided most to head to the nearest port, Mary ordered the second mate to hold the course for San Francisco, as her husband had planned. She took over navigating the ship, determining its position by chronometer and laying its course. When she wasn't performing captain's duties, she was caring for her husband and combing the medical books in the ship's library for a cure for his illness.

When the first mate learned of the situation, he sent an offer to Mary to take over command of the ship. She refused, she said, out of loyalty to her husband's judgment. When he then tried to foment mutiny among the crew, she reportedly called the crew to her husband's cabin and, sitting beside the unconscious captain, reminded the men of their duty.

After 136 days at sea, *Neptune's Car* docked in San Francisco on November 15, 1856. *Intrepid,* the clipper ship Captain Patten had initially set out to race against, arrived eleven days later.

Almost immediately after landing in San Francisco, the Pattens boarded a steamship bound for New York. From there they traveled to Boston, where Mary gave birth to their son, Joshua, in March.

The Committee of New York Insurance Officers, which had underwritten *Neptune's Car,* sent Mary $1,000 and a letter thanking her for her efforts and "for the large sum of money she had saved them." As word of the Pattens' story spread through the press, public donations also came to the family. The newly forming suffragist movement adopted Mary's valiant achievement as an emblem of women's capability.

In a reply to the insurance company, Mary explained that all the attention did not please her. What seemed extraordinary seamanship to others simply seemed second nature to her.

Mary's husband died at the Somerville Lunatic Asylum, just outside of Boston, less than six months after the birth of their son. Four years later, at age twenty-four, Mary died of tuberculosis. Nearly one hundred years after her death, in 1959, Patten Hospital opened at the U.S. Merchant Marine Academy at Kings Point, New York, dedicated to "Mary Ann Patten, Florence Nightingale of the Ocean."

Mary Ann Patten stands out in the written record as an exceptional seafaring woman, but there must have been hundreds of women in the nineteenth century who, like her, grew up at sea and were capable sailors. It was not the women who made their lives at sea, however, who gave competitive women's sailing its start. The advent of British Victorian upper-middle-class affluence and leisure time gave way to recreational and competitive boating. Traditionally, sailboat racing has been the province of the wealthy elite in this country, as well.

The oldest ongoing championship just for women in the United States is the Adams Cup. The Adams Cup is an annual event that continues to serve as the women's national championship of U.S. Sailing, the sport's governing body. It is an around-the-buoy, one-design yacht race that began in 1924 as the Hodder Cup. One-design races are held among more or less identical boats, set up to select the fastest sailors, not the fastest boats. (The broad category of sailboats most commonly used for racing is the sloop, which has one mast and two sails. Racing sloops are usually somewhere between ten and seventy feet long.) Each year, in the interest of fairness, the Adams Cup changes boat classes and sites. Elimination races among yacht clubs at the local, regional, and area levels across the country whittle down the field to ten entries over the course of several months.

Like women's sailing generally, the Adams Cup was long dominated by clubs from Massachusetts and New York. More recently, however, Amy Champman Kleinshcrodt, competing for the Buccaneer Yacht Club in Mobile, Alabama, won the Adams Cup, in 1977 and in 1980. Yachting being a sport that favors maturity and experience, Kleinshcrodt came back nearly twenty years later and skippered the winning boat in 1997 at age thirty-eight.

Kleinshcrodt's victories reflect the geographical diversification of sailing over the last few decades. As sailing has spread, there has been a national surge in the number of women participating in the sport. Despite the growth, one woman, Betsy Alison, has reigned as the most dominant individual in major women's team-sailing events over the past fifteen years. Broad-shouldered, big-voiced, and self-assured, Alison has demonstrated an exceptional ability to motivate teams of women. She won the Adams Cup three times between 1982 and 1989.

Alison has also left an indelible mark on the Rolex International Women's Keelboat Championships. Established in 1985, and held every two years, the Rolex International reigns as the world's biggest fleet-racing event for women. In 1997 eight countries competed, fielding a total of thirty-six boats. Alison has won the event five of the seven times it has been held.

Yacht racing divides into two general categories: fleet racing and match racing. Fleet racing is like a road race—a large group of competitors gathers at the start and heads to the finish. It's more a race against oneself than a game of strategy. Match racing, between two boats, is more like a boxing match. One is as focused on causing her opponent grief as she is on nursing her own boat for speed. Until 1997, match racing was a man's game; very few women were involved. Most notably, JJ Isler managed to sail her way to the top of the international elite match-racing circuit in the early 1990s and became the first woman to skipper a boat on the circuit.

In May of 1997, the Women's International Match Racing Association was formed to promote and support women's match-racing opportunities. Still in its infancy, the WIMRA has developed three major annual international events and is working to establish a program of smaller events. Betsy Alison has already begun winning in this new arena. Based out of Newport, Rhode Island, she had the top-ranked women's match-racing team in the United States in early 1998.

Pushing women's match racing onto the Olympic program was one of WIMRA's chief goals. Women's sailing got off to an excruciatingly slow start in the Olympics but has recently gained momentum. It wasn't until 1988, at the Games in Seoul, South Korea, that women got their own event for the first time. Women from thirty nations raced in the 470, a 15 ½-foot, two-person boat. As in other boat classes, the women competed in seven races over a marked course, with points awarded depending on order of finish.

It was a trial by fire, in some of the worst conditions ever recorded at an Olympic sailing venue. The U.S. team of Lynn Jewell-Shore and Alison Jolly led the field after the first six races. In the final race, they needed only to finish in the top fourteen to win the gold medal. "We were confident, but because of the horrendous conditions, we decided to race cautiously," says Jewell-Shore, who was twenty-seven at the time. Years later she still shudders when she sees videos of the race in the treacherous water.

Midway through the race, the Americans were sailing comfortably in the pack when they came around a buoy, looked down the course, and couldn't believe their eyes. Thirty-mile-per-hour winds and ten-foot-high waves were rushing toward them. "What we had been sailing in was a big challenge, but that stuff was frightening. I could see it coming up the course and just leaving carnage behind," says Jewell-Shore.

When the wind and waves hit the American boat, the jib toggle, or piece of hardware that connects the top of the jib to the boat, broke. Suddenly, the boat was only precariously upright. They turned head-to-wind in order to stop and stabilize the boat and then, says Jewell-Shore, "We argued for nearly twenty minutes about what to do next."

The women managed to temporarily repair the toggle, but by the time they were under way again, the pair had dropped to fifteenth place. "It was incredibly tense. But we just sailed our best, and we managed to finish ninth," says Jewell-Shore. "When it was over, we were so relieved, and Alison was so angry at her husband, who was in charge of maintaining our equipment, that it took a while for the victory to sink in!"

Two more women's sailing events were added to the Olympic program at the 1992 Barcelona Games. An American, Julia Trotman, won the bronze medal in the inaugural Olympic Europe dinghy race, a lightweight, one-person boat race. Women's sailboarding also debuted in 1992, just two Olympiads—instead of nine decades—after it was added to the men's program.

As women's Olympic sailing has begun to grow, so has women's competitive sailing at all levels in the United States. Girls' junior sailing is currently the fastest-growing contingent of U.S. Sailing. At the collegiate level, sailing, like all women's sports, is enjoying a period of development and recognition. Interest in recreational sailing is also increasing among women. Womanship is a women-run company designed to teach women sailing on boats that are staffed by women. Since 1985, the Annapolis-based company has taught nearly seven thousand women boat handling, sail trim, leadership, and confidence in on-the-water courses, and it reports a rising number of participants.

Expanding opportunities mean women are free to do everything from dabbling in weekend cruises to nurturing Olympic dreams to making their lives as professional sailors. The changes are not limited to the United States. Women all over Europe, New Zealand, and Australia are actively involved in recreational and competitive sailing—against other women, and against fields dominated by men—to an extent they were not twenty years ago. Isabelle Autissier of France is one of the most notable examples of a woman making her life in competitive sailing in a fashion only recently impossible. Autissier has had more success than any other woman sailing in the dangerous and demanding big-boat solo events against men.

If Autissier were a bit less pragmatic, she'd be a dead ringer for the Amelia Earhart of yachting. There is a physical suggestion of Earhart: sunny, boyish grin; short, curly hair; level, wide-set eyes. Autissier is an extraordinary adventurer, risk taker, and lone pioneer for women. She's also, like Earhart, a woman on intimate terms with her machine. And she nearly disappeared at sea. But unlike Earhart, there is little romantic about Autissier. She is a French marine biologist, who, when she's not at sea, keeps both feet firmly on the ground. "Anything is possible," goes one of Autissier's favorite adages, "but everything has its price."

New Year's Eve, 1994, Autissier was caught in a nasty storm, alone, aboard her sixty-foot sloop in the southern reaches of the Indian Ocean. She was partway through the second leg of the Around Alone Race, formerly named the BOC Challenge. The race is a single-handed, 27,000-mile trek around the world that ranks among the most difficult tests of self-reliance, intelligence, endurance, and true grit. Autissier had won the first leg of the race, from Charleston, South Carolina, to Cape Town by an unheard-of margin of five days—twelve hundred miles ahead of her nearest competitor. Her chances of winning the race then disappeared early in the second leg when a storm rolled her boat, *Ecureuil Poitou-Charentes 2*, and she was forced to head back to land for repairs. By New Year's, she simply had her eye on finishing the four-leg race. No small feat. Four years before, she had become the first woman ever to finish.

But, in one fell swoop, an enormous rogue wave rolled *Charentes 2* 360 degrees, dismasted her, pounded her to pieces, sent Autissier adrift, and shifted the sailor's focus from finishing to surviving. The only means of communication left on the boat that just moments before had been a marvel of modern technology was a satellite distress signal. Autissier triggered it, gathered what supplies she could, squeezed into the bow of her battered but up-right hull, and waited for help.

Her signal was picked up in Australia. Race officials pinpointed her coordinates, and the Royal Australian Air Force dispatched a fifteen-man search plane. Three hours into the search, Autissier was spotted standing on her deck, waving. The plane dropped her a survival kit, and radioed for the Australian Navy to send a destroyer complete with helicopter to perform the actual rescue. Autissier was soon back on land, but despite a week-long search by an Australian salvage crew, no trace of the rest of her boat was ever found.

"When you get into a bad situation and you get out of it, you can thank whoever you want, providence, God, whomever," said Autissier not long after the rescue. "I thanked the Royal Australian Air Force and Navy."

If you don't believe in luck, it follows that you don't believe in the concept of pushing your luck. Two years after her close call in the Indian Ocean, Autissier announced her third entry in the Around Alone Race, scheduled to begin from Charleston in July 1998 and finish there in May 1999. Her entry will be one in a fleet of at least twenty-five boats. If historical odds hold true, about two-thirds of those who start will finish, and, as has happened in the four previous races, a French boat—perhaps this time with a woman at the helm—will cross the finish line first.

In the meantime, forty-one-year-old Autissier set sail in the inaugural Gold Race in early 1998 to defend her rights to one of the most distinguished ocean racing records. She astounded the yachting world in 1994 when she completed the 13,900-mile clipper ship route from New York to San Francisco around the infamous Horn in sixty-two days, shaving fourteen days off the previous record set before the turn of the century.

While onlookers marvel at Autissier's nerve, she has a practically mathematical explanation for her extraordinary achievements in the raw and wholly male-dominated world of solo ocean racing. "The bigger the boat, the smaller the difference between men and women," she's fond of saying. It's true. On bigger boats, technological know-how, courage, and stamina rate as vastly more important than brute strength. Big-boat racing, as opposed to racing the smaller Olympic-class boats, is where women have achieved the most success competing against men over the years. But women have yet to win either of the two most prestigious big-boat races in the world, the Whitbread Round the World Race and the America's Cup, both team events.

The 32,000-mile, five-leg Whitbread is among the most grueling races in yachting. It was first established in 1973 by the Royal Navy Sailing Association of Great Britain and is held quadrennially. Until very recently, few women had competed in the race, and organizers clearly consider it a macho event, openly referring to it as a "man's race."

In 1990 Tracy Edwards of England won a spot in yachting history when she skippered the first women's team in the Whitbread. With twenty-eight-year-old Edwards at the helm, *Maiden* won two of the five legs for her class and completed the entire race. The effort silenced the critics who had said women don't have the skill or stamina to sail around the world. Edwards had competed in the 1985–86 Whitbread as the only woman aboard *Atlantic Privateer* and then decided to assemble a women's team for the next race. She painstakingly picked great sailors from all over the world and put a premium on their ability to work well together. Teamwork is a necessity when twenty-foot waves, skin rubbed raw by salt and wind, freeze-dried food, wet clothes, and sleep deprivation are all part of a day's work—day after day after day.

The success of Edwards's crew cut a path to the Whitbread for future women's entries, and they are now almost routine. American Dawn Riley skippered the all-female *Heineken* in 1994. Four years later, Team EF Education entered the 1997–98 Whitbread with a French skipper, Christine Guilleu, and an international all-female crew.

A back injury kept Edwards from the Whitbread after she skippered the first women's team in 1990. She worked for several years teaching business leadership and management courses—skills she had gained masterminding and skippering an expensive, comprehensive campaign for the Whitbread. Then—a self-described "teen rebel" who left home at age sixteen, drawn to the adventure of ocean racing—she came up with her next big idea.

In 1996 Edwards paid half a million dollars for *ENZA,* the boat sailed by Sir Peter Blake and Sir Robin Knox-Johnston when they set the nonstop around-the-world record in 1994. Under five-six, Edwards is a small, hearty, dogged woman, and she had purchased a very big boat. The ninety-two-foot catamaran is considered to be the fastest oceangoing vessel ever built.

Two years after Blake and Knox-Johnston set the circumnavigation record with *ENZA,* it was broken by Frenchman Olivier de Kersaus and now stands at seventy-one days, fourteen hours, twenty-two minutes, and eight seconds. It is that record that Edwards set out to break with an eleven-woman crew on a newly refitted *ENZA.* The boat was renamed *SunAlliance* after the British insurance company that kicked in 4.27 million British pounds to fund Edwards's dream to become the first women's crew to sail nonstop around the world and to do it faster than men ever had.

Edwards added two preparatory prongs to her goal. On July 1, 1997, her crew—which included one sailor from her original *Maiden* team—set a new world record for the fastest all-female crew across the Atlantic, of nine days, eleven hours, and twenty-two minutes. It was the third fastest transatlantic crossing ever. Frenchman Serge Madec holds the overall record of six days, thirteen hours, three minutes set in 1990 on a seventy-five-foot catamaran.

Inclement October weather interfered with Edwards's next warm-up exercise—the Round Britain and Ireland record. Instead, she aimed *Sun-Alliance* at the cross channel record (from Cowes to St. Malo), which she smashed by forty-five minutes with a time of six hours, forty-nine minutes, and nineteen seconds. Her all-woman team flew through the water at an incredible average speed of 22.7 knots.

Luck was not with Edwards's crew when they launched their final voyage in early 1998, however. Midway through the team's around-the-world attempt, they were close to a record-setting pace. As their boat approached Cape Horn in mid-March, pounding through typically nasty conditions, she was dismasted by a random, enormous wave. *SunAlliance* crashed to a halt. The team, with no hope of continuing its effort, was forced to limp to the shores of South America, leaving the task of a nonstop around-the-world voyage, and the record, to a group of women in the future.

The America's Cup is the other major yachting summit that remains to be scaled by women. Dating back to 1851, the America's Cup is the oldest, and among the most coveted, trophies in yachting. The tradition of racing every three or four years for the cup—an ornate, Victorian, sterling silver pitcher standing two feet high and weighing nearly nine pounds—began when *America,* a schooner representing the best of its young country's boat design and building capabilities, defeated a fleet of fifteen English yachts in a fifty-three-mile race around England's Isle of Wight. It was a stunning victory at a time when England was known for its naval acumen.

America brought the cup back to the New York Yacht Club. The club (the granddaddy of them all, dating back to 1844 and allowing women to join only in 1985) then began putting up the cup as a challenge trophy. The America's Cup is held as a series of races, first between two groups, the Defenders and the Challengers, with the two winners then squaring off in a final series. The United States has dominated the race, losing only twice in nearly a century and a half. American skipper Dennis Conner, who has won the cup three times, lost it to Australia in 1983 and to New Zealand in 1995.

The America's Cup was long dominated by extremely wealthy men who could afford to sink hundreds of thousands of dollars into boats and hire professional crews. Sopwiths, Vanderbilts, and Liptons glamorized the sport of yachting during the race's heyday in the first half of the twentieth century. But if the history of the America's Cup is one of the most venerable in sports, it is also among the most sexist. A handful of women, mostly wives and daughters of boat owners, played minor roles in early racing. But as women began to develop racing skills in the late 1930s, they were frozen out of the event altogether for fifty years. In the 1980s, two women made their way as backup crew members on boats. It wasn't until 1995 that an all-women's team, America[3], entered the race for the cup. The team, made up of many of the best female sailors in the country, shook the yachting world by racing neck and neck with veterans like Dennis Conner, who had twenty years of America's Cup experience under his belt.

Given the male-dominated nature of the sport, it's perhaps not surprising that so little is known about the women who sailed in the early America's Cup races. The first record of a woman sailing aboard an America's Cup boat came thirty-five years into the race. In 1886, British Challenger William Henn brought his wife aboard his boat *Galetea*. Mrs. Henn reportedly stayed in the plush cabin below deck for the duration of the racing, in the company of, strangely enough, her collection of pet dogs and a monkey. Seven years later, two young women, Lady Rachel Wyndham-Quin and Lady Eileen Wyndham-Quin, sailed aboard their father's boat, the British Challenger *Valkyrie II*. After the *Valkyrie II* lost, Lord Dunraven entered the race again in 1895, and again his daughters are listed among those aboard the *Valkyrie III*. It's unclear what exactly the young women did, if anything, on board. Most likely, they were simply "observers." It's a role that today may sound dull and inconsequential, but at the time it must have felt exciting and daring for a woman to board the exquisite racing machines and get a bird's-eye view of the action.

In that same year, 1895, a woman is listed for the first time aboard an American Defender. Hope Goddard Iselin, wife of syndicate manager C. Oliver Iselin, is the first woman on record with an active role in the America's Cup. Iselin served as "timekeeper" aboard victorious *Defender*. She operated a stopwatch and, among other things, tracked the time it took the huge 130-foot J-boats to complete their tacks. It was a crucial role that would have put her in the back of the boat among the afterguard (skipper, navigator, and tactician) in the thick of strategic planning and decision making. Four years later, Iselin was timekeeper aboard *Columbia*.

Mrs. William P. Burton appeared aboard the Challenger *Shamrock IV* in 1920, and by the 1930s, women seemed to be forging a place for themselves in the America's Cup. Elizabeth "Sis" Hovey was an early pioneer of women's yachting who grew up racing in Massachusetts and became the first American woman to skipper a boat in international competition in 1930. Four years later, while she was still in her twenties, Hovey's sailing experience and success won her an invitation to sail in the Defense trials aboard *Yankee*. A call to compete at the pinnacle of her sport was a significant turn of events in sailing praised at the time in the Boston press as "in keeping with modern trends in all sports."

The most interesting year for women in early America's Cup history came with the following race. In 1937, no fewer than five women were involved in the Challenger and Defense trials. And in the finals, two women,

Gertrude Vanderbilt and Phyllis Brodie Sopwith, competed against each other as timekeepers. Their famous, wealthy husbands, Harold S. Vanderbilt and Thomas O. M. Sopwith, skippered their yachts *Ranger* and *Endeavor II.* The rivaling, glamorous couples attracted a great deal of media attention, although there is little information about what the two women contributed to the racing. Stories focus on what they wore (team-issue jackets, slacks, and hats on board, tweeds and fur on land) and how they amused their husbands as tennis and golf partners.

Photographs accompanying the stories may tell more than the text. Even if the shots were staged, they show two women who are clearly comfortable and competent at sea. One photo shows Brodie Sopwith at the wheel of *Endeavor II;* she looks ahead intently while keeping her grip and stance firm as the boat heels steeply over to port. In another photo, she stands close behind her husband at the wheel. As she gazes through binoculars, presumably checking out the competition, he cocks an ear back toward her to hear her observations.

Another telling photo shows Gertrude Vanderbilt up on the high side, or rail, of *Ranger,* partially reclined and looking out over the water. The caption reads, "Mrs. Harold S. Vanderbilt, taking it easy on the deck of the *Ranger* . . . while her husband holds the wheel." But Mrs. Vanderbilt was not merely sunning herself. What the caption doesn't say is that she was doing what any good America's Cup sailor should have been doing: keeping her weight low and calm on the high side of the boat, so as not to disrupt its flight through the water, while paying close attention and waiting for the skipper's next call.

Women's growing capability as America's Cup sailors did not go unnoticed by men in the sport. Midway through the 1937 America's Cup finals, a story appeared in the *Boston Post* entitled, "Want Women Out of Yacht Race, Men Nautical Leaders Plan Rules to Ban Them From Part in International Events." In the story, "experts" register vague complaints about women corrupting the sport: "No matter how good a yacht expert a woman is, her presence unconsciously creates new problems." One "well known yachtsman" said, "This is a man's game and we want to keep it purely nautical. As soon as the women get on these J boats, you would think it was some kind of a social and fashion contest. . . ."

The criticisms seem a thin disguise for the sailors' fear of losing to women. The men met to draw up plans to bar women from future major yachting events, at least in part because they "objected to the idea that if the *Endeavor II* lifts the America's Cup, Mrs. Sopwith and Mrs. Sigrist [who sailed aboard *Endeavor I,* training partner to *Endeavor II*] would become their ladyships . . . when they help their husbands to bring the old mug back to England."

No official rules were passed, but women were conspicuously absent from America's Cup races for nearly fifty years following their brief zenith in the 1930s. A thaw began in the 1980s when Christy Steinman Crawford and Dory Vogel played important but somewhat low-profile roles in Dennis Conner's campaigns. In 1992, twenty-seven-year-old Dawn Riley fought her way onto a team of thirty men and impressed the skipper, billionaire businessman Bill Koch, with her talent and commitment. After Koch's team, also called America³, won the cup, he made the radical decision, true to his iconoclastic nature, that it was time to shake up the old-fashioned world of yachting by entering an all-women's team in the next America's Cup in 1995.

Koch's decision to stake his reputation and millions of dollars in seed money, equipment, and technology behind an unprecedented women's team was based in large part on his observations of Riley. "She was among the very best sailors on our team. She worked harder and performed in her position better than just about anybody," Koch said. "Watching Dawn made me believe a women's team could have a real shot at winning the America's Cup."

Dawn Riley would stand out in any crowd at five-six and 160 pounds of solid muscle, with a perfect dimpled smile, large piercing green eyes, and long blond hair. She grew up sailing competitively in Michigan, fighting her way onto boats full of men even as a youngster. One weekend every summer during her childhood, the women at the yacht club where her family sailed took over the boats from the men and put together all-women's races. One of the traditional events of the weekend was a bikini contest, which Riley entered at the age of fifteen. Standing in her bikini in front of scores of sailors, she was asked as part of the contest what she planned for her future.

"I said, 'In my future I plan on skippering an America's Cup campaign.' And they just absolutely laughed. They thought it was the funniest thing they had ever heard," explains Riley many years later. "I saw my first America's Cup race in Newport when I was thirteen, and it just stuck with me as something I wanted to do. I thought of it a lot, because in your dreams when you're a kid, anything is possible. I must have thought, 'If I say it out loud in front of all these people, maybe it'll happen.' But when they thought it was a stupid, crazy idea, instead of being discouraged it made me more determined."

Fifteen years and a lot of saltwater later, Riley quickly emerged as a natural leader on the women's team because of her extensive big-boat sailing experience. By the age of thirty, she had sailed in two Whitbread Round the World Races on all-female teams, once with Tracy Edwards and once as skipper. She was also the only woman on America³, the women's team with the same name, who had any firsthand knowledge of the seventy-foot-long America's Cup boats, whose masts reach 110 feet in the air, and which require sixteen people to sail. Most of the women on the team had experience racing much smaller two- to four-person boats, and the transition was a little like moving from paper airplanes to a 747.

Although initially dismissed as a joke and a sideshow to the main event, after six months of training, the women won their very first race against Dennis Conner, in what reporters described as "a milestone in sports history." Over the next several months, they went on to hold their own through a series of nearly thirty races with Conner and another team, PACT 95.

Through the process, the women captured the world's imagination—as pioneers, as underdogs, and as a symbol of women's capability. Good luck faxes and flowers arrived daily at the America³ compound from all over the world. Corporate sponsors—from Chevrolet to *Glamour* magazine to Hewlett-Packard—got behind the team to the tune of nearly $15 million. And during the year-long campaign, which required twelve-hour days, six or seven days a week, from sailors and support crew alike, America³ appeared in nearly two billion media impressions.

The team's major stumbling block turned out to be an internal leadership gap. Not that the team lacked good leaders. In addition to Riley, there was JJ Isler, also among the top handful of female sailors in the world, with a distinguished record as a world champion and Olympic bronze medalist in the 470 class in 1992. Isler was the first female skipper to break into the elite international match-racing circuit, a small, heady group of the world's very best competitive sailors. She practically grew up at the San Diego Yacht Club, and went to Yale, where she became the first woman to be named captain of the coed sailing team.

Tall and lanky with a mischievous sense of humor, Isler probably brought the most strategic, analytical mind to the America³ team. She was, like Dawn, a natural leader. But, perhaps reflecting yachting's old-fashioned mores, the all-male coaching and managing staff of America³ never turned over the reins of leadership to the women, and the women never forced the issue. When leadership problems developed aboard *Mighty Mary* midway through racing, the coaches' stopgap solution was to remove Isler from her position and replace her with a man, David Dellenbaugh, who had been tactician during the victorious 1992 campaign. Dellenbaugh performed heroically in a difficult role, but many fans of the women's team, and some of its members, felt betrayed by the crew change.

In the end, the women's team narrowly lost a chance to defend the America's Cup against New Zealand in a heartbreaking last showdown against Dennis Conner. In that final, deciding race, *Mighty Mary* led for five of the six legs and came around the final buoy by a substantial four-minute margin ahead of Conner's crew on *Stars and Stripes*. The television network following the race abandoned coverage at that point and switched to baseball spring training. Victory seemed certain for the women; the race was moving along at a snail's pace in very calm wind and seas.

But *Stars and Stripes* and *Mighty Mary* chose different sides of the course for their final leg, and Conner's gamble paid off. Down the left side came a very lucky puff of breeze that allowed *Stars and Stripes* to make up all of its lost ground on *Mighty Mary*—stuck in a wind hole—in a matter of minutes. *Stars and Stripes* crossed the finish line just a few lengths ahead of *Mighty Mary,* and, as Bill Koch remembers, "Those men cheered like they had just won the World Series." Their joy and relief were testimony to the fact that the women's team had been a real contender. It was the last time Conner's crew would cheer so heartily—they went on to lose five straight races, and the America's Cup, to New Zealand in the finals.

As team captain, Dawn Riley had played an instrumental role in bringing the women's team up to a competitive level in such a short period of time. "Dawn set the bar high, on and off the boat," says crew member Stephanie Maxwell Pierson.

Barely a year and a half passed after the women's final race before Riley had her arms around her next major challenge, becoming the first woman in charge of an America's Cup campaign. Riley based her campaign, dubbed America True, in San Francisco. She decided the team would be coed, with men and women competing together. "The idea is to pick the best person for the job, whether it's a man or a woman," explains Riley. Even though the next race will be in 2000 in New Zealand, building a campaign is a long process that requires raising $30 million, research and technology for new boat design, building new boats, and crew training. So Riley set up shop in the spring of 1997. Her campaign is one of more than a dozen around the world that will be vying for the cup in 2000. So far, hers is the only crew list with any women's names on it.

Skiing

Rhapsody in White
Jean Weiss

At the 1998 Olympics held in Nagano, Japan, Picabo Street ripped through the course of the Super G to win a gold medal by 1/100 of a second, a margin as thin as the hot-melon-colored suit she was wearing. The victory was stunning: not just because of Street's celebrity, or because the Super G is usually her weakest event, or because it's rare for an athlete to remain a top-level competitor after destroying a knee as Street had done only a year earlier. The victory was important because it showed how far American women's skiing had come. As Street stood on the podium to collect her medal, radiating all the fresh-scrubbed confidence you'd expect from a young woman who believes in past lives and auras and her inalienable right to excel, she earmarked the progress from a time when American women were competitors but not competitive to now, when they are first-place contenders. From the original American Olympic women's ski squad in 1936, when the well-bred Elizabeth Woolsey bested her teammates to place only fourteenth among the international lineup, to this: sixties love child Street gathering up her gold medallion. It was clear that in the United States, women's skiing had come a long way.

It took six decades, the span of time between Woolsey and Street, for American women to prove their worth as international competitors. The first mark of progress came in 1948 when Gretchen Fraser ended European dominance over Alpine skiing as the first American skier to win an Olympic medal. In the late 1960s, Suzy Chaffee led the women into the spotlight again when she abandoned Alpine in favor of the then relatively unknown form of skiing called freestyle. Thanks in large part to Chaffee, freestyle is now an established international event. A third leap occurred during the 1980s, when Tamara McKinney proved to the world that a ski racer's career could be sustained for more than a few seasons. In her decade-long reign, McKinney won eighteen World Cup races. Then came Picabo Street, the magnetic young woman who captured our hearts while capturing her gold. With flair and bravado, Street took us into the 1990s, establishing not only that American women could win, but that they could become wealthy and famous, too.

Yet Alpine and freestyle, arguably the most popular and visible forms of the sport, are only two strands in the rich history of American women's skiing. The deeply rooted Nordic and the renegade black sheep snowboarding also claim a stake. Though the journey has been less well documented, Nordic and snowboarding have changed dramatically for American women, especially over the past two decades. As snowboarding grows in popularity, some Alpine skiers are trading in their gear for the fat boards. Snowboarder Sondra Van Ert is a classic example of this trend. She left the U.S. ski team in the mid-eighties only to resurface ten years later as a world champion and Olympian of snowboarding. In her own way, Nordic racer Nina Kemppel sets a similar example for where American women stand as cross-country competitors. Kemppel continues a quiet rule over her U.S. contemporaries while falling far behind her European competitors.

There's a saying among ski bums that's offensive but honest. It goes something like this: I may sleep with you tonight, but don't count on me to ski with you tomorrow. This same fraternity has a second creed that sounds just as ludicrous: Skiing powder is better than sex. Ludicrous, that is, to everyone except those who've skied deep powder.

Skiing can become an obsession. To anyone who's lived in a ski town, this fact is painfully obvious. Talk of skiing dominates cocktail parties, newspaper sports pages, grocery store lines. Every season a new crop of freshly educated college grads trades its high-powered aspirations for waiting tables and a free ski pass. Sometimes they stay a few seasons. Sometimes they stay the rest of their lives. Middle-income families endure the financial hardships of an inflated ski town economy just so they can log forty days each season on the mountain. Some skiers never get enough. Why? Because, quite simply, skiing is like flying. There's the rush of gravity, a sense of weightlessness, a crescendo of speed and power that lifts one up and then knocks one down. There's an appealing element of danger. Just enough to feel as if every limit has been pushed. The slopes are precipitous, the visibility next to nothing. The chair, the gondola, or the tram could break down at any moment. It's a reasonable risk to take, but a risk nonetheless. One could lose control skiing on the mountain and crash into the hill, another skier, or, worse, a tree. People die skiing, though more often they break a leg or rip a ligament in their knee. Skiing requires split-second decisions about direction and terrain and style of turns. Moment to moment every skier is a hairbreadth away from success or failure. This is the appeal of Alpine and freestyle skiing—fast pace, dramatic decisions, speed, and varied terrain.

Skiing doesn't have to be difficult. Some people take it moderate and slow. They show up late to the ski hill, cruise all day on groomed slopes, check into the lodge for hot chocolate or to sit and read by the fire, then call it an early day. On any given ski mountain, there are choices of terrain. There are ungroomed powder slopes, slopes that have been sculpted all night by snowcat operators to make skiing easier, and bump runs that have been carved out and shaped by the tight turns of the skiers who have come before. Each section of a ski mountain is graded according to level of difficulty. Green circles mark the easiest way down a mountain; blue squares flag intermediate slopes; black diamonds indicate advanced terrain; double black diamonds are for extreme skiers only. While ski areas throughout the country subscribe to the same gradation of difficulty, the similarities stop there. One may find powder or icy terrain anywhere. There are exceptions, but a few generalizations are fair. Anyone who grew up skiing on the West Coast can attest to the fact that conditions tend to be deep, heavy snow on steep slopes, which packs out. Ski areas on the East Coast aren't as steep and tend to get less snow; they are renowned for their often icy conditions. The most extreme terrain and best, light-as-air powder is found in ski areas from Montana to New Mexico, along the Rocky Mountain range.

Skiing outside of resorts is another fun way to experience the sport. A growing number of people prefer to work up a sweat using Nordic's smooth, steady kick-and-glide, or skating, techniques. Cross-country skiing is easy to learn. It's also considered one of the best all-body muscular and cardiovascular workouts there is. Then there's backcountry skiing. Snowboarders, telemarkers, and Alpine skiers know that trudging with friends to the top of a mountain for a few hard-earned first tracks is even more satisfying than taking in the panoramic views at the top of every chairlift.

To be a good skier, to really make it past the intermediate stage, requires an aggressive attitude. To be a ski racer, it takes more. Starting at a young age is an invaluable advantage. For Alpine skiers, a low center of gravity and strong thighs lend an edge. For Nordic, endurance is the key. Freestyle skiers must be quick and agile. They also need to have rhythm. A commitment to a ski team and instruction from the best coaches are required. Experience on terrain throughout the country can prepare a racer for the unknown. In the end, though, it's a mental game. If a skier doesn't have it in her head that she's going to win, she won't.

* * *

Skiing isn't just about competition and thrill-seeking adventure. The sport was born from necessity. Prehistoric hunters used splintered logs to slide over snow-covered slopes while searching for prey. Rock carvings found in Russia dating back to 6000 B.C. show images of skis. The oldest pair of skis, now displayed in a Stockholm museum, dates to 3000 B.C. Written accounts from China and Scandinavia dating back five thousand years confirm the use of skis during war and the first informal ski competitions. The first recorded mention of women skiing is the ancient northern European myth of the goddess Skadi, a bow hunter who searched for game while gliding downhill on cross-country skis. Even the origins of modern skiing can be traced to Europe. The Norwegians developed the cross-country style known as Nordic mainly for transportation. It wasn't until the early twentieth century that skiing began to grow in popularity not just as a mode of transportation, but also as a sport. Gradually, skiers around the world adapted the sport to their terrain, developing different ski techniques. The Norwegians were accustomed to sloping, open countryside. The forested mountainsides of the Alps proved more complicated. It was necessary to develop the Alpine method and the technique called the Arlberg Crouch. Nineteenth-century Austrian ski instructors Mathias Zdarsky, Georg Bilgeri, and Hannes Schneider experimented with the Arlberg technique, which required a lift and swing of the body while bending the knees. This allowed skiers to safely navigate down steeps through trees. This style bred slalom, skiing through a series of gates, and downhill, high-speed skiing down a course. While Nordic continued to develop more quietly along solitary tracks in the backcountry, Alpine became fashionable. Fast, glamorous, and modern, Alpine was the centerpiece for winter tourism to posh ski resorts in the Swiss Alps, in Germany's Bavarian Alps, and in Austria's St. Anton and Innsbruck resorts. Skiers took to the slopes on large, heavy wooden skis and flimsy, leather lace-up boots, getting up the mountains on rope tows and T-bars. Because it required expensive travel, the sport's first enthusiasts were largely from the ranks of the privileged. Nonetheless, by the early part of the twentieth century, the sport was beginning to catch on with a broader population, and competition was the natural next step.

Skiing was a competitive sport for men as early as 1879, through ski jumping events held by the Norwegian military. Women skiers were four decades behind, competing for the first time during the 1920s. Racing through clubs and on college-sponsored teams, American women were quick to catch up with their male counterparts. Clad in tailored wool ski pants that fit neatly inside their low-cut, leather lace-up boots, they sported Tyrolean-style sweaters and jackets, flapper hats, ankle socks, and heavy wooden skis with cable bindings. Club racing brought recognition, credibility, and a place to experience racing to America's women skiers during this crucial decade, when Americans were beginning to compete with the rest of the world.

In 1924, the first winter Olympics was held in Chamonix, France, but the only venue allowed women was figure skating, in which eleven-year-old Sonja Henie made her debut. This was a disappointment to women skiers, who looked hopefully toward the next Olympics for the chance to compete. One week after the 1924 Games, the International Ski Federation was founded, a governing organization that lent credibility to skiing. The World Ski Championships' new official status paved the way for skiing's inclusion in the Olympics.

The next step came in 1931 when the International Ski Federation designated downhill and slalom as the two sanctioned events in international competition for men and women. Giant slalom, which is skiing between wider gates placed farther apart, was experimented with as early as 1935, though not sanctioned until 1972. (The Super G, a similar downhill race with gates, was accepted into competition even later, in 1987.)

Clubs, nationals, international championships: this was the women's race circuit until 1935. Then in 1936, women athletes—including Alpine and Nordic skiers—were invited to compete in the Olympics. But the United States had yet to form a women's Olympic team. Roland Palmedo, president of the Amateur Ski Club of New York, raised funds to partially finance the team and gave the task of selecting the racers to Mrs. Alice Damrosch Wolfe, herself a skier with experience managing women's teams in clubs throughout the United States. The selection process was informal, drawing from winners of the few women's competitions like the nationals and internationals and relying on word of mouth.

"In the summer of 1935 I wrote all the girls who had been on the 1935 International Ski Federation team plus the three best racers in the National championships at Mount Rainier, plus any other girl skiers I had heard of who seemed to be good enough to justify their training on an Olympic Squad," Wolfe recounts in the American Olympics Committee's account of the 1936 games. Wolfe's invitations sparked a flurry of early arrivals to train at St. Anton in the Austrian Alps, where the team was to be selected. The young women received financial assistance from money raised by Palmedo but primarily funded their own chance to try for the team. The official time to report was January 2, but most of the women showed up in early December. "I think all those girls thought about was training and getting into condition to make that team," writes Wolfe.

Eight women were selected for the American team and went on to Garmisch in Partenkirchen, Germany, a week and a half before the 1936 Olympics. Hotel bookings were tight as athletes assembled for the games, and the U.S. girls' team was housed in a tiny pension along with the German girls' team. Days later, Elizabeth "Betty" Woolsey, Clarita Heath, Helen Boughton-Leigh, and Mary Bird were the four Americans chosen to compete. Unfortunately, their enthusiasm and intense preparation proved inadequate when pitted against the Europeans, who benefited from a long tradition of skiing.

Europe was the epicenter of skiing, and European men and women were skiing's top competitors until after World War II. Not only was Europe the primary resort area; it was the place where the most innovative equipment was developed and instruction progressed. From that solid cultural base, European skiers were obviously going to be far superior to their American counterparts.

Betty Woolsey, the first among the American women, placed fourteenth in the downhill and nineteenth in the combined downhill and slalom. She ranked behind Germany, Norway, Switzerland, Great Britain, Italy, Austria, Holland, and Canada. Norway's Lail Schou-Nilsen won the downhill, taking third in the combined. Winning a majority of races, the German women dominated. In the combined event, Germans Christel Cranz placed first, Kathe Grazegger second, Hadi Pfeifer fifth, and Lisa Resch sixth. One can only imagine the Americans' disappointment laid bare before the Germans in that tiny pension on the evenings following each race. The pairing had been inauspicious. Four years later, the 1940 Olympic games were canceled because of World War II. The American skiers who had qualified for the Olympic team would have to wait.

At the onset of World War II, military forces around the world, from the United States to Russia, used skiing as a military tactic. Finland soldiers on skis led the way by defending their country against the Germans at the start of the war. The United States took note and recruited its best Alpine skiers for training in the 10th Mountain Division. Women's international skiing competition virtually halted. Resources were limited, and everyone was preoccupied with the war effort. Yet though competition suffered, the sport as a whole benefited from techniques and equipment developed by the military. After the war, those innovations were used to enhance recreational and competitive skiing. Improvements to over-the-snow transportation and cable-lift construction and the use of metal and alloy materials to construct chair lifts and rope tows made skiing easier and more fun. Wooden skis were replaced by faster lightweight metal skis, designed specifically for downhill and slalom. Lightweight synthetics like nylon replaced cotton and wool clothing. The public had access to flight, and travel to resorts became less expensive and available to the middle class. Skiing was no longer the domain of the wealthy.

Straddling this era of transition was the remarkable career of girlish, Cheshire-grinned Gretchen Fraser, who would be the first American to win an Olympic medal in skiing. Fraser was born in Tacoma, Washington, and learned to ski at her family-owned ski resort, Paradise Valley, one of three resorts on Mount Rainier that later consolidated into what is now Crystal Mountain. Fraser's parents were both from Europe: her Norwegian mother immigrated to the United States when she was twenty, her German father when he was twenty-two. The couple instilled their love of skiing in their daughter, a natural athlete who also played golf and tennis, rode horses, and flew airplanes. Eager for challenge, Fraser became adept at maneuvering a twin-engine Cessna, single- and multi-engines, seaplanes, and instrument-rating aircrafts. She also mastered the business of flying twin-engine aircraft and the Army jet trainer T-33, in which she won two air races.

In 1936 Fraser met and married ski racer Don Fraser and moved to Sun Valley, Idaho, where in 1940 they were named to the U.S. ski team. When Olympic competition halted because of the war, Fraser raced in national competitions, capturing the U.S. national downhill and Alpine combined championships in 1941 and winning the U.S. national slalom in 1942. Feeling as if she had nothing further to master, she retired and taught skiing, riding, and swimming to war amputees while her husband served in the U.S. Navy. When the war ended, Fraser's husband prodded her back into racing, convincing her, then twenty-nine, to attempt to qualify for the 1948 Olympics, to be held in St. Moritz, Switzerland.

With the war over, the Olympics drew audiences looking for celebration and sport. Fraser's twelve-year bid for the Olympics (she'd been a hopeful since 1936), paired with her age, old even by the competition standards of the time, made her a crowd favorite. She did not let them down. She stunned the world, who had yet to see an American, let alone an American woman, do well in international competition. She took second in the Alpine combined, a double race event no longer a part of racing. Her silver medal victory was the first medal won by an American skier.

Fraser responded to her victory with the declaration that she would take home a second medal by also winning in slalom. To do so, she had to beat Austrian Erika Mahringer, Europe's top-ranking female skier, who had beaten her in the Alpine combined on the first of two runs. At the second go-around, Fraser held the fastest time. However, four women, including Mahringer, were within a second of her. As she stood at the starting gate, ready to launch herself down the mountain for her second run, the starter's race phone went dead. She waited, shivering, for seventeen minutes, while a telephone line linking the top of the course to the bottom of the course was repaired. She nevertheless maintained her poise and concentration, running a perfect, controlled descent to a gold-medal win. Even today, athletes note the form and speed she maintained in spite of gear considered klunky and the debilitating technical difficulties she had waited through. Following the less successful bid of the women's Olympic squad in 1936, Fraser's show of force in 1948 became an inspiration for later generations of American skiers.

"I remember seeing pictures of her in Sun Valley," says eighteen-time World Cup winner Tamara McKinney, who made her mark in the 1980s as one of history's most accomplished Alpine skiers. "She just had the greatest technique: the good angulation of the knee, the aggressive stance. You could tell she was going for it in this picture. It looked very solid and balanced, and then you looked down and she had on these little short leather boots that would lace up." Fraser was inducted into the U.S. National Ski Hall of Fame in 1960. She died at seventy-five on the eve of the 1994 Olympics in Lillehammer, just over a month after the death of her husband of fifty-four years.

Competing alongside Fraser, finishing eighth in the slalom, twenty-first in the Alpine combined, and thirty-fifth in the downhill, fifteen-year-old Andrea Mead Lawrence had her first taste of the intensity of international competition. Lawrence had been skiing since she was three at the ski area her parents ran in Pico Peak, Vermont. She debuted in the 1948 Olympics as the team's youngest member. By 1950, the intelligent, well-spoken Lawrence had matured as an athlete under the tutelage of a Swiss ski instructor who worked at her parents' resort. She finished first in downhill, slalom, and combined at the U.S. nationals. A year later, she placed first in ten international competitions in a circuit that later became known as the World Cup.

By the time she arrived at the 1952 Olympics in Oslo, Norway, Lawrence had established herself as a champion, a reputation that she proved yet again. She won a first gold medal in giant slalom by an impressive 2.2-second margin. No one was quite prepared, though, for her even more remarkable slalom win. After falling during the first of two runs, she skied the course to a fourth-place finish. For her second run, she knew that if she was going to make it, she had to go for broke. She did, finishing two seconds faster than anyone else, an outstanding margin for slalom. Her combined scores won her another gold, making her the first U.S. skier to win two Olympic golds, a record that still stands. She had a chance for a third gold medal in the downhill race. Her split time was better than the other competitors, but she fell again; this time unable to regain the loss, she finished seventeenth.

With the exception of Fraser and Lawrence, Europeans continued to dominate both men's and women's Alpine skiing until Tamara McKinney's debut in the 1980s. The same was true for Nordic skiing. Northern Europeans, especially Norwegians, flourished in cross-country skiing competition until the 1990s, when Russian teams began to win. There are three primary competitions in cross-country: the standard distance races of fifteen to fifty kilometers; ski jumping; and the biathlon, a cross-country race with target shooting at intervals, derived from the military ski patrol race.

Excelling in cross-country was a source of intense national pride for the Norwegians. Not only did skiing begin in their country, the Norwegians, who won their independence from Sweden in 1905, viewed cross-country as a way for its citizens to develop athletic skills and strong moral character. A Norwegian household without several pairs of skinny skis lined up outside the mud room was a rare sight. Cross-country was Norway's equivalent of America's baseball. It was a common interest around which to rally. Perhaps in response to the Europeans' enduring command of Alpine and Nordic, and certainly related to the new popularity of recreational skiing on U.S. slopes, Americans turned their focus to freestyle. The newfangled discipline that combined dance, acrobatics, and skiing was the perfect match for America's less traditional skiing culture. And Suzy Chaffee was the perfect athlete to lead the way.

The first record of freestyle is traced to the nineteenth century in Telemark, Norway, where Nordic skiers had to master a series of techniques that included turning, jumping, and skiing straight downhill at high speeds. During the 1930s, Norwegian ski champions used skiing acrobatics as part of their training and performed acrobatics in skiing exhibitions. Ski instructor Mathias Zdarsky taught simple acrobatics in the European Alps as part of his ski instruction during the late nineteenth and early twentieth centuries. In 1926 Zdarsky's contemporary, the German medical doctor and figure skater Fritz Reul, wrote a book advocating acrobatics as the future direction for skiing. While acrobatics was accepted by the Europeans as a training enhancer for Alpine and Nordic skiers, they did not consider this style worthy of competition. In contrast, America's skiing culture was intrigued by the style, which grew out of leisure skiing. The sport debuted in the 1950s, when Stein Ericksen, an Olympic champion and accomplished acrobatic skier from Norway, immigrated to the United States and began showing freestyle at exhibitions. The four areas of freestyle competition are mogul; acroski, formally known as ballet; aerial; and combined.

Freestyle was perfect for Suzy Chaffee, because it paired three disciplines she was experienced in: dance, skiing, and gymnastics. Chaffee was born in 1947 to a father who was a ski jumper and a mother who was an alternate for the 1940 U.S. Alpine Olympic team. Her parents had her on the slopes by the time she was two. Unlike most other skiers, however, she studied classical ballet as well as logging long hours on the mountain. By 1965, when she'd qualified as a member of the U.S. Alpine ski team, she was also an accomplished dancer. In 1967, after she took fourth in downhill at the

World Ski Championship held in Portillo, Chile, she was the highest-ranked American woman in Alpine competitions. When the ski team traveled to the 1968 Olympics in Grenoble, France, Chaffee was their captain. Following the winter games, she decided she wanted a new challenge and switched from Alpine to freestyle.

Though fans had always been enamored of the glamour of freestyle, it had taken a decade for the style to receive recognition by the skiing establishment. Freestyle was considered excessively flamboyant. When a few competitors suffered severe spinal cord injuries, the sport's reputation took another hit—it was now considered dangerous, too. But in 1979 the International Skiing Federation finally acknowledged freestyle, in response to popular demand. Mogul and aerial events were allowed in the Olympics thirteen years later, in 1992. Though it took a while to win over the sports executives, it was much easier to win over audiences. The jumps, flips, and fast mogul maneuvering of freestyle skiing is a spectator favorite, and at its inception, Chaffee was a main draw.

Leggy, attractive, and vivacious, Suzy Chaffee was the perfect person to legitimize freestyle. Because there was no women's division in the early years of freestyle, she won three consecutive world championships, from 1971 to 1973, competing against the men. She also broke new ground as one of the first freestyle performers to add musical accompaniment to her routines. Though her athletic ability was impressive, in fairness, a good measure of her fame came from publicity off the slopes. She was Suzy Chap Stick, the ski bunny who promoted Chap Stick lip balm, and she also appeared seminude in a *Town & Country* photo spread. These promotional stunts proved that a woman athlete could earn substantial money. Chaffee also was an outspoken advocate of legislation that benefited women. In public appearances she promoted skiing and made it easier for the next generation of skiers to get attention.

In the 1990s, Donna Weinbrecht became the prominent woman freestyle skier. With a background as a figure skater and Alpine skier, Weinbrecht turned to freestyle in her early twenties, coaching herself for three years. In 1988 she finished first in the U.S. freestyle championships at Stratton Mountain, Vermont, and was named World Cup Rookie of the Year. She also specializes in mogul skiing and reigned as the U.S. champion between 1988 and 1992, winning the world championship in moguls in 1991 and an Olympic gold medal in 1992. Four years later, in 1996, she became the World Cup mogul champion.

At the 1998 Olympics, a third American freestyle skier, aerialist Nikki Stone, came to the fore when she won a gold medal, a feat made more remarkable by the fact that two years earlier she'd been told that a back injury would keep her from ever skiing again.

* * *

European women continued to dominate Alpine throughout the 1970s. Many people consider Austrian Annemarie Moser-Proell the best skier of that decade, although she didn't win an Olympic gold medal until 1980. The best American women skiers were Kiki Cutter, who in 1969 became the first American skier to win a World Cup title; Cindy Nelson, who in 1974 became the first U.S. skier to win a World Cup downhill title; and Barbara Ann Cochran, who won a gold medal in slalom at the 1972 Olympics. West Germany's Rosi Mittermeier, who in 1976 won Olympic golds in downhill and slalom, won a silver in giant slalom, and became the World Cup overall champion, was another force to be reckoned with.

Annemarie Moser-Proell began skiing at age four on a pair of hand-made skis carved by her father. At five feet, six inches, and 150 pounds, she was a strong, solid competitor. Between 1971 and 1975 she was the overall World Cup champion, a title no other woman has won more than twice. In the same five-year period, she competed in thirty-three downhill races, placing first twenty-one times and second eleven times. Her Olympic performances, however, were imperfect. At the 1972 Olympics in Sapporo, Japan, she lost two gold medals to Switzerland's Marie Therese Nadig, settling for a silver in downhill and giant slalom. American Cindy Nelson beat her in the World Cup downhill in 1974. The following year, in 1975, she retired for one year at age twenty-two, got married, and opened a café.

This window allowed Rosi Mittermeier to pull off her remarkable sweep in the 1976 Olympics in Innsbruck, capturing a gold in downhill, a gold in slalom, and a silver in giant slalom, making her one of the most decorated women in Alpine skiing. That same year, she became the overall World Cup champion. At twenty-five, she was the oldest Alpine skier competing. Her accomplishments are even more spectacular, given her accident-prone history. She barely survived her complicated birth; she nearly died at six months when a goat crushed her baby carriage and again at age two when she swallowed rat poison. As an adult, she broke her arm skiing into a tourist and nearly blinded herself colliding with a slalom pole while skiing.

Perhaps it was Mittermeier's success that prodded Moser-Proell out of retirement. It took her three years to get back into shape and back in contention. By 1979 she qualified again for the Olympics, in Lake Placid, New York. Competing in the downhill at the age of twenty-seven, Moser-Proell finally won her Olympic gold medal.

Alpine skier Barbara Ann Cochran deserves mention because of her gold medal in slalom in the 1972 Olympics in Sapporo, Japan. The course was treacherously icy, and only nineteen of forty-two entrants completed both runs. Cochran didn't have a long career, but her Olympic performance was encouraging for ten-year-old Tamara McKinney watching the Games from home. "That was the first Olympics that I consciously remember," says McKinney. "I was watching ski racing and thinking, 'OK, that's what I want to do.' When Barbara Ann Cochran won the slalom, I remember thinking, 'Someday I want to do that.'"

On the wall in Tamara McKinney's home in Squaw Valley, California, there is a photo of her maternal grandmother leaping off a ski jump wearing a long black dress. McKinney's mother, Frances, was equally passionate about skiing, providing every opportunity that she could for her brood of seven. The McKinney children grew up on the ski touring circuit, homeschooled and coached by their mother. The family lived from race to race, settling for the best accommodations they could find at each ski area. Sometimes that meant forgoing hot water and heat. The youngest sibling, Tamara, grew up taking her afternoon naps in a suitcase her mother would bring to the races. While the family toured the circuit, their father, former steeplechase jockey Rigan McKinney, bred horses at their home in Kentucky. Eventually, Frances's efforts paid off, when Tamara, her older brother Steve, and her older sister Sheila all qualified for the U.S. national team as teenagers.

A diminutive racer at five feet, three inches, and varying between 115 and 130 pounds, McKinney knew she had the talent. She just didn't know how to harness it at first. "I knew that I had the ability to create a lot of speed when I skied, but I really didn't know what to do with it," she says. "I just knew it was something that I needed to be true to."

Being true to her speed placed McKinney full-time in the World Cup circuit by the time she was fifteen in 1978. At her first major European event, she took third. Her next major win was the World Cup giant slalom title in 1981. Then in 1983 in the world championships held in Furano, Japan, she became the first American woman to win the World Cup title, in tight competition with defending champion Erica Hess of Switzerland and two-time champion Hanni Wenzel of Liechtenstein. McKinney skied in the 1984 Olympics, placing fourth in giant slalom. "I remember when I won my first race, and I was told, 'You are the best in the world today.' I thought, 'But you know what? I can do it again. I can do it again.'" says McKinney.

The next several years were emotionally McKinney's darkest, and they dramatically affected her skiing. Between 1985 and 1988, she lost her father to a stroke, her mother to cancer, and a brother to suicide. These sad events came on top of earlier family tragedies. When McKinney was fourteen, her older sister Sheila had slammed into a post while racing in a World Cup downhill, rendering her unable to walk or talk normally for an entire year. A few years after that, her brother had been seriously injured in a helicopter accident. Competition served as an anchor for McKinney. She won bronze medals in the combined events at the 1985 and 1987 world championships. At the 1988 Calgary Olympics, still healing from a broken left leg, she was unable to finish the giant slalom or the slalom. In 1989, though, she made her comeback. She took the gold in the women's combined at the world championships held in Vail, Colorado, beating the favored Vreni Schneider of Switzerland. That victory meant more to McKinney than all the rest, because of how much she'd overcome. "I'd been through so much more," she says. "In 1989 I came into the world championships with a lot of pressure, and I thought, 'Watch me. This one's mine.'"

Before retiring in 1991, McKinney had swept the 1980s World Champion Alpine competition, winning eighteen World Cup races—nine in giant slalom and nine in slalom. But she wasn't the only skier during this decade to make a name for herself. The same year McKinney placed fourth in the giant slalom, Debbie Armstrong surprised some of the finest skiers in the world by winning the gold at the 1984 Olympics. She was a twenty-year-old from Seattle with only a few races under her belt and a silver medal in combined from the 1983 U.S. nationals. She followed up her Olympic win by becoming the U.S. national champion in slalom in 1987 and qualified for the 1988 Olympics, where she failed to win another medal, and soon after retired from ski competition.

Diana Golden, a disabled athlete, also charmed the ski community. Golden began skiing as a child, but when doctors discovered cancer in her right leg, they amputated it to prevent the disease from spreading. She was devastated but decided that she still wanted to ski. A few months later, with her doctors' approval she was back on the slopes, using the same equipment as everyone else. The only difference was that she was using only one leg. She skied recreationally until her junior year in high school, when she caught the attention of a varsity skiing coach. She was asked if she wanted to ski on the team. The workouts were rigorous, but she kept up. Within a year, she'd qualified for the World Games for Disabled Athletes. Between 1986 and 1990, Golden won ten gold medals at the World Handicapped Championships and nineteen U.S. championship titles. In 1988 she won an Olympic gold medal in the giant slalom for disabled skiers. But the accomplishment she's most proud of came in 1987, when she ranked in the top ten in an open slalom race as the only disabled skier in the field. Golden's achievements as an athlete stand out beyond the fact that she was disabled. In 1986 she won the Beck Award as the best U.S. skier in international competition. Two years later, *Ski* magazine named her U.S. Female Alpine Skier of the Year and the U.S. Olympic Committee deemed her its Female Skier of the Year.

By the seventh decade of women's competitive skiing, women skiers had gained a reputation as a marketable commodity. The money started coming in. By the early 1980s, with the boom of the ski industry, an entire system was instated to subsidize skiers based on merit. In the United States, equipment companies supplied funds directly to the national team, which distributed a share to each skier. Skiers also earned prize money. Amateur competition rules that had limited an athlete's access to endorsements relaxed, and skiers were able to have their own personal sponsors. Suzy Chaffee had proved during the 1970s that a ski celebrity could get rich. At the time, her circumstances were unique. By the 1980s, several top-tier women skiers could anticipate lucrative earnings. It is estimated that McKinney's salary netted in the six figures for a number of years, enough to secure a comfortable retirement and allow her to turn to her family's second love, horse breeding and riding.

During the 1990s, skiing's future began to take shape with the rise of superstar Picabo Street. Street wasn't just a skier. She was a personality who became women's skiing's poster girl. To Street, her unprecedented wins were all part of some larger plan. "There are times when I'm really shocked and times when I'm like, 'This is what was meant for me; this is my destiny,'" she told *Skiing* magazine in 1995.

Street was born on April 3, 1971, in Triumph, Idaho, to Stubby and Dee Street. Classic sixties holdovers, they named her Baby Girl Street, but since the government wasn't enthralled about generic names on passports, Stubby and Dee picked the name Picabo, which in the Native American Sho-Ban tribe located nearby is supposed to mean shining waters. Street lived an unconventional childhood. She traveled through Central America with her family, took long domestic cross-country road trips, grew her own food, chopped wood, and was raised in a house with no television. The one convention was this: Like most children growing up outside of Sun Valley, she began skiing at an early age. She didn't start racing until her high school formed a varsity team, but the five-foot-seven-inch Street, who weighs in at 158 pounds, was aggressive and fast. When she made the U.S. ski team a year later, she was relying primarily on natural talent, winning the national junior downhill and Super G titles in 1988 at the age of sixteen.

Natural talent and nothing else began to look like laziness. In 1990 she was kicked off the U.S. ski team when she showed up for training unprepared and out of shape. She got her act together, rejoined the team, and in four years, between 1991 and 1995, rose from sixty-fifth to eighteenth to eighth to first rank in world downhill. Then she won her silver medal in downhill at the winter Olympics in Lillehammer. Her Olympic medal was followed by a string of victories at the World Cup during the 1994–95 season. After winning six out of nine downhill races, she became the first American woman to win the World Cup title.

Following a successful 1996 World Cup season, Street began training for the 1998 Games in Nagano, Japan. Then tragedy struck. In 1997, during a training run at Vail, Colorado, she spun out of control and tore the anterior cruciate ligament in her left knee. It's rare for an athlete to compete again at top level following such an injury. Yet with the help of the doctors at Vail's famous Stedman Clinic, as well as her trainers, Street believed that with aggressive rehabilitation she could regain her position and make it to the Nagano games one year away. It was a crapshoot, which she undertook with characteristic gusto. Just months before the Games, her comeback was on course. Then she knocked herself unconscious during a crash in Are, Sweden. Things looked bleak to everyone, but not to Street. Considering the complications, her hairbreadth 1998 Olympic victory was all the sweeter.

Street's topsy-turvy adventure toward fame soon became a smoother ride. Her bubbly joie de vivre has drawn in fans and lured the media. (Following the 1994 Olympics she said no to appearances on Jay Leno's and David Letterman's late-night shows but yes to *American Gladiators* and *Sesame Street*. In 1998 she changed her mind and was a guest on *Letterman*.) The corporate world has also taken notice of her public appeal. Street has endorsement deals with Nike, United Airlines, and Chap Stick. She's Nike's only female winter-sport athlete, and in 1998 the company introduced her signature Nike sneaker, the Air Max Electrify. Before her 1998 Olympic gold medal win, she told *Time* magazine that she wanted to become a talk-show host. "Every time I watch Rosie O'Donnell, I think about it more," she said. "I want to do that with athletes so that the world can see all these powerful and funny personalities."

While Street was grabbing the limelight at the 1994 and 1998 Olympics, other women quietly claimed their own victories. Thirteen-year U.S. ski team veteran and 1997 world downhill champion Hillary Lindh had a frank, humble attitude about her own brilliant career. For years Lindh provided the team's only real competition for Street, and though now they've patched up their differences, often their relationship was rocky. The two couldn't be more different. While Street fielded attention from the press, younger ski team members looked to Lindh as their role model. She was the calm, exemplary mother of the team.

Lindh competed in three Olympics and four world championships, capturing the 1986 world junior downhill championship, the 1986 and 1989 U.S. downhill championships, and the 1992 U.S. combined championship. In 1992 she became the first Alaskan to win an individual Olympic medal when she took the silver in downhill. She retired from the team in 1998, following her championship win and a string of equally impressive accomplishments. The Juneau, Alaska, native was born May 10, 1969, to a mother who herself had entertained Olympic dreams. "I think it's really neat that my mom grew up racing Nordic and Alpine," she says, "and though she didn't have anywhere near the opportunities during the fifties that I had, she passed that talent down to me and I was able to go to the Olympics."

There were other standouts during Picabo Street's skiing career. Canadian-born Julie Parisien, who competed on the U.S. ski team, won the silver medal in slalom at the 1993 world championships and took first in the giant slalom at the 1991 U.S. World Cup. American Diane Roffe-Steinrotter was the 1994 Olympic gold medalist in the Super G and the 1992 Olympic silver medalist in the giant slalom. German Katja Seizinger, the 1994 Olympic downhill gold medalist, was a top contender against Street entering the 1998 Olympics; at that point, Seizinger was the World Cup circuit's overall-points leader. U.S. ski team member Kristina Koznick in 1998 pulled in her first World Cup win in slalom just prior to the Olympics, only to disqualify herself in a bid for the bronze when she straddled a gate during her second slalom run. At the Nagano Games, however, while others received attention from the skiing community, the world seemed to have eyes only for Street.

Snowboarding and Nordic have had their own respectable journeys into the public eye. It's probably fair to say that snowboarding's route was more of a party-fest, while Nordic was a test of endurance. True to the nature of Nordic, athletes from that discipline continued to plod a solid, steady path, drawing fewer spectators to their less glamorous events. By the 1990s, when the Russians began to win over the Norwegians, the Americans still fell far behind in competitions, though the sport was catching on recreationally. Not so with snowboarding, where once again the open-minded United States became the center for development of a nontraditional event.

If freestyle was the Woodstock of the sixties, then snowboarding was the decade's mosh pit. The epitome of a fringe sport, it sprang from a young, rebellious generation. As early as 1913, however, sledders had fashioned the first snowboards from barrels. Leather straps secured the riders, who navigated the crude sleds using a rope tied to the nose of the barrel. In 1966 snow surfers, known as Snurfers, became the first mass-produced snowboards. Snowboarders steered their way down a slope by pulling a rope that was crudely attached to the board, which was similar to a large skateboard. Staples covering the deck provided traction for the rider's feet. Needless to say, Snurfers were difficult to control, prompting ski resorts to ban them from the slopes. Thus began snowboarding's cult pilgrimage to the backcountry that lasted through the 1970s.

By the late 1980s, snowboarding had nonetheless caught on, and by the 1990s, it was becoming the fastest-growing ski sport, spawning a U.S. team and exhibitions. Today, more than two and a half million people snowboard. In the meantime, ski resorts reopened their slopes to boarders—the moneymaking potential was too great to pass up. Then, a final gesture of acceptance: snowboarding was included as an official sport in the 1998 Olympic Games.

Like many snowboard enthusiasts, Sondra Van Ert started out as an Alpine skier. She made the U.S. ski team in 1984 when she was twenty, retiring two years later to finish a college degree in finance. For pleasure she tried snowboarding and got hooked. She loved the floating sensation she got when boarding through powder and the G forces she felt when generating a turn. Van Ert was considered relatively old to compete; nevertheless, she joined the U.S. snowboarding team in 1995 when she was thirty-one. In 1997 she placed first in grand slalom at the world championships in San Condido, Italy. She also placed first in the 1996 and 1997 World Cup competitions. In the 1998 Olympics, she was the top contender for a gold medal in the snowboard giant slalom. Although she ended up placing twelfth, she was proud to be an Olympian and proud to be a boarder. "We're a real varied bunch of people," she says of the snowboarding clan. "For me it's been a lesson, having people judge me because I'm on a snowboard. If they saw me still wearing my U.S. ski team uniform, they'd be drooling. Instead, I'm on a snowboard and they think I'm scum. That really bothers me. I think the Olympics is enriched by having snowboarding. Snowboarding is still in its infancy. The athletes are only there because they love it. The snowboarders still come down to the crowd smiling and waving and congratulating the people who did better than they did. It embodies what the Olympics is supposed to be."

Nordic ski racing entails grueling mileage through isolated countryside and enjoys quite a different reputation. "Freestyle and snowboarding are very, very glamorous," says U.S. Nordic ski team member Nina Kemppel. "And we certainly are in the shadow of the obvious giant, Alpine skiing. You have to really be a fairly secure person to go out and put everything on the line in a 10K in the woods where no one can see you. That's what we do. We go out and hurt our bodies because we love this sport."

Kemppel, an Alaskan native, has been on the U.S. team for nine years and is considered the best U.S woman Nordic skier. Internationally, she has competed in two Olympics and finished in the top twenty in two World Cup events. Because in the United States Nordic skiing receives relatively little funding, Kemppel and fellow team member Kerrin Petty live in Norway so they can train with top-level Norwegian and Swedish clubs.

While Norwegian women swept the field during the 1970s, Russian women prevailed during the 1990s. Russian Lyubov Egorova is one of the most decorated athletes in the history of the Winter Games. She has won the gold medal in numerous Olympic competitions, including the 5-kilometer classical in 1994; the 4- and 5-kilometer mixed relay in 1992 and 1994; the 10-kilometer freestyle pursuit in 1992 and 1994; and the 15-kilometer freestyle in 1992. Following the 1997 world championships, Egorova's career came to an abrupt halt after she failed a drug test and admitted that she had used a banned substance. Her gold medal win in the 5K competition was revoked, and she was suspended from competition until 2001. Soon after, she announced her retirement.

In the fall of 1997, Alpine skier Jill Sickles Matlock, snowboarder Bonnie Zellers, and telemark skier Kasha Rigby ventured into New Zealand's Mount Aspiring National Park to climb Mount Aspiring, then descend on their respective boards. Though the trio's plans were waylaid by bad weather and only Matlock made it up and down the peak, their North Face–sponsored expedition was a symbol of several future trends in women's skiing, one of which is the adventure off piste. More and more, backcountry skiing is preferred by skiers seeking to push the limits of their sport. There's higher risk, due to avalanche danger, unstable terrain, and exposure to bad weather. Backcountry skiing also offers a more solitary experience when compared to skiing at crowded, lift-accessed areas.

The fact that Matlock, Zellers, and Rigby all began as Alpine skiers at groomed ski resorts is also typical of the adventure skiing trend. After reaching a pinnacle, all decided to move into what is called extreme skiing. At thirty-four, Matlock was one of the best off-piste Alpine skiers in the world. In 1994 in her first backcountry skiing competition, she won the U.S. Extreme Skiing Championships. In those competitions, the skiers select their own course down a mountain. They are judged by the difficulty of the line they choose and how successfully they ski it. Since her first win, Matlock has taken fifth, second, and third in the World Extreme Skiing Championships and first in the 1996 U.S. championship. Rigby is one of the best women in the world in telemark skiing, a free-heeled style of downhill skiing that traces back to Nordic roots. In 1993 she took fourth place as the sole telemarker in the U.S. Extreme Skiing Championship. As a snowboarder, Zellers claims more first descents than any other woman in the world, among them the Col du Aiguille Verte and the Puobel Couloir in Chamonix. In 1990 she was named snowboarder of the year by *International Snowboard* magazine.

Trips like this generate a lot of interest. This is good news for women who wish to raise enough money to support their adventure trips, as these women did through North Face. In fact, the all-women's trip was considered important enough to become a *Women's Sports & Fitness* magazine cover story.

Whether the credit goes to Picabo Street's outsized ego, Title IX legislation securing equal access to sports for girls and women, or the fans who proved the popularity of women's sports during the 1998 summer Olympic Games in Atlanta, the corporate world now knows that women's sports generate revenue. Top athletes like Street can become celebrities. Athletes like Matlock, Rigby, and Zellers can get money to fund their adventures. But perhaps even more significant is how the accomplishments of the elite have transformed the sport for the average skier. Whether Alpine, Nordic, freestyle, or snowboard, whether downhill at a ski area, skating on a track, or touring in the backcountry, all women can enjoy the opportunities and respect earned by a century's worth of dedicated women: a century spent floating over snow.

Figure Skating

Gaining an Edge
Michelle Kaufman

Women's figure skating has been around for nearly a century, and still the debate rages: Is it a sport or is it a beauty pageant? Seemingly dainty young women glide across the ice in glamorous sequined dresses, their faces in full makeup, their hair perfect, their nails manicured. They spin, bend, leap, and stretch their fingertips like ballerinas. They make it look easy when they launch their bodies off the ice on the edge of a blade, twist three times in the air, and land softly on the back edge of the opposite blade. They smile afterward, flower bouquets in their arms, waiting for judges' marks, and then they wave to the crowd, like Miss Universe contestants.

But most people don't see these women after their performances, drenched in sweat, gasping for air, massaging their sore muscles. Most people don't see these women in sweatshirts and mittens, training at six A.M. in bitter cold rinks, jumping and falling, jumping and falling, jumping and falling, until they land just right.

The sport still goes by its original name, ladies figure skating, despite all the strides of women's liberation. Style and elegance and "ladylike" behavior are still expected of women figure skaters in the modern era, in addition to the physically grueling triple lutz jumps, dizzying spins, and combination jumps. Judges award two sets of marks, one for technical merit and one for artistic presentation. Scores range from 0.0 (not skated) to 6.0 (perfect), and the two marks are weighted equally. Female figure skaters must exhibit power and athleticism and at the same time look like porcelain dolls.

It is a sport that, despite its name and image, has been a declaration of freedom for nearly a century's worth of female skaters; for what could be more liberating than gliding across a giant sheet of ice for four minutes, all alone, soaring into the air, attempting daring trick after daring trick with no net underneath, and landing cleanly on a single blade? And in what other sport could a woman make a million dollars in 1939?

When precocious eleven-year-old Sonja Henie showed up on the world figure skating scene in 1924, she had no idea that she would change the sport forever. Even after her death, her daring moves and theatrics would live on in the skating of Dorothy Hamill, Nancy Kerrigan, Tonya Harding, Michelle Kwan, and Tara Lipinski, skating's current star.

Lipinski became the youngest Olympic figure skating champion in history when she won the gold medal in Nagano, Japan, at the 1998 Games at the age of fifteen. She was sixty days younger than Henie was when she won the 1928 Olympics.

Seventy years separated their gold medals, but watching gutsy Lipinski—all eighty pounds of her—leaping and darting across the ice, a giant smile across her face, was like watching a crackly, black-and-white Sonja Henie film reel come to life; except that Lipinski was landing jumps Henie never even dreamed about, jumps that had been reserved for men for nearly a century.

Henie joined the sport in 1924, when women skaters wore extravagant hats and bulky skirts that covered their ankles. Skating was, after all, an outdoor sport in those days, and heavy clothes protected women from the blustery winds, snow, and rain that often fell during competitions and training sessions. But the main reason women skaters wore long skirts was that exposing their legs would have been considered unladylike. Female skaters were discouraged from jumping because their knees might be exposed if their voluminous skirts flew up. Judges were known to deduct points at the glimpse of a thigh or kneecap.

At the time, figure skating was a favorite sport of kings and queens, movie stars, czars, and princesses. It was a graceful alternative to speed skating, a favorite sport of the European masses, and by the early 1900s, exclusive figure skating clubs were being formed all over Europe. The rich and privileged delighted in the sight of elegantly gowned women gliding across ice and tracing figure eights. The skaters' feet rarely left the ice, and that's exactly how the establishment liked it.

Henie, a dimpled, blond Norwegian, would revolutionize skating fashion, introduce athletic moves never before tried by women, add sex appeal and theater to what had been a demure sport, and expose figure skating to mainstream sports fans. Although her personal life didn't glide as smoothly as her skating performances, she would become hugely successful. By the time her career was finished, she would make far more money than baseball players Babe Ruth, Roger Maris, and Lou Gehrig combined. She made her first million dollars by age twenty-six and was worth an astonishing $47 million at the time of her death.

There were earlier pioneers in women's skating. British housewife Madge Syers rocked the establishment when she showed up with her husband, Edgar, at the 1902 men's world championships and entered the competition. There were no written rules to prevent a woman from competing, so the judges reluctantly allowed her to enter.

Syers, a champion swimmer and equestrian, skated better than her husband, and the judges awarded her a silver medal behind the great Ulrich Salchow, after whom the back-footed jump is named. Salchow reportedly was so impressed with Syers that he gave her his gold medal. The International Skating Union, determined not to be embarrassed again, immediately banned women from the event and four years later formed a women's championship, which Syers would win easily twice before winning Olympic gold in 1908.

American Theresa ("Tee") Weld, the 1920 Olympic bronze medalist, was the first woman to attempt a salchow jump and was reprimanded by judges for completing moves "unsuitable for a lady." Her early career was interrupted by World War I, but she would end up winning six U.S. titles in singles, nine U.S. pairs titles, and six U.S. ice dancing titles. Charismatic Charlotte Oelschlagel of Germany made a good living as a show skater in the late teens and early 1920s. She made her New York debut in 1915 and spent the next six years skating to packed audiences at the Hippodrome. But it was Henie who would earn the title Queen of the Ice, a title she has never relinquished.

Sonja Henie was born April 8, 1912. Her father, a wealthy Oslo fur merchant, owned the city's first automobile. He bought his daughter a pair of skates for Christmas when she was eight years old, and three years later, she pouted off the Olympic ice in Chamonix, France, with a last-place finish. Skating was a sport for adults, and judges frowned on the idea of a young girl entering such a prestigious competition.

The age issue would remain a contentious one for decades to come. Some judges in the 1990s disapproved of youngsters such as Michelle Kwan and Tara Lipinski, who raced past their peers in the novice and junior divisions, mastered the necessary tests with ease, breezed through regional and sectional championships, and entered senior-level world competition at age thirteen. Though they could jump as well as the best women in the sport—better, in most cases—their tiny bodies and childlike presence on the ice made many judges and fans wince. International judges often deducted artistic points from Kwan and Lipinksi during their first year as seniors, a reminder that they had to wait their turn.

Like Kwan would decades later, the young Henie was determined to win over the judges in her day. After that last-place Olympic finish, she begged her parents for more lessons, and they obliged. "Papa Henie," as her wide-girthed, imposing father was nicknamed, would do anything for his Sonja. It is often the case in individual sports such as figure skating, gymnastics, and tennis that the families of sports prodigies reach a point where they must decide whether to pull their children out of school and send them out of town to train with more prestigious coaches. Sonja traveled with her mother to Germany, England, Switzerland, and Austria to train under the best coaches and ballet teachers. No amount of money was too much for the Henies to spend if it meant their Sonja would be happy. Papa Henie was his daughter's biggest promoter and choreographed her every move on and off the ice. He even capitalized on his daughter's talent, going so far as to demand that a fancy car be donated for her to ride in and then turning around and selling the car for a profit.

Parents of modern-day skaters continue to make sacrifices in the name of the Olympic dream, and a costly dream it is. A national champion-caliber skater can spend upwards of $50,000 per year in training costs. There are coaches and choreographers to pay, tutors to hire, ice time to rent, dresses to buy, plane tickets to reserve, and skate boots to upkeep.

Lipinski's parents agreed to live apart so that Tara and her mother could move from Sugar Land, Texas, in search of better skating coaches. Nancy Kerrigan's parents double-mortgaged their home so she could continue taking private lessons. Shelby Lyons and her parents shared a one-bedroom apartment—Shelby slept in a walk-in closet—so that the teenage skater could train in Colorado.

In Henie's case, the time away from home paid off. When she arrived at the 1927 world championships in her hometown of Oslo, she was still relatively unknown. By the time the event was over, she was one of the most famous athletes in Europe.

Six women skated before Henie in that competition, all of them older than eighteen, all of them in ankle-length skirts, and all of them very serious as they traced their figures. The crowd applauded politely for each competitor. Then the public-address announcer introduced Henie, and the fourteen-year-old skated to center ice wearing a huge smile and a dazzling, tight-bodiced, white dress with a thigh-length bell skirt and white bloomers underneath. She grabbed each side of her skirt and curtsied while jaws dropped. Her mother had designed the dress not only to draw attention, but also to give her talented daughter more freedom of movement. "It had no folds or furbelows to confuse the picture of my movements," Henie wrote in her autobiography, *Wings on My Feet*. "If I never remembered any thing else I ever wore, I would remember that trim white velvet dress with its bell skirt."

But it was Henie's performance, more than the length of her skirt, that fans and judges would remember for years to come. Not only did she skate faster than anyone else and complete what were then considered difficult jumps—back-to-back single axels—but she seemed to float across the ice, dramatizing each figure with facial expressions, head movements, outstretched fingertips, and delicate swings of her free leg. It was clear that afternoon that Henie's inspiration had come from her favorite ballerina, Russian Anna Pavlova. Her love of dance also showed in her free-skating program, which was choreographed like a ballet, joining together her spins and jumps with elegant dance steps and tippy-toed sprints across the ice.

Henie's 1927 world title was not without controversy. There were five judges—three from Norway, one from Germany, and one from Austria. The Austrian and German judges gave first place to Herma Planck-Szabo of Austria, and the three Norwegians gave their vote to Henie. As a result of the protest that followed, the International Skating Union instituted a rule, still in effect, that allows only one judge per country in international events. Despite the rule, judging controversies continued. During the cold war, eastern bloc coaches were known to band together—"I'll give your girl 5.8s if you give my girl 5.8s."

But judges rarely disagreed on Henie after that 1927 world championship. She was clearly the best skater in the world and would win ten consecutive world titles, a feat matched only by salchow to this day. She also won seven consecutive European titles and won the Olympic gold medal in 1928, 1932, and 1936. By the time she retired, she had won 1,473 cups and medals.

Over those years, Henie would introduce figure skating to the masses and become one of the most well-known entertainers in the world. She especially enchanted young girls, who didn't have many sports role models at the time. When Henie entered the sport, women wore traditional black skating boots. She switched to beige boots and then white, and little girls everywhere followed suit.

In Norway, she drew crowds of thousands at docks, trains, just about anywhere she appeared in public. A crowd of thirty-five thousand showed up for an exhibition before the 1928 world championships in Bergen. A rowdy Henie crowd outside an exhibition in Sweden surrounded the car she was traveling in and had to be quelled by the military; a police escort was necessary whenever she traveled to the United States. In 1932, at the Olympics in Lake Placid, New York, scalpers got five dollars for tickets to Henie's performance, a hefty price considering it was the heart of the Great Depression. Joe Williams, a New York–based sportswriter of that era, wrote that Henie was "undoubtedly the biggest individual draw sports has ever produced."

Henie never shied away from the attention. She was known to travel with dozens of glitzy skating costumes and lavish jewels. She usually carried ten pairs of skates, most of them lined with expensive chamois. And if there was a camera nearby, she was flashing her trademark smile. By the time she retired from amateur skating in March 1936, Henie counted among her fans Queen Mary, King Edward VIII, and Norway's King Haakon, who telegraphed her before each performance. Crown prince Friedrich Wilhelm of Germany gave her his diamond stickpin.

Even Adolf Hitler was a Henie fan. The Nazi leader twice invited Henie and her parents to lunch at his home near Munich, and he presented her with an autographed, silver-framed photo of himself. Those visits were not well received by the Norwegian public. There were rumors that the Nazis were instructed not to harm the Henie property during the occupation of Norway. Though Henie never publicly praised Hitler, she didn't speak out against him, either.

In 1945, after newspaper stories questioned her loyalties, she reportedly donated $45,000 to the Norwegian war effort, but by then her image had already taken a hit. Her association with Hitler didn't scare off Hollywood promoters, however. Henie had made it no secret that her ambition was to be a movie star. She wanted to combine skating and theater on the silver screen, and promoters were tripping over themselves to sign her. "I want to do with skates what Fred Astaire is doing with dancing," she said. "No one has ever done it in the movies, and I want to."

Sixty years later, television promoters are doing the same thing with modern ice skaters, realizing that few shows draw ratings numbers higher than figure skating. Sports agents scout potential clients at the junior-level competitions, sign contracts with them as teenagers, and help them earn hundreds of thousands of dollars before they're eighteen.

Dennis Russell Scanlan, a New York promoter with connections in the movie business, got Henie a U.S. barnstorming tour after the 1936 Olympics. She headlined shows in New York, Chicago, Pittsburgh, St. Louis, Minneapolis, and Boston for $20,000 per night. Always afraid of being injured, she had her precious legs insured by Lloyds of London for $5,000 a week, the largest sum the company would underwrite. She also forbade women in her traveling troupe from wearing bobby pins, as they might fall out onto the ice, causing her to trip.

In 1936, 20th Century Fox offered Henie a five-year contract for two movies a year, each for about $125,000. Her first movie, *One in a Million,* was a huge success, and by 1939, the *Motion Picture Herald* ranked her the number-three draw in Hollywood, behind Shirley Temple and Clark Gable. Henie also figured out before most athletes that money could be made in merchandising, and she made over a million dollars on royalties from dolls and souvenirs.

The popularity and opulence of Henie's traveling Hollywood Ice Revue grew with each movie's success, although Henie was not so popular among her peers. She was a shrewd businesswoman, and her brash demeanor rubbed people the wrong way. Trained actors were irked that Henie, an athlete with no acting experience, could command monstrous movie deals.

The more money she made, the more lavish her lifestyle became. She enjoyed daily massages. In a day when most women didn't drive, she loved cruising around in one of her two cars—a Mercury Cabriolet and a sixteen-cylinder Cadillac. She was a perfectionist and was rarely satisfied with the quality of ice she encountered on her tours, so in 1949 she bought her own Zamboni ice-resurfacing machine for $10,000, becoming one of only three people in the world to own one. The tractorlike contraption traveled by train wherever she went. "She's really the one who got the word out there about my dad's invention," said Richard Zamboni, son of Frank, who built the first machine. "She'd stop in some city, and a few days later, we'd get a call from the arena saying they wanted a machine like Sonja Henie's."

She also was fastidious about her skate blades, and the only person she trusted to sharpen them was Eddie Pec, who lived in New York and would travel by train to Henie's dull blades whenever he was needed. Henie never slowed down. She made eleven movies between 1938 and 1960, and stayed in shape by playing tennis, skiing, and swimming. In fact, in 1935 she won the Norwegian national tennis title. She was always thin—five-foot-two and 110 pounds—but her muscular calves hinted at her strength. No woman of her day skated faster than she did or jumped higher. She raised athletic standards for the female figure skaters who came after her.

At age forty, Henie was still wiggling her hips in hula skirts, hamming it up with audiences, and skating full-speed in midriff-bearing costumes. She became a U.S. citizen in 1941. After two divorces, she married her teenage sweetheart, Norwegian Niels Onstad, a ship owner.

Henie considered a comeback to competition at age fifty-three, but it never happened. The ice queen was diagnosed with leukemia in 1968. Her shapely legs slowly lost their form. Her chubby cheeks became sunken. Though she remained draped in jewels throughout her illness, the sparkle in her eye was dimming. Henie died in her husband's arms on an ambulance plane from Paris to Oslo on October 12, 1969. She was fifty-seven.

Amateur figure skating in Europe collapsed after Henie's retirement in 1936. World War II was tearing Europe apart, and most of the great skaters and coaches were from Germany, France, and England. People had more important things to worry about than whether they could land a salchow, so rinks closed and coaches found themselves unemployed. Sequined costumes and shiny skate blades gathered dust while European girls struggled to survive the terrors of war.

Meanwhile, in the United States and Canada, the sport thrived, virtually unaffected by the war. Dozens of European coaches crossed the Atlantic in search of work, and North American skaters began to dominate world competitions. Thousands of little American girls, inspired by Henie's movies, signed up for skating lessons in the 1940s.

In 1947, at the age of eighteen, Barbara Ann Scott of Canada became the first North American to win a world title, and in 1948 she won the Olympic gold medal. Scott was the fastest spinner the world had seen. She was also one of the hardest working, having trained twenty thousand hours prior to the Olympics. Scott was known to practice outdoors in slush and subzero temperatures and often scraped snow off the ice herself. As a pro, she routinely did twelve shows on weekends.

The line between skating and entertainment got blurrier during Scott's career. Figure skaters began to pay as much attention to costumes and music selection as they did to the difficulty of jumps and spins, a trend that continues to this day. Skaters often sift through hundreds of music pieces before they find the perfect one, and world-class skaters spend several thousand dollars per year purchasing the perfect beaded and sequined dresses.

Scott, like Henie, liked wearing furs and jewels. The two skaters developed an intense rivalry, the likes of which wouldn't be seen again until the Tonya Harding–Nancy Kerrigan conflict of 1994. Though female skaters seem dainty and ladylike in their elegant costumes, their rivalries are often as fierce as those between heavyweight boxers. When Scott was twenty-three and Henie, at thirty-nine, was in the latter years of her career, Scott's press agent was quoted as saying, "Barbara Ann has such pretty legs compared with Sonja's."

After the war, while the European skating community tried to regroup, Scott and a couple of U.S. women dominated the amateur ranks. Tenley Albright, a polio victim and surgeon's daughter from Massachusetts, won two world titles and the 1956 Olympics. Carol Heiss, a blue-collar girl from Queens, New York, won five world titles—1956–60—before winning the Olympic gold in 1960. She attempted an acting career but quit after making her only movie, *Snow White and the Three Stooges*, to become a skating coach.

American dominance came to a halt when tragedy struck in 1961, and the tremors were felt all over the skating world. America's next generation of skaters—the entire U.S. team—was killed on February 15, 1961, when the plane carrying them to the world championships crashed in Belgium on its way to Prague, Czechoslovakia. Eighteen skaters, sixteen officials, coaches, judges, and family members were aboard. There were no survivors, and the competition was canceled in their memory. On that plane was one of the world's most promising skaters, sixteen-year-old Laurence Owen, the daughter of ten-time U.S. champion Maribel Vinson Owen, also killed in the crash. The younger Owen had just won her first U.S. title and was favored to win a world medal. The elder Owen had become the first woman sportswriter at the *New York Times*.

It took nearly a decade for skating to become popular again in the United States. Not only had the top-name skaters died in the crash, but also the glamour sport no longer seemed in tune with the emerging youth counterculture of the 1960s. How could an American teenager get excited about silly skating routines when friends were fighting for civil rights and dying in Vietnam? How could feminist women embrace a sport in which female athletes wore makeup, hairspray, sequins, and skirts?

But the sport still had its stars, with the two top American names being Peggy Fleming and Janet Lynn. Fleming, one of the sport's most glamorous and balletic skaters, won three world titles and the 1968 Olympics. Her family sacrificed to advance her skating career, moving from Cleveland to Pasadena, California, to Colorado Springs. Fleming's mother designed and sewed all of her costumes. She was best known for a gorgeous move in which she would go from a spread-eagle line—legs spread, arms and feet pointing outward, leaning back—into a double axel (the only jump taken from a forward position) and then back into a spread-eagle. She won the 1968 Olympic gold despite botching the double axel, signed a $500,000 contract with the Ice Follies, and appeared on television commercials for soap and panty hose. She eventually joined Dick Button as a network skating commentator.

In 1971, a blond pixie with a radiant smile spurred a dramatic change in the way figure skating was judged. Janet Lynn, an Illinois schoolgirl, would go down in history as the most memorable skater never to win an Olympic medal. Lynn could never master compulsory school figures, a tedious portion of the competition that accounted for 50 percent of the final score and required skaters to etch six of forty-one possible figures on a patch of ice in an empty rink. Judges would then crouch down and measure the figures with rulers, giving points for precision of carvings, which the television viewing audience never saw.

Lynn won five consecutive national championships from 1969 to 1973. Her powerful and creative free-skating programs mesmerized audiences, but her mediocre school figures always dragged down her marks. Before the 1972 Olympics in Sapporo, Japan, Lynn graced the cover of *Newsweek* magazine, and inside was the following prediction: "Lynn is a virtual cinch to enchant the Sapporo audiences with her dazzling free skating—and almost equally certain to fall short of the points accumulated by Austria's Beatrix Schuba in the dull compulsory competition."

Lynn floated across the ice, danced into her jumps, fell into a flying sit spin, spun around on the ice in a sitting position, smiling through it all, and the Japanese crowd was silent—its greatest display of honor. But the gangly, clumsy Trixie Schuba of Austria had built up a huge lead with near-flawless compulsory figures, and she won the gold medal despite a seventh-place finish in the free-skating event. Even the generally polite Japanese fans jeered at the decision.

A year later, responding to public outcry about Lynn's bronze and the scoring system, the International Skating Union introduced the short program and reduced the importance of school figures. Skaters would be required to complete seven elements during a short program (two minutes), and that would count for 20 percent of the total score. Figures would drop to 40 percent, and the long program would be worth 40 percent. School figures decreased in value as the years went on and were finally abolished in 1991.

Lynn stayed in the sport that 1973 season and signed a $1.45 million deal with the Ice Follies, making her the world's highest-paid female athlete at the time.

By 1976 the tumult of the sixties had subsided; Americans were celebrating the bicentennial and seemed ready again to embrace traditional values and clean-cut entertainment. Television and the emphasis on free skating over compulsory figures made figure skating more exciting for fans.

Enter Dorothy Hamill, an insecure, nearsighted nineteen-year-old who was born in Chicago, Illinois, and grew up in Riverside, Connecticut, near Greenwich. Her father, Chalmers Hamill, was an executive at Pitney Bowes. Hamill received her first pair of skates as a Christmas present when she was eight years old. She tried them out on a neighborhood frozen pond and was jealous of the kids who could skate backwards. She begged her mother, Carol, for group lessons and before long was receiving high praise from her instructors.

She hired a personal coach, and in 1976 she was ready to show the world what she had learned. Wearing thick glasses, she conquered compulsory figures at the Olympics in Innsbruck, Austria, and then ditched the glasses for uncomfortable contact lenses to perform a near-flawless free skate to win the gold medal. Unlike Henie, Hamill had neither the money nor the personality for flashy dresses, so she wore a simple $75 pink knit dress sewn by a friend's mother—a far cry from the $13,000 designer dress Nancy Kerrigan would wear eighteen years later.

A television audience of millions fell in love with Hamill, the girl with the perky wedge haircut. Skating fans were further endeared to her when she had to squint to see her scores (eight 5.8s and a 5.9 in technical merit and all 5.9s in artistic impression). In the months following the Olympics, women and girls everywhere asked their hairdressers for Dorothy Hamill wedge cuts, and the hairdo became as popular as she was.

The public adulation overwhelmed Hamill; she was never comfortable with her celebrity status. From the time she began skating in second grade, she was shy and unsure of herself. She frequently burst into tears before competitions and suffered long battles with stage fright and loss of confidence. "She is critical of herself to the point of being negative," said her coach, Carlo Fassi. "I keep telling her if you want to convince the judges that you're the best, you must first convince yourself."

Hamill's fragile psyche was evident during a world competition in Munich in 1975. Unhappy with scores awarded a West German skater before her, the fans booed. Hamill, about to start her free skate, thought the boos were for her; tears streamed down her face, and she left the ice. When she realized her mistake, she smiled shyly and went back to center ice to begin her routine.

Despite her insecurities, Hamill always appeared confident once the music began. A 1974 *Sports Illustrated* article describing her U.S. title–winning performance said: "Her assurance and speed made the competitors who preceded her appear to have skated in slow motion. Her high, clean double lutz came not after but out of a dazzling display of footwork so neatly accomplished that the judges might have missed it."

Hamill's most famous move was a delayed axel jump in which she seemed to hang in the air before completing the one-and-a-half revolution. She also prided herself on high-speed spins. At the time, her moves looked impressive—but the world had no idea how much more athletic female skaters would become. Hamill was the last Olympic champion to win without a triple jump. (Two decades later, teenagers Michelle Kwan and Tara Lipinski each included seven triple jumps in their long programs.) Hamill's Olympic gold-medal routine probably would not even earn a U.S. junior title in 1998.

Upon her return from the Olympics, Hamill's hometown of Riverside held a parade in her honor and renamed the town's ice rink after her. Neighbors remembered her as one of dozens of young girls who took up skating as a hobby. More than 100,000 children take group skating lessons in the United States, and hundreds of those develop such a passion that they begin taking private lessons. From those hundreds, the best twenty-five or so in each category (novice, junior, senior) advance to the regional championships. The best four from each region make it to sectionals, and then a field of about twenty make it to the national championship.

Hamill had been through all the ranks and finally reached the pinnacle of her sport—that glorious, spine-tingling moment listening to the national anthem from atop the Olympic medal podium. She was asked to give speeches and pose for thousands of photos, and she immediately signed with an agent. A female figure skating champion, especially one with a squeaky-clean image, stood to become a millionaire. The Ideal Toy Company manufactured Barbie-like Dorothy Hamill dolls, and little girls all over the United States rushed to toy stores to get them.

One of those little girls was Kristi Yamaguchi, who would mention the doll when she won the 1992 Olympic gold medal sixteen years later. Yamaguchi was born with deformed feet that required braces and corrective shoes, and when doctors suggested she take up a sport, she remembered Hamill and chose figure skating. Though Yamaguchi was one of the most athletic and artistic skaters of all time and a fan favorite on post-Olympic skating tours, she was not swarmed with endorsement deals. Some marketing experts surmised that corporate America was not ready for a Japanese-American to endorse their products. But over the next few years, Yamaguchi would reap benefits from her gold medal. She made several hundred thousand dollars performing for professional ice shows, coauthored the book *Figure Skating for Dummies,* and was named spokesperson for the 2002 Winter Olympics in Salt Lake City.

Hamill signed a $1 million-a-year contract with the Ice Capades in 1976. She would do thirteen shows a week, eighteen to twenty-three weeks per year. She moved to Hollywood, California, and married Dean Paul Martin, the son of Dean Martin, at a lavish wedding attended by many of the biggest film and TV stars. Tabloids chronicled her every move, and the mercurial Hamill didn't respond well. Her marriage to Martin ended in divorce after two years, and in 1987 she married Ken Forsythe, a sports physician and former member of the Canadian Olympic ski team. They purchased the Ice Capades but sold it a few years later. In 1995 Hamill and Forsythe divorced, and in 1996, Hamill filed for bankruptcy.

Despite her financial troubles, Hamill always looks back fondly on her skating career in interviews and continues to follow the sport closely. She said she finds it "incredible" that the top skaters in the 1990s don't do school figures, and she marvels at the athleticism exhibited by Kwan's and Lipinski's generation.

Canadian Petra Burke, the 1965 world champion, was the first woman to land a triple-revolution jump, and Dianne de Leeuw of the Netherlands landed a triple at the 1975 world championships. But the first woman to consistently land triples in competition was American Linda Fratianne. The Los Angeles native had tremendous spring and strength in her legs, and she landed triple toe-loops and triple salchows with ease. Each style of jump—loop, salchow, lutz, and axel—requires the skater to take off from a different blade edge, and Fratianne could do everything but the triple axel. She was the best jumper of her day and so determined to beat rival Anett Potzsch of East Germany at the 1980 Olympics that she got a nose job and had her teeth fixed for judge appeal. Potzsch won anyway; Fratianne had to settle for silver.

Athletic young women all over America tried to emulate Fratianne and spent countless hours mastering jumps Hamill hadn't even thought about ten years earlier. The bar had been raised, and women's figure skating would never be the same. Elaine Zayak, a sixteen-year-old American, unleashed six triple jumps at the 1982 world championships and narrowly beat the statuesque East German Katarina Witt. Shortly thereafter, the International Skating Union, fearful that women's skating would lose its beauty and become a boring jump-off, introduced rules that limited the number of jumps a skater could repeat in a program. They also began to require women to include a spiral in their routines. The spiral is a graceful one-footed move in which the skater glides across the ice with one leg fully extended behind her. It would become Nancy Kerrigan's trademark move in the early 1990s.

The institution of the new rules favored Witt, one of history's most artistic skaters, and she would dominate the sport from 1984 to 1988. Witt was born in East Germany in 1965, and by the time she hit puberty, her model-like looks made her a crowd favorite. Much to the dismay of her more athletic rivals, Witt was able to win with only three triple jumps in an age when jumping was the rage. She won the 1984 Olympic gold medal over reigning world champion Rosalynn Sumners and received more than thirty-five thousand love letters in the following months. Marriage proposals came almost monthly as Witt won the next four world titles.

Witt won Olympic gold again in 1988—the first repeat champion since Henie—but this one wouldn't come so easy. It was a classic matchup between Witt and Stanford premed student Debi Thomas, who was seeking to become the first African-American athlete to win a medal in the Winter Olympics. Thomas, born in 1967 in New York, grew up in northern California and became fascinated with ice skating while watching ice clown Mr. Frick at a local show. She begged her parents for lessons, and they enrolled her at a nearby rink. She was a natural, and in 1986 she became the first African-American woman in history to win a gold medal at the world championships. The rivalry between Witt and Thomas grew fierce, and, ironically, at the 1988

Olympics both women chose to skate to the music from *Carmen*. Witt went first and gave a brilliant artistic performance, but her lack of technical difficulty left the door open for Thomas, who had upset her at the 1986 world championships.

Thomas unraveled under pressure, however, landing badly on her second jump and missing two more jumps later in the program. She seemed to give up after the second fall, and a worldwide television audience watched, stunned, as her dream shattered in four minutes. She was so upset when she left the ice that she brushed past her coaches. "The whole reason I came here was to be great," she said afterward. "After that [the falls], I couldn't be great." Thomas eventually got over the loss, finished medical school, and became a physician. She also opened the door of the lily-white sport for future black skaters such as Surya Bonaly of France, a former gymnast known for her back flips and quadruple jump attempts.

Witt retired after the 1988 Olympics and joined the pro circuit, and Japan's Midori Ito took center stage after becoming the first woman to land a triple axel in competition during the 1989 world championships. Ito, a tiny fireplug, first turned heads in the early 1980s, when she landed a triple-toe-loop–triple-toe-loop combination at age twelve, a phenomenal achievement.

Right about the same time, halfway around the world at a nondescript rink in Portland, Oregon, a gutsy little girl in hand-me-downs was landing the extremely difficult triple lutz jump as a novice skater. It was hard to believe that a ten-year-old with severe asthma could master a jump that Olympic champions Henie, Hamill, and Fleming never even tried. But those who knew Tonya Harding were hardly surprised. The diminutive blonde had no fear. There wasn't a fragile bone in her body. Harding's father, Al, bought her a .22 rifle when she was in kindergarten and chopped off the stock so it would fit in her tiny hands. She hunted deer, drag raced, played pool, and chain-smoked as a teenager. She was skilled enough as a mechanic to rebuild a car engine.

The ice rink was Harding's frozen oasis, the one place she could escape a troubled childhood. She dropped out of school briefly in eighth grade, reenrolled, and then dropped out for good in tenth grade.

Harding was the only child born to LaVona Harding, then a waitress, and her fifth husband, Al, who struggled to hold a steady job. LaVona Harding couldn't afford to buy Tonya lavish costumes, so she sewed them herself. The dresses were often garish and unsophisticated. Harding's music selections were unconventional. Judges cringed at her style, but they couldn't ignore her tremendous talent. "I wasn't born with a silver spoon in my mouth," Tonya would say later. "My mom made my school clothes from polyester blends, and the other kids made fun of me. I never had fancy dresses like the other girls. The other girls would have a new dress for each competition, and I had to wear the same ones over and over. It was embarrassing."

What Harding lacked in sequins she made up for in guts. Other girls skated with more grace, but she was the only one brave enough to challenge boys with triple axels at age fourteen. The leap requires the skater to take off from one blade, do three and a half revolutions in the air, and land backward on the opposite skate blade. Conventional wisdom said that a woman's body was not fit for this rigorous a jump. Harding would disprove that theory at the 1991 U.S. championships, where she became the second woman in history to land the triple axel in competition, which helped her vault over the more graceful Yamaguchi for the gold medal.

It was also in 1991 that Harding filed for divorce from her husband of one year, Jeff Gillooly, though the couple ended up reconciling for a time. Harding made headlines later that year when police found her brandishing a baseball bat at another motorist at a busy intersection. She got another visit from the Portland police two years later, when a neighbor in her apartment complex heard a gunshot in the parking lot. Police found Harding, Gillooly, and a loaded gun in their pickup truck. Harding insisted the gun went off accidentally; the weapon was seized.

Meanwhile, on the opposite U.S. coast, a shy teenager named Nancy Kerrigan was making a name for herself in the Boston area. Like Harding, Kerrigan was more powerful than she was graceful. She learned to skate playing hockey with boys, and she preferred jumping to dancing. And, like Harding's, Kerrigan's family was not rich. Her father, Dan, was a welder. As Kerrigan got more serious about skating, her father worked odd jobs, took out loans, and refinanced the house to pay for her hobby. Kerrigan's mother, Brenda, was her biggest fan, although she never saw her skate. A virus took her eyesight in 1970, shortly after Nancy was born.

Harding and Kerrigan were a year apart, and their paths had crossed since they were juniors. Harding always felt that Kerrigan was favored by judges because of her more traditional family background and her Katherine Hepburn–like cheekbones. The rivalry intensified after the 1992 Olympics, which Yamaguchi won. Ito took the silver, Kerrigan won bronze, and Harding, who fell on the triple axel, finished fourth. Shortly before those Olympics, Kerrigan had her gap-toothed smile corrected. Everyone raved about how beautiful she looked. Harding had her smoke-stained teeth bleached. Nobody noticed.

Madison Avenue and the skating establishment expected Kerrigan to be the next ice princess. She had worked hard on her artistry and added graceful steps between her jumps. Her trademark spiral was the most impressive the sport had ever seen. By 1993 she was being called a gold-medal favorite, and a month before the 1994 Winter Olympics in Norway, she had already secured endorsements with Reebok, Campbell's Soup, Evian, and Seiko. Magazine and newspaper stories raved of Kerrigan's elegance and her gorgeous skating dresses, which were designed by Vera Wang, a New York fashion designer and former skater.

Harding and Gillooly, her on-again, off-again husband, watched from a distance and seethed. Didn't anyone notice that Harding was the first American woman to land a triple axel? Wasn't it a great story that this poor girl with asthma had made it in a rich sport? And everyone knew how much a gold medal was worth. The winner of the 1994 Olympic figure skating crown would make millions of dollars, perhaps grace the cover of a cereal box, visit late-night talk shows, and be the headliner in upcoming tours. Gillooly wanted to see Harding rake in the dough. So he and three friends concocted a plan. An injury to Kerrigan's knee would knock her out of the Olympics. Gillooly offered his pals $6,500 to do the job. They agreed and flew to Detroit, where Harding and Kerrigan were competing in the 1994 U.S. championships.

On the afternoon of January 6, 1994, as Kerrigan was leaving a practice session at Cobo Arena, a man assaulted her and whacked her on the right knee with a metal baton. She fell to the floor and wailed, "Why me? Why now?" She withdrew from the competition, and her Olympic chances looked grim.

Harding won the U.S. title and an Olympic berth two days later. She said she was disappointed that Kerrigan was injured because she was looking forward to "beating Nancy's butt" at the Olympics. A day after Harding's victory, an anonymous caller told Detroit police that some Portland men connected to Harding had plotted the attack on Kerrigan. On January 19, Gillooly was charged with planning and bankrolling the attack, and his buddies signed confessions. Harding was also implicated and arrived at the Olympics under a cloud of suspicion. The U.S. Figure Skating Association tried to ban her from competing, but she hadn't been charged, so she was allowed to compete.

The Nancy-and-Tonya saga gripped much of the world for weeks. The story led network news and tabloid television shows and made the front page of most major newspapers. Photos of Harding topless showed up in British tabloids.

Harding showed up at the Olympics out of shape and finished tenth in the short program. The largest television audience in history tuned in for the long program, and Harding gave fans plenty to talk about. She was known to have equipment problems at the most inopportune times, so it came as no surprise when she went out onto the ice, missed a jump, and burst into tears as she skated toward the judges' table to show them her broken skate lace.

They agreed to let her get a new lace and start over. She finished in eighth place after falling on the triple axel.

Kerrigan, meanwhile, ignored her sore knee and skated the performance of her life. It was good enough for a silver medal behind Oksana Baiul of the Ukraine. Hundreds of flowers and stuffed animals covered the ice when Kerrigan finished her routine. She smiled, picked up the flowers, and waved at the crowd, looking like the perfect ice princess. Harding watched from a sky box, her head buried in her coach's shoulder, her face drenched in tears.

Shortly after the Olympics, Harding pleaded guilty to hindering the prosecution in the attack of Kerrigan. She paid a $100,000 fine to the state of Oregon and was sentenced to four hundred hours of community service. The U.S. Figure Skating Association banned her for life. Gillooly and his buddies went to jail. In the end, Harding would have more headlines than she ever craved. She would go down in history as one of the most famous skaters of all time, and she would bring more attention to the sport than anybody since Sonja Henie.

"It was absolutely mind-boggling that figure skating became so popular," says thirty-year veteran coach Frank Carroll, whose students include Michelle Kwan. "As much as we sometimes put down Tonya Harding, women's sports in general owe her a great debt of gratitude. It was a terribly negative way to go about it, but she did really do a lot for women's sports."

Television ratings for figure skating skyrocketed during and after the 1994 Olympics, trailing only the National Football League. The 48.5 CBS rating for the Nancy-and-Tonya showdown was the third highest ever for a sports program of any kind. Sports fans who never before cared about skating were all of a sudden discussing Kerrigan and Baiul and Harding over their lunch breaks and on radio talk shows. Newspaper sports sections that previously buried skating news inside were displaying figure skating on the front, alongside football and basketball. The networks took notice, and dozens of made-for-TV skating specials sprung up in the months following the Olympics. Forty skating web sites appeared on the Internet.

With the increased interest in the sport came big money for every figure skating star but Harding. Sold-out arenas meant hundreds of thousands of dollars for marquee skaters such as Kerrigan, Yamaguchi, and Witt. The made-for-TV specials were paying as much as $20,000 for one evening's work. Not since Henie's day had figure skaters been so marketable.

The new generation of skaters that followed in the mid- to late 1990s entered the sport knowing millions of dollars were waiting for the Olympic champion. Sports agents knew that, too, so they began scouting junior-level skaters, shmoozing with their families, and trying to guess which little girl would wear gold in 1998 in Nagano, Japan. The two skaters they targeted were Michelle Kwan and Tara Lipinski.

Kwan was born in 1980 in Torrance, California, to Hong Kong immigrants Danny and Estella Kwan. The family ran a Chinese restaurant, where Michelle and her older sister, Karen, helped out after school. Kwan's love affair with figure skating began at a local mall, and after a few sessions, she asked her parents for private lessons. Her discipline and athleticism were immediately evident to coach Frank Carroll, and he knew this girl would be a star. He also soon learned that she would stop at nothing to make the Olympics, even if it meant going behind his back to take the senior-level test after he advised her to stay in juniors one more year. Kwan took the test while Carroll was on vacation, passed, and at age thirteen stormed on to the national figure skating scene.

A few years behind her in juniors was Lipinski, a tiny, daring girl from Sugar Land, Texas, who was dazzling fans with her triple jumps. By the time Lipinski was eleven, she had outgrown her local rink, and coaches suggested she move north to train at an elite skating club. Her father, Jack, vice president of a Houston-based oil refinery, couldn't leave his job, so he agreed to live alone with the two dogs while his wife, Pat, moved with their only child to Delaware. After a spat with the Delaware coach, Team Lipinski moved to West Bloomfield, Michigan, a Detroit suburb, to train with Richard Callaghan, who also coached men's world champion Todd Eldredge. The Lipinski family would remain split for four years and charge up $1,000-a-month phone bills, but Jack and Pat insisted it was worth it.

Both Kwan and Lipinski had to win over judges who were turned off by their little-girl looks. After Kwan finished fourth at the 1994 world championships, her coach, Frank Carroll, suggested that his talented pupil begin wearing makeup and pile her ponytail up into a more sophisticated bun. Her parents were opposed to the idea. They didn't think their daughter was old enough to wear lipstick and mascara. The coach, and Kwan herself, finally convinced them, and within a year she was receiving high artistic marks for her more mature presentation, a routine in which she portrayed the seductress Salome. At four-foot-eight and eighty pounds, Lipinski looked even more childish than Kwan on the ice. Though she mastered seven triple jumps, her skinny legs didn't get high off the ground, and some judges remarked that she belonged in juniors. Like Kwan, she pulled her ponytail up into a bun, began wearing more makeup, and worked tirelessly on improving her artistic impression.

By the time Kwan and Lipinski took over the Olympic stage in 1997, they had hired agents, appeared on dozens of TV specials, toured the country for more than $500,000 apiece, secured commercial endorsements, and written autobiographies.

Figure skating had become the most high-profile of all women's Olympic sports, and Olympic hopefuls such as Kwan and Lipinski faced pressure unlike anything felt by their predecessors. When Lipinski upset Kwan for the 1997 world title, the media immediately questioned whether's Kwan's best days were behind her. When Lipinski fell during her short program at the 1998 U.S. championships, a photo of her mistake made the nightly news and appeared on the front of hundreds of American sports sections.

No longer did skaters show up at the Olympics as unknowns and leave as stars, the way Fleming and Hamill did. By the time young women got to the Olympics in the 1990s, the spotlight often had been shining on them for years, and the Olympic rings could feel as suffocating as nooses.

The nation watched as Kwan and Lipinski skated brilliantly to finish one-two at the 1998 U.S. championships. They arrived in Nagano, Japan, in February 1998 as co-favorites to win Olympic gold, with Kwan holding a slight edge. Nicole Bobek, one of the most glamorous but inconsistent skaters in U.S. history, had worked her way back from injuries to become a bronze-medal favorite. American skating fans—and CBS television executives—had their fingers crossed for a 1-2-3 USA sweep.

The only question seemed to be whether Kwan or Lipinksi would take the gold. Kwan is more artistic, the pundits said. Her photo graced the covers of *Newsweek* and *Sports Illustrated.* Television analysts and newspaper columnists all over the world predicted that if Kwan didn't fall, she'd win. Feeling the intense pressure, Kwan opted not to stay in the Athletes Village at the Olympics and, instead, spent the week holed up with her parents at a hotel. She arrived in Nagano several days after the Opening Ceremony. Lipinski, meanwhile, marched in the Opening Ceremony, posed for photos with sumo wrestlers, stayed in the Athletes Village, answered e-mail fan letters every day, and bopped all over Nagano in the days preceding the women's skating competition. She told reporters that she wanted to "truly experience" the Olympic spirit and that she was having the time of her life. Her coach, Richard Callaghan, could hardly believe how calm she seemed in the days preceding the biggest moment of her skating career. "It's like she's a regular teenager for certain times of the day, but when she gets on the ice, everything changes," he said.

Kwan admittedly took the cautious approach, figuring a clean program would be enough to win. She did only two of her triple jumps in combination and skated slower and tighter than she had at the U.S. nationals. Her strategy failed. On the night it mattered most, Lipinksi skated her heart out. She became the first woman ever to land a triple-loop–triple-loop combination jump in competition, and she made sure to do it directly in front of the judges' table. She skated fast, without fear, and nailed five triple-combination jumps as the roar of the crowd intensified. When she finished, she sprinted on the ice and shrieked with joy like a kid getting out of school for summer vacation.

In a departure from the past, the judges favored athleticism over artistry and awarded the gold medal to Lipinski. She became the youngest Olympic figure skating champion in history. "It's a sport," Lipinski's father would say afterward. "If they wanted it to be ballet, they'd call it ballet." Kwan's eyes brimmed with tears as a silver medal was draped around her neck. "I should have done a harder program," she said afterward. "But c'est la vie. I learned a life lesson that no matter how hard you work, and how much you want something, you don't always get it."

On the other side of the room was the giddy Lipinski family, finally together after so many nights apart. Oh yes, and Tara's agent, who was eager to get her projected $10 million career started. Lipinski would spend the next few weeks taking limousines from talk show to talk show, giggling at the Grammy Awards, mingling with stars at the Oscars, hawking Barbie dolls, and showing off her medal to schoolchildren. Seven weeks after her gold-medal peformance, she announced that she was turning pro, that she wouldn't continue Olympic-level training. She had earned her Olympic gold, and love of her family was more important than pursuing another medal. "It was really hard for my family to be apart," she said. "When I came back from the Olympics, having my mom and dad together, going to movies and malls was such a relaxed feeling. I don't want to be twenty-two and not know my dad."

Lipinski embarked on a sixty-six-city tour that earned her an estimated $15,000 per night. She insisted that she'd like to try harder jumps in coming years, maybe even a quadruple jump some day, and her tiny body suggests it's possible. In Fairfax, Virginia, a twelve-year-old named Elizabeth Kwon was already raising eyebrows for the 2002 Olympics. She hit four triples as a novice, and the agents are starting to call.

Will the pressure to master increasingly challenging jumps diminish artistic presentation in the future? Will skating go the way of gymnastics, where young female athletes are considered over the hill when their hips fill out and they can drive themselves to practice? Will all the made-for-TV skating specials oversaturate the market and dilute the sport? Nobody knows for sure. But one thing is certain—the spirit, athleticism, and glamour that Lipinski demonstrated in Nagano could be traced straight back to Henie, who decades before managed to break the ice for all women skaters while she tiptoed daintily, smiling with every calculated move.

Swimming

$\mathcal{F}$rom Gold Spangles
to Gold Medals
Karen Karbo

In the one hundred years or so that women have been publicly recognized as swimmers, the sport has evolved from a vaguely illegitimate but glitzy entertainment to a legitimate and somewhat monotonous show of strength and speed that occupies our attention for a few weeks every four years. Whether celebrating the triumph of marathon swimmer Gertrude Ederle's 1926 English Channel swim in a ticker-tape parade down Fifth Avenue, buying a forty-nine-cent ticket to Billy Rose's Aquacades to watch hundreds of female water ballerinas—the first synchronized swimmers—dive and stroke in spangles and sequins, or sitting in the dark bewitched by a glistening twenty-foot-tall Esther Williams, people in the first part of the century were captivated by the spectacle of women in water. Meanwhile, the wallflowers of swimming, the women who wore tank suits, not spangles, and hacked up and down the pool at their local women's swimming club, began to gain the world's attention at the summer Olympics. The showgirl swimmer was then superseded by the girl jock; the saucy, buxom Aquabelle of the Hollywood movie was replaced by the disciplined teen machine, a college girl who earned great grades and big endorsements and had no life outside the classroom or the pool. Today, swimming, like everything else, has splintered into subcultures: marathon swimming, which takes place in open bodies of water, challenging swimmers to travel ungodly distances in cold water amid sharks and pollution; synchronized swimming, the direct descendant of the Aquacade and an underappreciated Olympic sport; and the aspect of swimming we usually think of when we think of the sport of swimming, Olympic racing, which presents every four years another crop of Wheaties box cover girls.

* * *

The first women swimmers in modern history emerged in England at the end of the nineteenth century. The English—by which I mean English men—were extraordinarily proud of their swimming abilities. They held contests in frigid rivers, the colder and swifter the better. One Victorian report on the sport claims: "There is no instance of any foreigner, civilized or uncivilized, whose achievements in the water surpass those of the British." These swimmers were largely from the upper classes, educated at public school. The Romantic poets of the time—Shelley, Keats, and Coleridge— the same guys who experimented with opium and puffy shirts, were also drawn to swimming. Byron self-prescribed swimming to take the edge off his never-ending restlessness. In 1845, in the first modern swim meet, two Native Americans traveled to Britain to beat the field using a windmill-like stroke that was a rudimentary crawl, the father of the freestyle. While Flying Gull and Tobacco were trouncing the breast-stroking English with their weird overarm stroke, the women of their tribes were back home helping their men measure the depths of rivers. The women's heights were noted; then they would walk in until the water covered their heads. This was the closest they came to swimming.

The women swimmers of the time were generally one of two types of women: eccentric British adventuresses, many of them intrepid Victorian travelers like Mary Kingsley who felt freer swimming in the lakes and rivers of Europe and Africa than they did at home in England, where they were excluded from the public baths and sniggered at if they dared take a swim at the beach; and wild girls, for whom swimming was the equivalent of bungee jumping, or extreme snowboarding. These first female swimmers were women on the fringes, women willing to hurl themselves into the water in bathing suits that exposed their flesh. They were brazen, wanton. Since swimming involved stripping down to what amounted to no more than your underclothes, it was thought to be highly improper. Indeed, the sight of a woman swimming in public drew circus-sized crowds. In the United States, in the first part of the twentieth century, a woman could be arrested for entering the ocean without her stockings. A woman named Etheldra Bleibtrey, the first American woman in history to win a gold medal (in the 1920 Olympics in Antwerp, Belgium, the first year American women competed in swimming), was once arrested for swimming in the nude. She had taken off her stockings in order to wade in the surf at Manhattan Beach, California.

When women decided they wanted to enjoy swimming too, it created the same consternation the navy is now experiencing when considering the question of how to accommodate a female on a submarine. Male swimmers grumbled more or less unanimously. They detested the imposition of a bathing suit, then called drawers. For one thing, swimming represented to many of them an escape from domesticity, represented in part by women. Women, by their insistence in wanting some of the action, were ruining the fun.

Women's bathing costumes—they resembled something you'd find in the closet of Little Miss Muffet—were the height of modesty while dry. When wet, they clung to the female form in a way found so shocking that, according to swimming historian Charles Sprawson, "The bathing machines which towed swimmers out to deeper water were now equipped with 'modesty hoods,' the invention of a Quaker to save the embarrassment of those troubled by the sight of women emerging from the sea in soaking costumes."

In addition to the bathing suit dilemma, the doctors of the day thought swimming to be terrible for the womb, inhibiting conception. If a woman was pregnant, swimming would certainly damage or abort the fetus (how ironic that swimming is now thought to be one of the most healthful activities an athletic woman can do while pregnant; I swam until the morning of the evening I delivered my daughter). The greatest concern, however, was the potential for unbridled sexuality that might spring from splashing around in a bathing outfit. No matter that the outfit consisted of bloomers, skirt, and shirt and was often made of serge or wool, fabrics more conducive to drowning than swimming.

In the years that followed, swimming went from being a daring outlet for a few female renegades, to one of the top pastimes of the average American woman. This is due in part to the effects of World War I. The cliché newsreel footage of the era shows both mothers and ingenues gamely taking the place of men in the office and on the assembly line. Likewise, as the boys marched off to war, the lifeguard stands were left empty. As young recruits abandoned their pools, lakes, and beaches for the battlefields of Europe, women were forced to pick up the whistle, don the pith helmet, and get ready to be bored stiff. (Most lifeguarding, as anyone who has done it for more than a week during the summer will tell you, mostly involves breaking up fights during Marco Polo.) It wasn't the act of lifeguarding that was stimulating to women, but the fact that to become a lifeguard a woman had to earn her American Red Cross life saver's certificate, and that whet her appetite for swimming. During the late teens and early twenties tens of thousands of mostly young women became lifeguard certified.

Meanwhile, in 1914 the AAU, the Amateur Athletic Union, dipped its toe into women's sports by entering women in competitive swimming races. Three years later, in 1917, the year women won the vote and the United States officially entered the war, a court reporter named Charlotte "Eppie" Epstein rented the small pool in the basement of the Hotel Terrain in Brooklyn, New York—one of the only chlorinated pools in the city—and formed an organization dedicated to training women for competition, the Women's Swimming Association of New York.

Although women were allowed to compete in the Olympics in 1916, it wasn't until 1920 that the Americans could put together a female swim team. Eppie's personal credo informed the training of that first women's team; next to the highly specialized training methods of today's Olympians, her ideas were simple and exact: 1) stick to the dress code; 2) behave; 3) compete, whether you feel like it or not.

The primary benefactor of this advice was fourteen-year-old Aileen Riggin (now Soule), who at ninety-two years of age is the oldest living Olympian and to this day remains the only female Olympian in history to have won medals in both diving and swimming. In the first Olympics in which American women competed, in 1920 in Antwerp, Belgium, she won a gold medal in springboard diving; four years later, in Paris, she took a silver in diving and a bronze in the backstroke. The gold she won in Antwerp was earned under circumstances that border on the surreal. The event was held in a canal, in fifty-two-degree water. Between dives the four-foot-ten, sixty-five pound Riggin had to be rubbed down by her teammates to avoid hypothermia. When they weren't competing, the team, composed of both young girls like Riggin and older women, some as old as forty, who were married with children, toured the battlefields of the recently liberated Belgium, collecting war souvenirs that included bullets and German helmets. Although the women's swimming events were roughly the same as they are today (the 100-, 220-, 440-, and 880-yard races became the modern-day 200-, 400-, 800-, and 1,500-meter races), Olympic diving was far less complex. Diving was still primarily a way of entering the water in order to swim, and the most difficult dive performed was the swan dive, even in the men's competition. The female divers had no coach to speak of, and the concept of training was as far off as the invention of the microchip. Soule, who is the current holder of three backstroke world records in the 85–89 age division of the Masters—an organized worldwide swim club for adults—has said that the divers just sort of picked it up themselves. The place where they had the first trials was a tidal pool in New York, where the depth of the water varied with the tides; the divers bent their elbows when they entered the water in order to break the dive, or risked breaking their necks.

While the presence of women in the Olympics helped erase the stigma of woman-swimmer-as-exhibitionist, it wasn't until a few years later that the idea gained complete public approval. When it did, it wasn't an Olympian who popularized the sport, but a fifteen-year-old German-American butcher's daughter named Gertrude Ederle, who joined the Women's Swimming Association with the purpose of learning the proper way to swim. Ederle would go on to hold twenty-nine world records in just about every distance for which there was a race, but it was her swim across the English Channel that put her name in the history books.

By the time Ederle made her first attempt to swim the channel, in 1925, only five people—all men—had managed to complete the twenty-one-mile swim. During Ederle's first try, she was seized with a horrible case of seasickness and pulled from the ocean a mere seven miles into the swim. On August 6, 1926, after coating her body with her own concoction of olive oil, lanolin, and Vaseline, she entered the water in Cape Gris-Nez, France, for her second try and emerged fourteen hours, thirty-one minutes later in Kingsdorn, on the coast of Dover. Her swim was a record, nearly two hours faster than the five men who had previously swam the channel. This was even more remarkable because a storm blew in during her swim, dragging her about fourteen miles off course.

In the early days of competitive swimming, endurance, not speed, was the contest. Without goggles or any accurate way to forecast the weather, a swimmer dove in and hoped for the best. Now an English Channel swim is planned with the aid of a computer that calculates the effect the channel's notorious tidal currents will have on a swimmer's time, the better to plot a course. It's not unlikely to begin a swim at nine P.M., on one of the handful of days in either July or August when the channel is warm enough and the tides are right. The air temperature might be, say, fifty-five degrees, the water temperature, if you're lucky, the same. Every hour the support boat may feed you with the aid of a bamboo pole, or a shuffleboard stick. You eat the yolk of an egg, some milk and glucose, a mashed peach.

The conventional wisdom about why women make such splendid marathon swimmers is this: Women are reputed to have greater endurance than men, a higher threshold of pain than men, and, regrettably for those who aspire to wear hip huggers and matte jersey gowns, more fat. More fat equals more buoyancy and greater insulation against the cold. The assumption that there is parity between men and women in endurance swimming is evident by the fact that in most organized long-distance swims there are no separate divisions. In 1997, the winner of the 16th Annual Manhattan Island Marathon Swim was a twenty-eight-year-old Australian named Tammy van Wisse, who in seven hours, fifteen minutes, and fifty-seven seconds dodged several passenger ferries and a prison barge to take first place. A guy took second.

America's fascination made Ederle one of the first athlete-celebrities. She was honored by a ticker-tape parade in New York City attended by 2 million people. She was offered a $200,000 contract to appear on the stage. In 1926 dollars, a working-class man could expect to make that much in a lifetime. But the swim exacted a price: her ears were damaged in the channel swim, and by the age of twenty-seven she was deaf.

Florence Chadwick, born eleven years after Gertrude Ederle, in San Diego, California, took the idea of long-distance swimming one step further. She was a swimming prodigy who swam across San Diego harbor all by herself at age six. In 1950 she swam the English Channel, where she smashed Ederle's record by over an hour. At the time of this first swim she was thirty-two years old, elderly by any athletic standard. She swam the channel a few more times, just for the fun of it, then became the first woman to swim the twenty-one miles between California and Catalina Island. In 1953 she crossed four channels in five weeks—the English, the Bosporus, the Dardanelles, and the Strait of Gibraltar.

The marathon swimmer has more in common with a mountain climber than a marathon runner. The swimmer, like the climber, is at the mercy of the elements. Distance for the swimmer is nothing, temperature everything. Marathoners routinely spend a day and a half in water not much warmer than fifty degrees. The degree of pain endured by the distance swimmer is more akin to the ongoing ordeal of childbirth than to the relatively short agony endured by racers during the final few crucial seconds of a sprint.

As forty-nine-year-old Diana Nyad, the one time world-record holder for the longest swim in history (102.5 miles, between the Bahamian island of Bimini and the coast of Florida), wrote in an essay for *Esquire* entitled, fittingly, "Mind over Water," "I have put more grueling hours into swimming than someone like Jimmy Connors will ever know in a lifetime. I don't begrudge him his talent in that particular sport. There is simply no way he could comprehend the *work* that goes into marathon swimming."

To train for her greatest challenge, becoming the first person to cross the shark freeway between Cuba and the United States, Nyad swam in the ocean for eight hours a day, followed by a ten-mile run. On a marathon morning she might eat a half dozen raw eggs and as much cereal, toast, and jelly as she could hold. Once in the water, she would stop every hour for a protein drink worth about thirteen hundred calories; still it took only roughly three minutes for her blood sugar to drop below standard metabolism levels. After a twelve-hour swim she would be seventeen pounds lighter. And this is if things went well. Many times, the ocean or lake reminds the swimmer that she has no business there. In Nyad's first attempt to swim around Manhattan, the current was so strong that she was caught swimming in place beneath the Brooklyn Bridge for over an hour. Mild seasickness is not a reason to abort a swim; Nyad has swum while throwing up, once for thirteen hours on end. Her rationale was this: When you're seasick on a boat, the advice is to get into the water; when you're seasick in the water, there's nowhere to go, so you might as well keep on swimming.

Nyad ultimately failed in her journey across the Strait of Florida (which, by the way, is always conducted inside a sharkproof cage). Seventy-nine miles and more than forty hours into the swim, her body was so swollen by jelly-fish stings that she was forced to stop. Last year, Australian Susie Maroney completed the swim between Cuba and Florida, and although she was hauled from the water twelve miles short of the Florida coast, she was within U.S. territorial waters, and so she was granted the record. She spent thirty-seven hours inside her sharkproof cage, swimming 88.5 miles. For the last several miles her companion was a forty-foot sperm whale.

Thirty-nine-year-old endurance swimmer Lynne Cox, while not Wheaties box famous, has used her status as one of the world's top open-water swimmers to draw attention to political causes. In 1987 she swam 2.7 miles across the forty-degree water of the Bering Strait, between Little Diomede Island in Alaska and Big Diomede Island in what was then the Soviet Union, to demonstrate how "close" we really were. In 1994 she conducted what she called a "peace swim" across the Gulf of Aqaba to unite Jordan, Israel, and Egypt. To dot the *i*, she intentionally swam against the current.

Until the mid-1930s, the visual appeal of the female swimmer hadn't been fully exploited. Both Aileen Riggin and Gertrude Ederle had been celebrated for their achievements, not because they looked seductive—or, more impor-tant, made swimming look seductive.

Prior to both Riggin's Olympic success and Ederle's channel swim, an Australian named Annette Kellerman was the first "motion picture mermaid." Kellerman's show involved diving into large aquariums and, in a rudimen-tary synchronized swimming routine, executing balletic moves and flirting with the fish. She participated in breath-holding contests (her record was three and a half minutes), and, in a stunt designed to attract publicity rather than show off her long-distance swimming prowess, she swam down the Seine, attracting a half million spectators. Kellerman was also a diver of some re-nown, and in a 1914 movie called *A Daughter of the Gods*, she unwittingly broke the world high-dive record by diving over a hundred feet.

The mermaid shows put on by Annette Kellerman drew crowds, but it was sideshow stuff, a novelty act more along the lines of sword swallowing or fire eating. In 1939 impresario and entrepreneur Billy Rose launched the all-swimming eponymous extravaganza, Billy Rose's Aquacades, the high point of the 1939 New York World's Fair and the eventual inspiration for Hollywood's swimming musicals of the late 1940s and early 1950s. He hired world-class competitive swimmers, young and attractive men and women willing to give up their amateur status for his show. Johnny Weissmuller, who never lost a race during his five-year amateur career and would go on to beat his chest handsomely in a number of tiresome Tarzan epics, was one of Billy

Rose's greatest stars. So was Rose's second wife, world champion backstroker
Eleanor Holm.

In today's sport culture, Holm's romantic story would make a sports
agent salivate, though it's unlikely that an Olympic swimmer who routinely
broke records the way Holm did would have the time or the energy to lead a
life like hers. Born in Brooklyn in 1913, the five-foot-three Holm earned a
gold medal in the 100-meter backstroke in the 1932 Olympics. In the quali-
fying heat, she smashed the world record by several seconds; over the next
two years she broke every world record in the backstroke at every recorded
distance.

At sixteen, she was a showgirl, and in 1933, at age twenty, she married
jazz singer Art Jarrett. For several years, she trained for the 1936 Olympics
during the day and sang with Jarrett in clubs at night. She liked to joke that
her training secrets were champagne and cigarettes.

In those days transporting an Olympic team overseas meant a leisurely
transatlantic cruise. For two weeks aboard the SS *Manhattan* Holm drank
and gambled and carried on most nights until daybreak. Word of her unseemly antics reached the USOC, and upon her arrival in Berlin she was
summarily booted off the team. Considering the "crime," the ban was exceedingly harsh: she was barred from all future amateur swimming contests
for the rest of her life. It is said that she cried on Hitler's shoulder, then went
on to become the toast of Berlin without ever putting on a swimsuit.

Holm's marriage to Art Jarrett ended in 1938; shortly thereafter she
married Billy Rose and starred in his first Aquacade, held at the Cleveland
Fair, in Lake Erie. Holm's ensemble consisted of silver high heels, a swimsuit covered with silver sequins, and a matching floor-length cape. Even
though women hadn't worn skirts and bloomers for some time, and the far
more practical one-piece suit (instituted by the Women's Swimming Association of New York) had been accepted as a legitimate part of the sport, the
effect of a spotlight fixed on a woman in such a form-fitting costume was
still titillating.

Holm's performance was a demonstration of her world-record backstroke. It was said that on many nights she unofficially broke her own records.
Sometimes she would find herself swimming through large schools of min-
nows, and if she didn't sprint, they tried to wriggle into her swimsuit. Holm
was the star of the Aquacades through 1940. In 1954 she divorced Billy Rose
and moved to Florida, where she still lives.

Holm's Aquacade replacement was an exuberant young Californian
who had no Olympic medals to her credit, though she had earned a spot on
the 1940 Olympic team. In the same way the U.S. boycott of the Olympics
in 1980 would forever alter the careers of a generation of young swimmers

who needed an Olympiad in which to showcase themselves at the height of their strength and skill, the cancellation of the 1940 games because of World War II forever altered her career. Esther Williams wound up becoming a star of the screen rather than a star of the pool.

Although the Aquacades folded a year after Williams signed on, the instant she became available she was snapped up by MGM. She went on to star in many silly, lavishly photographed movies with titles like *Bathing Beauty*, *On an Island with You*, *Dangerous When Wet*, and *Million Dollar Mermaid*. Indeed, by the early 1950s, she was a million dollar mermaid: at the time the film was shot she was one of the highest paid actors in Hollywood.

The essence of star quality is and has always been indefinable and endlessly debatable. A review of one of her films in a New York paper summed up Williams's appeal like this: "Miss Williams is no actress, but she is extraordinarily graceful when she gets in the drink." She conferred a mixture of glamour, graciousness, and California wholesomeness on a sport that, for women anyway, was still in the throes of finding an identity in the American imagination. She also unwittingly founded the sport of synchronized swimming.

That the Americans have dominated "synchro," as it is known around the pool, since its Olympic debut in 1984, has made little difference in our public perception of it. Although in Atlanta in 1996 the American team triumphed with a perfect score of 100, stroking and spinning to the classy strains of *Fantasia*, synchro has failed to strike much of a chord in the world of swimming. Perhaps, like beauty pageants, it seems a product of another era.

But it's a demanding sport: You need to have the heart and lung capacity of a competitive swimmer and the ability to tread water better than any water polo player. You've got to be able to hold your breath while executing moves that would give a gymnast pause. Sometimes you do all this upside down. And while other athletes are allowed, even encouraged, to look as if they're feeling the burn, the performance of a synchronized swimmer is marked down if she appears winded.

The current American champion is Becky Dykoen-Lancer, who in 1993 won an astonishing nine consecutive Grand Slams—a trio of first-place finishes in solo, duet, and team competition in a single meet. Due to a change in the synchro swimming rules for 2000, Dykoen-Lancer won't be able to compete in singles or even duets, which have been discontinued. Instead, she will be part of the eight-woman American team. People inside synchro swimming say this will be the equivalent of watching Mary Lou Retton compete among a troupe of high school gymnasts. The rule change reflects a desire to accommodate the tyranny of television—how much more exciting it is to watch eight women "blossom" and "corkscrew"

and, as the Americans did in 1996, impersonate a violin, playing one leg
with the other while treading water upside down—and acknowledges the
reality that there may not be enough world-class synchronized swimmers
to hold solo and duet competitions.

In the early 1960s tastes in Hollywood movies changed. Esther Williams's
star fell, and along with it the idea of swimming as something sensuous and
glamorous, an escape from the strictures of civilization. Although female
swimmers had been regularly breaking one another's records since 1916, the
first year the AAU held national championships, the image of the dour competitive swimmer up on the starting block swinging her powerful arms around
to loosen her shoulder joints had been overshadowed by Hollywood's version of the girl swimmer—playful, comely, somewhat inscrutable, always
traditionally feminine. As the world became increasingly enamored with the
modern Olympics, televised religiously every four years with greater and
greater fanfare, our image of the great swimmer gradually narrowed to someone who spent the time between Olympics imprisoned in a pool, preparing
for a race that would last mere minutes. Swimming, which came to mean
almost exclusively Olympic swimming, gained respectability while suffering
a loss of personality. No one save people inside the closed world of competitive swimming can tell the athletes apart, and fans of swimming, sportscasters, and sports journalists distinguish among the bobbing white swim caps
by devising superlatives: the first, the most, the only.

The first swimming superstar of the modern Olympic era was Australian Dawn Fraser. Born in 1937, Fraser was the first woman to swim the 100-
meter freestyle in under a minute. She was also the first woman to win three
gold medals, all in the 100-meter free, in consecutive Games, beginning in
1956. Her third medal was won in the 1964 Olympics in Tokyo, a mere six
months after her mother was killed in a car accident. (Fraser had been driving and suffered a chipped neck vertebra.) She was twenty-seven years old,
geriatric by today's standards, when fourteen-year-old girls routinely occupy
the top tier on the victory stand.

In an activity that was beginning to seem closer to a religious practice
than a sport, Fraser was rowdy in the old-style tradition of Eleanor Holm.
She liked to have fun. She shot off her mouth, claiming that if she'd been
allowed to swim naked, she would have broken every world record on the
books. In the 1964 Tokyo Olympics she refused to wear the regulation swimsuit, claiming it wasn't comfortable and hindered her performance. Then, in
what she said was simply a practical joke, she stole a Japanese flag from the
emperor's palace by climbing a fence and plunging into the moat. She was
arrested and later released, and in a move that shows how little a sense of

humor swimming officials had even in those days, she was banned from the sport for *ten* years. Even though the ban was lifted after four years, her career was finished.

That kind of unruly spunk has more or less disappeared from the public lives of world-class swimmers, for several reasons. The late 1950s and early 1960s saw the beginning of new conditioning techniques; training intensified. Goggles were invented, swimsuits streamlined. Rudimentary studies were launched on the prime age for female swimmers; extreme youth won out. Donna de Varona was thirteen when she qualified for the 1960 Olympic team. Although she failed to medal—she went on to win two golds in Tokyo in 1964—she was slapped on the cover of *Sports Illustrated* anyway. World records in every event steadily ticked downward.

There are limits, however. Limits in how much technology can improve performance, limits to how fast a human being can propel herself through water. The closer Olympic swimming comes to reaching those limits, the more it takes to bring down the existing record. It takes more training, more luck, more science than it did forty years ago to shave a few tenths of a second off a world record. Dawn Fraser's 1956 world record for the 100-meter freestyle was 62.0 seconds. The current record is an Olympic record held by Jingyi Le of China, 54.01 seconds. In forty more years it's unlikely that the record will drop a full eight seconds. Entire teenhoods are sacrificed to shave off a tenth of a second.

Prior to 1970, the story of excellence in competitive swimming was told by the numbers, the records for men and women marching down millisecond by millisecond in a similar fashion. From 1964 until 1971, a time in which no new discoveries were made that would enhance performance, few records were broken in either men's or women's events. Likewise, both men's and women's events were dominated by the United States and Australia. "The Star-Spangled Banner" was just about the only tune played during the award ceremony for men's 100-meter and 200-meter events, while the Australians routinely had their way with the longer distances. Again, the women's story is similar; Australians like Dawn Fraser and America's Donna de Varona reigned in short and long distances alike.

Then in 1972 came Kornelia Ender and the women of the German Democratic Republic, whose shoulders and arms bulked suspiciously. The numbers in the women's events ceased representing excellence and gave evidence instead of an aberration: drug use.

Before then, the GDR, as East Germany was known, had never been a presence in world-class swimming. Prior to the 1976 Summer Games in Montreal the East German women had never won a single gold medal in

Olympic competition. That year, they grabbed gold in eleven out of thirteen events and set eight world records. Ender, through no fault of her own, came to represent all that was warped about the East German swimming program, a program that relied on a Draconian training regime that robbed children of their childhood and then—although this didn't come out until much later—gave them drugs disguised as vitamins in order to give them every physical advantage.

By age eleven Ender had enrolled in a special school for gifted athletes; there, she swam seven miles a day under the supervision of both a coach and a doctor. By thirteen, she was formidable—five-eleven, 167 pounds—and was the anchor for two East German relay teams, both of which won silver medals in 1972. For the next four years, she was the master of both freestyle and butterfly sprints.

By 1973 she held *ten* world records in the 100-meter freestyle. In one race, the world record plummeted from 58.25 to 55.65 seconds. I remember watching Ender swim on television with some friends from my college swim team; we were still teenagers ourselves, and no one we knew looked like that, nobody. We saw these soft, unformed teenaged faces, faces not unlike our own, sitting atop Herculean shoulders, massive pectorals and deltoids. Ender went on to win four gold medals in the 1976 Olympics in Montreal and set a mind-boggling twenty-three records during her career. (Her record in the 100-meter free was broken by fellow East German Barbara Krause in 1980 and then by Kristin Otto, another East German.) In Montreal, she won two gold medals and smashed two world records in the space of twenty-eight minutes.

As the 1972 Games progressed, jaw-dropping amazement gave way to innuendo. Creepy rumors emerged that Ender's natural gifts had been enhanced with "vitamin cocktails" that included enough anabolic steroids to increase a female swimmer's testosterone by as much as three times that of a normal woman.

One of the most outspoken critics was the American Shirley Babashoff, who was bested by East Germans in every event in which she competed. She won a total of five silver medals and never won a gold. When Babashoff complained that there was something suspect about the East Germans' performance, she was accused of being a bad sport.

For the next eight years, the East German women were invincible. In 1988, at the Olympics in Seoul, Kristin Otto collected six gold medals, breaking Kornelia Ender's record by two. Again, there was talk about steroid use and again it was swept aside.

When the Berlin Wall came down, the secret of the East German women's swim team came out. Although no names were named, several eminent coaches went on record as saying that steroid use was quite prevalent among the women in the 1970s. *Swimming World* reported in 1994 that according to Dr. Warner Franke, a German biochemist and member of the national board of review investigating the situation, papers found in the files of the secret police "prove without a doubt that every single East German world-class athlete was doped." Ender has denied all knowledge of any drug use and never tested positive for drug use. She is quoted as saying, "You must understand that no one, not the swimmers or coaches or doctors, ever spoke about drugs. Sports officials never talked to us about anything. We never questioned what we were being given."

As for Shirley Babashoff, after her frustrating experience at the 1976 Olympics, she enrolled at UCLA. But the commitment and focus necessary for continuing to swim at her usual championship level eluded her. She left school after a year and wound up working as a mail carrier for the U.S. Post Office. Her response to the confirmation of what she already knew fifteen years ago: "What's the statute of limitations on cheating?"

The Olympic committee is currently considering repealing the medals won by the East Germans in the early 1970s, since the evidence of their drug-enhanced performances has become incontrovertible.

If the history of women in swimming has been skewed by the use of performance-enhancing drugs, it was deformed by the American boycott of the 1980 Olympics and the tit-for-tat boycott of the 1984 Games by the Soviet Union. The effect of the first boycott is obvious: swimmers who had qualified for that Olympic team had to hope that they were still good enough to qualify four years later. When the Soviet Union, as well as the rest of the eastern bloc, failed to show in 1984, it deprived athletes of the chance to prove themselves against the world's best swimmers. Careers were unmade. Nancy Hogshead, who at age fourteen set the American records in the 100-meter and the 200-meter butterfly, in 1978 had moved to Florida at age fifteen to train full-time for the 1980 Olympics. Mary Terstegge Meagher, another swimmer whose competitive life was forever compromised by the back-to-back boycotts, in 1981 set world records in the 100-meter and 200-meter 'fly that stood for fourteen years. She was sixteen years old.

The only American swimmer for whom the boycott, in retrospect, seemed a mere inconvenience was a young woman considered by many to be the Michael Jordan of women's swimming, Tracy Caulkins.

Caulkins, now thirty-five, had qualified for that 1980 team as a seventeen-year-old high school senior, arguably at the peak of her powers. Unperturbed, she went on to college at the University of Florida, where she continued to develop, astonishing the swimming community by winning more titles (forty-eight) and breaking more records (sixty-two) than any U.S. swimmer in history. Even more impressive was her versatility. Being a champion at that level usually means specialization, as a sprinter, or middle-distance swimmer, or an expert in the long course. In 1984, swimming five hours a day, six days a week, Caulkins set records in the 100-meter breaststroke, the 200-meter butterfly, the 200-meter individual relay (the most demanding event, which requires the swimmer to swim fifty meters each of freestyle, breaststroke, backstroke, and butterfly), and the 400-meter individual relay. She was also a member of the record-breaking 800-meter relay team. Although she had yet to set foot inside an Olympic Village, Caulkins was the best female swimmer in America. Some thought she was one of the greatest swimmers who ever lived.

In the same way that Eleanor Holm and Esther Williams embodied the ideal of the female swimmer in their time, Tracy Caulkins was the "perfect" swimmer of her time. On a world-class swimmer's résumé, besides the list of medals won for particular events, there is often mention of her grades when they are good, reflecting an entire life colored by intense focus and discipline. These days, a great swimmer is more likely to be an academic overachiever than a party girl. In addition to everything else she did, Caulkins was an Academic All-American in both 1983 and 1984.

In 1984, in Los Angeles, Caulkins set a new American record in the 400-meter individual medley on opening day, then went on to win two more gold medals. That year she was named Female Athlete of the Year by the USOC. Satisfied by her achievements, at twenty-one Caulkins retired.

The girl who broke Tracy Caulkins's record in the 400-meter individual medley was a fifteen-year-old named Janet Evans. The story of her greatness has become a comfortable tale of swimming destiny. Born in 1971, at one year she was already at home in the pool. By the time she was five she was racing, and before she was out of high school she held three world records.

We fell for Janet Evans in Seoul, in 1988, because she had a gorgeous, ear-to-ear grin and because she appeared to be the Girl Least Likely. We loved her because she was so small and lean as a whippet—at fifteen she was only five-three, weighed less than a hundred pounds, and had almost no body fat—and had a peculiar windmill stroke that looked as if it belonged to a cartoon character. In Seoul, she took gold medals in the 400- and 800-meter freestyle and the 400-meter individual medley. Her fourth gold came four years later, making her one of the only women to win gold medals in two consecutive Olympic Games. After the Olympics—always a difficult is-that-all-there-is time for champions—Evans dutifully went home to California and enrolled at Stanford University, where she was expected, like Caulkins, to plow through the water for four more years, grabbing medals and academic honors along the way.

Swimming at that level, year after year, all one's young life, in fact, is not simply exhausting, it's a virtual impossibility. Only a handful of people know what it's like to prepare for an Olympic swimming race. You train in the morning and then again in the afternoon. You swim five, six, seven miles a day, six days a week, for four years. At least. A school holiday means two practices that day instead of one. Sometimes you train so hard you pass out. You are an amateur expert in the science of hydrodynamics, which studies the effectiveness of swimming strokes, the way humans can maximize their speed in water. If you are male, you shave your chest, your legs, everywhere. Tiny bubbles affix themselves to a single hair shaft, creating drag, forcing you to work harder. If you are a woman, you are singular among most other athletes in that you don't mind a little body fat, for fat floats.

What goes on in your head during those hours upon hours in the swimming pool? According to both marathon swimmers, who slog away in large, open bodies of water, and competitive swimmers, who swim imprisoned in pools whose length, depth, and lane markings are legislated by the governing bodies of swimming, a lot of singing goes on. One guy I knew in college, an Olympic swimmer, swore by "Smoke on the Water." Childhood is revisited, past conversations edited, sexual fantasies pondered. Promises are made, treats are promised, if you can just get through the workout. Strangely, few swimming champions ever mention visualizing themselves up on the medal stand.

On the day of the race there is nausea. Watch the starter; pace yourself by finding marks in the pool: the three-foot mark on the side, the edge of the drain, an unidentifiable blotch on the bottom. Take a long, long time to undress, as long as they'll allow, hoping to cook your opponent. If she's prone to nerves, you'll know. If she's prone to nerves, you'll be able to cook her by making her wait. Try an intentional false start, if you dare. Then the gun goes off, and you go, and mostly you can't remember the rest.

Stanford swimming was not it for Evans. Though she got As and dragged herself to practice, when the NCAA instituted new guidelines reducing the amount of time a college athlete could train, Evans left school. Trading in her college eligibility for product endorsements and sponsorship deals, she moved to Austin, Texas, to train with a new coach. But she suffered the fate traditionally reserved for elite gymnasts. She grew, and she grew up. Although she won a gold in 1992 in Barcelona in the 800-meter freestyle, when she only silvered in her other race, the 400-meter, and failed to make the relay team entirely, audiences were disappointed.

* * *

Currently, the headline races of Olympic swimming, the short, flashy freestyle sprints, are ruled by the Chinese, who, like the East German women in 1972, came from nowhere to sweep the sprints in Barcelona in 1992. Again, there were young girls—although unlike the Germans, these girls were naturally tiny in build and stature—with enormous arms and backs, smashing world records. Although no Chinese woman has ever tested positive for drugs during the Olympics, they have tested positive ten times in world-class races, and in 1995 China was banned from competing in the Pan Pacific Games. Performance-enhancing chemicals are technologically ahead of the tests used to test them, the same way that the best burglars have the skill to dismantle the finest burglar alarms. Jingyi Le holds world records in both the 50- and 100-meter free, although Amy Van Dyken of the USA beat the Chinese swimmer to win the gold in the 50-meter free in Atlanta in 1996.

Janet Evans still holds records in the longer freestyle distances, although in Atlanta in 1996 she was whipped in the 800 by the self-styled, brash up-and-comer, sixteen-year-old Brooke Bennett, who, with her six earrings marching up one ear, her self-imposed tattoo limit of three, and her public dissing of Evans—she's been quoted as saying, "Janet knows there's someone else coming up to take her place"—has already mastered the all-important modern skill, crucial in athletics, of capturing ink. Bennett is not yet a great swimmer, but she is a sassy one, a throwback to flag-stealer Dawn Fraser. She's a girl with her own mind and a big mouth to go with it, as essential as a tank suit to competing, not just for medals but for media attention.

Still and all, the sport of swimming remains essentially impenetrable, because it will always be something done alone. When I left swimming for running, I was thrilled with the options. You could jog alone or with someone else. If you were with someone else, you could have a conversation. You could listen to music on a Walkman. Although you can buy a sort of Walkman that goes under water, it remains a mere gadget. Swimming is silent. No music, no conversation, save your own infernal thoughts.

Equestrian Sports

The Highest Risks for the Boldest of Athletes

Jackie C. Burke

Kathy Kusner feared sabotage as she prepared to ride in the 1971 Maryland Hunt Cup, arguably the world's most difficult steeplechase. She knew the all-male race committee—indeed, the male population in general—were displeased that a woman had entered this last bastion of manliness in the horse world. Considering that the first woman to enter the Boston Marathon was pushed out of the race by an irate male spectator only a few years before, Kusner said she "could envision someone pulling my horse's bridle off and chasing him away, leaving me standing there with no horse."

The Maryland Hunt Cup began in 1896 when the male ancestors of the 1971 race committee challenged one another to a race crossing the most daunting boundary-line fences that divided their Green Spring Valley hunt-country estates. Frankly, Kusner was not what the race founders had envisioned for their annual test of manhood. She was a slight brunette as pretty as Elizabeth Taylor in *National Velvet,* and as bold as the character the superstar portrayed—a girl who rode in the Grand National Steeplechase by disguising herself as a boy.

The committee held a midnight meeting on the eve of the race. Turney McKnight, one of the younger members of the group, as well as a lawyer, advised the board that there was no legal justification for prohibiting her participation as the Hunt Cup was open to amateur riders, and Kusner, a member of the 1964 and 1968 Olympic jumping teams, was an amateur in the ever watchful eyes of the U.S. Olympic Organizing Committee. As the first woman to hold a Maryland Racing Commission jockey's license and the holder of a National Steeplechase rider's license, she had the credentials generally required of Hunt Cup riders. Clearly, she had a legal right to ride. McKnight convinced the committee to allow Kusner to ride that

year and to avoid the predicament in the future by officially limiting the
race to gentlemen riders.

Ironically, Kristine Linley Matlack, McKnight's half-sister, had been
the one to name Kusner as her jockey. Matlack had been raised in the tradition of strong women—her mother skied in the Olympics—and as a racehorse owner and now a veterinarian, she believed her horse, Whackerjack,
would have his best chance with Kusner in the saddle. With a World and a
European Women's Jumping Championship in her trophy case, Kusner said,
"I had ridden in races for fifteen years, and I knew I could jump."

On race day the two women received permission to saddle the horse at
the van they had hidden at a neighboring farm to prevent tampering before
the race. However, when Whackerjack got to the paddock, he was forced to
plod around for almost an hour carrying the heavy saddle and lead pad needed
to bring the petite Kusner's riding weight up to the regulation 165 pounds.
Matlack says, "I guess they thought it would tire out the horse to carry all
that dead weight for so long. It didn't matter—he finished fifth, about where
we expected." Whackerjack had been shown by Linley Matlack in both hunter
and open jumper classes. He was not quite a "big time" show jumper, nor
did he have the heart or foot (speed) to be a top racehorse. What he did have
was the careful, canny ability to handle the Hunt Cup's huge timber jumps—
solid and ranging up to five feet, three inches in height—and one of the best
jumper riders in the world on his back. Kusner gave him a safe, sure ride over
the twenty-one fences and four-mile distance that made the event a marathon as well as a jumping contest.

After she pulled up, someone in the crowd rushed over and tried to grab
Kusner's saddle. Because riders must carry their own gear to the scales and
weigh back in with all equipment used, she could have been disqualified.

In subsequent years women have ridden in the Hunt Cup, steeplechasing's toughest challenge, on a regular basis and a number have won, starting with Joy Slater Carrier in 1980 and including Elizabeth McKnight,
Turney's wife, the winner in 1987, but it was Kusner that did it first so women
riders could follow.

The history of man and horse goes back a long way, and the relationship
between the two has been far reaching. Horses enabled ancient man to expand his hunting and trading territory, to make war on or escape from his
enemies, and to travel. Archaeologists and historians speculate that nomads
of the Eurasian steppes first mounted up sometime between 6000 and 3000
B.C. The first solid evidence of a horseback rider that can be accurately dated
is a Mesopotamian cylindrical seal carved in 2150 B.C. Man used the horse

not just for labor and travel but also for sport. Hunting on horseback was thought to build character and to serve as a school for life and for war, as was polo, which dates back at least twenty-five hundred years. Polo scenes were found etched on eighth-century Chinese tombs. Interestingly, they pictured women as both teammates and opponents of men.

Ancient art and literature also confirm that women hunted beside men, queens with kings. Greeks, Romans, and Celts even named their hunting deities after women. Perhaps the earliest women warriors were the Amazons of classical Greek legend, who bred and raised horses in Scythia, near the Black Sea. Great riders, they were the first to employ cavalry techniques. Queen Boadicea, a fearsome rebel leader mentioned in Caesar's *Commentaries on the Gallic War,* drove fleet-footed horses hooked to light chariots into battle against professional Roman legions, and Joan of Arc rode astride the thunderous warhorses of the Middle Ages to lead the French to key victories against the English during the Hundred Years War.

In the late 1300s, women's horsemanship suffered a major setback when the sidesaddle was invented. This impractical but "appropriate" style of riding continued to hinder women into the twentieth century. Led by the example of prominent women on sidesaddle like Anne of Bohemia, queen to Richard II of England, Catherine de Medici, and Queen Isabella—who pregnant with her first child managed to raise an army, to stem civil discontent, and to lead her troops in successful defense of invasion by Portugal—the female population rode sidesaddle because of growing popular opinion that it was the only fitting way for a lady to ride.

The sidesaddle handicapped the women who followed the hunt, especially after the nineteenth century, when the sport changed from slow processions with little or no jumping to one that rivaled steeplechasing in speed and obstacles to be crossed. Women of Victorian England could no longer keep pace as the course became too difficult when fields were fenced to enclose stock and drained for more efficient farming. But women continued to hunt in France through unfenced woods, in Ireland with its devil-may-care attitude about how you might get across the country, and in wild, wide-open America. In the states, it is estimated that more women hunted in 1800 than in 1900, and that as many women as men hunted in 1939. By this time older women in the hunt field still clung to the sidesaddle, but as before, practicality overcame piety in America at the turn of the century and young girls were being taught to ride astride on the cross saddle again.

Of course there were those who disapproved of women riding astride. Belle Beach wrote in her 1912 *Riding and Driving for Women* that a woman's thighs were too round and too weak to ride astride, and that the thought of a grown woman wearing pants was preposterous. But the change back to the cross saddle was partially motivated by economics as well. Custom-made sidesaddle equipment was too expensive for the growing middle class turning to riding and hunting for recreation.

Hunting as a rural pastime had gained popularity with the formation of the Master of Foxhounds Association in the late 1800s. Women were often invited and sometimes led the hunts. Mrs. Gertrude Rives Potts was recognized as the first woman master of foxhounds not long after the Association was founded. As Master of Foxhounds, an honor, a vocation, and an athletic pursuit, Potts imported and trained a pack of English foxhounds, bred and schooled her own horses, organized a hunting staff, and enlisted the consent of seventy-two neighboring landowners to form a suitable country for the Castle Hill Hounds. On hunting days, in the early 1900s, she rode out from her Virginia Piedmont estate before daylight, followed foxes deep into the Blue Ridge Mountains, and returned home with the hounds after dark. By 1928, ten women masters had followed Mrs. Potts's example. In 1995, 120 of 170 U.S. hunts were led by women.

Two of the most respected and longest-serving American masters of foxhounds are Nancy Penn-Smith (Mrs. John) Hannum of the illustrious Mr. Stewart's Cheshire (Pennsylvania) Hounds, who began as a young woman barely out of college and celebrated her fiftieth year as master in 1995, and Mrs. Theodora Ayer Randolph, who served as master of the Piedmont (Virginia) Hounds, America's oldest organized hunt, from 1954 until her death in 1996.

Mrs. Randolph's longtime huntsman Albert Poe relates a story from his first year with the Piedmont Hounds. He said that back in 1954 the hunt field obstacles consisted of huge stone walls and high post-and-rail fences. The first time he rode up to one of the five-foot-high walls, he stopped and tried in vain to lower the heavy telephone pole that hung over the top. Mrs. Bettina Belmont Ward, who rode up front with Mrs. Randolph that day, yelled for Poe to "jump or get out of the way." Poe says admiringly, "Those women were game!"

Horse shows in America and international jumping competitions in Europe were first held as the new century dawned. Polo, too, which followed British officers back from India, then jumped the big pond to America, and in 1896, the first international polo match was played in the U.S. Informal steeplechases hosted by hunt clubs sprung up everywhere, and in 1901 the first international show jumping contests were held in Europe, regulated by the host nation, with esteemed riders, both men and, sometimes, women, invited to participate. Horse sports including dressage, jumping, and "the military" were added to the Olympics in 1912, which replaced the annual World Cavalry Games. Shortly thereafter the Federation Equestre Internationale (FEI) was formed to regulate riding competition at the Olympics and other international competitions. But its primary interest was men's competition, so the women were forced to come up with alternate means of participation. Women moved into these new venues an inch at a time, shocking crowds by riding astride at the New York National Horse Show at Madison Square Garden in 1921 and in England's biggest international show in 1922.

During this time American women also began to organize polo leagues in Seattle, Santa Barbara, Colorado Springs, Omaha, Philadelphia, Baltimore, and Long Island. By the 1930s, they held their own "Ladies Races" at hunt-sponsored steeplechases and sometimes raced against men in cross-country races also sponsored by hunt clubs. A growing number of women also rode in international jumping events in special classes. In 1934 the American Horse Shows Association was formed to provide standard rules and begin recording results. The records show that while more men are listed among the winners during this time, the younger generation was dominated by girls performing well against the boys in horsemanship classes. Mary Hirsh was awarded a race horse trainer's license in 1936; Margaret Cotter won the 1941 Jumper championship at the New York National Horseshow.

By 1936, the FEI formally invited women to enter all international events making them subject to the same rules as men, though the FEI remained strong in its conviction about women in Olympic competition. Critical mass among women had been reached during the days of World War II, when able-bodied men were away and women like Judy Johnson were granted jockey's licenses, rode in steeplechases, took over the operations at stables, and saddled up in almost every category of horse competition. When the soldiers returned, the leisure class of men who had devoted their lives to horses were forced to work full time, and the women were not forced to surrender supremacy of the stables. But because men still held the reins of power for decisions regarding the Olympics, U.S. Polo, and state racing commissions, women weren't permitted equal access to most horse sports until much later.

In 1947, for instance, when the U.S. cavalry was disbanded, the members of former military teams—all men—were, by special orders, permitted to represent America in all-military Olympic equestrian events.

Not until 1949, when the U.S. Equestrian Team was formed, were open tryouts held for the 1950 Olympics. Two of the three riders selected for the first USE and jumping team were women, Carol Durand of Kansas City and Norma Mathews of California. In 1952 women joined the Olympic team in dressage as well. In 1968 American women were permanently granted jockey's licenses. During the 1970s and 1980s, it was not Title IX, lawsuits, or vocal advocates that brought about change, but women who knew they were good enough for the highest levels and just kept competing and winning until even all-male committees had to agree.

Equestrian sports are diverse if they are anything. Each subculture has its own special style of competition, its own ruling body, its own stars, and its own outstanding women. The three Olympic disciplines, jumping, dressage, and eventing, as well as those outside Olympic sanctions—racing, steeplechasing, and polo—each tell a story of struggle for women, and ultimately a tale of triumph.

Dressage, which is riding elevated to an art form, can best be described as ballet for horses. Competition bears certain similarities to figure skating. The Olympic test calls for specific movements, including correct demonstrations of the walk, trot, and canter at various speeds and in various configurations. Small circles and quick changes of direction require strength, balance, and precision. The test is performed in a regulation-sized arena before a panel of judges, who score correctness, smoothness, and grace.

In Europe, dressage has been practiced since the sixteenth century, when monarchs built indoor riding schools like the Spanish Riding School of Vienna. Some of the movements performed there are now included in the Olympic tests, such as the pirouette, a full circle at the canter in which the horse does not progress forward but spins around his hocks, and the piaffe, a trot in place. The concession to permit women to enter dressage didn't affront the male rule makers' egos. Men never felt very territorial about dressage, according to Donnan Sharp Monk, a member of the 1968 U.S. dressage team. Monk, whose former husband, Michael Plumb, rode on an unprecedented six Olympic eventing teams (and in the Alternate Olympics in 1980), says that back then it was assumed that anyone who could jump, jumped, and the rest did dressage, which is a little slow for the American lust for speed and excitement. The French word does not even have an English equivalent.

A photo in a riding magazine of Fritz Stecken performing the piaffe so inspired Marjorie Haines Gill that she took her entire $1,500 savings and moved to Long Island in 1951 to study under the German master. Before World War II, no one in America had even heard of dressage, save cavalry officers who had witnessed it in the Olympics and even had competed, though with a notable lack of success. After the war European experts like Stecken came here as refugees and began to ply their trade.

Haines was fresh out of art school, just twenty-one but with a lifetime of experience riding hunters and jumpers. Now a master of yoga and an experimenter in natural healing methods, she has always been a deep thinker and a seeker of the spiritual center. Dressage seemed to her like a new source of communication with the horse. Stecken selected Haines as the most promising of his handful of students and assigned her to ride Flying Dutchman, a grand old German horse that had been in training for the 1940 Olympics, then was liberated and sent to America by General George Patton, who spared such animals from slaughter by the approaching Russian armies.

There were so few American riders who wished to ride on the 1952 dressage team that tryouts were not held. Inspectors just visited the candidate's stable and watched each one ride. Haines, with just one year's dressage experience, was selected for the U.S. team and sent to the Helsinki games. She caught pneumonia on the boat going over, and Flying Dutchman became ill with shipping sickness and was saved by an Argentinean veterinarian traveling with his nation's team. Upon arrival in Europe, a weakened Haines found herself in a thoroughly hostile environment. The military and the male establishment might have selected a woman to ride on the team, but that didn't mean they liked it. The Germans weren't particularly welcoming, either, to an American mounted on one of their best horses.

Haines was very much on her own, with little solace and no coaching help, as Stecken, for political and financial reasons, could not accompany her. She was also ill prepared. Before traveling to Europe, she had never ridden a grand prix test of the sort used in the Olympics; indeed, she had never even watched one ridden to know how it should look. Haines had simply been mounted on a perfectly schooled horse and taught the Olympic-level movements. She says, "We Americans trying to ride dressage must have been a funny lot to those well-schooled Europeans. I just kept trying to remember what Fritz told me. That's all I could do."

Flying Dutchman's courage and Haines's natural talent shone through. They placed a respectable seventeenth, and the U.S. team placed sixth, a ranking America had bested only once since 1912, when the event was sanctioned by the IOC.

Haines was not the only woman to ride at Helsinki, and perhaps Lis Hartel's story is even more dramatic. Hartel, a Dane, was struck by polio in 1944 and told she would never ride again. With maximum effort she disproved this diagnosis, though she remained paralyzed below her knees and had to be lifted into the saddle. Hartel captured the attention of the world press when she won the individual silver medal in dressage in 1952. She recalls, "It was the first time women had competed equally with men in the equestrian games, and this really brought my name into the limelight worldwide, because not only was I a woman, but a handicapped woman!"

Hartel won the World Dressage Championship in 1954 and in the 1956 Olympics qualified for a ride-off for the gold, which never took place as the Swedish judge, hearing of the tie, scurried back and changed his score to give his countrymen both the individual gold and the team gold. She then retired from Olympic competition, but has continued to encourage the development of dressage around the world and mainstreaming the handicapped.

The dressage woman of today has challenges beyond riding skills and an invitation. She needs organizational talents and fund-raising efforts as well. Michele Gibson, a 1996 Olympian, was able to compete because the owner of the dressage horse she rode in the 1996 Olympics read an article in the Sunday *Atlanta Constitution* about the three years she had spent training in Germany as a working student. With Peron, a horse schooled to the Prix St. George level, the classification just shy of the Olympic Grand Prix, and the funds raised by friends through demonstration performances and generous donors, Gibson returned to Germany for three years' further training. With major European victories in her pocket, Gibson was the belle of the ball at the 1996 Olympics in her native Georgia. With the handsome bay stallion, she placed fourth individually and won the team bronze—in both cases equaling the best USET finishes in dressage.

Dressage demands patience and the ability to be in simpatico with the horse—the ideal picture in the dressage ring is one of perfect accord, in which the horse seems to imagine what is required without visible cues from the rider—there are certain to be more women competing by the 2000 Olympics. Donnan Monk concludes, "Dressage is a perfect sport for a woman. Women ride with their minds, not their bodies. They can get into a horse's head and bond with the animal."

Unlike dressage, which is subjectively judged, jumping is objectively scored, with penalties for knockdowns, falls, refusals, and exceeding the time limit for the course. For the Olympics the best three of the four rider's scores count toward the team tally, and at least three scores must be posted for the team to remain in contention. Jumping is dangerous and falls are not uncommon, given the size of Olympic jumps—over five feet high and seven feet wide on the first round—and the difficult juxtapositions of the sixteen to twenty obstacles. Men, wishing to protect women from harm, waited a little longer before permitting women to get into this venue. They didn't hesitate to borrow their well-schooled horses, however, and Pat Smythe, an English jumper, twice was forced to relinquish her horses to the men who were allowed to compete.

Smythe, a young English woman, began her climb to fame during World War II in Red Cross gymkhanas. She won the assortments of children's games on horseback and beat adults in the jumping classes as well. In 1945, when Smythe's father died and she and her mother lost their home, moved to rented rooms, and ran a riding school in nearby fields, the prize money that Smythe won in jumping classes helped make ends meet. Smythe began to win jumping events at the larger county shows and, at age twenty, was invited to tour Europe with the 1947 British squad. So successful was her international debut that she was asked to lend Finality, the small and sensitive mare she was riding, to the 1948 Olympic team for a man to ride. Smythe, raised to make sacrifices during wartime, went along, though the male riders had no success with Finality. She says, "It took really good hands to ride Finality. She wouldn't take any bossing or bullying." Smythe qualified for the 1952 Olympic team, but because rules still prohibited women in jumping, she again agreed to lend her horse, this time a large, excitable Thoroughbred named Prince Hal. Hal was no more fond of male riders than Finality had been, and when Hal was returned to Smythe, he was thin, in poor condition, and so nervous it took months of patient work to get him back in form.

Smythe was not the only woman sidelined in 1952. Carol Durand, who had been selected for the very first USET jumping team in 1950, was sent to Europe with her two horses in hopes she would be permitted to ride in the Olympics. But rules changed to permit women to ride only in dressage, so one of Durand's horses was named reserve for the Helsinki Games and the other was assigned to her best friend and horse-training buddy, Arthur McCashin. McCashin finished thirteenth in the Olympics and the team won the bronze medal.

Neither McCashin's son, nor Durand's husband, nor her former groom remembers her being unduly vexed or disappointed by her exclusion from the Olympics. It was the type of thing women had come to expect. Durand took part in eight team victories during the fall 1953 tour and was named Individual International Champion at the New York National. She quit the team after that, even as the rules changed to permit women to ride in the 1956 Olympics. "Riding on the team and traveling to the different horse shows took so much time away from her husband and young son. I think she wanted to stay home with her family," Kathi Fordyce, who groomed for both Durand and McCashin, speculates.

Smythe was still around, however, and finally got her chance to compete in the Olympics in 1956. The coach, so eager for her horses at two previous Olympics, now demanded she leave Prince Hal at home, even though the horse had won many international classes and set a number of women's high-jump records. She was forced to ride Flanagan instead, "a common little Irish horse," with only one year's international experience. Even so, she placed tenth best of sixty-six riders, helping win the team silver medal. "The coach didn't like me or my 'temperamental' horses," Smythe explained. "The Olympic jumps were so high and distances between fences so long—the standard distance of an 'in and out' is twenty-four to twenty-six feet; at Helsinki two fences, nearly five feet high and well over five feet wide, were placed twenty-nine feet apart—that the course favored the big, powerful German horses. Prince Hal could have bounded over the course. I think he would have won the gold medal, given a chance." She rode on the British squad again in the 1960 Games, then retired from competition, married, and raised a family.

No American women came forth to follow Durand's early efforts until 1958. Four male riders—William Steinkraus, Hugh Wiley, George Morris, and Frank Chapot—carried the jumping team through the fifties, but by the next decade the talent pool had become shallow and the tryouts for the United States Equestrian team were finally open in 1958. Kathy Kusner was among those at the trials. Team coach Bertlen de Nemethy, a Hungarian, had not come from a tradition of women riders but selected Kusner for further training. His wife, Emily, observed, "When he saw Kathy, he knew what he had."

Morris and Wiley both dropped off the team before the 1964 Games, opening berths for Kusner and Mary Mairs, a later addition to the team, then only twenty years old. Both rode again in 1968 when the U.S. team placed fourth, one quarter of a point off a medal, over an excessively difficult course that accounted for over one hundred faults by the winning team (compared with an average of twelve at other Games). In 1972 Kusner rode on the U.S. squad that came within one quarter of a point of winning the gold.

During Kusner's ascendancy in the jumping world, Melanie Smith, a young Memphis Pony Clubber, was practicing and dreaming of riding on the team. Doors began to open for Smith when former Olympian George Morris took an interest in her. She was selected to ride on the 1980 USET jumping squad only to experience the disappointment of so many athletes when President Carter decided that the United States would boycott the 1980 Olympics. Smith contented herself with an individual bronze for the Alternate Games and once again made the team in 1984. That year, Smith and Leslie Burr-Howard joined two male riders to claim team gold medals, the first won by Americans and by women.

In the 1984 Games, only three of the ninety or so riders were women, and each won a medal—Smith, Burr-Howard, and Heidi Robbiani, the individual bronze winner representing Switzerland. In 1996, again three women won medals—Leslie Burr-Howard and Anne Kursinski helped the United States win the team silver, and Alexandra Ledermann of France won the individual bronze.

Though women have not yet won the individual gold in Olympic jumping, they have proved themselves the best in every other big class in the world. Both Smith and Burr-Howard have won the World Cup, and Burr-Howard has won the richest jumping class in the world, the 1997 $725,000 du Maurier

Class at Calgary, Canada. Even compared to these prizes, Burr-Howard has said there is no thrill like representing one's nation in the Olympics, especially in your own country.

Young jumper rider Alison Firestone has already enjoyed the excitement of winning some of show jumping's top prizes and may yet parlay experience gained under a USET developing riders' grant to Olympic gold. Developing riders' grants offer invaluable international experience by permitting riders like Firestone to represent the United States in second-tier European competitions. Firestone started riding jumpers at age eleven. She won the World Cup in 1997 and 1998, and at twenty-one she was rated number one in the 1997 Samsung World Cup Series. So far as the Olympics go, Firestone said she takes each day at a time.

William Steinkraus, America's first individual gold medal winner in jumping, says that winning the gold is like catching the brass ring. The fact that women have not won is probably a statistical anomaly, especially considering that in America women are regularly selected for American Olympic teams, and those of other English-speaking countries as well, but they are rarely or never chosen for European or South American teams.

Rules banning women from participating in the Olympic three-day event, considered the most dangerous and physically challenging equestrian venue, took the longest to change. In the early years, eventing, as it is now called, was simply referred to as "the military." The three-day tests incorporate simplified versions of both dressage and jumping, the other two Olympic disciplines, as well as a grueling endurance test. Dressage, ridden on day one, was originally held to prove the obedience of an officer's horse for the parade field; the cross-country of day two measured a horse's fitness to carry a courier over any terrain; and stadium jumping on the final day assured the horse's fitness to continue after the exertions of the endurance phase.

The endurance test at the Olympics consists of four phases. Phases A and C are roads and tracks, with a combined length of up to twelve and a half miles, taken at a trot. Phase B is a two-mile steeplechase course ridden at racing speed. The final, D phase is a challenging cross-country course that can exceed four miles and include up to thirty-two obstacles that are a maximum of three feet, eleven inches high, six feet wide at the top, nearly ten feet at the bottom, and solid in nature. Each phase has a time limit, with penalties assessed for overtime and additional penalties allotted for refusing or falling at obstacles on the steeplechase or cross-country.

The sport is extremely taxing and can be dangerous. Injuries are commonplace and deaths not unheard of. Two Olympic-level riders have died in recent years as the result of falls while competing, including Amanda

Warrington, one of America's brightest hopes. In the Olympics, three of the four team riders must finish, so competitors who fall on cross- country often remount and finish even with broken bones to keep their nation's team in the running. (Even HRH Princess Anne fell on the 1976 Olympic course, suffered a concussion, and completed the course to register a score for the British team.)

As the FEI rules did not ban women from any competitions except the Olympics, women rode in and even placed in the very first nonmilitary, international three-day event in 1949 at Badminton, England, which with its diabolically difficult cross-country jumps is still considered the toughest in the world. In 1951 Jane Drummond-Hay (now Whitely) placed second and was promptly asked to lend her horse to men on the 1952 Olympic team, since women were not permitted to ride. Margaret Hough won Badminton in 1954, and agreed to donate her carefully trained horse to the 1956 Olympic team as an alternate.

In 1956 Sheila Willcox won second place at Badminton and when Olympic selectors asked for her horse, the twenty-year-old Miss Willcox said no. High and Mighty was her only horse, and if injured, a very real possibility in such a dangerous sport, she would have nothing with which to compete. Willcox was so vilified by the press that she finally agreed to sell her beloved horse, though it was reported that the horse was lame and would not be used for the 1956 Games. Willcox says, "The trouble was, none of the men on the team could ride High and Mighty. He was really just an overgrown pony. If you didn't stir him up, which none of the men could do, he'd think, 'Well, too bad, I'm not doing that!'" Willcox bought her horse back for his sale price and, to prove he was perfectly fine, won Badminton the following year by the largest margin ever recorded. Willcox won Badminton for a third straight year on a different horse, lest there be any doubt of her ability.

The IOC was still not convinced that women should ride on Olympic teams because they feared a woman would not be capable of continuing if she fell on course, that she might not be able to compete due to gender differences. Willcox says, "I always delighted in walking up to an old colonel—the kind who barks—and saying, 'Guess what? I'm having my period, and look at me, I'm still standing!'" In 1964 the FEI voted to drop the rule that banned women from the Olympic three-day, though British members of the committee still voted against the change. Most credit Willcox's excellence and accomplishments as provoking the change. Ironically, she was never selected for the British team because she was quite unpopular with the selection committee, going back to the time she wouldn't hand over High and Mighty. She was still winning in 1971 and still hoping to make the Olympics when her riding career ended with a fall at the Tidworth three-day that crushed her T-6 vertebra, broke T-7, stretched her spinal cord, and left her paralyzed. Though she was given no hope of walking again, she has beaten the odds and, though badly crippled, is ambulatory.

So it was that American Lana du Pont became the first woman ever to ride and also the first to medal in Olympic eventing. Du Pont (now Wright) says that that honor should have gone to Willcox or one of the other great British women. She says, "I was just lucky to be in the right place at the right time with the right horse."

Du Pont became interested in eventing while still at Oldfields Preparatory School. She told her friend Donnan Sharp Monk about the sport, and they followed their interest to the USET training grounds in Gladstone, New Jersey, where riders in all three Olympic disciplines gathered for coaching. Neither can say now what they were doing there, since women back then were not permitted to enter the three-day. Monk said they were welcomed because they brought along Richard Watjen, an excellent dressage coach who helped team riders in every discipline. Watjen convinced Monk to specialize in dressage, but du Pont refused to switch. When the 1964 team trials were held, she says, three experienced riders were clearly the best, and she and Billy Haggard, who had been on a Pan-American team, were about equal fourths. When rules changed that year to permit women to ride the Olympic three-day event, she found herself on the team, headed for Tokyo. Haggard, in a sportsmanlike gesture typical of him, sent his horse Bold Minstrel to Tokyo for Mike Plumb to ride.

Du Pont had little international experience. She didn't know how to ride the Olympic course, but she was too shy to ask her team members for help, and the coach who had accompanied the team did not consider it his duty to walk the cross-country course or to counsel the riders. During the competition she fell in the middle of a jump because of mud caused by a heavy rainstorm. With a leg up from Donnan she went on and, in spite of a second fall, finished the course, proving false all those theories about a woman's lack of courage to carry on in the face of adversity. She rode in stadium jumping the final day (learning only later that her horse had broken his jaw in their first fall) and stood on the podium afterward to collect a team silver.

It was quite a while before other American women followed du Pont. In eventing, as in jumping, a few good riders had carried the U.S. team for a decade, and none were in the wings to follow. When Jack le Goff was hired as coach for the USET, a talent search was held and a number of women were selected for further training. A democratic Frenchman, le Goff had seen women coming to the forefront in his sport before moving to America. When it came time to name teams, he didn't hesitate to include Mary Ann Tauskey on his gold medal–winning team for 1976; Karen Stives and Torrence Watkins, individual bronze medal winner, for the Alternate Olympics in 1980;

and those two again on the gold-medal team of 1984, with Stives winning the individual silver. By the time le Goff retired, capable riders of both sexes in this country abounded.

American women have ridden on every Olympic team since 1976. Karen Lende O'Connor rode on the team in the 1988 Olympics, and in 1996 she joined her husband, David, Bruce Davidson, and Jill Henneberg on the podium for the team silver medal. The husband-wife duo of Team O'Connor have the organizational skills, as well as riding skills, to solicit and manage a steady stream of international-level horses. Their vast experience leads to more wins, which leads to more horses.

As with jumping, it is the English-speaking countries—the United States, Canada, Great Britain, Ireland, Australia, and New Zealand—that give women a chance to compete internationally. Still, women are proportionately underrepresented in eventing at the Olympics, though not to the degree seen in jumping, and not at all on the medal podium. While women have not yet won the individual gold in eventing, women have captured Badminton and its American cousin, Rolex, Kentucky, as often as men.

Women have needed courage, determination, and even a lawsuit to get a toehold in the racing world. Jockey licensing, granted by state-appointed racing commissions, and steeplechase licenses, doled out by the National Steeplechase Association (NSA) weren't offered to women until forced to by the courts in 1968.

Betty Bosley Bird was not permitted to ride in the 1947 Maryland Hunt Cup, though her horse, Count Stefan, finished second, and in the 1953 Hunt Cup her entry, Marchized, won. Had the times been different, Bird undoubtedly would have been granted a jockey's license, and so would Sally Roszel, one of her leading rivals in ladies' steeplechases.

Roszel was a leading lady steeplechase rider from the 1940s to 1960 on the highly contested Virginia point-to-point circuit, informal steeplechases held by hunts which offer one race on each card for women. She was also one of the best exercise riders around. Roszel schooled steeplechasers for top trainers both at the Maryland tracks and at Stephen Clark's in Middleburg, Virginia, until she was brought to the attention of management by male pros who complained that they were losing business to her and demanded that Roszel be ruled off. "I don't want to sound bitter, but I was really disappointed when I could no longer ride at the track. I really loved to jump a horse over a big fence." In the 1950s women started making inroads on the stable side of the racetrack. By the 1960s, a number of leading trainers had taken on dependable, quiet women, naturally lighter in weight than men, to work their high-strung young thoroughbreds.

Each August Kathy Kusner took a holiday from touring with the USET jumping team to gallop horses at Saratoga Springs, New York, where the best trainers in the world converge for the one-month race meet. The trainers for whom Kusner rode every morning told her, "If only you had your jockey's license, we would let you ride in the afternoon [in the races]."

Kusner says, "Of course they would say that. They had nothing to lose. I didn't have my license."

Each year, Kusner longed to ride as a jockey and hoped one of the exercise girls who rode year-round would take the plunge and apply for a license. Kusner said she didn't have the time because she had a whole other life with the jumpers. Finally, though, in 1967 she saw that the clock was running out. She was already twenty-eight years old, and if she was going to have a chance to race, it was now or never.

Kusner asked racing stewards in West Virginia what it would take to get a license. They welcomed her interest and told her to hire a lawyer for assistance with the application process. Through a friend she procured the services of Audrey Melbourne, who was a moxie lawyer with knowledge of the racetrack. The one thing, though, was that Melbourne was licensed in Maryland, so the case would have to be filed there. Kusner remembers Audrey saying, "This isn't going to be a problem," and admits she's never let her forget that.

Melbourne, who now sits on the Maryland Circuit Court, the first woman ever elected to that position, says that she knew Kusner's application would be turned down and that the Maryland Racing Commission would deny that they refused on the basis of sex. Steinkraus, Kusner's fellow Olympic team member, recalls with admiration, "The racing commission lectured the two women like they didn't know anything about racing. Melbourne listened patiently, then took them off at the knees."

Rhetoric notwithstanding, it took one full year for the process to work its way into circuit court. The racing commission contended that Kusner "simply didn't ride well enough," even though she had ridden in any race that would permit women riders since age sixteen, worked for a number of top racehorse trainers, and passed every competency test demanded by the racing commission.

Kusner says, "What was always so frustrating was that I was being denied solely because I was a woman. I know men who were granted their license promptly, though they had no riding background simply because they were short."

Melbourne says that although it has long been believed that this was tried as a sexual discrimination case, it was not. She presented it as an administrative law case—that is, the state offers licenses for a profession, and a qualified applicant was unfairly denied. Melbourne proved her case with such simple and sure logic that no other qualified woman has since been denied her jockey's license in the United States. "To say it took the court thirty seconds to decide the case would be an exaggeration. It took nine seconds for them to find in my favor," Kusner says. The case also had implications in numerous foreign countries.

Kusner missed the opportunity to be the first woman to actually race at a pari-mutuel track as she was sidelined shortly after receiving her license in October 1968 by a broken leg suffered riding for the United States at the New York National. But that November, Penny Ann Early, exercise girl for trainer Willard Proctor, was entered in a race at Churchill Downs in Louisville, Kentucky, the track that hosts the Kentucky Derby each May. The day Early was to ride, a Derby atmosphere pervaded, with the stands and the pressroom full. When it came time for her race, instead of walking out to the paddock with Early, the male jockeys staged the first boycott of the track's ninety-four-year history. Stewards switched Early's race to the final race of the day and worked frantically to persuade the men to ride. Finally, in order not to lose the betting handle (the track's portion of bets placed), they ruled that Early would have to be replaced by a man.

Barbara Jo Rubins was slated to race at Tropical Park (now Calder) in Florida January 15, 1969. While Rubin waited for her opportunity huddled in the Red Cross trailer that served as her makeshift changing room, a brick was hurled through the window. She had been named to the last race of the last day of Tropical Park's meet. She figured that if the jockeys boycotted, as it was rumored they would, Rubin could simply mount up, walk across the finish line, and, as the only finisher, be declared the winner. The crowds would have their show. Instead, the jockeys boycotted during the fifth race and caused chaos in the packed stands. Once again, the stewards replaced the woman with a male jockey. This time, though, they fined the boycotting jockeys $100 each and sent word out that the next time the penalty would double, then redouble until the men got the message. Jockey's Guild representatives advised men not to accept rides if they were unwilling to compete against women.

"Their excuses were so lame," rider Diane Crump recalls. She had been working with thoroughbred horses since the age of thirteen, but says that she had never imagined women would ever be permitted to ride as jockeys. Then she heard about Kathy's lawsuit and thought, "All right, I want to ride races right now!"

Crump was entered to race in 1968 at Hialeah, Florida, unexpectedly, by a trainer she scarcely knew. When she learned of her entry from a fellow exercise rider at Gulfstream Park Race Course, she had to borrow racing equipment. Crump was escorted to the paddock by armed guards to ward off aggressive crowds who hurled bottles as well as insults. George Johnson,

Jr., supervisor of the Florida State Racing Commission, was determined to put an end to the male jockeys' shenanigans. He said, "God help them if they cause trouble this time." Nothing untoward occurred. Crump rode a horse not figured to be a factor to finish tenth in a field of twelve, then came back less than one month later and won at Gulfstream Park.

The first woman to win a pari-mutuel race was Barbara Jo Rubin, on February 22, 1969, at Charles Town, West Virginia. She then won nine of her first eleven races in spite of rough riding and fouls by male jockeys, whom she never called up before stewards because she says that the men were testing her, and if she had snitched, it would have been the end of her career.

Robyn Smith is one of the best remembered of the early women riders, both because she was the first woman to be a leading jockey on the highly competitive New York race circuit, and because the beautiful rider with the looks of a fashion model is Fred Astaire's devoted widow.

By 1969 three women were entered to ride in an NSA-Sanctioned steeplechase at the Middleburg, Virginia, spring races. When Ready Snodgrass, Katherine Kingsley (then Chatfield-Taylor), and Mary Ryan raced in Ladies' point-to-point races, they were well known and respected by the male steeplechase jockeys, who had no qualms about riding against them. Since the NSA had lost against Melbourne, there was no reason not to assign the women to mounts for the 1969 Middleburg, Virginia, Spring Races. They already had won races on these mounts and the women were the best-qualified riders, period. "When I heard I was entered, I grinned all over, then was scared to death," Snodgrass said. If stage fright set in, it was not because she sensed this to be a historic moment. "I was young, dumb, and happy— just doing what I liked to do best." While none of the women placed that day, they did not cause any problems on the racecourse, and soon after more women were granted licenses. Perhaps because of the discrepancy in the numbers, or more likely because neophyte riders are not given many mounts, the first race won by a woman was a long time in coming.

Barbara Kraeling McWade took the honor at Radnor, Pennsylvania, in 1975, aboard Fuzz Ears, a horse that she owned and trained under the watchful eye of mentor Lovell Stickley. Wins followed for women picking up speed after Joy Slater Carrier's win (aboard a family-owned and -trained horse) in the Maryland Hunt Cup, and proved that women jockeys really could do anything. After that, the most prestigious steeplechases started falling into the hands of women on a regular basis, including the title of champion jockey, which is given to the rider who accumulates the most first-, second-, or third-place finishes throughout the year.

Blythe Miller is one of the most successful jockeys of the 1990s. She won the overall jockey's championship in 1994 and 1995, after just missing the title in 1993. The daughter of steeplechase trainer Bruce Miller and Nancy

Miller, a professional horsewoman who runs a fox-hunting barn, Miller began her steeplechasing career while studying interior design at Mount Vernon College and jogged five miles per day to train for races on the weekends. After graduation, she turned down offers from design firms to follow her first love, riding fast and true over steeplechase fences. In 1996 her title slipped away to her brother Chip, but she still averages nearly $500,000 per year in purses in a sport with many fewer races than are offered at the flat tracks. To bring the steeplechasing story full circle, the 1997 title went to Archibald Kingsley, son of Kassie Kingsley, and her son George was 1998 leading Virginia point-to-point rider.

The most famous present-day woman jockey is Julie Krone, many times leading rider at a number of the biggest tracks and the first to win one of the Triple Crown races, capturing the Belmont in 1993. By 1996, she had won $53 million in purses. Jockeys receive pay for each horse raced regardless of its finish, along with 10 percent of purses for winning rides and 5 percent of second-place finishes. Stakes carry the richest purses, from $25,000 for a minor race to $300,000 and up for a Grade I event like those of the Triple Crown. Comparisons among professional athletes regularly find jockeys to be the fittest of all tested. Krone says that race riding blends aerobics with the mental discipline of yoga and the flexibility of gymnastics. One of the keys to her success is that she figures out how each horse would like to be ridden.

There have not been as many success stories for women on the race-track as there have been in other equestrian venues, perhaps because racing is the most dangerous and intensely physical of all such sports. Taking a fall while racing is a little like standing on top of a car (horses' backs measure five to six feet off the ground) and jumping off while traveling at forty miles an hour, then being trodden upon by ten or so oncoming quadrupeds, each weighing in excess of a thousand pounds and shod in steel shoes. Steeple-chasing adds to deadly speed the element of jumping, in which a scrum of eight to fifteen horses leap fourteen to twenty-one fences, four to five feet in height. On average, one in every ten rides ends in a fall. Not only is it dangerous, but it requires a lot of experience, and quite a lot of money.

Experience is acquired with time and effort and, for those of more modest means, opportunity may be obtained through 4-H riding programs or the U.S. Pony Club, an organization dedicated to teaching horse care as well as horsemanship. Pony club programs started such riders as Melanie Smith and Karen O'Connor on paths that led all the way to the Olympics.

Equestrian sports have a mystique about them that have always drawn women to the sport. Little girls love horses, captivated by their beauty and power; women love the freedom they feel in the saddle; females love the equality of the competition. There is the emotional bond between a woman rider and her horse, and women love the empowered feeling they have in the stable, on the track, and in the ring.

Today the vast majority of participants in most horse sports are women. Girls outnumber boys in the Pony Club by at least ten to one and in the American Horse Shows Association by better than eight to one. Even in racing, steeplechasing, and polo, where one sees a predominance of men, women are beginning to catch up. Twenty colleges from Stanford to University of Virginia to Cornell to Texas A&M boast of women's polo teams.

The secret to accomplishments in riding sports is believing in one's own talent and not taking no for an answer. Kathy Kusner, who charted her way through unbroken ground in more than one riding field, was told repeatedly that she couldn't possibly do the things she proposed to do. Defiantly and confidently she refused to give in. "If I want to do something, and I'm not doing it now, what have I got to lose by trying?"

Gymnastics

*T*he Battle Against Time and Gravity

Jane Leavy

In 1956, when women's gymnastics was still the province of grown women, Agnes Keleti of Hungary arrived at the Olympic Games in Melbourne, Australia, with a higher purpose. Sixteen years earlier, she had been an aspiring young gymnast when Adolf Hitler's pursuit of a master race forced the cancellation of the 1940 Olympics. It had been much more than an inconvenience to her, the loss of the proverbial athletic dream. Agnes Keleti was Jewish.

In 1941 she was expelled from her gymnastics club, along with all other non-Aryan competitors. When the Nazis occupied Hungary, her family went into hiding. She survived the war, living on forged papers purchased from a Christian girl. She worked in a munitions factory and later as a maid for the Nazi-sponsored deputy commandant of Budapest. She smuggled food to her mother and sister living underground in a safe house operated by the Swedish humanist Raoul Wallenberg. They survived, thanks to Wallenberg. But her father died in the gas chamber at Auschwitz.

When the war ended, Keleti, then twenty-seven, went back to gymnastics. In her last training session before the Olympic competition in London was to begin, she tore a ligament in her ankle. She watched the 1948 Olympics on crutches.

Four years later, she made her belated Olympic debut in Helsinki, the first Olympics to feature individual gymnastics competition for women. Keleti stunned everyone but herself by winning the gold medal on the floor exercise, a silver in the team competition, and a bronze medal on the uneven bars.

Keleti returned to Hungary, her Olympic career seemingly complete. But history intervened once again. By 1956, the Hungarian insurrection against the communist regime was reaching its zenith. Having lived through

the Nazi occupation, she wanted no part of communism. Gymnastics offered
a path to freedom. Defying both time and gravity, she tried out for her third
Olympics. Again, she made the team.

The Soviets invaded Hungary less than three weeks before the Games
began. While Soviet troops were putting down the uprising with tanks and
shells, Agnes Keleti was in Melbourne becoming the oldest gold medalist in
gymnastics history. She was thirty-five years old.

Keleti never returned to her homeland. After the 1956 Games, she received political asylum in Australia. Later, she moved to Israel, where she
became the national gymnastics coach and the mother of two sons at the age
of forty-one and forty-three. "They didn't believe I could win a gold medal
when I was thirty-five, and I won four," she once said. "My children were
just two more gold medals."

> *"Oh, my God, thirty-five?" says Nadia Comaneci.*
> *"Should I know her?" asks Mary Lou Retton.*
> *"Wasn't she Yugoslavian or something?" says Kerri Strug.*

It is neither particularly surprising nor particularly damning that modern gymnasts know nothing of Keleti. In the world of gymnastics, 1956 is
*pre*history, a time remembered vaguely in sepia tones and grainy black-and-
white, sixteen-millimeter film. The transcendent beauty of the human form
in unexpected motion hasn't changed since then. But everything else about
gymnastics has, thanks in large measure to Comaneci, Retton, and Strug.

Comaneci, with her seven perfect 10s at the 1976 Games in Montreal,
raised the bar for everyone, establishing perfection for the first time not just as
a goal but as a real possibility. Retton, who was then seven, watched at home
on television in West Virginia and announced, "I can do that." And she did.
By becoming the first U.S. gymnast to win the Individual All-Around competition at the Olympics in 1984, she laid claim to the sport for a generation of
American girls like Kerri Strug, who grew up watching *her* on television.

Twelve years later, at the 1996 Olympics in Atlanta, Strug vaulted into
national consciousness by completing a one-and-a-half twisting Yurchenko
vault on an ankle shorn of ligaments. It was an athletic profile in courage
and brought to gymnastics a new dimension of gallantry. But it also raised
questions about the trajectory of the sport and the women in it. Will they,
should they, continue to embrace the male ethos that dictates "Ya gotta play
hurt"?

Gymnastics today is a combination of unsurpassed beauty, daring, and
risk. In a sport defined by the difficulty of combinations, this is the most
difficult combination of all. Every four years, these flying nymphettes soar
to prominence, performing flips and twists, layouts and saltos, Tsukaharas

and Yurchenkos, terms of art that briefly become household words. It doesn't matter if we can't define them. We know what they are—astonishing.

The trajectory path of human performance always has been higher, faster, farther. Pushing the envelope is what we do. But in women's gymnastics, higher, faster, and farther has also meant smaller, lighter, and younger—adulthood held in abeyance. In the last twenty-five years, high-octane performances have been fueled by high-tech developments in training and equipment. The exercise floor on which Comaneci performed was little more than a wrestling mat. Today's gymnasts perform on spring-loaded exercise floors and balance beams.

They fly through the air feigning the greatest of ease, routinely defying physics and credulity. In fact, for every landing they "stick" in the crucible of competition, there have been hundreds more practiced in the gym. In Keleti's day, practice consisted of a couple of hours two times a week. She took up gymnastics in order to make herself strong enough to play the cello. Today elite gymnasts put in forty-hour workweeks. Injuries due to overtraining and metabolic changes that stave off puberty threaten their all too brief careers.

Baseball players get three strikes; quarterbacks get four downs. Gymnasts get one shot. One bobble, one misstep out of bounds, one ill-timed growth spurt, and a career can be over. The margin for error is as slim as the athletes themselves. The pressures, physically and emotionally, are enormous. Because the window of opportunity for success is so small and can close so fast, elite gymnasts live in a kind of suspended animation. The sport demands and rewards monastic devotion, a singularity of purpose and focus that may serve well later in life but doesn't allow much for growing up.

It is a hothouse existence, protected and rarefied, pressured and stifling. Retton's wedding was a turning point in her life, she once said, not just because she was getting married but because, for the first time, she was making all the decisions. "You're mature one way and very immature in other ways," she says. "You spend your childhood basically in a leotard."

The urge to tumble, flip, and fly is as old as the gods. Throughout history there have been those with the uncanny ability to flout the natural laws that ground most mortals. That is what makes them so compelling. Everyone loves the daring young man on the flying trapeze.

Modern gymnastics is the hybrid offspring of two ancient and opposed pursuits: entertainment and fitness. It is an elegant carny act performed in unadorned leotards. Western tradition has always embraced the concept of a fit body and a fit mind—for males. In ancient Greece, gymnastics was an integral part of the Olympics and an indispensable part of a young man's schooling, a means of building strength and overall health.

Plato endorsed the value of physical exercise for men and women alike. "I assert without fear of contradiction that gymnastics and horsemanship are as suitable to women as to men," he wrote in *The Laws*. But he was ahead of his time.

For women, acceptance of such unseemly behavior came grudgingly and in fits and starts. Physical daring was tolerated as long as it was theatrical, spectacle as opposed to competition. The earliest gymnasts were performers who combined acrobatics and dance. They entertained royalty as far back as the pharaohs. Bas-relief images of female acrobats can be found at the temple of Queen Hatshepsut in Karnak (circa 1480 B.C.)

By the Middle Ages no great European court was without acrobats and tumblers, jesters and jousters. But, by then, the role of women was already constrained by notions of modesty, frailty, and virtue. Renaissance women played the lute. They did not stand on their heads in public.

In the 1800s Frederick Jahn, of Germany, the father of modern gymnastics, popularized the notion of building strength through working out. The equipment he invented and promoted—parallel bars, vault, and horizontal bar—was used exclusively by men. He called his exercises "turnen"—from the French word for tournament. They later became mandatory for all German soldiers.

As the new century approached, attitudes toward female fitness began to change. Vassar College made physical education mandatory in 1886. The exercises were not for public consumption or even artistic merit but aids in the battle against disease, particularly tuberculosis.

Ladies gymnastics made its Olympic debut as an exhibition sport in 1904, when women clad in long skirts and high collars performed field exercises with wands and barbells. The first official Olympic competition did not take place until 1928. Teams of eight women competed in a group exercise performed with clubs, canes, ropes (then called portable apparatus), on the vaulting horse, and in a free exercise with the apparatus of their choice. The gold medal was won by the Dutch, five of whom were Jewish. Only one survived the Holocaust. The others perished along with their children at Sobibor and Auschwitz.

The 1928 competition was considered experimental and was not held again in 1932. Two years later, the first world championships for women took place. And two years after that, women were finally allowed to compete on the uneven bars.

Individual Olympic competition for women, as we know it today, did not exist until 1952, also the year the Soviet Union made its Olympic debut. It marked the beginning of forty years of Soviet and eastern European domination in the sport. Soviet team officials refused to allow their athletes to live among the sweaty capitalists in the Olympic village in Helsinki. They erected a scoreboard in their fenced-in camp to keep track of the medal race between the United States and the USSR. When the Americans went ahead near the end of the games, the board was wiped clean.

The Soviet team won its first of ten consecutive gold medals in Helsinki, a string broken only by its boycott of the 1984 Los Angeles Games. The inaugural gold medal for the individual all-around was also won by a Soviet, Maria Gorokhovskaya, a tradition handed down to Larissa Latynina (1956, 1960) and to Lyudmila Tourischeva (1972).

The most famous of the Soviets was the least athletically accomplished. Olga Korbut became a cult figure in the West without winning the all-around competition. At four-feet-eleven and eighty-five pounds Korbut was the first female gymnast to take advantage of her diminutive size. In 1972 the Munchkin of Munich awakened the Western world to the possibilities of physics and sinew, and, in the process, challenged the prevailing cold war wisdom: better dead than red.

Korbut had qualified for the Soviet team as an alternate and was a substitute in the team competition. Everything about her was unexpected: her pigtails, her smile, her age. She was seventeen but looked much younger. In a matter of days, she reversed centuries of precedent—making female gymnasts more visible than men. On the first night of competition, she executed a half-backward somersault off the high bar and caught the lower one on the way down, a move she called the "flik flak." The world gasped.

Two days later, she fell from the bars—and from medal contention—weeping when the judges announced her score: 7.5. Only the staunchest nationalists were unmoved when she returned to competition less than twenty-four hours later with her impish smile, dancing pigtails, and technique intact, winning gold medals on the balance beam and floor exercises.

At the White House, President Richard M. Nixon told her she had done more to ease global tensions than the diplomatic corps had in five years. "We all thought the Russians were robots and had no emotion," Mary Lou Retton recalls. "We saw this little Russian girl crying. It was, 'My gosh, they really do have feelings.' I'm not sure she changed gymnastics technically. But she brought attention to it. She brought it popularity."

She seized center stage for women's gymnastics and set it for Nadia Comaneci.

Nadia Comaneci was discovered on a playground in Moldavia at age six. She was a kindergartner in Onesti, Romania, doing what kindergartners do. "Upside-down stuff," she recalls.

The not yet legendary Bela Karolyi was an unknown gymnastics coach looking for supple bodies around which to build a gymnastics super power—and a name for himself. He would make Comaneci a star—and, later, Mary Lou Retton and Kerri Strug. The world would come to know him as the Transylvanian Svengali of women's gymnastics, the master of motivation, manipulation, and prime-time hugs.

But when he discovered Comaneci, she remembers, "he was just a big tall guy, no mustache. I knew his wife, Marta. She was choreographing a play for us called *The Cherry Tree*. We had to dress up as cherry trees. You just had to bend and dance."

Bend and dance, she could. She was light and lithe, mentally unyielding, and impossibly limber. She changed everything about the sport: the vocabulary, the equipment, the body type, the expectations. Before Nadia, gymnastic champions were long, elegant, athletic *artistes* who aspired to grace and perfect lines. Comaneci aspired to the impossible. Before Nadia, there were no "releases"—those breathtaking midair, look-Ma-no-hands maneuvers that are now standard fare in every competition. Comaneci made degree of difficulty the new standard by which all comers would be judged.

At four-eleven and eighty-six pounds, she was deadly and dazzling. She served notice at the 1975 European championships by dethroning five-time Soviet champion Lyudmila Tourischeva. A year later, she arrived at the Olympic Games in Montreal with a solemn demeanor—"a solemn wisp," *Time* magazine called her—and a rag doll she tried to hide behind during press conferences. The sport would never be the same again. "How did I change it?" she asks now. "I did something that they thought could not possibly be done. I like to do things nobody else does. If someone says, 'It's impossible,' I try it."

In gymnastics, Karolyi once said, eight years is the same as one hundred years. The back flip Olga Korbut had performed on the balance beam four years earlier was so unprecedented it wasn't included in the International Gymnastics Federation Code of Points, the regulations that stipulate the value of each move on the four required apparatuses. Today's gymnasts routinely perform three back flips in a row on the beam.

Comaneci's historic performance on the uneven parallel bars in Montreal was so unprecedented it defied existing technology. She debuted the Comaneci salto on the first evening of team competition. The routine was elegant, airy, and lethal. Pushing off the high bar, she whirled through the air in a front salto, and then with her legs in a straddle position, recaught the bar. She was a white blur of continuous motion, soaring above previous norms.

The crowd waited silently, anticipating the unprecedented. A roar went up as the number 1.0 flashed on the scoreboard. "It stayed like this a long time," she recalls. "I thought, what is this? Really? A one?"

The perfection of her routine was so unanticipated, technology did not allow for a score of 10. But those in attendance knew what they had seen—history. By week's end, she had accumulated seven perfect 10.0s and five medals: three gold, one team silver, and one bronze.

She returned home and was proclaimed the youngest ever Hero of Socialist Labor. Headlines hailed her as "Nadia, the Golden Girl of Romanian Sports, a Symbol of the Free Life of Our Youth."

"It didn't mean that much then, what I was accomplishing at age fourteen," she says now. "It was satisfying. I was the coolest kid there. I got to travel. If you ask if I realized what I did then, I had no clue."

Suddenly, every gymnast had to be fourteen years old and weigh eighty pounds. In 1956 the average age of the women on the U.S. Olympic gymnastics team was nineteen; two of the team members were even married. Their average height and weight were five-four, 124 pounds. In 1980, no one on the Soviet team even reached five feet. By 1992, the average U.S. gymnast was sixteen years old, stood four-nine, and weighed eighty-three pounds.

Gymnastics became the province of pixie pygmies, lithe, young daredevils whose physiques resembled those of children. Success in the elite ranks came to demand the hormonal repression of womanliness, supple, prepubescent bodies. Absent inconveniently developed breasts and hips, they could get around on the equipment unencumbered. They could manage giant swings on the uneven parallel bars without hitting their heads on the way down.

Even Karolyi, now retired to his ranch in Texas, laments this extreme, which is somewhat odd because he created it. In 1996 the International Gymnastics Federation voted to raise the age for Olympic competitors to sixteen. Not surprisingly, the change met with skepticism in some very knowledgeable quarters. Comaneci says, "Well, I would not be history today if they had done that before."

So great was her popularity after Montreal that her theme music from the American soap opera *The Young and the Restless* became an immediate hit and was renamed "Nadia's Theme."

Her life was not without its soap opera plotlines. When Karolyi was removed as national coach in 1978, it was widely rumored that she tried to kill herself, which she denies. "I knew I wouldn't be able to win without Bela, so I faked drinking bleach, hoping he could stay," she has said.

It is hard to imagine a coaching change provoking thoughts of suicide. But in gymnastics the relationship between athlete and coach is unique, partly because the athletes are so young and partly because training is so intense. They are dependent on their coaches for their safety, their schedule, their sense of self.

After Comaneci, it became the norm for young girls to move away from their families to live and to train. "It wasn't directed to be trend changing," Karolyi maintains. "We were working in a small mining town in Romania. There were no other age of kids except elementary kids."

This is more than a bit disingenuous. Younger girls are not only more physically flexible, they are more psychologically pliable—coachable, in the sporting vernacular. It is no wonder that Comaneci worried she couldn't win without Karolyi.

Dom Professor, as she called him, was reinstated as national coach in time for the 1980 Olympics. Comaneci returned to competition and to form, losing fifteen pounds she had gained since Montreal. Her results in Moscow were almost as spectacular as they had been four years before: this time two golds and a controversial silver medal in the Individual All-Around.

Comaneci needed a score of 9.9 on the balance beam to tie the Soviet leader for the gold. She had already earned a 9.9 and a 10 with earlier performances of her beam routine. For her, a score of 9.9 or better *was* routine. She went through her program with only the slightest wobble. When it was over, the judges were as silent as everyone else in the arena. They refused to vote. For twenty-eight minutes, they debated her score. Finally, it flashed on the screen: 9.85, thanks to 9.8s from the Polish and Soviet judges. No doubt the Soviet bloc judges remembered how she had upstaged Korbut at the Olympics four years earlier.

Like figure skating, gymnastics is a subjective sport, and like figure skating, infinitely political. Judging controversies, storied examples of partisanship and incompetence, are legion. In 1977 Romanian dictator Nicolae Ceausescu sent an ambassador to retrieve the team from a competition he deemed too politicized. Comaneci and the other Romanian athletes were grabbed off the mat midway through competition and flown home in Ceausescu's personal plane.

Even by those standards, the twenty-eight-minute delay in Moscow was unprecedented. "It was bizarre that it took so long," Comaneci says. "I knew we were competing in Russia. It wasn't like I expected to win."

Karolyi defected to the United States on March 30, 1981, the day President Ronald Reagan was shot, bringing with him the training methods he had employed in Romania and the reputation for making champions. Comaneci did not see him again until the 1984 Olympics when she traveled to Los Angeles as an honorary member of the Romanian delegation. Romania was the only communist country not participating in the Soviet-led boycott. Worried that Comaneci would defect, and ruin their public relations bonanza, the Romanian government had her followed.

She saw Karolyi just briefly. He introduced her to the new "Nadia," Mary Lou Retton, an encounter that proved stunningly anticlimactic. "I think she said, 'Hello,'" Retton recalls.

"I had a chaperone twenty-four hours a day," Comaneci says. "I was afraid to talk to him. Afraid to do two steps. Defecting didn't even occur to me."

Until November 1989, that is, when she walked six hours through mud, ice, and darkness to the Hungarian border. The government sent security forces to her house to seize her trophies. "But they weren't prepared because there were so many," she says. "They came only with their hands in their pockets. They put a seal on the door so my brother cannot go and remove things until they come back the next day with bags. The next day didn't happen because the revolution started." A year later, a Romanian journalist visiting the United States called and said he had a present for her from her brother: her medals. "Only the important ones," she says. "Olympics, Worlds, and Europeans."

The defector who arrived in Montreal, the site of her greatest success, was not the waif with pigtails the world remembered. She'd put on a lot of weight and too much makeup. The stiletto heels did not help her image, already sullied by a reported affair with Ceausescu's son, Nicu. When it was learned that the man who had arranged her midnight flight, and with whom she intended to live, was the married father of four children, she was branded a homewrecker and worse. "Sometimes I would think that maybe it would have been better if I had been killed trying to escape," she said in 1990.

But for Nadia, there was to be a fairy-tale ending. She soon returned to larger-than-life status, appearing on a ninety-foot billboard in Times Square, in an advertisement for Jockey underwear. "I brought my mom to see it," she recalls. "*Entertainment Tonight* wanted to see her reaction. She said, 'Oh, my God, you have no clothes on.' I said, 'Mom, I have some.' It was a big shock. It was a very good thing for me to do. People remember me as fourteen. It was a good thing for me for them to see me as a woman."

So much had happened, it was hard to believe she was the same woman-child who had visited Times Square fifteen years earlier. That had been her first visit to the United States. She was competing in the America's Cup at Madison Square Garden. Photographers asked her to pose with American gymnast Bart Conner, the winner of the men's competition. "They said, 'Just lean over and give her a little kiss on the cheek,'" she remembers. "So he did."

All she remembers of that first kiss is "some little blond guy." All the Americans were little blond guys. Years later, when Conner asked her to marry him, she was so surprised that he had to ask her again.

Today, they run a gymnastics school in his hometown, Norman, Oklahoma, and conduct exhibitions and clinics around the country. She does charity work for Romanian adoption agencies and orphanages. She is thinking about having children, thoughts that cause her to ruminate on her own childhood and its alleged hardships. "My kid is going to be born with everything," she says. "I come from a very poor family. My parents did really hard work. In Romania, people always said, 'Oh, gymnastics is very, very hard.' I am thinking, 'If this work is hard, what about my parents? What do I have to do? A couple of flips. I get a salary that is bigger than my father had.'"

Only one thing troubles her in retrospect: the image of her as a grimly determined gremlin. "I'm watching those tapes from 1976," she says. "I'm waving, smiling. Everybody says I'm not smiling. Mary Lou is different. What do they want me to do? Tell jokes all the time? I like to smile at the end."

Watching Comaneci's 1976 performance on TV in Fairmont, West Virginia, was seven-year-old Mary Lou Retton, a hyperkinetic child who was always running into things. To minimize the damage, Lois Retton had enrolled her daughter in an acrobatics class. Only for Nadia did she sit still.

"I was sitting in a split," Retton recalls. "I was in acrobatics at the time. I knew right away ballet wasn't my thing. I said, 'Mom, I'm going to be just like her. I'm going to go to the Olympics.' She patted me on the head and said, 'Yes, honey.'"

Retton's awe was unfettered by any awareness of gravity or her own short, muscular body, which did not conform to the prevailing Nadiaesque form. Karolyi once described her in his inimitable English as "a small, little junky kid." You'd think she was the Paul Bunyan of the balance beam. At four-nine and ninety-two pounds, she wasn't exactly what you'd call huge, except maybe for her smile. She was physically ebullient.

Before Retton, Karolyi's girls were "airy, tiny, little kids flying," he says. "Mary Lou dominated by physical expression, by performance rather than a physical look. It changed a trend and gave again back to the sport, which I always thought was the right thing to do, regardless of size, weight, color, the right to be contenders for the highest awards."

She was eight when she appeared in her first gymnastics meet. After performing on the first apparatus, the uneven bars, she jumped for joy when the scoreboard registered 1.0. Just like Nadia in Montreal! Unfortunately, her score really was 1.0.

Still, she proved to be a natural. "It's easy," she once explained. "When you get older, you start to get scared. When you're small, you're so stupid. If the coach says do something, you're going to do it."

It wasn't long before she began agitating to move to Houston to train with Karolyi, lecturing her parents on the virtues of Bela-style discipline. Her mother was reluctant to let her go. The Rettons were a large Italian family who believed closeness was a function of proximity. Lois Retton fretted over missed proms and other perks of teenage life. Mary Lou pointed out that she wasn't old enough to go to the prom anyway. "She makes it seem like I miss more than I do," she said at the time.

Her father, Ronnie, was the third guard on Jerry West's famed University of West Virginia basketball team and, later, a shortstop in the New York Yankees farm system. He never made it to the majors. "We've got to give her the chance," Ronnie told his wife.

Mary Lou was fourteen when she arrived at Karolyi's gym. She wasn't the "it" girl then. No American had ever been the "it" girl. Apart from Cathy Rigby, the first American to medal in world class competition (silver medal, balance beam, 1970 world championships), and Marcia Frederick, the first American to win a gold medal at the world championships (uneven bars, 1978), U.S. gymnastics had always been an afterthought.

Muriel Davis Grossfield, a three-time U.S. Olympian (1956, 1960, 1964) who won seventeen national titles, had never even performed on a regulation balance beam before the 1956 games. "When I started in gymnastics, I knew everybody in the sport within six months," she says. "There were no gymnastics in public school. We ran around doing exhibitions and trying to teach the teachers. Then we'd show up at a meet and be judged by the people whom we had just taught."

Membership in U.S. gymnastics grew from 7,000 mostly male gymnasts in the mid-1960s to 32,000 in 1980. As of 1996, there were 67,000 members, 55,000 of them female, largely because of Mary Lou.

The year before the 1984 Olympics, no one had even heard of her. Dianne Durham, the first African-American U.S. national champion, was the doyenne of Karolyi's gym. Retton was injured and didn't compete in the 1983 World Championships. Twelve months later, the roles were reversed. Durham suffered a career-ending knee injury and never even made it to the 1984 Olympic trials. Retton became Karolyi's great small hope.

If Comaneci was a butterfly, Retton was an irrepressible force of nature. Nothing stopped her: not even knee surgery a month before the trials. She was a blithe spirit, amiably explaining to reporters why it was a good thing to have moved away from home. Her family name had once been Rotundo. "As in fat," she said then. "If I lived at home I'd weigh three hundred pounds."

She used press conferences to lobby heavily for an introduction to actor Matt Dillon, upon whom she had a crush. Wherever she went, she created a sensation. Fifty teenyboppers lined up to watch Retton get a complimentary haircut from sponsor Vidal Sasson. "Don't bald me," she pleaded, as the hairdresser snipped and photographers snapped.

Not quite bald, she made her getaway, leaving behind fifty little girls who scrambled for locks of her hair. Her mother, Lois, watched with pride and ambivalence. "I'm afraid I've lost her to the world and it will never be the same again," she said.

Two weeks later, her words proved prescient. It is hard to believe in retrospect that the Olympics was Retton's first major international competition. She led the Americans to a silver medal in the team competition and was ahead of Ecaterina Szabo of Romania by .15 of a point when competition in the Individual All-Around began. Retton and Szabo were in different groups that night, competing on different apparatus at the same time. The competition in Pauley Pavilion had the heightened quality of a three-ring circus as spectators tried to keep both gymnasts within view. Retton fell behind on the first two rotations, her weakest, Szabo's best. "My beam and bars—Lord, they were not very difficult—except for me now," Retton says. She laughs a huge laugh—a ten.

Szabo, who had been one of Karolyi's girls in Romania, went to the uneven parallel bars for her last performance. In midair, her legs were infinitesimally askew. And on her dismount, she took a step back, an automatic deduction of a tenth of a point. A 10 would have meant the gold medal. The 9.9 she received meant that Retton needed a 10 on the vault to win.

Retton paced madly on the sideline waiting for her chance on the vault. *Her* vault. She owned the vault. No one else in the world approached it with her speed or recklessness. No one else soared 11½ feet in the air. "She unloads in competition," Karolyi always said.

Unload she did. She flew through the air like an exclamation point, declaring with her perfect landing—and her perfect score—that gymnastics now belonged to America. Just to make the point emphatically clear, she did it again. She stuck that landing, too. And, in so doing, she says, "I brought hope and faith to American little girls."

Karolyi, the lovable, megalomaniac guru, leapt across the barrier—a move he had been seen practicing the day before—and wrapped Mary Lou in the red-white-and-blue hug seen round the world. A hard-bitten reporter accustomed to willowy, teary-eyed sixteen-year-olds, asked Mary Lou if she shed any tears at those two perfect 10s. "Nah," she replied, "I was too happy to cry."

Karolyi says, "I am still calling her the sunshine of my coaching career. She lighted up. Everyone wanted to be the second Mary Lou."

* * *

Watching at home on television with her best friend, Kerri Strug was upended by what she saw. Gymnastics was already in her soul. She had watched the TV movie about Comaneci so often she knew all the lines by heart. But it was Mary Lou who took her breath away. "I know I didn't say, 'I can do that,'" Strug says now.

Her friend was rooting for Szabo. "She liked Szabo because she was pretty," Strug remembers. "I said, 'Are you crazy? You're supposed to root for the American.'"

Strug actually had met Retton once at Karolyi's gym, where her older sister had trained one summer. Like Retton's first meeting with Comaneci, it wasn't exactly a transcendent moment. "I didn't pay attention to Mary Lou, to be honest," Strug says. "Dianne Durham was the one I wanted to see. I remember they were on bars. Dianne Durham kept missing. Mary Lou didn't."

Strug was never expected to be the next Mary Lou. She was always among the best but never quite the best. "I was always second fiddle," she says. "If they took two girls to the finals, I was third. If they took three, I was fourth."

She moved away from home to train with Karolyi when she was thirteen. Like Retton's mother, Melanie Strug did not want her daughter to go. "I said, 'Absolutely no,'" she recalls. "My husband said, 'If she wants it so badly, you can't say no.'"

Actually, you can. But it gets harder as the emotional and financial investment grows. As a deterrent to big-headedness, the Strugs insisted that Kerri eat dessert on her birthdays and avoid watching gymnastics videos at home. Comaneci, who now sees things from a coach's perspective, says, "Most of the time things happen when parents are pushing. The kid feels the pressure from the parent. We have it at school. You can see them watching through the glass."

At the 1992 Olympic Games in Barcelona, Strug was fourteen, the youngest member of the U.S. team. She missed the All-Around finals by .014 of a point, finishing fourth among the Americans. Karolyi retired, and Strug bounced from gym to gym and injury to injury. The next four years were the worst of her life. In December 1993 she severely tore a muscle in her stomach. Her parents ordered her to come home. She didn't compete again until the summer of 1994, when she slipped from the bars and injured her back: a stress fracture of the L-4 vertebra. "I landed on my stomach with my legs over my head like a 'C,'" she says. This time her father, a heart surgeon, was alarmed. "An arm, a leg, it heals," Strug says, "but a back is different." She recuperated, however, and Karolyi unretired to coach the new presumptive "it" girl, Dominique Moceanu, who took to signing autographs, "1996 Olympic champion, for sure." Strug returned to Karolyi's fold.

Of the seven members of the 1996 U.S. team, she was the only one who arrived in Atlanta without an agent or a book deal. She had signed a letter of intent to attend UCLA where she hoped to compete as an amateur. Though eighteen years old, she was Karolyi's baby. That's what he called her, what he calls her still.

A week before the Olympics, Mary Lou Retton visited the not yet "Magnificent Seven" at their training camp in Greensboro, North Carolina. She reminded them of their mission. Kim Zmeskal, another Karolyi wunderkind, had become the first American world champion in 1991, winning the All-Around title against a field that included the Soviets. Unlike Retton's 1984 Olympic medal, there were no asterisks attached to Zmeskal's title. Shannon Miller had followed suit, winning the world championships in 1993 and 1994. Only one thing had eluded American gymnasts: the Olympic team gold medal.

By all accounts, Retton's pre-Olympic pep talk was stirring. "It made everything inside you well up," says Kathy Kelly, women's program director for USA Gymnastics. "She told them to feed off it, soak it up, don't be afraid."

Retton, a truly motivational speaker, has admitted that sometimes she fudges a little when telling the story of those two Olympic vaults, just to heighten the suspense for the audience. Could she do it? Would she do it? In fact, she never had any doubt. "C'mon," she told the 1996 Olympians. "I did that millions of times in the gym. Show your stuff. Surprise them."

And Strug did. She was the last U.S. gymnast on the last apparatus on the last day of team competition. Like Mary Lou, the vault was her event. For once, politics hadn't dictated the order of competition. She was up last, batting cleanup. Dominique Moceanu, the fourteen-year-old with the autobiography already in print, had inexplicably sat down on the landings of both of her vaults. Whether the Americans would win their first-ever gold medal in team competition was in Strug's hands and feet.

She remembers nothing of what transpired in the air above the vault on her first attempt, only the ominous sound and searing pain of her too-short landing. The ankle bone pushed forward in the joint, tearing the medial and lateral ligaments. She hobbled the length of the mat, trying to feel her foot, while Karolyi implored her to shake it out.

Reporters heard her ask, "Do I have to do this?" She remembers asking a different question, the competitor's question: "Do we need this?" Meaning did the Americans need her to make the second vault in order to win the team gold. "You can do it," Karolyi replied.

None of the U.S. coaches, and none of the athletes, knew the truth: the gold medal was already theirs. Strug's second vault was completely unnecessary. "In the excitement of the moment, they forgot how to add," says Jackie Fie, president of the women's technical committee of the International Gymnastics Federation, who was sitting at the judge's table. "We knew she didn't have to do the vault. I was wondering why she went again. I thought, 'Gee, that's brave when she really doesn't have to.'"

Strug had thirty seconds to decide. There is no injury time-out in gymnastics. The judges record the score, the green light flashes, and you go, because that's what gymnasts do.

Pain is a given in gymnastics. Injuries are a way of life. Shannon Miller competed in Atlanta with an injured wrist. Moceanu had a stress fracture in her right tibia. Strug's ankle was taped *before* the evening's competition began, due to chronic shin splints.

"The vault hurts when you land it right," Bart Conner says. "Kurt Thomas always used to say, 'Make it hurt, baby.' Because in order to stick the landing you have to grind your heels into the floor."

Strug's teammates stood in a circle, holding hands and saying a prayer. She reminded herself how many times she had done this in the gym. The green light flashed, and she went, holding the landing on her bad foot long enough to show the judges she had completed the vault. Then she collapsed in pain. "It was the defining moment of the 1996 Olympics," Retton says.

Not a single elite athlete questions Strug's decision. All would have done the same. It's the moment she had trained for eight hours a day, six days a week since age thirteen. Asking her to hold back would have been like asking the rain not to fall. It is telling, however, that Retton, now the mother of two little girls, isn't sure she'd want her daughters in the position of having to make the decision Strug had to make.

Dr. Bill Sands, a sports physiologist at the University of Utah, estimates that when Strug landed the second vault, she placed nearly a thousand pounds of pressure on the already unstable ankle joint. "Looking back, it wasn't a smart move," says Strug's teammate Jaycie Phelps. "But when you're in the moment, you're in the moment. You don't want to be distracted."

You don't want to be informed or prudent. And, most definitely, you don't want to think twice. Dispassion is not rewarded by the Code of Points. "The athlete is going to do it for the team and for herself," says Phelps. "The coach isn't going to say, 'Don't do it.' I don't know who could say it." An independent physician, perhaps, without a vested interest in the athlete's performance? Mary Lou Retton strongly believes it is time for gymnastics to institute an injury time-out. But, as Jackie Fie, of the women's technical committee, says, "We're in a money-driven sport. You can't get things across that would be beneficial to the athlete."

Strug isn't sure it's a good idea. "It's better I didn't know how bad it was," she says. "It would have made me cautious and intimidated."

Single-mindedness is the distinguishing characteristic of all great champions. Ron Miller, a physicist who also happens to be Shannon Miller's father, says, "There's something in the person. People spot that, and it can be used against them. I hope the sport would mature enough to where the girls who have that talent not be exploited, where the desire of the athlete to perform is handled for the benefit of the athlete.

"The sport is immature. There's no player's union. These are little girls. They are used by the various federations, parents, and coaches. The system itself has no real protection. No one in the system is looking out for the girl."

Immediately after her vault landing, Strug was swept up in Karolyi's telegenic arms and a blitzkrieg of sudden fame. *Saturday Night Live* came calling and *The Rosie O'Donnell Show* and *People* magazine, too. Mary Lou offered her home phone number and said to call any time, which Strug has from time to time. "I'm, like, all this from one vault?" Strug recounts.

The 1996 gold-medal win, the torque of her life changed forever. Before the Olympics, she never had time to go to birthday parties. Two months later, she was sitting next to Chelsea Clinton at the President's fiftieth birthday bash. Before the Olympics, she didn't own a single pair of heels. Two months later, Rosie O'Donnell's staff was outfitting her in DKNY. And strangers were stopping her on the street, asking to pick her up the way Karolyi had. More often than not, she agreed.

Strug posed with her teammates for the front of the Wheaties box but parted ways with them soon after. Her parents insisted that she honor her commitment to attend UCLA in the fall of 1996 instead of touring with the Magnificent Seven, a decision that didn't exactly endear her to her teammates. In the past when her mother described her to friends as socially immature, they often replied, "You don't know how lucky you are that she isn't going to pot parties." Still, the Strugs knew it was time for her to grow up. "My parents said, 'We love you and we're glad about everything, but you're still our kid. You need to go to college when it's appropriate.'"

Now little girls on gym mats all over the country crowd around her picture, wanting to touch it, as if some of what she has—some of what she did—will rub off on them. The older brother of one of those little girls was mightily offended when an unthinking parent procured an autographed photo for his sister but not for him. "But, Mom," he said firmly, "she was in the Olympics."

To some, Strug's performance is a moral exemplar, a belated proof that female athletes—and women gymnasts in particular—are made of the same right stuff as their male counterparts. "Her impact was so different than the two others, Mary Lou or Nadia," Karolyi says. "The others, they were tigers, always fighting. Kerri turned totally out of her nature, against her nature actually, under the incredible moment of the Olympic games.

"Always they are nice, they can smile, they can do good gymnastics. But when it gets rough, they run away and break down crying. This bothers me. Kerri was the last probability to come out and show to the world the heart of the tiger. It was ironic, but she was the one."

To others Strug's second vault was as troubling as it was inspiring. That very week, the *New England Journal of Medicine* published a sobering article documenting how great the damage to young gymnasts can be. The *Journal* warned that "overtraining, injuries and psychological damage are common consequences" of gymnastics training, particularly at the highest levels of the sport.

After the vault, one of the authors of the *Journal* article told the *Washington Post*, "The real concern is that this kind of thing is happening every day. These kids are destroying their bodies and we're letting them do it."

We live in a nation that genuflects before the god of stoicism. Playing hurt is the true national pastime. "Sucking it up," to use that uniquely inelegant phrase, is the skill we most admire. Except when it comes to little girls. Then we're not so sure how tough we want them to be. Strug chafes under this implicit double standard. "If it's a little boy, it's fine, he's tough," she says. "When it's a gymnast, they're being abused and ruining their bodies."

A highly critical book by Joan Ryan, published in 1995, *Little Girls in Glass Houses*, detailed the deaths of two American gymnasts: Christy Henrich, who weighed less than fifty pounds when she died of multiple organ failure due to anorexia and bulimia in July 1994; and Julissa Gomez, who broke her neck on a vault when she was sixteen and died three years later.

Defending World champion Yelena Mukhina, of the Soviet Union, who fell while practicing her floor routine and broke her spine sixteen days before the 1980 Olympics. She was permanently paralyzed from the neck down, unable even to speak for six months. A Chinese gymnast was paralyzed during the 1998 Goodwill Games while warming up for vault.

Is it any wonder Strug's mother felt sick to her stomach before every competition? Or that Shannon Miller's father could barely breathe after once watching his daughter miss the vault completely? "Her coach, Steve Nunno, reached over and caught her," Miller recalls. I said, 'Well, he's earned his pay this week.' Steve says, 'Oh, we practice that all the time.'"

Injuries are only the most visible part of a Gordian knot of health issues that plague gymnasts. In the last decade, sports medicine specialists have identified a constellation of interrelated symptoms called the Female Triad— disordered eating, amenorreah, and osteoporosis caused by thin, brittle bones. It is common among female athletes who train at high intensity, not just gymnasts.

But in gymnastics, the need to remain light can lead to compulsive dieting, poor nutrition, and eating disorders such as anorexia and bulimia.

Cathy Rigby, now better known as Peter Pan, was twice hospitalized after her gymnastics career was over when her weight dropped below eighty pounds. Lowered percentage of body fat staves off the hormonal imperatives of Mother Nature, delaying or interrupting puberty, a phenomenon known as amenorrhea. It was a fact of life for Strug, Miller, and also Retton, who two children later has no apparent ill effects.

USA Gymnastics team doctors say the reproductive system kicks into gear once training is suspended. But because prolonged amenorrhea can cause early onset of osteoporosis, all team members are counseled at age sixteen about potential long-term side effects. Their bone density is tested. They are also offered low-dose birth control pills and calcium supplements.

In 1994 USA Gymnastics formed a Task Force to Study the Female-Athlete Triad. An Athlete Wellness Program was established, as a result of which height and weight information on athletes is no longer disclosed. An athlete's cookbook was published, videos and educational seminars sponsored. A curriculum called the Athlete's Wellness Program has been developed.

The intent is to make attendance mandatory for all coaches in order to receive a safety certification from USA Gymnastics. "One of the complaints is that the governing body has no teeth," says 1972 Olympian Nancy Thies Marshall, who now manages the Athlete's Wellness Course. "But they do have teeth. They can regulate who can be on the floor coaching."

But in a realm populated by underage perfectionists who are encouraged to believe that a perfect body leads to perfect tens, the potential problems are obvious. Old habits die hard. A year after the Olympics, still tiny and barely able to see over the dashboard of her new BMW, Strug cruised Olympic Avenue in Los Angeles in search of her favorite frozen yogurt at the Big Chill, confiding that she splurged twice a week. Nonfat, of course. But empty calories still.

As Ron Miller says, "Gymnastics is probably the most unfair sport there is. In other sports, if you get bigger, there's a place for you. In gymnastics, if you don't fit a very constrained body type and size, you don't have a future. The mechanics don't allow for it. In this sport, if you make a mistake on the vault, just once, you can be dead. It's very unforgiving." There is a place where the limits of sinew and physics meet. Mary Lou Retton says flatly, "We've reached the physical limit in gymnastics."

Every four years after the Olympics, the International Gymnastics Federation rewrites the Code of Points. And each time they make it harder. Even the great Nadia looked at the Code of Points issued after the 1996 Olympics and thought, "Oh, my God, I'm glad I'm not competing."

The twists and turns of Strug's Yurchenko vault are so many, and so complex, it is almost impossible to follow, even in slow motion, performed by one of her many stuffed bears. Yet immediately after the Games, officials devalued it. "You can't get a 10 even if you do it perfectly," Strug says. "They've made it too hard."

She sighs, momentarily indulging in the incredulity the rest of us feel all the time. "And now there's five or ten kids doing a double! After a double full, I don't see how it can get harder without us killing ourselves."

Each year the sport becomes exponentially more difficult. As a child, Comaneci practiced a move on the uneven parallel bars named for Agnes Keleti. Today's gymnasts have never heard of it. Kerri Strug does remember learning one of Nadia's revolutionary pikes when she was eight years old.

"You can't compare what Nadia and Olga did to what I did," Retton says. "It's black and white. Their most difficult things were considered compulsories in 1992 and 1996."

And now, thanks to a 1994 decision, there are no more compulsories. The intent may have been to decrease the work load, but, Retton says, it won't work. "They're not going to cut down on the time in gym. They're just going to do eight hours of optionals."

In gymnastics, compulsories are the foundation on which the architecture of daring is built. They are the basic skills necessary in order to be able to do the hard things safely. "If you eliminate those, then you're going to have people trying harder and harder things that they are not able to do," Strug says. "If there are no compulsories, there's no reason to have good flexibility. If you don't have good flexibility, it's easier to get hurt."

The question is how to protect athletes from themselves, and how to protect those little girls watching at home on television who would be the next Kerri Strug if they could. Ron Miller would place limits on training. "With football and baseball, there's a limit," he says. "The NCAA can't have them hitting a baseball eight hours a day."

He proposes a twenty-hour week and a mandatory off-season, an idea Retton rejects as unworkable and unenforceable. Strug advocates a dual scoring system like the one used in figure skating, in which athletes receive two sets of marks: one for technical merit and one for artistic presentation. But skaters will tell you there's plenty of room for political manipulation in that system.

Improved equipment offers some help. The International Gymnastics Federation mandated women's use of thicker, twenty-centimeter mats for better shock absorption starting in January 1998. Male gymnasts have been using them for fifteen years.

The problem, as Comaneci sees it, is this: "Little kids will always go for the hard stuff, the acrobatic stuff. They're not that lovely to the eyes. They just tumble. Because they can."

And audiences will demand it. "They don't want to see cartwheels," Comaneci says. "They're going to say, 'OK, that's nice, but where are the hard tricks?'"

She should know. She created the expectation. If she was in charge, she'd rewrite the rules so that gymnasts don't get rewarded for simply repeating a skill with a high degree of difficulty. "Say you do a double lay-out on the floor," she says. "You can't do it a second time unless it's combined with something else. That way you'd have to create something from artistry."

Retton agrees. "Instead of giving extra points for extra daring, they need to give it for originality and creativity," she says. "Everyone's doing the same stuff. They need to be rewarded for doing different things, not hard things—original things. So we don't have the serious injuries that everyone thinks are going to happen. It's scary."

Unlike figure skating, which has done an enviable job of creating and prolonging professional careers, there is no afterlife in gymnastics. Most female gymnasts are has-beens by the age of twenty. In the wake of the 1996 Olympics, two rival gymnastics tours took to the road, one headlined by Strug, Conner, and Comaneci, the other starring the Magnificent Seven (minus one). But, Conner says, there was not enough interest to support both tours. His tour folded.

Figure skating is marketed on the sugarplum sex appeal of sleek, young ice queens. It is no coincidence that they are coached to "sell" their programs to the audience. There is nothing particularly sexy, however, about an eighteen-year-old prepubescent body. Women can't relate to it. Men *don't* relate to it. Comaneci, Retton, and Strug are exceptions to the rule: personalities who continue to make money off gymnastics. Retton remains a fixture in the firmament of American celebrity, one of those athletes on a first-name basis with the American public. Strug was among the glitterati feted at *Time* magazine's seventy-fifth anniversary bash in 1998. But Olga Korbut lives and coaches in virtual anonymity in Atlanta, coping with a thyroid problem attributed to exposure to fallout from the nuclear reactor accident at Chernobyl.

Muriel Grossfield remembers a time when gymnasts, like Agnes Keleti, were allowed to mature and grow in the sport. "I learned how to be an athlete after I became a coach," she says. "I was better at age twenty-eight than when I retired at age twenty-four."

As the rules are currently written, there is no place for the older woman in gymnastics. Retton believes that the International Gymnastics Federation did not go far enough in raising the age limit to sixteen. If she had her way, you'd have to be eighteen, old enough to vote and drink, in order to compete in the Olympics. "If they want to see high-flying, Evel Knievel types, tiny, pigtailed girls, the age will stay low, which is where it will probably stay," she says. "Where I'd like to see it go, is older. I would have loved to stay in it. So you can make a career out of it, instead of just a childhood."

It's a revolutionary concept: women dominating women's gymnastics. A thirty-five-year-old Olympic champion? Another Agnes Keleti? Retton giggles at the thought. "Not after two children," she says. "You tell Nadia, if she'll do it, *I'll* do it."

"Yeah, right," Comaneci says.

Soccer

*F*rom the Suburbs to the Sports Arenas

Elise Pettus

Soccer is often referred to as the world's game because of its popularity among so many nations. It has also been known as the people's game for its popularity among the working class and poor. But for all its connotations of inclusion, soccer until recently was largely available only to the members of the world who happened to be men.

The sport has always had a reputation for rigor and roughness. In fact, its rise as a popular sport began when the ancient Greeks organized games to strengthen their warriors for battle. As a tool for military conditioning, the game was played well into the late Roman empire. A millennium later, soldiers of the British colonial army brought soccer to the continents of Asia and Africa.

The rise of soccer as the premier international men's game has been a steady development over the past century and a half. By contrast, the rise of soccer as a women's game has been meteoric. The history of women's international soccer is a mere fifteen years. And while other sports such as women's tennis and swimming can look back fondly at a heroine for each generation since the 1920s, the female stars of soccer—April Heinrichs, Michelle Akers, and Mia Hamm—have shared the field for much of their respective careers.

It may just be coincidence that in this country, women did not play soccer in numbers until the 1970s—the same decade they were first recruited to join the ranks of men in the U.S. Army. Across the Atlantic, the earliest celebrated women's soccer teams owed their very existence to war. While British men were fighting World War I, many sisters, wives, and daughters went to fill their shoes at work, particularly in the factories that manufactured weapons and equipment. To occupy their breaks and to keep their spirits up, women workers began playing pickup soccer games in the factory yards.

In 1917 the women at a Preston weapons plant called Dick, Kerr organized themselves into a team and called themselves the Dick, Kerr Ladies. It was one of the early leaders, Grace Sibbert, who first proposed the women play a match. Game proceeds, she suggested, could go to wounded soldiers at the front.

The British football association initially supported Sibbert's proposal as a novel, if offbeat, way to raise funds for an inarguably good cause. On Christmas Day, ten thousand viewers came out to the local league grounds to watch their first football game. Viewers were mainly curious to see females play a sport so closely identified with the essence of British maleness and athleticism. But the match raised good money, and the next match drew more viewers as word spread that the players weren't half bad. Factory teams began forming in other parts of Britain to play against each other and to challenge the Dick, Kerr Ladies. Soon what had begun as a quirky idea became a popular form of wartime entertainment as well as a major source of income for charities devoted to the wounded and the widowed.

The women's games were so popular that the matches continued to sell out after the war was over. Male players returned home to become fans and even trainers of the teams. Companies began recruiting female players and promising them jobs on the assembly line. In 1920 the Dick, Kerr Ladies played to a sold-out stadium of fifty-three thousand, while over eight thousand disappointed viewers had to be locked out. In 1921 Britain boasted 150 active women's teams.

In 1922, the Dick, Kerr Ladies traveled to North America. Although in Canada they learned that women were not allowed to play soccer, there were plenty of matches to be found in the States—as long as they were ready to play men. Many of these all-male opposing teams included professional and semi-professional players. Nevertheless, as they made their way down the eastern shoreline, the women won three, lost two, and tied three of their well-attended games. Newspapers covered their games in Massachusetts, Rhode Island, New York, and Maryland, with a mixture of amusement and surprise. Occasionally, reporters took swipes at the team by implying that the men had only allowed the women to win.

The Dick, Kerr players came home to a chilly reception from the British Football Association, the guardian institution of men's soccer. Concerned that the women players were stealing viewers and dollars away from the men's game, the group banned women from all of its playing fields. Without those sizable venues, it would be difficult to gather a crowd, let alone raise significant money for charity. And when the "fathers of football" raised public suspicions about the team's expenses and fund-raising integrity, the women were in no position to fight back. Dick, Kerr and the rest of the women's teams were largely managed by men who did not involve them in the finances. Despite the women's adamant denials of financial wrongdoing, the innuendo was enough to undermine their appeal, and gradually the women were forced back onto the sidelines of sports. By 1925, the first wave of women's soccer had already effectively ended.

In the United States, a time line published in a 1930 book on women's athletics shows soccer being introduced to American college women in 1919, just after "natural dancing" and before "clogging." But actual play was limited. First, there was concern that excessive physical strain might actually make women sterile. Second, while there was thought to be nothing wrong with a genteel round of badminton, the idea of women kicking and scrambling over a ball in the dirt was unsavory, if not ridiculous, to many.

In 1918 a group called the Committee on Women's Athletics was appointed to define rules for several emerging women's sports and to keep them within the boundaries of safety and propriety. The rules for women's soccer aimed chiefly at taming the men's version. Playing periods were made shorter, and players were highly restricted to certain areas of the field to defeat the need for rigorous running.

According to officials of the time, physical exertion wasn't the only element to be feared. Emotional stresses could be harmful, too. Dudley Sargent, a kind of turn-of-the-century Dr. Spock, embraced exercise for women but cautioned against competition. He expounded that if women were allowed to let school rivalries fuel them the way men did, they were apt to drive themselves to collapse. The proper place for women's team sports became the "field day," for which students were assigned to teams within the school and played each other one day out of the year. Any natural drive in women to compete was thus met and safely countered with lessons on teamwork and unity.

In soccer, as well as other team sports, field days were largely the rule for women up through the 1950s. Occasional "meets" between colleges such as Radcliffe and Smith required players to form two teams, each with a mix of players from both schools. Soccer as an intramural sport was offered at several top women's colleges, but a greater number of women were using soccer drills in field hockey practice than ever actually joined a soccer team. During the feminine fifties, soccer was still considered too manly a sport for most girls.

It was also during the fifties that America began its migration to the suburbs. Those new postwar communities with their grassy open fields were great incubators for America's love of sports. Although most of those fields beckoned mainly to boys, some of their sisters began playing, too. Some played baseball, and others played soccer, even if it was only in their own backyards.

In 1964 the American Youth Soccer Organization was founded to provide support and set standards to meet the burgeoning interest in the game. Already, certain areas of the country were becoming strongholds for soccer. In northern Virginia, Washington, north Texas, and Tennessee soccer programs initially sprang up around concentrations of Europeans or South Americans who had settled in the area. If money and space allowed, the programs soon blossomed into full-fledged leagues. The South, especially, drew players from abroad or from the northern states who were seeking the warm weather for year-round play. There were plenty of interested children to coach, and by the late sixties, it became increasingly common to find girls' teams as well as boys' teams in communities where soccer had taken hold.

The 1970s were a bright decade for soccer in the United States. Following American excitement over the 1966 World Cup (which England won), the North American Soccer League was founded to administer the professional men's games. Throughout the next ten years, the game grew steadily more popular. In 1978 Pelé, the world-famous star of the Brazilian men's team, came to the United States to play for the New Jersey Cosmos. For the first time, soccer matches drew almost as many spectators as baseball. Moreover, the soft-spoken, clean-living Pelé was an ideal role model for American boys and girls. But while talented boys might look to a future with the national team, few girls could see playing soccer beyond high school.

Girls' club teams in American suburbs did not translate to college varsity teams until five years after the landmark Title IX decision. Phil Pincince, a talented soccer player from Rhode Island College, got his first postgraduate job at Brown University. In 1976 Brown was one of a growing number of colleges that had a women's club soccer team, but Pincince decided in 1977 that it would have the first bona fide varsity team in the country. Brown's first team was made up of a few experienced players and many who were learning the game. "We had a wide range of talent," says the coach. "Some were tennis players who picked up the sport fairly easily, a few had experience playing club soccer in their hometowns, and there was a handful of amazing athletes who would still be considered great today." Pincince increasingly drew players from strong soccer states like Tennessee, Florida, and Virginia, as well as newer hotbeds growing in Massachusetts, Connecticut, California, and Washington State. Pincince called around the Northeast to see if other colleges had teams that were looking to compete on a varsity level. He found a Canadian college team that had been in existence a few years already, and there were new teams starting up at Tufts, Plymouth State, Harvard, and Yale. The Brown team finished its first season in 1978 with a winning record of 13–1, losing their only match to the Canadians from Lake Champlain. During the following fall, there were enough women's teams to enable Brown to host the first Ivy League championship, drawing newly hatched teams from Harvard, Dartmouth, Princeton, and Yale (Brown lost to Harvard in the finals). Through Pincince, Brown reigned as a kind of epicenter for women's college soccer in the late 1970s. In 1979 he helped to organize the first Eastern Regional Championships, which took place on Brown's campus.

That was the year that Anson Dorrance, a former soccer player for the University of North Carolina, took a walk with the head of school athletics. They dropped by a women's club soccer team practice. "Do you think these girls have potential?" the director asked him. Dorrance, a bright, wiry-framed twenty-six-year-old, was rarely at a loss for words, but he could respond only with a shrug. He was already coaching the men's team to help pay his law school tuition, but when the director offered him a full-time job to build a women's varsity team, Dorrance accepted. He welcomed the challenge and looked forward to the freedom he would have to shape this team from scratch. Law school, he decided, could wait. Almost immediately after Dorrance took the position, he began shaping not just his new team but also the future of women's soccer.

In 1980 UNC was one of about twenty women's colleges that were putting together their first women's soccer teams. Dorrance and his peers discovered that their first challenge as women's coaches was to create what generations of women's "physical education" teachers had worked to prevent: a team of hungry female competitors. In the team's first year, Dorrance had no scholarship money, but he did manage to recruit one player. The fledgling Tar Heels played mostly club teams from North Carolina and neighboring states. When some of the club teams trounced his newly hatched squad, he simply offered their starring players a spot on his team when they graduated from high school. In his second year, Dorrance was able to offer a free room to the next two recruits, and the following year he could even offer a little money.

In 1981, with less than fifty collegiate teams across the country, Dorrance and a Colorado coach, Chris Lidstone, felt their new teams were ready for a championship. But the NCAA, the ruling body of college athletic competition since 1950, wasn't likely to grant them one. The organization was at best lethargic about women's sports initiatives. It also had a long list of championship requirements, including a minimum pool of eighty teams. So Dorrance and Lidstone turned instead to the smaller Association for Intercollegiate Athletics for Women, an alternative organization founded in 1971 specifically to organize and promote women's intercollegiate competition. Though the handful of national teams fell short of even the AIAW minimum, the coaches' request for an AIAW-sanctioned and -sponsored national championship was heard, considered, and granted.

The first national women's soccer championship was held at UNC in 1981. Twelve teams were invited for a week-long festival of soccer events and games. The Tar Heels won the finals, beating Central Florida 1–0.

Coaching women was new to Dorrance, and there were a few things he discovered early on about the difference between coaching women and coaching men. Women were likely to be better listeners. They tended also to be more open to learning new things. On the other hand, it often seemed that being liked mattered more to women players than being the best. Sometimes the two seemed mutually exclusive. As he discovered in his third year as coach, a single outstanding player with a no-holds-barred attitude could wreak havoc on the intricate dynamics of the team.

Ten years before she came to UNC, April Heinrichs was a cherub-cheeked, rambunctious seven-year-old living in Littleton, Colorado. Her father was a fireman. Her mother did odd jobs around town. The family had little money for extracurricular activities for their children, but when they dropped their daughter off at a community soccer program, they hoped it might focus or even relieve some of her excess energy.

Heinrichs excelled at soccer. Later, she discovered that she excelled at softball, too. And basketball and track. She played all these sports in school. But as a high school junior, she dreamed of winning a scholarship to play college soccer. The problem was that in 1980, the year she applied to college, universities with strong women's teams, like Brown, Harvard, the University of Central Florida, and the University of Connecticut, weren't even looking at players from Colorado. They were scrutinizing players from Dallas, northern Virginia, and Seattle, the so-called soccer centers, where strong traditions of competitive club soccer had already produced top college players. Heinrichs even wrote to Dorrance at UNC. He wrote back, but not with good news. Heinrichs accepted a basketball scholarship at Mesa College in 1981. But each weekend, she drove home to play with her club soccer team, the Colorado Bandits.

In December, Heinrichs's team flew east for a tournament at Brown University, where another finalist coach saw her play. Although her team lost their games, Heinrichs stood out as the single most talented player on the field. The coach called Dorrance and told him there was a player from Mesa he had to consider. The following spring, Dorrance flew to Denver on a ticket equal in price to his travel budget for the year and caught up with Heinrichs playing an indoor match with her club.

Dorrance was stunned by Heinrichs's ability. He had never encountered a player as strong or athletic as the scrappy and unspoiled Heinrichs.

He made her an offer. Shortly afterward, Central Florida made her an offer as well. Heinrichs didn't visit either school before deciding on UNC, where she decided she would get the better education. There was, she said, one little thing she wanted to know. "How does the team get along?" she asked several times of the UNC coach. "I don't know," Dorrance answered somewhat impatiently. "Fine, I guess." All his male players had ever needed to know was would they get scholarships, and would they start. To the question Heinrichs posed, all he could think was "Who cares?"

Heinrichs arrived for the 1982 preseason in a battered pickup truck she had driven from home. She was awed by the gear her teammates dragged from their parents' station wagons. Aside from her cleats, her soccer equipment consisted of a pair of cheap tennis shoes for running, training, and everything else. "At home, we couldn't afford more than one pair of shoes," Heinrichs recalls. "The notion of having two and three pairs of shoes was amazing."

Most new recruits had names that team players had heard of through their local soccer networks. Heinrichs, on the other hand, appeared to be a farm girl out of nowhere. But when she stepped onto the field, the farm girl changed completely. Within the first few practices, Dorrance finally understood why she had been so anxious to know about how the team got along. She stood head and shoulders over the other players in skills. And she played and practiced with a level of intensity that none of his players had ever seen.

The Tar Heels all saw themselves as highly competitive. They were, after all, the best in the game, having won the first national championship. But Heinrichs's competitive drive was ferocious. Instead of backing down in the face of a growling senior, or passing the ball as quickly as possible, Heinrichs growled back and took the ball around her. Impatient when a goalie was slow to retrieve the ball after a score, Heinrichs would push past her and run into the net to grab it. In short, her teammates thought she was annoying. They resented her the way her teammates had at home.

"April refused to be mediocre in order to be well liked," her coach recalls. "She just wasn't afraid to compete and to be the best she could." Rather than allow her teammates "to put her in her place," Dorrance grabbed an opportunity to lift the competitive standards of the team. He began to work to bring the players up to her level of play and develop in them the extraordinary mental toughness she possessed. To raise their competitive drive, he developed a system for ranking each player in every drill and posting a list at the end of the day. He created what he liked to call "a competitive cauldron" to nurture soccer excellence. And Heinrichs became the leader of the squad.

A balance had to be struck, of course, between this new level of intensity introduced by Heinrichs, and the chemistry that was just beginning to work for the team on the field. "We had to get these players to compete against each other and still get along," Dorrance wrote in his book *Training Soccer Champions*. Players had to be able to battle each other like gladiators on the field and then revert to being friends in the locker room. The competitive arena was fierce, but Dorrance encouraged them to leave the fighting on the field, and eventually the players learned to do it. He created an atmosphere in which players also earned respect for their support of other players on the team. The combination of increased competition together with a strong team bond would prove to be a long-standing formula for victory.

After the first collegiate championship had proven itself a success, the NCAA decided that women's national soccer championships were a good idea and took charge of the annual event. The money, power, and prestige of the NCAA effectively squeezed out the smaller AIAW, which had given intercollegiate soccer its start. Eventually, the women's organization folded. But women's college soccer was already on its way. The number of teams and the level of play were rapidly climbing. But even as other teams around the country improved, the UNC Tar Heels took home the NCAA trophy every year, except for 1985, a year that Heinrichs was recovering from a knee injury.

In 1985 the Olympic Committee and the U.S. Soccer Federation hosted the first Olympic Festival for women's soccer in Baton Rouge, Louisiana. Players were chosen from each state to compete at a regional level, and then the regional players met at the festival to compete under the eye of Mike Ryan, the man chosen to select a national team. Ryan had a long history in soccer, having coached some of the earliest club teams in Seattle, an established hotbed of soccer talent.

Heinrichs couldn't compete in the festival; her injury had taken her out of the game for most of her junior year. But another young standout showed up in Baton Rouge. Her name was Michelle Akers.

At nineteen, Akers was a tall, lanky college sophomore at Central Florida, the school that often placed second to UNC in the final four. She had been recruited from Seattle, where she had already made her reputation as an exceptional player. The daughter of a psychologist and a female firefighter who divorced when she was eleven, Akers grew up playing football and soccer with her dad, her brother, and the boys at school. In the first grade, she announced her plans to become a wide receiver for the Pittsburgh Steelers. Her teacher pulled her aside to tell her girls didn't play professional football. Akers swallowed her disappointment and turned her focus to soccer.

Akers was passionate about winning and rarely had to worry about losing. On occasions when she did, however, she didn't take it well. When she was eight, she reportedly beat up a neighborhood boy for outrunning her in a race. As a soccer player in her early teens, it was not uncommon for her to handle a loss by stalking off the field in a sulk. As she grew older, she learned how to keep her emotions in check. While the rest of her team would be in the locker room shouting with disgust at a recent loss, Akers would be likely to sit by herself, utterly silent, keeping her feelings inside.

As Akers grew up, she also learned how to control her competitive engines so that she could go full throttle at will. On her high school team, the Flyers, she was a singular terror, as she trucked toward the goal with her wiry hair flying like a lion's mane. By the time she got to Central Florida, word had already spread that she was a soccer phenomenon. But when she turned to another freshman the first week of school and confided her doubts about making the team, it was clear that she didn't always feel as confident as she appeared.

Akers did make the Central Florida team and impressed all her teammates with her energy, discipline, and hard work. To some of her teammates, she seemed friendly but slightly aloof. When she was elected team captain during her senior year, she accepted it reluctantly. She didn't relish making speeches. As one of her teammates recalls, "Michelle wanted to be left alone to do her best."

But that rarely happens with athletic phenoms. And it didn't happen with Akers. In 1985 she was among those picked by Ryan to play for the national team.

The new women's national team included six starting players from UNC and the rest from other schools. In August of that year, they traveled with Ryan to Italy for their first international tournament. With almost no training before the trip and no idea what level players they would be facing, they lost 3–0 to England, tied Denmark, and lost to the Italian team 1–0.

The following year, Anson Dorrance was hired by the U.S. Soccer Federation to run the team tryouts and to coach the national team. His first choice: April Heinrichs, who was back from her injury and playing well again. Once again, Dorrance decided to develop his team based on Heinrichs's fearless attitude and her style of play. Michelle Akers also made the second-year team, but Heinrichs, now a senior, was the leader. Akers later recalled the day she got over her fear of Heinrichs. A ball went out of bounds off Heinrichs's foot, and the younger Akers called her on it. Heinrichs denied it, but after Akers shouted back, she simply handed over the ball. The young Akers was stunned when she realized that she had won this little showdown. That day, Akers felt she had arrived as a full-fledged member of the team.

During the next two years, new players joined the group. Players such as Julie Foudy, Joy Fawcett, Kristine Lilly, Carin Jennings (later Gabarra), and Carla Overbeck would eventually play key roles on the U.S. team. All of them were under twenty (with Foudy as young as sixteen) and had much to learn about international competition. But they were all outstanding athletes, and they were all exceptionally fit. They came to develop the competitive hunger and mental toughness that would make their strength unique.

Heinrichs was still a major influence on the team. She was known for the way she could dribble the ball through opposing traffic and take it all the way to the goal. Akers was known particularly for her tireless chases for the ball, her powerful headers, precise passes, and cannonball shots on goal. And though few Americans were watching their earliest games, the U.S. women were just beginning to show what they could do.

In 1986 and 1987, the team traveled to places like China, Sardinia, and Taiwan. With a tiny budget, they had little time to train together, so players learned to take responsibility for their own fitness and training regimes. Sometimes the team members didn't meet up with each other until they arrived at the airport before a trip. Many of the players held jobs outside of soccer to pay their bills and had to ask for special leaves for every game. Heinrichs, for instance, was engraving name tags at a Texas supermarket until she was lucky enough to get a coaching job at William & Mary College. All too often, team members got fired from jobs that couldn't wait for their return from a game.

Travel accommodations were simple, and food was often strange and hard to eat. On one trip, the team lived on Snickers bars donated by a company sponsor. Their uniforms were castoffs from the men's U-16 team. The reason for the boys' rejection: the socks had run in the wash, leaving the once white shorts a powder pink.

Nonetheless, as early as 1986, the team won its first title. After a brief training camp in Minnesota, they played the inaugural North American Championships, beating Canada 2–0 to win the trophy. When the team returned to Italy in August, they won two games and made it to the finals before losing the trophy to the hosting team. On the international field, they were rookies who still had a lot to learn. They routinely got kicks and bruises in their effort to save balls that were rolling out of bounds. And sometimes the kicks came from opponents being protected by bad referees.

But the U.S. women were beginning to see their own progress, and despite the hardships of travel, they were hungry for more international competition. During down time on their trips they would muse about the future. In 1986 the idea of a championship on par with the men's World Cup—the most revered of all international sporting events outside the Olympics—was a fantasy. The joke between Dorrance and his team members went like this: If he was still alive by the time a Women's World Cup became reality, he would apply for a job as suitcase porter for the team, just for the chance to be there. But maybe it wasn't such a fantasy, maybe Dorrance just needed to see that there were more players out there, better players, who might help make it possible.

Mia Hamm was only fourteen when Anson Dorrance first saw her play on a soccer field in north Texas. Right away, Dorrance has said, he knew that she could become one of the greatest soccer talents in the world.

Mariel Margaret Hamm was born in Selma, Alabama, to an air force pilot-instructor named Bill and his wife, Stephanie, a former ballerina. She was second to the youngest in a family of four girls, until her parents adopted two Thai-American boys. The eldest boy was eight, and Mia, at five, looked up to him right away. When Garrett Hamm immediately picked up sports, his little sister joined in. She recalls being babysat on the sidelines of the soccer field. Garrett was the first to discover his sister's soccer talent. He always allowed her to play in his games, and he picked her to be on his team. He knew that she was fast, and he called her his secret weapon.

Soccer was a game her father loved and encouraged his children to play. Following the lead of her brother, Mia was playing as early as five. She played several sports until, following her brother again, she chose to spend most of her time on soccer. Her family moved frequently, as Bill Hamm was transferred to new bases. And wherever they settled—California, Virginia, and then Texas—she joined a soccer team as soon as she could.

In 1986 the Hamms were living in Wichita Falls, Texas, and Mia was chosen to play on the U-16 state select team that was part of a growing nationwide Olympic Development Program. The coach for North Texas State University saw her play at a tournament and was so impressed that he called Anson Dorrance and told him he just had to come and see her play. When Dorrance got to Texas, he decided to see if he could pick out this marvel on his own. As he watched the girls scrimmage, one of them took a pass and accelerated so quickly that she left all the others behind. She controlled the ball with the power and precision of a much older player.

The following year, when she was just fifteen, Hamm joined the national women's team. As a new player in 1987, and the youngest by over a year, she often started as a forward but never made a goal. Audiences did notice her lightning pace and her agility with the ball; as a rookie, however, her youth coupled with her competitive intensity occasionally undermined her. She was shy, and though she was generally gracious, she needed to be alone before her games. If anyone should trespass on her private time, she could get snappish or abrupt. Sometimes she would get impatient with herself and shut herself off from the others. Toward the end of the year, at a tournament in Taiwan, Dorrance put it to the teenage Hamm that she would have to earn her stripes if she really wanted to rank among the best. She would have to work hard, hone her skills, and learn to be a better team player.

At seventeen, Hamm went to UNC and joined the Tar Heels while she played on the national team. Because she was still a minor, Dorrance and his wife became her temporary guardians for the year. At North Carolina, she took Dorrance's challenge and worked her hardest to become a pillar of the team.

During her four years as a forward for the Tar Heels, they won four national championships. Hamm scored 103 goals, earning herself the title of all-time leading scorer of the Atlantic Coast Conference. Between her sophomore and junior years, Dorrance recalls, she made great leaps forward both on and off the field. A new boyfriend who played soccer meant more leisure time spent kicking the ball in one-versus-ones. She was also succeeding in taming the sometimes overwhelming pressure she put on herself to excel. "Like anyone who is remarkably great," says her coach, "Mia has an inner ambition that drives her constantly to prove herself, so she can almost never be truly content." But she was developing a new level of confidence and discipline, which she would bring to her performance on the national team. One day when the team was on hiatus, Dorrance spied her practicing sprints all alone. "A champion," Dorrance told her, "is someone who is bending over backward to exhaustion when no one is watching." Mia Hamm was beginning to prove herself a champion.

Hamm was still only a sophomore when, to the surprise of Dorrance and the U.S. team, FIFA, the global administrators of soccer, granted approval for an international Women's World Championship, to be held in 1991. Although they didn't call it the Women's World Cup, that is what it was. What had been, since 1930, the planet's highest soccer award for men would now be available to women. And the U.S. team thought they might have a chance to win it.

Team USA was making its reputation as a young, fit, and scrappy group with a powerhouse personality. With Heinrichs as the U.S. team captain, Akers as the leading striker, and forwards Carin Gabarra and Mia Hamm, the team had a formidable offense. Joy Fawcett and Carla Overbeck presented a tough defensive wall. Midfielders Julie Foudy, Heinrichs, and Kristine Lilly launched creative attacks that often caught the opponent off guard. They had, recall some spectators, a psychological edge that enabled them to pounce on the other team's weak points and push through to victory.

Before the inaugural event in Guangzhou, China, U.S. Soccer granted the team money for an unprecedented three-week training camp. The camp in Florida was a luxury they hadn't had before any previous matches. Though still a good deal shorter than the men's training camps, the women were pleased. They had learned early on, out of necessity, how to train themselves whenever the team was apart. In fact, being part of the team meant knowing how to be your own coach. Besides, recalls Heinrichs, they couldn't imagine spending more time together without straining their relationships, not to mention their ties to their families, friends, and jobs.

When the women arrived in China on November 17, 1991, they were feeling strong. But in the eyes of the other nations, the United States was still a third-world power as far as soccer was concerned. The American men's team hadn't made a decent showing at the World Cup in forty years. The rest of the world simply didn't think the United States could take its soccer seriously. Even the U.S. Soccer Federation failed to send over any of its representatives for the first three rounds. When the U.S. team walked out into the Guangzhou stadium, they looked up to see the biggest crowd they had ever played before. From the field it appeared to be a sea of Chinese faces, but if they strained, they could make out a tiny speck. That speck represented the handful of Americans—mostly family and friends—who had come to see them play.

The U.S. team won their first game when Carin Gabarra scored two goals and Mia Hamm scored one to beat Sweden 3–2. In their second game, they trounced Brazil 5–0. Throughout, Heinrichs served to motivate and galvanize her team, yelling at them to push and work harder. She scored two goals in the semifinal match against Germany, which the USA won 5–2.

Akers began slowly, with no goals at all until the second game. But when she scored her first goal against Brazil, she seemed to ignite. She scored two more in the next game with Japan and then a remarkable five against Taiwan. She stood out in her ability to scare down her opponents, to go after every airborne ball and win it. At times, her coaches worried that she was putting herself at risk—she chased balls even when it didn't matter, and if she was downed by an opponent, she never stayed down the way players from the other countries did. She pulled herself up and threw herself back into the fray. In the final match, against Norway, she seemed to explode with her energy and will. She scored the only two goals of the game, winning the cup for the United States in front of sixty-five thousand soccer fans.

The eighteen women on the team had won their country its very first world cup title. They were now soccer champions of the globe. Their victory made headlines in China, throughout Asia, and even in Europe. The women flew home deliriously happy. But when they got here, their nation seemed to welcome them with a big "So what?" There wasn't a hint of fanfare on their arrival. "It was hard," recalls Lauren Gregg, the team's assistant coach and a former team member herself. "It reinforced for us that we weren't playing just because people were watching or because we were being paid a lot of money." That was for sure. The players left each other at the airport and returned home to college exams and lost jobs. It was hard not to feel disappointed. No one at home seemed to have been watching.

But someone had been watching. Soon, they began to hear mutterings within soccer circles that Michelle Akers was to soccer what Michael Jordan was to basketball and Billie Jean King was to tennis. The U.S. Soccer Federation wanted to hear from the new women's team. Within months, Umbro, a leading soccer equipment company, approached Akers to sign a major contract for her endorsement. Although Heinrichs had signed a contract with Lanzarra before the tournament, her benefits consisted mostly of free equipment (which, given the team's budget, did not go unappreciated). Now a soccer company was willing to give up hard cash for the endorsement of a woman soccer player.

For many members of the team, this would usher in a new chapter in their lives as professional soccer players. But for Heinrichs, the moment she lifted the world cup trophy was the highest moment of her career. Immediately afterward, she faced the lowest. For the past three months, her knee had been failing her. It was, it turned out, not an anterior cruciate ligament tear, so common to soccer players and women players especially, but a rare degenerative cartilage problem that showed no promise of improving. At twenty-eight, Heinrichs had carried the team from its fledgling years to its victory over the world. Now, just when the world was beginning to notice, she had to walk away. In the fall of 1991, she retired as a player from the U.S. women's team and went to coach the women's soccer team at the University of Virginia.

The five-ten, 150-pound Akers was now widely considered to be the best soccer player in the world. There was still no mainstream press coverage in the United States of American men's or women's soccer. But Umbro worked to publicize Akers and women's soccer by flying her around the country for speaking engagements, seminars, and autograph signings. In 1991 5.7 million girls and women were playing soccer in the United States. Now they had a role model they could read about in soccer magazines and maybe even meet.

Akers had matured a great deal from the retiring personality on the Central Florida team. She stepped into her role as first ranking diplomat for American women's soccer and worked hard at it. Julie Foudy, the garrulous and outgoing midfielder, also won an endorsement after graduating from Stanford and forgoing plans for a medical career to stay with the team. Hamm was the first female soccer player to sign a contract with Nike. But Akers was in large part the front-runner, spending months on the road for soccer events and appearing regularly on the covers of soccer publications.

The year following the world cup, the number of college-age female players doubled from 300,000 to 600,000. More and more women—the earliest, athletes from the national teams—were now coaching women's soccer at colleges around the country. They could inspire their players with dreams of becoming a Michelle Akers.

Toward the end of 1992, however, Akers's energy was beginning to drag. She was so accustomed to giving 150 percent that it took her a while to notice that her body wasn't delivering what she asked of it. She began to experience regular headaches, intestinal upset, and dizziness, all of this accompanied by a bone-numbing weariness that never seemed to let up. Through the rest of that year, she tried to push herself beyond the pain. She had always relied upon her will to get her body to do what she wanted. But this time, it didn't seem to work.

In 1993 Akers was playing a match in Texas when she suddenly appeared to glaze over. The crowd noticed her unable to respond as the ball came her way and whizzed on by. Then she collapsed. Later at the hospital, she was diagnosed with Epstein-Barr virus, which the doctors later changed to chronic-fatigue immune-deficiency syndrome—an illness with no known cause or cure.

It was also in 1993 that the International Olympic Committee voted to admit women's soccer into the pantheon of official Olympic sports for 1996. It was a spectacular victory, won in no small part by the singular efforts of an Atlanta woman who had never even played soccer till she was thirty. Marilyn Childress, the manager of a precision machine shop in Atlanta, Georgia, was too old to be a beneficiary of Title IX, but as an amateur league player she had become involved in organizing and promoting the woman's sport at the state and national levels. When, in 1991, the Olympic Committee first announced that women's soccer was "highly unlikely" to be part of the upcoming Olympics, Childress didn't believe they had given it serious enough consideration. She immediately went to work to prove that women soccer players were ready for the Olympics and that the public was ready for them. She did copious research, enlisted hundreds in support, and organized an international "test game" in Atlanta. With the help of Akers, Heinrichs, and the politically connected parents of team member Amanda Cromwell, Childress eventually changed the minds of soccer administrators all over the globe.

For the American players, the announcement was thrilling news. Eight national teams would face off against each other at the upcoming Games in

Atlanta. The U.S. women may have been among the only Americans to witness their achievement in China, but now all of their country would have a chance to see them play on the world stage.

Women's soccer was beginning to win real support in the United States, largely because of the recent success of the national team. Elsewhere, however, women were still fighting their own battles to try and get into the game. A few countries, especially in Scandinavia, had welcomed women to soccer early on. Denmark, Sweden, and Norway, for instance, started women's teams in the 1970s and generally encouraged women with funding and support. But in many other countries, particularly those considered world soccer powers in the men's game, women were still shut out.

Of the three biggest soccer nations in South America, Argentina, Uruguay, and Brazil, only Brazil entered a women's team in the world cup—which was itself remarkable given that in a country almost half the size of South America, there were only three hundred women playing the sport at all. China actually had a history of women's soccer dating back to the Tang and Song dynasties (A.D. 600–1300). The sport was encouraged for schoolgirls back in the 1920s and emerged as a competitive game in the early 1980s. But while the Chinese boasted technically excellent players, the women's national team was disbanded after their world cup loss in 1991.

In England, home of the Dick, Kerr Ladies, a ban on women's soccer managed to stifle the sport for several decades. Until 1993, when the Football Association formed a division to oversee and promote the women's game, there was little growth. Even today, England's national team continues to suffer from what seems to be a general lack of enthusiasm for British women in cleats. Then, of course, there are countries where tradition or religion prohibits women from playing altogether. In Iran, the world began to see a ray of hope for Iranian women's rights, for example, when in 1994 women were allowed to attend soccer matches as spectators for the first time since the Shah was overthrown.

Unlike male players, female players around the globe shared a bond in their struggle to advance their young sport. They developed a cooperative spirit that often transcended national boundaries and created excitement about international exchange. Several members of the U.S. team played for a few months a year with professional teams in countries like Italy, Sweden, and Japan, where established women's leagues offered opportunities for consistent and challenging games. Even in those countries, their championship status made the U.S. women highly visible role models. As they prepared to play both the Olympics and the world cup, the players took their responsibilities seriously as representatives of their game.

As the World Cup approached in 1994, Michelle Akers seemed to be hitting her peak as a superstar in the public eye. She was a celebrity guest at the men's World Cup in 1994, and a celebrity guest to Sweden, where she had spent three summers playing on one of the top Swedish teams. On the field, however, she was struggling just to continue to play for her team. She was determined not to miss the Olympics. Neither could she consider skipping the 1994 World Cup. While chronic-fatigue experts inveighed against physical overexertion, Akers tried to find a training regime that would maintain her as a world-class athlete but wouldn't bring her to collapse. Now, with her health and energy on a kind of roller coaster, and an impending divorce from her husband, she was forced to cut back her time as a spokesperson so she could devote all her time to her game. Even then, her symptoms sometimes kept her out of practice and out of the gym.

In the meantime, new players were joining the team. Shannon Mac-Millan, a midfielder, and Tiffeny Milbrett, a forward, both came from the Portland Pilots soccer club in Oregon. Tisha Venturini, a outgoing midfielder, arrived from California. In August of 1994, Anson Dorrance stepped down after eight years as U.S. coach to return to the Tar Heels full-time. Stepping into his shoes was Tony DiCicco, formerly the goalkeeper coach and assistant to Dorrance since 1991. Lauren Gregg continued as assistant to DiCicco. To help them in their bid for a second world cup, DiCicco also hired April Heinrichs, who had made such a contribution to their first world cup win.

The women achieved a major victory when the U.S. Soccer Federation voted to give the team money for a six-month residential training camp in Florida, and for the first time, the female postcollegiate players would actually earn a small salary. It was a huge relief to players used to pleading with bosses to keep their jobs or leaning on family for cash to tide them over. But it also demanded that the players—several of whom were now married—leave their families for half a year. Furthermore, while twenty-four players would sacrifice all the other facets of their lives for the entire training period, only eighteen players would then go on to Sweden.

For the most part, the U.S. team felt confident upon their arrival at the World Cup Games in Sweden. In the months and weeks preceding the match, they had begun to be the focus of attention from international soccer reporters and fans. The matches would even be broadcast on ESPN.

Akers had made the team, but it had been a terrific struggle. Six minutes into the very first game of the cup, however, she collided head to head with a Chinese player and fell to the ground unconscious. She ended up with both a concussion and a twisted knee. One of the rookies, Tiffeny Milbrett, got an earlier than expected chance at the big time when she ran in to sub for the ailing forward. Milbrett scored, but the match ended up in a 3–3 tie with China.

In the next round, the team played with Akers's name scrawled across their socks. They conquered Denmark 2–0. Next they beat Australia, and in the quarterfinals they beat Japan. But Norway was a formidable opponent, and although Akers was back for the semifinals, her knee was still not up to par. Forward Carin Gabarra also happened to be suffering from pleurisy. After Norway scored an early goal, the U.S. team fought hard to make it up. Akers, who had outscored any player, with eighty-two goals scored in eighty-eight international games, failed to make one that day.

It was the quiet Mia Hamm who emerged during the World Cup Games as a player of remarkable all-around talent. Switching positions as needed from forward to midfielder to goalie, she initiated most of the team's offensive drives. She made three assists and two goals, one of which she made during the final game after a spectacular sixty-yard solo run down the field.

But despite Hamm's skill, the team simply didn't show the chemistry that had always been palpable during their very best games. Their plays seemed somehow tentative. In the end, the United States came in third behind Norway and China. For the women of U.S. soccer, it was a crushing defeat to lose their world title so soon.

After the loss, they examined their play and decided it was time to make changes. They would need to take into better account the evolution of the game as it was being played around the globe, while building and maintaining their own unique strengths. Coaches DiCicco and Gregg used the loss as a springboard to raise the team to the next level. They had less than twelve months before the Olympics to transform themselves into world champions again.

In January they went back into their training residency, where they would stay until the games began in July. The team's game strategy had always relied largely on their ability to send the ball long from behind and run up for an attack at every possible opportunity. Now there was a new focus on the players' ability to keep the ball in possession. The new system depended on strong ball skills on the part of the defense and the midfielders. They worked on being able to flip their defensive tactics, depending on the play of the opposing team.

Once they laid the groundwork for this new, more sophisticated game, the coaching staff felt they risked losing the scrappy, offensive drive that had always made them winners. They then went back and sharpened the players' aggressive edge and psychological strength by returning to the competitive passing drills, timed sprints, and individual rankings from the days of April Heinrichs.

In the months before the Olympics, a buzz was building about the U.S. team despite their recent loss. Now safely through her teens, Mia Hamm was beginning to eclipse Michelle Akers in public popularity. Hamm was both a dazzling player and a well-spoken soccer representative. Supremely modest about her own talents, she always responded to the phrase "best soccer player in the world" by pointing to the rest of her team's accomplishments. Her youthful, pony-tailed image was suddenly gracing the windows of Nike stores in major U.S. cities.

"Through the years of hard work," says Lauren Gregg, "it often seemed as though we were preparing ourselves for contests we never knew would happen." They knew about the Olympics, of course, but for most of the players, it wasn't until they stepped off the bus in Georgia that it really struck home. They were going to play for their nation in the greatest contest on earth. Goalie Briana Scurry made an offhand promise to her teammates: "If we win, I'll run naked through the streets of Athens."

Because there weren't enough stadiums in Atlanta, the women's soccer games were scheduled in faraway fields around the country to avoid the congested center of the Olympic village. They played their first match, against Denmark in Birmingham, Alabama, where thirty thousand spectators cheered them and celebrated with a week of events in their honor. After beating Denmark, they went on to play Sweden in Orlando, Florida, where Hamm twisted her ankle and had to be carried off the field by stretcher. They won the match anyway and then faced China at the Stadium Complex in Washington, D.C. Without Hamm in the lineup for their first match with China, the Americans tied the game. After a tie, it is determined who moves to the next round by how many goals the team has accrued in total. Luckily, the United States had accumulated enough points to send them to the semifinals against their arch rival, Norway.

All but six of the eighteen U.S. Olympians had played on the team that lost to Norway in 1995. They were determined not to let Norway steal another world title away. But after the first twenty minutes, Norway scored a goal to lead the game and kept their lead into the seventy-sixth minute, when finally Akers scored a goal from a penalty kick. Then the teams remained tied until the full ninety minutes were up and the game continued into sudden-death overtime. In the center of their pre-overtime huddle, Akers lay on the ground in a desperate attempt to save some strength to finish the match. In perhaps the most dramatic minutes of women's Olympic soccer, the U.S. women hung on until in minute ten, third-year midfielder Shannon MacMillan scored a goal to win the game.

The final against China was to be played at Sanford Stadium in Athens, Georgia, on August 1. No amount of practice had prepared them for the feeling of stepping into a stadium with 76,481 spectators. It was the largest crowd ever assembled to watch a women's soccer game. Most of the people there had driven hours to see the match. Fans carried banners with the players' names emblazoned across them. There were men in the crowd emblazoned in war paint with "I Love Hamm" and "Hamm is Good" splashed across their chests. Americans were roaring with adoration for the American women of soccer.

The Chinese team had pulled themselves back together and worked hard since their World Cup loss in 1991. They were fast, skilled, and extremely fit players. Eighteen minutes after the game began, Shannon MacMillan scored a goal, but the Chinese took one fourteen minutes later. The game remained tied at 1–1 until the last twenty-five minutes when Tiffeny Milbrett made a goal on an assist from defender Joy Fawcett. Screams of fans shook the bleachers during the last twenty minutes as the U.S. team fought to hold on to their lead. Suddenly shouts of "USA, USA" turned to an almost deafening roar as the final whistle blew. The American women had won the Olympic gold. America had seen them play and had reason to like what they saw. Before heading into the crowd of reporters and congratulaters, the team took a lap together around the field to celebrate their feat in a moment of unity and closeness. Women's soccer had finally arrived in the United States.

Despite the intense enthusiasm from the stands, the games were never broadcast as part of NBC's Olympic prime-time coverage. *New York Times* writer George Vecsey wrote in his Monday column following the final match that NBC "dissed this skilled and charismatic team," and in a characteristic line calculated to diss the network back on the women's behalf, he concluded, "Something is happening, but you don't know what it is, do you, Mr. Peacock?"

If the network missed its chance to catch the players on the pitch, it didn't diminish their star appeal. Hamm's star rose to new heights as the undisputed queen of post-Olympic soccer. Already one of the faces of Nike, she would soon appear in TV commercials for Pert Plus Shampoo. Later, Power Bar, Pepsi, and Earth Grain breads would also sign contracts with the celebrated striker, making her the first female soccer star to show commercial appeal to companies outside of her sport. Her appeal wasn't limited to advertisers, either: she appeared on *David Letterman*, on *Regis and Kathie Lee*, and on *People* magazine's list of the fifty most beautiful people in the world. She was voted favorite female athlete in an ESPN/Sportzone Internet poll—over Martina Hingis, Sheryl Swoopes, and Tara Lipinski. Hamm treated each opportunity to appear on TV or in magazines as a chance to sell the game, and she proved herself a cool and competent spokeswoman. She was able to handle the attention without allowing the spotlight to stay on herself for long.

The women's triumph at the Olympics didn't benefit only the stars. Every member of the U.S. team currently benefits from at least one endorsement contract, and every one of them has become a role model for hundreds of younger players around the world. An increasing number of publications have devoted themselves to covering women's sports, and two focus simply on women's soccer, *Women's Soccer World,* an international magazine, and *Network,* put out by the Women's Soccer Foundation.

In 1995 the number of women and girls playing soccer in this country approached 7.5 million. An expansive Olympic Development Program now boasts almost 15,000 players trying out each year and 5,000 state-level select players nationwide. At the same time, an expanding network of club teams like the Dallas Sting, the Portland Pirates, and the Cincinnati Hammer are developing powerful female players who are going on to first-division collegiate and national teams. Women's collegiate soccer now includes over five hundred schools, which celebrate the end of their year with the NCAA championship each spring (UNC has won the championship title all but three of its fourteen years).

Battles remain to be fought at the top and the bottom of the American soccer ladder, however. It is still primarily a white, middle-class, suburban sport, and efforts are just beginning to bring soccer to kids in inner cities. Programs like Soccer in the Cities get help from sneaker companies as well as from luminaries like Mia Hamm who spend time coaching and developing urban indoor soccer leagues.

America's best players are finding that they have to battle to stay in contention themselves. Of the eight nations that sent teams to the last Olympics, all but two—China and the United States—run women's leagues for their top competitive players. U.S. Olympic team members and coaches say that they need a league that can offer consistent top-level competition. Without it, their championship status may soon start crumbling away. Currently, the best women players in the country must keep up their game by moving to a country that has a league (as Michelle Akers, Briana Scurry, and others have done), by playing on men's club soccer teams, or by joining the W-league, an open women's amateur league, where, they say, the level of play varies greatly from game to game.

Plans to launch an eight-team professional women's league in 1998 unraveled when the U.S. Soccer Federation (now known as U.S. Soccer) failed to give support at the time the league organizers needed it most. With Mia Hamm, Julie Foudy, and most of the U.S. team committed to play in the fall, and with several major sponsors lined up, the last-minute cancellation came as a letdown for the women and their fans. Alan Rothenburg, the U.S. Soccer president, has intimated that his organization might be more supportive in the year 2000, after the 1999 World Cup Games to be hosted here in the United States.

The next World Cup tournament will be a pivotal event for women's soccer in North America. There is potential to expand soccer's American audience dramatically. As many as seventy national teams will be hoping to qualify for a berth in the thirty-two-game championship. And for three weeks of the summer, the games will be played in eight cities across the country.

Of course, American television will be a key ingredient. Most of our televised soccer now comes to us from Spanish-speaking countries. Already, ESPN is signed to broadcast all of the thirty-two games, and ABC is committed to televising at least the opening, semifinal, and final matches. When they do, millions of Americans will finally have the chance to see their own world champions in action.

Some of those watching will be young girls who hope to play for the United States themselves someday. It is likely to be the very first time they see their role models on the international field. They, and thousands of other girls watching, might be unaware that fifteen years ago there was no such thing as a women's national soccer team or that twenty-five years ago a girl's opportunities in soccer were largely confined to her own backyard.

Today, girls make up 40 percent of the participants in youth soccer around the country. In Heinrichs's youth, female players could count on few supports other than themselves and, if they were lucky, their parents. Today they are likely to find opportunities and reinforcement from their schools and communities, as well as the general culture. Labels such as "tomboy" no longer distinguish the girl who plays soccer. In the pages of contemporary children's books, everyone from the Berenstein Bears to the Boxcar Kids plays soccer. Recently, they were joined by America's favorite doll when Barbie Soccer Coach was released in 1997. Today, there is even a rapidly growing network of soccer leagues for the proverbial soccer mom.

The image of the female soccer player is changing, and it is also changing us. Mia Hamm's long, shiny hair swinging in commercials for Pert Plus is a kind of semaphore. Being a soccer player, it tells us, doesn't mean we won't grow up to be women. The image of Hamm and her teammates working together out on the field from match to match and season to season sends an even stronger message that many girls and women are beginning to believe: Being a soccer player can help us grow up to become better women.

Ice Hockey

*I*n From the Cold

Barbara Stewart

Standing at center ice in the Big Hat arena in Nagano, Japan, the members of the USA 1998 Women's Olympic Hockey Team stood tall, their faces beaming with pride, many of them clutching their gold medals while they sang along to "The Star-Spangled Banner." Their voices were choked with emotion, and few could hide their tears.

Across the ice, the Canadian players were crying too. They had put up a good fight in the gold-medal game but had come up on the short end of a 3–1 score. It had been a war of sorts, with both teams shouldering the hopes and aspirations of their countries and every single player profoundly aware that they were part of sports history. In fact, this game had been the culmination of a hundred-year struggle to gain recognition and respect for women's hockey—and in many ways, all female athletes in North America—in a society where the sport was often viewed as, at best, a curiosity. Not bad, *for girls,* the sportscasters and rink-side pundits would say, with a wink. But now "the girls" had brought their game to the premier sporting event in the world and shown that it could be every bit as exciting, and every bit as ugly, as the men's game.

The two teams had been going at it all year long. Leading up to the gold-medal game, the U.S. and Canadian Olympic teams had butted heads fourteen times over the course of the 1997–98 season. The series was dead even, at seven games each. But the Americans had held the upper hand in the two months leading up to the Olympics, winning five of seven games. They had a lot to prove. For ten years, the United States had played in Canada's shadow. Team Canada had won every world championship, all four of them, since their inception in 1990. In fact, Canadian women owned the sport—and that didn't sit very well with the Americans. To add to the pressure, the American men's team was on the verge of being knocked out of medal contention. For the first time, Olympic organizers had allowed countries to field teams of professional hockey players, and many hockey commentators expected Team USA—bolstered by superstars like Brett Hull, Chris Chelios, and Mike Modano—to take home the gold. But the team had played poorly from the very start and would ultimately finish with a 1-and-3 record in the preliminary round. That wasn't good enough to advance to the finals, and Team USA extended its losing streak to eighteen years; not since 1980 in Lake Placid, when the United States won gold over the vastly superior squad from the Soviet Union in the fabled "Miracle on Ice," had an American team taken home a medal in Olympic hockey. So now it was up to the women.

While the heat was on the American team, they at least had the advantage of going into the tournament as underdogs. No such luck for Team Canada. They were the odds-on favorite to win gold. The experts predicted it. Their fans back at home *expected* it. And the players themselves wanted it more than anything. After all, hockey was Canada's official winter sport and unofficial religion. In 1972, when a professional team made up of Canada's best men beat the Soviets in a dramatic eight-game exhibition series, the whole country celebrated; schools, businesses, even the government shut down for the day: everyone was home watching the deciding game. Historically, Canadian teams dominated Olympic hockey—from the very first Olympic Winter Games in Chamonix, France, in 1924, when Team Canada beat Switzerland 33–0, Czechoslovakia 30–0, Sweden 22–0, and Great Britain 19–2 on its way to a gold medal. But Canada hadn't won Olympic gold in hockey for forty-six years. Many believed that Canada's time had come again.

The fact that they were playing Team USA didn't make things any easier for the Canadians. While Americans tend to think of Canada as its friendly neighbor to the north, Canadians often feel overwhelmed living next door to this economic and political giant. Hockey was one area in which Canadians felt themselves superior, but this facade of confidence was starting to crack. A year and a half before the Nagano Olympics, at a Canada Cup tournament—the unofficial world cup of hockey—Canada's best men players lost in the final to Team USA. The Canadian hockey world was stunned, and the pressure was on the women's team to defend their country's honor. "We don't want to hear the American anthem," Canadian forward Lori Dupuis told reporters in the days leading up to the Olympic showdown. "We don't want to see them hooting, hollering and saluting their fans. We want to win the final for those reasons and for the gold medal."

The Canadian and the American women had already met once in Olympic competition, in what turned out to be a goal-filled, action-packed affair clouded by controversy. On paper, it was a meaningless game, held on the last day of preliminary competition, after Canada and the United States had both secured their spots in the gold-medal game. The Canadians started off strong, outworking and outskating their bigger, slower opponents. But as they built a 4–1 lead over two periods, the Americans began to up the ante. They hit a little harder, skated a little more aggressively, pushing the no-bodychecking rule in women's hockey to its absolute limit. Soon the teams were trading cheap shots—an elbow here, a butt end there. By the third and final period, things were getting rough. In all, referee Manuela Groeger assessed forty-eight minutes in penalties, unheard of in women's hockey, including a high-sticking double-minor to Team USA defender Vicki Movsession and a ten-minute misconduct to her teammate Angela Ruggiero—the U.S. star defender of the future—for checking from behind. But the aggressive play paid off; the United States scored six unanswered goals in the third period, on their way to a 7–4 rout. The players kept at it, though, even after the final whistle sounded. Several of them milled around, trading verbal jabs. Suddenly, things got ugly. Sandra Whyte, a Team USA forward, said something in the midst of an argument with Team Canada top scorer Danielle Goyette. Goyette exploded, slamming her stick against the protective glass before storming off the ice. A few minutes later, Goyette's teammates found her sobbing in the dressing room. The Canadian players alleged that someone—they didn't mention Whyte by name—had made a derogatory comment to Goyette about her father, who had died from Alzheimer's disease on the day before the Olympics began. The public may never know what really happened, but one thing was for sure, the gloves were off, and no one knew exactly what would be in store for the gold-medal game.

Both teams seemed tight as they started the gold-medal final game. They were playing cautious hockey, neither team wanting to make that one mistake that would lead to the all-important opening goal. The period ended with the teams knotted at 0–0, and the shots were almost even, nine to eight in favor of Canada. But Team USA took control in the second period, led by the aggressive play of their captain, Cammi Granato—whose brother Tony had made his own mark as an NHL player. Under intense pressure, Canada's Nancy Drolet took a tripping penalty just forty-six seconds into the period. Canadian goaltender Manon Rheaume played brilliantly, keeping the American power play off the board until, with only five seconds left in the penalty, Gretchen Ulion banged in a goal: 1–0, Team USA. For the rest of the period the Americans were all over their opponents, outshooting them 11–4, and it was only thanks to Rheaume's solid goaltending that Team USA didn't run up the score. Team Canada pressed hard early in the third period, but U.S. goalie Sarah Tueting was equal to the task. Just when it seemed Canada might tie things up, the momentum of the game changed. The usually mild-mannered Danielle Goyette ran into Elizabeth Brown, a Team USA player, right at center ice. Referee Mara Zenk gave her a two-minute penalty in the box. On the ensuing power play, Shelley Looney scored, to put the United States up by two. With less than ten minutes to play, the Canadian cause seemed all but lost. But they started to press, and with five minutes left to play, U.S. defender Tara Mounsey knocked a Canadian forward to the ice. Referee Zenk sent Mounsey to the penalty box for two minutes. A minute later, Goyette redeemed herself by potting Canada's only goal, fed to her from Hayley Wickenheiser, who would later reveal she was playing with a strained knee and a fractured elbow. This set the scene for a wild finish. Canada took charge of the play, but Tueting was sensational. With two minutes left to play, Canadian forward Stacy Wilson took a pass from Karen Nystrom and found herself all alone in front of the American net. She drilled a shot, but Tueting was up to the task. With one minute left to play in the game, Canadian coach Shannon Miller tried a desperate play. She pulled goaltender Rheaume in favor of an extra skater. Canada came close a couple times, but with eight seconds left, Sandra Whyte lifted the puck into the empty Canadian net. The game ended 3–1. Sports history had been made; Team USA had won the first ever Olympic gold medal in women's hockey.

Few sports have had as difficult a time gaining acceptance as women's hockey. Many people—men *and* women—have viewed the sport as a second-rate parody of real hockey, the men's game. In Canada and the northeastern United States, where ice hockey as we know it developed, women have been a part of the sport from the very beginning, often competing head-to-head with men. In no other team sport can women make this claim; not soccer, not rugby, not football. The only other team sport that has had a persistent female presence in its history is baseball, but even that has qualifications. Women's baseball enjoyed a certain vogue during the war years, but the public looked on it as a novelty, a curious diversion to fill the space while most male baseball players were engaged in more serious business overseas. Otherwise, women were relegated to the softball diamond, baseball's slower, softer cousin.

But hockey was a different matter. Men and women have been playing organized hockey for more than a hundred years, although the game's roots go back several centuries. Old drawings, photographs, letters, and sketches offer evidence to indicate that people were playing a form of hockey even as the first settlers were arriving in the new world. Many played with a ball instead of a puck and used crude sticks shaped more like canes, with very few rules. No one has been able to pinpoint the exact moment of the birth of modern hockey, but a widely told story sets the first game somewhere in the winter of 1853, when a group of bored British soldiers decided to play field hockey on a frozen pond just outside the gates of Windsor Castle, in England. Rumor has it that Queen Victoria herself watched the game and was terribly amused. Sports historians believe that the modern game of hockey developed simultaneously at different spots in North America; communities in New England, Montreal, Ottawa, and throughout southern Ontario have all laid some claim to being the birthplace of the game. What we do know is that hockey really took shape in the 1880s, when a group of students from Montreal's McGill University first put the rules of hockey on paper. Borrowing from lacrosse, field hockey, and rugby, they came up with a rough and tumble version of ice hockey. The game was quite different from the one we see today; they used a ball instead of a puck, and each team could have up to fifteen players at any one time, instead of the current six. Women were right there, skating and stick-handling alongside the men. In fact, one of the earliest known "action shots" of people playing hockey is a photograph in Canada's National Archives taken around 1889, which shows several young women in full skirts and fur hats, hunched over their hockey sticks, enjoying an afternoon game of hockey. This gives a good idea of the kind of recreational environment that nurtured hockey in its infancy. Unlike other team sports, which were often developed to help create a structured play environment for young boys—and prepare them for a regimented, team-oriented life in the military—hockey grew up as a purely social event. In the long, cold, Nordic winters, outdoor rinks were cheap and plentiful and provided the central medium for human contact. That's where friends would get together to relax, chat, have a pleasant skate, and maybe catch a game of shinny, an informal variation of hockey, a kind of keep-away on skates, with no teams and few rules.

By the 1890s the die was cast. Hockey was no longer just a recreational activity; now it was a serious sport, with leagues and championship trophies and scoring awards, and an emphasis, particularly in the men's game, on competition and victory. By 1892 the best amateur men's teams in Canada were competing for the fabled Stanley Cup, that enduring symbol of hockey supremacy, which is now awarded annually to the National Hockey League's championship team. But as the sport become "serious," the segregation between male and female players grew. Even as men's leagues were sprouting up, female athletes were embracing the game, and all-women teams were becoming the norm. History books record that the first all-female match was played in Barrie, Ontario, some sixty miles north of Toronto, in 1892, and two years later, the venerable McGill University allowed female students to play hockey among themselves, provided they had a guard on the dressing room door, no boys watched, and they were "comfortably and warmly dressed" in long dresses and heavy wool sweaters. By the turn of the century, women's teams could be found as far west as Vancouver and Seattle, right through to New England and Canada's maritime provinces. The stage was set for the men's and women's game to develop on separate paths that would cross each other time and time again.

The 1920s were the golden age for women's hockey in North America. By now, there were hundreds of senior amateur, college, and junior-level teams and leagues—there was even a national championship, reminiscent of the Stanley Cup—and female players were earning public attention for the first time. However, because women's hockey lacked the same kind of media profile as the men's game, those women who wanted to carve themselves a niche in the world of sport had to turn elsewhere to get noticed. Canada's Bobbie Rosenfeld best exemplifies the era. As a standout athlete, weaned on a diet of hockey, she had to turn to track and field to make her mark in the public imagination.

Born in Russia in 1905, Fanny "Bobbie" Rosenfeld arrived in Canada one year later. Her parents settled in, fittingly, Barrie, Ontario, a port city at the westernmost point of Lake Simcoe. Early on, Bobbie proved herself to be a gifted athlete, excelling at half a dozen sports: hockey, softball, tennis, golf, basketball, and track. It's been said that the best way to sum up her sports accomplishments is to say that she wasn't good at swimming. She was a born athlete. Although not tall, no bigger than five feet five inches, nor particularly heavy, she was wiry and muscular. She had a curious look to her: her head was slightly too large for her body, and she wore her hair in a close-cropped, flapper style, even years after it had been fashionable. But perhaps her most striking feature was her eyes: dark, focused, burning with intensity. She was famous for her competitive flare, not that she was physically aggressive with her opponents—she was always gracious, on and off the playing field—but because of the way she gave her all. While other athletes gained a popular following through their colorful personalities, Bobbie remained earnest and relatively low-key. But it was this intensity that appealed to the public.

Bobbie first caught the public eye in 1920, when she was barely fifteen. She was playing in a softball tournament with her team when someone convinced her to enter an exhibition hundred-yard dash. She won the race, unaware that she had beaten out Rosa Grosse, then Canadian champion in the event and an eventual world-record holder. Grosse was furious—and the two athletes remained rivals throughout their careers—but Bobbie's win caught the eye of many of the country's sporting elite. From that race, her fame spread, and soon after, she moved to Toronto—Canada's economic and social heart—to take a job in a chocolate factory and compete at the highest levels possible in track, hockey, softball, and tennis.

By 1922 she had a national reputation. She was considered by many to be the finest sprinter in Canada and was well on her way to being a world-class runner. Before she hit her twentieth birthday, she set the world record in the 220-yard event: twenty-six seconds flat. But that honor was taken away a short time later when officials discovered that the track was exactly one yard short of the international standard. But Bobbie persevered. A few months later she helped her company-sponsored track team, the Patterson Athletic Club, win the Ontario Ladies Track and Field Championships, the most prestigious women-only sporting event in the province. In a single afternoon, the club came first in the 220-yard race, discus, long jump, and 120-yard hurdles and had second-place finishes in the javelin and the 100-yard dash. Not bad, considering Bobbie was the only entrant on the Patterson team. The papers heralded her accomplishment, but she was only warming up.

Fittingly, the highlight of this tremendous athlete's career came at the 1928 Olympics in Amsterdam. These were the first Olympic Games in which women were allowed to compete in track-and-field events, and the change did not go unnoticed. Pope Pius XI himself denounced the move, believing women unsuited for this sort of intense athletic competition, while the founder of the modern Olympics, Baron de Coubertin, personally protested women infringing on the "solemn periodic manifestation of male sports." But Bobbie Rosenfeld didn't seem to care one way or the other what anybody thought. This was her chance to shine on the world stage, and she wasn't going to let the opportunity slip through her fingers. She made her own way to the Olympic trials in Halifax, on Canada's eastern coast, competing in shorts and a YMCA T-shirt she'd borrowed from her brother, and her father's socks for good luck. The socks must have worked: She set Canadian records in the 200, the discus, and the broad jump. Successful at the trials, she moved on to the real thing, the Amsterdam Olympics. Her first event was the 100 meters. It was a close race, with four of the six runners only a few inches apart at the finish line. Bobbie finished neck-and-neck with the American sprinter Betty Robinson, but the judges awarded the gold medal to Robinson, and, under the protests of the Canadian coach, Bobbie Rosenfeld took second. Her next event was the 400-meter relay, which Bobbie and her teammates

Ethel Smith, Myrtle Cook, and Florence Bell won handily, in 48.4 seconds, a record that was to last until the 1950s. Bobbie might have been content going home with a gold and a silver medal, but she saved her greatest triumph for the end. Though she was known primarily as a short-distance runner, Bobbie's coach inserted her into the 800-meter event at the last minute. He didn't expect her to win; he just wanted her to offer some encouragement to Jean Thompson, the seventeen-year-old runner who'd been trained for the event. Running ninth in the final stretch, Bobbie pushed until she was right on Thompson's tail. The younger runner was starting to falter, but Bobbie paced her on to finish a respectable fourth. Bobbie Rosenfeld was fifth, although it was obvious to anyone who watched the race that she could have passed her teammate at any time. The race was in controversy. Some of the runners reportedly collapsed at the finish line, overcome with exhaustion, although other reports observe that the women were no more tired than the men at the end of the event. In any case, many critics pointed to the race's aftermath as proof that it was unsafe for women to compete in track and field; the "weaker sex" simply couldn't take the strain, they said. Bobbie disagreed. "Any girl who satisfactorily passes a medical examination and who accepts and practices the correct methods of training is capable of running the 800 metres," she told a reporter from the Canadian news magazine *Maclean's*. Then she added with characteristic understatement, "Even though I did not train specifically for it, there was no undue effort required to enable me to finish." The detractors won the day, however, and the women's 800-meter race was banned from the Olympics until the 1960 Games in Rome.

While Bobbie Rosenfeld could claim ownership of Olympic medals, world records, and the mastery of half a dozen sports, she never stopped playing her favorite sport, hockey. She'd learned the game on the outdoor rinks and frozen ponds back home in Barrie, honing her skills—as did most of the best female players in the sport—by playing alongside the boys on the rinks and ponds in unorganized games. Throughout the 1920s and into the early 1930s, before arthritis ended her career, Bobbie was the driving force behind the Toronto Patterson Pats, one of the first dominant forces in women's senior amateur hockey. By the 1920s women's hockey was well established in Canada and even in parts of the United States: the University of Minnesota had as many as three women's hockey teams at one time. In 1924 the Ladies' Ontario Hockey Association (LOHA) was formed by a group of senior amateur women hockey players, including Rosenfeld, and that league became the model for the dozens of women's teams that competed for local, regional, and, eventually, national championships. But despite the widespread acceptance of the sport, a sense of novelty persisted.

There was a pervasive notion that athletic competition was somehow masculine, and commentators bent over backwards to stress that these female hockey players were just "regular" girls. The result was a kind of coy irony that undermined the sport. "The Ottawa lassies who crossed sticks with the Patterson's pats looked more like a school girls' team," wrote Alexandrine Gibb, a former athlete herself who was female sports reporter for the *Toronto Star*, in her coverage of the 1929 Ladies' Ontario Hockey Association finals. "They must have picked all the beauties from in and around Ottawa and taught them how to play hockey. From the tiny Olive Barr in goal, with her fair hair and innocent, child-like face, to the tallest defence girl, they were all easy to look at," she continued. This kind of patronization persisted, despite the fact that the best women players at the time, and this certainly includes Bobbie Rosenfeld, could have easily earned a place on top-level men's teams. The men simply wouldn't allow it. Ability or not, when it came to hockey, the sexes were segregated.

During the 1920s and 1930s several female sportswriters, most of whom were former athletes themselves, had weekly and even daily columns in Canada. Phyllis Griffiths wrote for the *Toronto Telegram*, Bobbie Rosenfeld had a daily in the *Globe*, Alexandrine Gibb wrote for the *Toronto Star*, and Myrtle Cook wrote for the *Montreal Star*. And they all wrote about the most popular women's sport: hockey. Today, the lack of publicity, media coverage, and recognition of female hockey players by sports editors is striking; the sports section regularly reports on the NHL and every minor league going, but never carries regular summaries of the Central Collegiate Women's Ice Hockey Association in the United States or Canadian senior leagues like the modern-day Ontario Women's Hockey Association.

Why has women's hockey consistently been overshadowed by the men's game? There are undoubtedly a lot of complicated answers to that question, but perhaps Rosenfeld personified many of the issues. Her very presence in the game was something of a novelty. Certainly her name brought people in to watch hockey games, but her fame had come not through her prowess on the ice but through her achievements on the track, particularly at the 1928 Olympics. The fact that her reputation transcended the sport, and that her fame as an athlete eclipsed that of virtually any amateur male athlete in Canada at the time, probably left some people with a sour taste in their mouth. And it didn't help that she was rather openly, for the time, a lesbian; in the eyes of some, this did not "set a very good example" for young hockey players. Worst of all was that Bobbie played the game like a man; she was physically and mentally aggressive—not one to break the rules but the kind of player who didn't slow down when someone got in her way. In short, she understood the nature of the sport completely. In terms of strategy, hockey is a team sport like no other. In some sports—baseball, and even football to a certain extent—individual players have their personal territory clearly defined: the pitcher has the mound; the quarterback has a place secure behind the offensive line. But hockey is an entirely fluid game, a team sport that relies on individual players to constantly adjust, restore, and maintain their proper position. The aggressive player has a competitive edge; she can get in position for a shot on net, and she can play an effective defensive role by pushing, bumping, and outpowering her opponent. The result is that while other sports could easily be modified to fit the more socially acceptable image of the passive female athlete, it's impossible to change or to "tone down" hockey without changing its very nature. Rosenfeld understood that and used her own competitive intensity to its full advantage.

Bobbie Rosenfeld's domination of the sport of women's hockey was to be short-lived. She led the Toronto Patterson Pats to numerous LOHA and national championships, but within a year of her triumphs at the Amsterdam Olympics, she was stricken with crippling arthritis. She spent eight months in bed and another full year on crutches. To some, it was further proof that women simply weren't built for the athletic life. But, always the competitor, Bobbie fought back. By 1932 she was back playing the sports she loved, earning the hitting title in her softball league and winning honors as the top player in the LOHA. Her illness had taken its toll, though. She was noticeably weaker and played under constant pain. When questioned about her medical problems, she would just shrug her shoulders. In 1933 the arthritis flared up again, and Bobbie Rosenfeld was forced to retire from sports once and for all. She took a job on the other side of the fence, as a sports reporter for the *Toronto Globe*, and kept her hand in the game she loved by becoming a prominent hockey coach—helping her beloved Patterson Pats to maintain their place as a dominant force in women's hockey—and league organizer. Her achievements were not forgotten. In 1949, sixteen years from the last time she shot a puck or nailed a home run, sportswriters named her Canada's Woman Athlete of the Half Century. It was her proudest moment, capping a career that paved the way for Canadian women athletes to come.

Thanks to pioneers like Bobbie Rosenfeld, women's hockey enjoyed steady growth throughout the 1920s and 1930s. Ontario, Quebec, Alberta, and the Maritimes all featured numerous leagues catering to all levels of play, short of professional clubs. While it's difficult to know the exact number of female players at the time—no adequate records were kept—informal reports suggest that the sport was at least as popular as it is today. The dominant teams of the 1930s included the Red Deer Amazons of Alberta's Ladies Hockey League and the legendary Preston Rivulettes, one of the most famous amateur sports teams in Canada at the time. The Rivulettes, from a town in southwestern Ontario now known as Cambridge, began as a women's softball team and turned to hockey on a dare. Formed in 1931, they quickly developed into the top team of the LOHA, supplanting Rosenfeld's Patterson Pats, and went on to dominate the national scene as well. They won the national Dominion Women's Hockey Championship ten years in a row and over that time amassed a record of 350 wins, 3 losses, and 2 ties. Their games were often sellouts, and players like Hilda and Nellie Ranscombe, Myrtle Parr, and Marm Schmuck enjoyed press coverage unparalleled in the history of women's hockey. But with the start of the Second World War, everything changed. Canada entered the war in September 1939, and very quickly men's and women's hockey teams began to fold across the country as people geared up for the war effort.

Almost overnight, women's teams and leagues disappeared, in what has to be one of the most dramatic shifts in the history of North American sports. One moment, the women's game was almost as strong as the men's in terms of distribution and participation; the next, female players were few and far between. Even after the war, men took to hockey again as if nothing had happened, while women's hockey floundered. To cite just one example, directly before the war, Montreal alone supported dozens of women's teams; after the war, it had one three-team league. In the early forties and fifties, the few top women's teams that survived—the Moose Jaw Wildcats, the Winnipeg Canadians—were forced to play men's teams to find adequate competition. Much has been made of the socioeconomic reasons for the decline of the women's game—men had returned from war and pushed women back into their role as passive observers—but this interpretation leaves a lot of questions unanswered. Women's hockey had thrived in the years before the war; why was it pushed to extinction after it? And why, in the backlash against women in sports, was women's hockey hit so hard?

The answer may lie in the very practical consequences of the war. It had brought greater industrialization, particularly to southern Canadian cities, and of course this meant greater urbanization. With less and less available space outdoors, hockey players had to rely more and more on indoor arenas. In other words, more players were competing for much more limited ice time. In the flux of sexual politics at the time, women's hockey lost out. The men's game was deemed far more serious and important, and men who controlled the hockey leagues and municipal arenas cut back on the ice time allotted to girls and women. The fifties were the golden age of professional hockey in North America, when the sport regularly drew more fans than basketball or football. In Canada, the sport took on a mythic dimension as millions of hockey fans from one side of the country to the other tuned in to listen to sportscaster Foster Hewitt and his weekly coast-to-coast radio broadcast, "Hockey Night in Canada." Names of NHL stars like Maurice "the Rocket" Richard, Ted Kennedy, Jacques Plante, and Gordie Howe resonated in the ears of young hockey fans. And suddenly it became the dream of every Canadian boy to play in the National Hockey League. To accommodate this dream, women's hockey programs had to be sacrificed.

The difficulties encountered by female athletes in the fifties and sixties are characterized in the story of one little girl who became front-page news in Canada, all because she wanted to play hockey. Her name was Abigail "Abby" Hoffman, and in 1956 she made a simple decision that was to have lasting consequences. The nine-year-old decided that she wanted to play hockey at a competitive level. She enjoyed playing head-to-head with her brothers on the corner lot and felt herself to be as good as, if not better than, many of the boys. Abby didn't see any other girls in the neighborhood playing hockey; it was mostly a boys' environment in those days. That didn't stop her. She hated to be left behind and decided that she wanted to play hockey too.

Abby saw an ad in the newspaper for a new boys' league starting at the University of Toronto, and she asked her parents if she could play too. Her mother called and found out it was for boys only, but the family decided to go down on registration day and check things out for themselves. Abby's mother left her in the line and went to track down an official who could explain why her daughter wasn't allowed to play. When Abby got to the front of the line, she signed up like everyone else. "I didn't think I was doing anything wrong. I just wanted to play hockey. When I registered, I showed my birth certificate for age confirmation. No one bothered to look at my sex," Abby recalled.

In a few weeks, an official from the Toronto Hockey League called Abby and assigned her to a team of nine-year-old boys. So she started the season as "Ab" Hoffman, becoming one of the top defensemen in the league. She cut her hair short and went to the arena with all her equipment on so she wouldn't have to change in front of the boys. At the end of the season, she was selected to the league all-star team and was required once again to bring in her birth certificate for inspection. This time, the officials wondered what was up. They called her mother, assuming that Ab had brought in her sister's birth certificate by mistake. But there was no mistake, her mother explained. Abby wanted to play competitive hockey, and her parents wholeheartedly supported the idea. The resulting story made headlines across the country: "Star Defenseman in Little League a Girl," announced the March 8, 1956, *Toronto Star*. Many of the league officials wanted to ban young Abby from hockey, but cooler heads prevailed. She was allowed to finish the season, although the league decided to furnish her with her own private dressing room.

The following season, though, league officials effectively squeezed Abby off the boys' team and convinced her to join a girls' team instead. But the games were few and far between, and the competition didn't measure up. Abby soon quit the game to find a sport that would allow her to reach her potential. Like Bobbie Rosenfeld before her, she turned to track and field as a stage where women were permitted to strive for excellence. Within a few years, young Abby Hoffman was one of the top distance runners in Canada, setting her sights on the international field. Eventually, she made her mark in track and field, winning gold in the 800 meters at the 1963 and 1971 Pan-American Games and top prize in the 880 yards at the 1966 Commonwealth Games as well as making the trip to four Olympic Games. After retiring from competitive sports, Abby remained involved in amateur athletics. She earned a master's degree in political science and eventually put her education and experience together to take the role as director general of Sport Canada, the country's national amateur sports organization. Despite her achievements, there is an air of sadness to her story, the tale of an athlete who came to a sport she loved—hockey—just at the moment when the doors were closed to any woman who wanted to take the game seriously. Years later, Abby recalls being shocked by all the attention. She wasn't trying to make a political statement, she says; she was just doing what came naturally. "My whole family was sports-oriented and athletic," Abby explains. "I had two older brothers that played hockey, so it was easy for me to play with them. The tennis courts across the street doubled as an ice rink during the winter months. And most importantly, no one in my family ever said to me, 'A girl shouldn't play hockey.'"

Slowly, women's hockey began to rebuild. The sixties saw limited growth, particularly at the college level. Women formed varsity teams at Ontario universities in Kingston, Toronto, Guelph, and London and began practicing again at the University of Minnesota. By 1967 there were eight teams in the Ontario women's varsity league. Still, the game was slow to catch on outside of the university forum, and now women's hockey faced a new challenge in the form of a sport called ringette. Ringette took the old idea of the segregation of the sexes in hockey to its logical conclusion; a new sport, based on hockey but less aggressive, was "designed" specifically for women. The game was played on the ice, with skates and sticks; but the sticks were straight, and instead of a puck, there was a rubber ring. Players would shoot and stick-handle by placing the end of their stick in the middle of the rubber ring. Otherwise, the general design of the game was similar to hockey—although all forms of body contact were strictly forbidden. The growth of ringette in Canada was astounding. The sport originated in the early 1960s; twenty years later, there were almost fifteen thousand registered ringette players. Women's hockey didn't fare nearly as well. By 1983, almost one hundred years after women started playing hockey, there were just five thousand players regis-tered in Canada, and a fraction of that in the United States.

Why did ringette succeed while women's hockey faltered? For one thing, it was considered a "safe" version of hockey. In those days, body check-ing was permitted in the women's game, and many parents were reluctant to enroll their daughters in such a rough sport. In fact, it's probably no coinci-dence that the sport of women's hockey really began to take off in 1986, the year organizers voted to ban hitting. But the other reason for the relative success of ringette was simply a matter of public perception; ringette was seen as a "girls' game." Why would any female want to play the boys' game of hockey? Judy Diduck offers a good example. She played on four Women's World Championship teams for Canada and was a driving force on the Olympic silver-medal team. She learned her craft playing ringette. It wasn't a matter of choice, as Judy has explained in interviews. She didn't know women's hockey existed, so ringette was her only option. She started playing ringette when she was ten years old and gave it up in 1990 to play hockey, when she was twenty years old.

So women's hockey limped through the 1960s but began to show some signs of life in the 1970s. Women's leagues started sprouting up again out-side of varsity arenas in Ontario, British Columbia, and the northeastern United States, and there was even talk out of California of a women's pro-fessional ice hockey league. It was an age of expansion in professional sports, and even pro hockey, whose owners are notoriously slow to change, man-aged to follow the trend. The National Hockey League doubled from six to twelve teams in 1967, continued to grow throughout the seventies, and faced some stiff competition with the advent of the World Hockey Association in 1972. This rival professional league immediately started raiding players and fans from the NHL. It was a rocky time for professional hockey, with fran-chises coming and going with alarming speed. But all the activity did have the effect of bringing the game of hockey to more fans, particularly Ameri-cans living outside of the eastern states. With more exposure, and more arenas, more young people began to pick up the game.

By the late 1970s women's hockey in Canada was starting to get orga-nized. Women established administrative organizations for their sport in most of the provinces, and in 1977 the Canadian Amateur Hockey Association—the national administrative body—allowed female players to register for the first time in its sixty-three-year history. Meanwhile, in the United States, women's hockey remained almost solely the domain of the colleges. Brown University in Providence, Rhode Island, led the way. In 1964 Brown had been the first U.S. college to have a female hockey team, and in 1975 Brown broke new ground again by sanctioning the first varsity women's hockey team in the United States. By the end of the 1970s there were a handful of women's varsity hockey programs scattered across the states—including Cornell University and Hamilton and Ithaca colleges, all in New York; the University of Minnesota; and Providence College in New Hampshire—but many of these teams had to turn to Canada to find any competition. Finally, in 1977, the Ivy League set up the first women's intercollegiate hockey schedule; American female hockey players finally had a league of their own. The rest of the world was starting to pick up on the sport as well. The seventies saw women's teams spring up in Finland, Germany, Sweden, and even Japan, and by the end of the decade Denmark and Switzerland were added to the list.

By the eighties, the public seemed more comfortable with the idea of women playing competitive hockey. By 1986 there were over 1,000 girls' and women's teams in Canada and some 120 teams in the United States. By the end of the decade as many as forty thousand girls and women were playing organized hockey in North America. And in the 1990s the growth was unprecedented, perhaps doubling each year in the early part of the decade. Once again, a lot of forces were fueling this renewed interest in women's hockey, not the least of which was the continuing fallout from the social revolution that had reached its peak in the late 1960s. With the rise of feminist politics, women no longer accepted old notions of their "place" in society that kept them from striving for social, academic, business, and athletic goals. But as always, practical forces were at work too. The trend toward greater urbanization had continued unabated since the war, and thousands of new indoor arenas with artificial ice—many of them in shopping malls—had sprung up across the continent. In the meantime, the popularity of hockey as a participation sport for boys was in decline. In part, boys just had a lot more activities to choose from. Hockey has always been an expensive game to play, and in the uncertain economic climate—Canada was in the midst of a long economic recession—many families found the costs too high to bear. And the sport was earning a rather deserved reputation for being far too rough, to the point of being dangerous. In an age of rapid expansion of professional hockey, the sport had reached its lowest ebb. Both the NHL and the WHA had their fair share of legitimate stars, but the leagues were heavily padded with unskilled players who were often more adept at fighting than anything else. Many young players were emulating their professional heroes, to the detriment of the game. So the situation was completely reversed from the end of the war; now, there was lots of ice, with fewer and fewer players to use it. By the mid-1980s, the hockey establishment decided that maybe female players weren't such a bad idea after all.

Still, organizers had yet to resolve two long-standing issues: segregation and body checking. The body-contact rule was supposedly in place to encourage a "higher" level of play, emphasizing skating and puck-handling skills. But that logic doesn't quite flow: body checking, if properly enforced by the referee, hardly diminishes the skill level of the game. Beneath the surface, the no-intentional-contact rule seems to be a throwback to the old days of women's hockey, when officials were paranoid that somehow the rough-and-tumble sport would destroy the athletes' femininity. While the body-checking debate was yet to be settled, the old question of segregation was still creating problems. From the earliest ages, hockey organizers have encouraged boys and girls to play on separate teams. Since virtually every top-notch female player will tell you that she developed her skills playing with boys, that strategy seems designed to limit the overall development of the women's game. And the fact that such a policy remains the official position of both USA Hockey and Hockey Canada—the national hockey administrative organizations—is highly questionable. Certainly, the legality of the strategy has been challenged. In 1985, in a story reminiscent of young Abby Hoffman, twelve-year-old Justine Blainey took the Ontario Hockey Association to the Supreme Court of Ontario over the right to play hockey in a boys' league. For Blainey, the issue wasn't a matter of sexual politics; it was simple common sense. "It was crazy," she said in a 1993 interview. "In the girls' league, I played once a week at a rink 20 miles away; while in the boys' league, my brothers played every other day, in our neighborhood, with far better players."

On top of those practical considerations, Blainey felt that her skills were being stifled in the girls' league, where slap shots and body checking were outlawed. "There's nothing wrong with checking if it's done properly," Blainey said. "But there's a no-intentional-body-checking rule in women's hockey, and that just means the players are trickier and use other forms of checking you can't see. Some players, such as myself, prefer to play hockey with checking—the body contact can be exhilarating."

The courts took almost three years to sort out Justine's case, in which the Supreme Court of Canada, the top judicial office in the country, eventually came down firmly on her side, granting the right for girls to play on boys' teams, even though hockey officials continued to encourage females to join their own leagues under the guise that it was somehow better for them. Justine herself played her first game on a boys' team in January 1988 and kept on playing with them until she reached the University of Toronto, where she joined the varsity women's team.

The first Women's World Championships added to the public profile of women's hockey. The idea for the championships began to percolate in 1987, when the Ontario Women's Hockey Association organized an informal, unsanctioned world tournament, featuring teams from both Ontario and Canada, the United States, Sweden, Switzerland, Holland, and Japan. Three years later, the International Ice Hockey Federation, international hockey's governing body, sanctioned the first official Women's World Championships. First held in Ottawa, Canada, in 1990, the championships focused attention on female hockey players from around the world and captured its fair share of the media spotlight. Canada dominated that first international forum, which also included teams from the United States, Finland, Sweden, Switzerland, Norway, Germany, and Japan. The Canadians, led by scoring sensation Angela James of Toronto, outscored their opponents 61 to 8 on their way to a gold medal. The American team had a great run as well. Paced by an outstanding goaltender named Kelly Dyer from the powerhouse Assabet Valley women's hockey program in Concord, Massachusetts, and a talented teenager named Cammi Granato, Team USA won four straight in the preliminary round, outscoring their opponents 50 to 15. They gave Team Canada a scare too in the final, taking an early 2–0 lead, before the floodgates opened and the Canadians—dressed in uncharacteristic pink and white uniforms—scored five unanswered goals for the win. Fans were impressed by the game's pace and skill, and even *Sports Illustrated* declared that women's hockey "is not the pajama party you might imagine."

By the time of the second official Women's World Championships, in Tampere, Finland, in the spring of 1992, the sport was firmly entrenched, and women's hockey was well on its way to becoming one of the fastest-growing participation sports on the continent, if not in the world. Once more, the event caught the attention of the sporting world. Again, eight teams competed, with China and Denmark taking the place of Japan and Germany. Canada dominated once more, but other teams—particularly the United States and Finland—showed tremendous improvement.

These two world championships gave women's hockey a whole new public profile, and the sport blossomed. By 1992 there were more than one hundred club and varsity teams at U.S. colleges alone—a dramatic increase for a sport that, ten years earlier, numbered one hundred teams in the entire country. In Canada and the United States, enrollment was at a high. At the time of the first world championship, there were 8,100 female players registered in Canada and some 5,600 in the United States. Five years later, the Canadian figure had almost tripled, nearing the 24,000 mark, while the U.S. numbers had gone through the roof; in 1995, there were more than 20,000 females registered in American hockey programs, almost four times the number in 1990. And outside of North America, existing programs were expanding as new countries were entering competitions. By the mid-1990s, China, Russia, Czechoslovakia, Latvia, Australia, Italy, Norway, and France all had national-level women's hockey programs of one kind or another. As the sport has gained in popularity, a new kind of player has emerged, the career athlete known for her hockey playing alone. Unlike the old days, when female hockey players like Bobbie Rosenfeld and Abby Hoffman had to go outside their sport to seek recognition and personal excellence, players like Cammi Granato of the U.S. National Team have proved that women's hockey is capable of producing stars all on its own. Among this new breed of female hockey stars, though, one player stands out: Manon Rheaume, who broke down every previous stereotype by breaking into men's professional hockey.

Manon Rheaume's love affair with hockey started at a very early age. Like lots of young goalies, she came to the position by default. Her older brothers, Marlon and Pascal—who now plays for the NHL's St. Louis Blues—needed a moving target to shoot at while practicing in the basement, so they recruited Manon. Soon afterward, her father was looking for someone to play goal for his boys' team, when Manon stepped forward. And at that moment a little girl's dreams crystallized; she wanted to become the first female hockey player in the NHL.

In her early days, Manon became quite accustomed to breaking new ground, and by age eleven she had created a media sensation in her home province of Quebec by becoming the first girl to play in the prestigious Quebec Peewee Hockey Tournament. In 1991 she made history again by suiting up for the Trois-Rivieres Draveurs of the Quebec Major Junior Hockey League, hockey's equivalent of college basketball. Manon took to the net halfway through the game, with her team tied with the tough Granby Bisons. Over the next seventeen minutes, she faced thirteen shots and allowed three goals. Not great, by any stretch of the imagination, but it was a start and certainly got the eye of the hockey world. One of the people who took notice was Phil Esposito, former hockey superstar, who had taken over the general manager's job for a fledgling NHL franchise, the Tampa Bay Lightning. Esposito—whose flamboyant style had earned him the nickname "Trader Phil" around the league—decided that Manon deserved a shot at the NHL. Impressed by her skill, and sensing a story the press would love, Esposito brought her down to Florida for a tryout, where she impressed scouts by holding her own for a period in an intersquad game.

A few days later, on September 23, 1992, she was given the chance to play in an NHL preseason game against the St. Louis Blues; once again, she fared OK, stopping all but two of the nine shots she faced in the period. More impressive, though, was her grit. She stood her ground against some of pro hockey's toughest competitors, who were determined not to let her off easy.

In the end, the exercise proved very little. Manon was a competent goalie but nowhere near NHL caliber, which prompted some critics to point to her as proof positive that women didn't belong in the men's game. Most observers just considered the move one of Esposito's little publicity stunts, designed to gain some attention in a town where ice hockey was the farthest thing from most people's minds. But Manon took the opportunity seriously. "I've always concentrated on my job as a goaltender, not on making it to the NHL," she states. "I know some people thought it was some kind of stunt, but I also know that I earned the respect of a lot of the players, and that means the world to me."

Manon's flirtation with the big league was short-lived. Tampa Bay quickly signed her, then sent her down to their International Hockey League farm team, the Atlanta Knights. She played two games with the Knights, allowing seven goals in just over one hour of total playing time and earning another place in the record books: the first woman to ever play in a professional hockey regular-season game.

Meanwhile, Manon was carving a niche for herself as a sports celebrity; even *Playboy* got into the act, offering the attractive young goalie $1 million to pose in the nude. A devout Roman Catholic, she turned it down. Certainly, her fame vastly overshadowed her results on the ice. She bounced around the minor leagues, earning a handful of starts and some competent but lackluster statistics. In a way, her situation was the complete opposite of that faced by Bobbie Rosenfeld; Manon Rheaume was famous, not because of her athletic prowess, but *because* she was a woman playing hockey. That's not to say she wasn't skilled. In women's hockey, Manon remains one of the dominant players in the world, leading Canada to two world championships and a silver medal in the Olympics, while maintaining a goals-against average that rarely crept above 1.00. It wasn't simply that men's hockey was that much better than the women's game; it's a rougher sport, to be sure, and the shots are faster. But the flow of the game is completely different, and Manon had developed a style of play that's best suited for the female game.

"The tryouts for the NHL and the Canadian national women's team were two very different experiences," she says. "When I'm playing with women, I have to adjust my timing because the shots on goal are slower, but the women also tend to keep the puck in play much longer. The women's game has helped me play with the men because it has forced me to learn how to concentrate, while the men's game has taught me how to move on my feet and be more aggressive."

Ironically, it took Manon's experience playing with the men to finally help bring women's hockey the recognition it had sought for so long. With a bona fide star, who transcended the game by capturing the imagination of an entire continent, women's hockey was standing at the edge of a new era.

As the final buzzer sounded, Team USA's players threw their sticks and gloves into the air. Unlikely as it may have seemed two weeks previously, they'd just defeated the women's hockey powerhouse, Canada, 3–1 for the first women's hockey gold medal at the 1998 Olympics. Forward Karyn Bye, a five-time national team member and 1995 USA Hockey Women's Player of the Year Award winner, grabbed an American flag and wrapped it around her shoulders as her teammates skated around the ice, hugging each other and waving to their fans. For the most part, the Canadian women stared glumly at the ice, fighting back the tears that would finally break through as teams lined up for the medal presentation.

While the weeks ahead would hold highs and lows for both teams— for the United States, a White House meeting with President Clinton and even the team photo on the front of a Wheaties box; for the Canadians, a heroes' welcome at home, followed quickly by the dismissal of head coach Shannon Miller—it was clear that the real winner was women's hockey. Given the chance to showcase the sport, the players proved up to the task. Even the Team Canada members realized that something important was going on, something bigger than any single game, bigger than the Olympics itself. Canadian coach Shannon Miller, the usually reticent ex-cop, was overcome with emotion. She cried along with her players as they stood at center ice listening to their rivals sing "The Star-Spangled Banner." But she had a change of heart when she saw Team USA captain Cammi Granato with her medal draped around her neck. "I had a feeling of joy go through my body," Miller told a reporter from the *Toronto Sun*. "I realized an Olympic gold medal was being hung on a female hockey player. I couldn't believe the impact it had on me." Miller was right. For her, the game had come and gone. But for women's hockey, it was only just beginning.

Things look bright indeed. Women's teams are already gearing up for the 2002 Winter Olympic Games in Salt Lake City, Utah, which promises to be a media showcase for the defending gold medalist, Team USA, and for the sport in general. Meanwhile, there's talk around the NHL of forming a women's professional league, along the lines of the Women's National Basketball Association. With all the interest and activity, the future promises to be an exciting one for women's hockey, finally paying full dividends to the pioneers of the sport, who took on the men at their own game and, through their toil and tears and decades of frustration, proved their sport to be a worthy opponent.

Basketball

$\mathcal{N}$ot Quite the Game Intended

Shelley Smith

Sylvia Crawley tied a bandana over her eyes and began dribbling the basketball. Thirty feet from the basket, the six-foot-five Crawley took off in a sprint, reached high with the ball as her feet left the ground, and slammed it through the net. It was the first-ever slam-dunk contest in women's professional basketball, held January 18, 1998, during halftime of the American Basketball League's All-Star game. As she landed, Crawley, whose nickname is Apollo oo, broke into a wide smile, ripped off the bandana, and pumped her fist in the air. The sold-out Disney Wide World of Sports Arena in Tampa, Florida, rose to its feet and cheered wildly.

Fourteen years earlier, Georgeann Wells had become the first woman to dunk in a college basketball game. Now, in 1998, there was an entire contest.

"This," Crawley said, "is an amazing day."

Crawley's winning dunk came on the heels of another amazing day in women's basketball history. Nikki McCray, who had helped lead her professional basketball team, the Columbus Quest, to the first-ever ABL championship, was defecting to the other women's professional league, the WNBA, for a reported $250,000-per-year contract. At a packed press conference, McCray, who was the ABL's Most Valuable Player in its inaugural season, also announced that she was signing a $1 million contract with Fila, which was designing a Nikki McCray basketball shoe. "I saw a great opportunity with the ABL, and now I see one with the WNBA," McCray said. "Isn't it wonderful to have a choice like that?"

As America prepares to enter the twenty-first century, women's basketball has never been healthier or filled with more promise. Tickets to the 1998 Women's Final Four college basketball tournament in Kansas City sold out in a matter of hours. Nearly thirty-four thousand people jammed the Georgia Dome in 1996 to see the U.S. women's Olympic team play against Australia. U.S. Olympic star Dawn Staley became the first woman whose portrait was painted on a giant Nike billboard, her athletic likeness caught in mid-stride atop a nine-story building in Philadelphia. Another Olympic basketball star, Sheryl Swoopes, got her own Nike shoe the same year she became pregnant and was featured on the cover of one of the two women's sports magazines to emerge in 1997. The number of high school girls competing in basketball has tripled in the last twenty years and so has attendance at Division I women's games.

The 1990s have, indeed, been packed with opportunity and choice for women playing basketball on every level. Where once women basketball players had to coach, retire, or move overseas to play beyond the college level, they now are being courted by not one, but two professional leagues in the United States, both offering lucrative salaries. Where once a female professional player had to fund-raise or work another job to play and stay financially afloat, she is now being flooded with endorsement offers. Where once it was laughable to think about even the college championship final being televised, there are up to ten women's collegiate and professional games on television each night. Where once women who played college basketball had to search far and wide to find a school to play for and then pay for her own schooling, full scholarships are now awarded at every major college and university that fields a women's basketball team. And, perhaps most important, where once young girls wanting to play the game were forced to join boys' teams because there weren't enough girls to form a league, girls are now on waiting lists across America to join girls' leagues, which have sprung up like weeds. And they no longer have to take the name Lakers or Knicks or Rockets. They are the Sparks or Monarchs or Comets. At last, women's basketball no longer takes a back seat to the men's game—in fact, an argument can be made that women's basketball has even surged ahead. "To me, the best pure basketball I see today is among the better women's teams," says legendary coach John Wooden, whose UCLA men's teams won ten NCAA championships over twelve years. "It's the game as I like to see it played, without so much showmanship."

The women's game could never have gotten to this remarkable stage without pioneers, women who sacrificed and struggled, women who refused to give in to society's strictures and slights, women who ignored perceptions and attitudes. From the beginning women's basketball has survived because of the people who envisioned a future for the game and a place for its players.

* * *

It is doubtful that when he invented basketball in 1891, Dr. James Naismith ever imagined that the game would grow to such proportions for men, much less women. But basketball had a certain appeal to women, a certain flair even when played at the snail-like pace that was adopted back then. Senda Berenson, a Smith College physical education instructor, first introduced women's basketball at the collegiate level, believing the game to be a good way to teach independence and instill confidence in her students. She devised a version of the game quite different than what the men were playing. Where men were playing five players against five players on one regulation-sized court, women, under Berenson's rules, used three courts, with two players per team in each court. Men were allowed to dribble and pass and run both ends of the floor. Women, however, were limited to just one dribble before a pass had to be made. Men wore short pants and long-sleeved shirts, while the women wore heavy bloomers and thick, black stockings. Because even that was considered immodest attire in those days, the women voted unanimously not to allow any men—except the school's president—to watch them play.

Berenson's game caught on quickly. There was an immediate attraction between basketball and women, who, through Berenson's vision, were given a way to experience competition, a chance to participate in a sport without compromising their femininity and, therefore, their acceptance in society. Many people at that time believed that physical exertion was dangerous to women, that it could damage women's reproductive organs and cause problems with childbirth. Women were thought to be fragile and weak and incapable of strenuous activity. But basketball at a slower, scaled-down level wasn't a physically demanding sport, and so it was deemed an appropriate activity.

Administrators at the pristine Vassar College made women's basketball a field day event in 1896, the same year the first official collegiate game was held between California-Berkeley and Stanford. No men were allowed into that game, either, but the Armory Hall was jammed with hundreds of cheering women as Stanford won, 2–1. The game also surfaced in the ordinarily conservative South around the same time it was flourishing on both coasts. Clara Gregory Baer introduced basketball to girls at her school, the Sophie Newcomb College, in New Orleans, a sophisticated and obviously progressive institution. In 1895 Baer published "Basquette," the first set of basketball rules for women. And in 1901 she became the editor of the inaugural women's basketball publication, *Basket Ball for Women*, published by the Spalding Athletic Library. By 1919, the bounce pass was introduced, halves were shortened to fifteen minutes each, and a basket with an open bottom replaced the closed basket with a pull chain. Coaching (except during half-time) was still forbidden.

In this somewhat stilted environment, the game thrived and spread. Women's basketball was featured in the Jeux Olympiques Feminines in Monaco in 1921, with teams from Italy, England, France, Norway, and Switzerland competing for the title, eventually won by England; and even at home in the United States, the game was increasing in popularity as more and more girls were introduced to athletics. By 1925 thirty-six states held high school tournaments, and a year later, the Amateur Athletic Union, the governing body for athletic teams competing outside the university or college arena, sponsored the first-ever national women's basketball championship.

The AAU became extremely important during the 1930s, when the country slid into an even more conservative phase. During that time intercollegiate competition was banned from most higher-education institutions, administrators there believing sport to be a waste of time for young women, who should be focusing on more proper endeavors. But basketball had already worked its magic. Many women, enthralled by the sport, refused to buy into conservative America's thinking. All around the country, women began to form amateur and industrial leagues sponsored by local companies or smaller colleges and governed by the AAU.

When World War II broke out, and women entered the workforce in record numbers, the number of company teams increased, too. Recruiting for talent became fierce. It was not unusual for a company to try to steal a player from another company based on her skills on the basketball court. Companies also stole players based on their looks. The part of America still not quite ready to accept women on athletic merits was willing to accept them on their physical merits. In order to attract crowds, companies outfitted their teams in sexy uniforms and held beauty contests at halftime. Players were encouraged to wear makeup and curl their hair and not sweat so much as to look masculine. Often these women posed for glamour-shot photographs—the first athletic pinup girls.

One of the most popular teams of that era was the all-black Tribune Girls, a team sponsored by the *Philadelphia Tribune*. Ora Washington was tall and lean and one of the best overall athletes in the city. Born in the Germantown section of Philadelphia in 1898, she first became a champion tennis player, winning nine singles tennis championships in the all-black American Tennis Association. She retired from tennis because her skills and strength were too much for younger players, who grew weary from losing lopsided matches. Not to hurt the growth of tennis nor quit athletics, she changed sports and learned to play basketball.

Upon joining the Tribune Girls, Washington was an immediate hit. She was dominating and quick and led the team in scoring for most of her eighteen seasons. The Tribune Girls played "boys'" rules—three players from each team under one basket and three players for each team under the other. They traveled around the United States, dazzling the crowds that swarmed the gymnasiums and school-yard courts, and lost only six games in nine years. There was no money in tennis or basketball back then, so Washington earned her living by cleaning houses. When she retired from the team, she devoted the rest of her life to helping youngsters interested in both sports, giving free clinics throughout Germantown.

In 1934, at the Tulsa Business School, a young woman of Cherokee descent named Hazel Walker helped revolutionize the sport. With her amazing skills and captivating personality, Walker led her team to the AAU championship that first year. By the time her amateur career was finished, she would be named an All-American eleven times, establishing herself as the greatest player of the 1930s and 1940s. Walker played for several different AAU teams, including Lyon Oil, Louis & Norwood Flyers, and the Little Rock Dr. Peppers. But it was her own signature team, the Hazel Walker Arkansas Travelers, that dazzled the country and captured the hearts of young girls, helping to perpetuate the interest in the game. "The first time I saw her play it was in my hometown of Aberdeen, North Carolina," remembers Elva Bishop, who later produced a documentary on the history of women's basketball for public television. "There were less than two thousand people there, and they were playing against the town's best male athletes. To see her play, to see that women can be that good, it changed me forever."

Walker's team played in a different town every night for six and a half months, traveling by station wagons from gym to gym. It was sometimes dangerous—there were several robbery attempts—but Walker's players were not deterred from pursuing the game they loved. "We had a gun, and we weren't afraid to use it," says Frances "Goose" Garroutte, one of Walker's teammates. They also had to fight the stigma that came with being a woman player. "Women traveling alone in those days were considered trash. It wasn't proper for women to be athletes, and people didn't know much about them. They expected a bunch of rough-looking women, and they were always surprised. Hazel knew up front what to expect, and we helped people understand that you can look like a lady, act like a lady, and still play ball."

Hazel left the Arkansas Travelers to join one of the more eccentric teams to spring up during that era—the All-American Red Heads, which barnstormed around the country playing ad hoc men's teams. All the players had red hair, "by God or by bottle." "These women are as deft at handling the ball as they are a lipstick," said one television announcer, commenting during one of their games. Orwell Moore took over sponsorship of the Red Heads in the 1950s. He says, "People loved to watch our team play. School kids would flock to see the Red Heads' cars. We had 17,500 people come out at Chicago

Stadium once when we were there. We always tried to sell girls' basketball wherever we went." Various versions of the Red Heads would tour the country for fifty years.

By far the most successful company-based team during this era was sponsored by Hanes Hosiery, then a small company based in North Carolina, whose star was Eunice Futch, who was raised in Jacksonville, Mississippi. "I was recruited by Hanes when I was in eleventh grade, fifteen years old," recalls Futch. "They wanted me to come to North Carolina and finish high school. That didn't go over real well with Mother and Daddy, so I waited until I graduated on January fifteenth in 1947 and started my first game on January twentieth." Futch was part of every game Hanes played en route to a four-year, 102-game winning streak. Hanes' streak would be broken in the 1950s by the Hutchinson Flying Queens from Wayland Baptist College, which posted a 131-game winning streak. "Women players were highly motivated and good students," remembers Harley Redin, the Queens' coach. "They all signed a contract saying they wouldn't smoke, drink, or dance. They did it because they wanted to play basketball."

Several players from both the Hanes and Wayland teams were members of the first U.S. team at the women's world championship basketball tournament held in Santiago, Chile, in 1953, which beat Chile 49–36 to claim the title. Most of the team, however, were from the Nashville Business College. The team established itself in the 1950s as the most successful AAU team in history, led by Nera White, named All-American fifteen straight years and the first woman inducted into the Basketball Hall of Fame in Springfield, Massachusetts. White could drive both ways, reverse dribble, and she had a hook shot that could hit from thirty feet. She was also one of the most unselfish players on the team. "She cared more about and took more pride in helping a teammate get open, to get the open shot than she cared about scoring herself," remembers teammate Doris Rogers. "She was the most talented basketball player I'd ever seen." "She would definitely be a superstar today," says another teammate, Sue Gunter, who coached the 1980 U.S. Olympic team. "She could do things on the court that I thought were impossible."

Nashville won the AAU championship eleven times, in 1950, 1958, 1960, and from 1962 through 1969. Its coach, John Head, coached that first world championship team in 1953 and also the team in 1957 in Rio de Janeiro, where the U.S. women edged the Soviet Union 51–48 in front of forty thousand screaming fans. The demise of the NBC team came in the 1960s, when three major rules revisions helped take the game to a more exciting level. The unlimited dribble was legalized; more than two players from each team were permitted to rove the entire court; and stealing the ball was permitted. This helped pick up the pace of the game and allowed women with speed and quick hands to excel. However, the founder of the NBC team, school president

Herman O. Balls, was vehemently against the rules revisions and disbanded his team in 1969. "There are several things that entered into my decision," Balls said. "It is well known that my team will never play men's rules. I think it is fundamentally wrong and if persisted in, will eventually destroy girls' basketball."

In 1971 the version of the game that Dr. Naismith invented—five players on a team on one court, with everyone allowed to run, dribble, shoot, and block—was adopted for women. Finally, basketball, as it was meant to be played, was deemed appropriate. It signaled an acceptance not yet experienced and established the framework for growth within the sport and within the perception of the sport.

By far the biggest lift came in 1972, when Title IX was passed. The law mandated that schools receiving federal funds must provide equal programs—including athletic programs—for boys and girls. The bill, signed by President Richard Nixon, was a major breakthrough in women's athletics. The Association for Intercollegiate Athletics for Women was formed just after Title IX was signed, becoming the governing body for all women's sports at the college level, setting up tournaments and league-play formats for colleges across the country. This was an organization separate from the NCAA, designed to help bring athletic programs into compliance with the new law. Most women's athletic departments were barely more than an office with a staff of one or two and equipment handed down from the men's program. "They talked about equality," remembers Mary Grace Colby, the first women's athletic director at the University of Santa Clara. "I had a broken chair, a phone, a desk, and two used tennis rackets when I got the job. And things didn't change for a long time."

Title IX legislation did send a message that America was serious about providing equal opportunity for female athletes, but it was a message that wasn't well received or even acknowledged in many parts of the country. Changing rules is one thing, but changing attitudes proved to be something very different. Even with the law, many schools at every level weren't interested in taking the steps to bring their programs into compliance. The common belief among those administrators was that athletic programs for women were not high-priority budget items and certainly not worth adding at the expense of jeopardizing the funding for men's athletic programs.

Part of the problem was fueled by the country's growing concern about homosexuality and women's athletics. For years the most popular sports for women were gymnastics, tennis, and figure skating, all individual sports, which many in society believed were the acceptable athletic activities for young girls. Team sports, on the other hand, weren't considered as appropriate because the play was too manlike. A common perception was that girls playing boys' sports wanted to be boys, and the resulting homophobia was rampant. "Use of society's fear of homosexuality was one of the only tools left to keep women from playing sports," says Donna A. Lopiano, executive director of the Women's Sports Foundation. "There were those who felt threatened by Title IX."

Homophobia created mini-dramas across the country as many communities pressured their local athletic directors not to add girls' basketball at their schools for fear that the schools would be overrun with lesbians. College coaches began using lesbianism as a negative recruiting tool, telling parents and athletes to stay away from a certain rival school, for example, claiming the school—correctly or incorrectly—was a "gay" school. This resulted in a number of young women shying away from playing basketball for fear of jeopardizing their popularity or being labeled gay. Homophobia may well have robbed society of some of its best basketball players by scaring off the girls who simply weren't willing to fight common perceptions and stereotypes.

There were other hurdles facing women's basketball at that time as well. One of them was the media and its coverage of women's teams, which was, in most cases, nonexistent. Sports editors argued that their readers didn't want stories about women's games and pointed to the small crowds as proof. Coaches and players argued, on the other hand, that if newspapers began covering games, writing stories about the competition and the players, that more people would choose to attend. It was a catch-22. Eventually, under pressure from the school administrators and the women's sports community, newspapers began sending reporters to games, but their stories were generally buried inside the sports section and kept short. "I kept thinking we needed to change attitudes," remembers Marian Washington, who played for the Raytown Piperettes under the AAU system and took over the women's program at the University of Kansas in 1973. "Finally, I just said let the law govern and abide by the law. If we wait for attitudes to change, we'll be waiting a long time."

It was during this era of transition and challenge that small colleges began to emerge as dominant women's basketball forces. Larger schools didn't have an interest in women's programs mainly because they were not part of the school's strategic athletic plan, which was male dominated and, generally, football motivated. But administrators at schools like Old Dominion and Louisiana Tech, for example, which didn't have football, saw an opportunity to excel athletically by establishing a strong women's basketball team. Given a budget for recruiting and scholarships to give to women players, coaches at these schools were able to attract top players and become successful.

Small southern schools dominated the AIAW in the seventies. The College of Immaculata won the first three AIAW national championships, between 1972 and 1975, and Delta State University, known as "the little school that was good," won the next three. It wasn't until 1978 that a larger school, UCLA, won the title. Four years earlier, UCLA had the foresight to sign Ann Meyers, who became the first woman ever offered a full basketball scholarship by UCLA, a bold move by a school that was dominating the decade in men's basketball.

Meyers was raised in Southern California and grew up playing the game with her older brothers. The sixth of eleven children, she always could find a good pickup game on the family driveway. She battled many of the stereotypes that were prominent during the years she was learning to love the game. "I got teased a lot. I was a tomboy. I didn't fit in with the girls," she says. "I always had short hair. The boys didn't really accept me, yet they liked me because I was a ballplayer. I was caught in the middle."

In high school, Meyers excelled in seven sports, but it was in basketball that she captured the national spotlight. After leading UCLA to the National Championship, she became the first woman to earn a salary from the NBA when she signed a $50,000 contract with the Indiana Pacers a year later. She didn't make the team, however, and after a brief stint with the New Jersey Gems of the Women's Professional Basketball League (which folded in 1980) she became a commentator and mother, marrying Hall of Fame baseball player Don Drysdale.

That Meyers was recruited, offered a scholarship, and signed with UCLA was nevertheless instrumental in the development of women's basketball. It sent a signal to the country that it was time for America to provide equal opportunity to women athletes. That a major university sent the signal was equally important, setting precedent and standards for other major universities. The message had ever wider ramifications overseas, as the international community began to understand the growth and popularity of the women's game.

For the 1976 Olympic Games in Montreal, the Federacion Internationale de Basketball (FIBA), the governing body for international basketball competition, had decided to increase the men's field from twelve to sixteen teams. More important, however, it decided to add, for the first time ever, a six-team women's basketball event as well. It was a major breakthrough for women like Meyers who were playing the game in relative obscurity. For years they had worked to get women's basketball added to prestigious international competitions. In 1972 and 1974, U.S. teams were formed to play exhibition games against the Soviet Union. When it was announced that the event would be added to the Montreal Games, more than 250 girls crowded the gym at Queens College for tryouts.

Meyers was one of them. So was Nancy Lieberman, an eighteen-year-old high school phenomenon who was invited to try out for the historic team. Lieberman grew up spending summers in New York, taking the A-train from Brooklyn into Harlem to play street ball against the city's best male players. "I was always told I wouldn't make anything of myself. My brother was an A student—he was going to be a doctor. I was just an athlete. I had to learn to depend on me. So I took on an arrogant attitude—not to hurt people, but just to keep striving," she says. Armed with street-ball skills and relentless determination, Lieberman made the Olympic team, and when the U.S. women's team won the silver medal (losing to the Soviet Union in the finals), she became the youngest basketball player to win an Olympic medal. Following the Olympics, she signed with Old Dominion and led the school to two national championships, and she became the first woman to play in a men's professional league, spending two seasons with the Springfield Flame of the United States Basketball Association. In 1987 she joined the Washington Generals, a team that traveled and played against the Harlem Globetrotters. "Since there was no professional women's league at the time, I thought it was my only chance to make basketball my career," she explains.

It was, at the time, her only chance to continue playing the game that had taken her from Brooklyn to the Olympics. There were several attempts in the late 1970s and 1980s to establish women's professional basketball in the United States, but nothing ever succeeded, mainly because the critical television contracts couldn't be negotiated. TV executives didn't think women's basketball was a worthy investment, and cable television had yet to emerge as a viable option.

The Women's Basketball League, which began in 1978, had eight teams in its first year and expanded to fourteen teams in its second season. Organizers, initially, were encouraged by the interest. But the novelty wore off as the players were criticized for not being as dynamic as their male counterparts and for appearing "unfeminine." In an attempt to save the league, organizers scheduled exhibition games against teams of Playboy Bunnies and sent players to modeling courses, but with the losses nearing an average of $250,000 per team, the league folded in 1981. Three other leagues folded during this time before they even got started: the WABA lasted one season; the Ladies Professional Basketball Association lasted a month in 1980; the Liberty Basketball Association, which adopted 9.2-foot baskets and spandex uniforms, lasted one exhibition game.

With nowhere to continue playing, Lieberman and Meyers both turned to sports broadcasting. Lieberman worked as a basketball commentator on women's basketball for ESPN and Prime Sports. Years later, when another professional league was started in 1995, she joined the Phoenix Mercury of the Women's National Basketball Association. After two years of play she retired as a player and became head coach of the WNBA's Detroit Shock.

By the 1980s the growth of the industry that allowed Lieberman and Meyers limited opportunities to have basketball careers expanded to present more venues for college basketball and fiery Cheryl Miller. Miller was the third of her parents' five children. Like Meyers, she learned the game from her brothers, especially Reggie, who was a star at UCLA and then with the Indiana Pacers, and she learned how to compete from her parents. Her mother, Carrie, had played on an all-black basketball team as a teenager and encouraged her daughter to play the sport she had loved as a girl. Her father taught her to fight the racism and sexism that restrained a young black girl who wanted to play sports. In an interview with *Ebony* magazine, Cheryl explained that as an eleven-year-old, she had been passed over by one of the local boys' teams after showing up the coach's son and learned early. "Dad told us that if a white coach had to choose between a black athlete and a white athlete of similar skills, he would choose the white athlete. Every time. The moral therefore was that it was not enough for us to be good—we had to be flat-out better. A lot of people look at Reggie and myself and think that we are cocky and arrogant, and maybe we are, but only in the sense that we believe in ourselves and our talent," she says.

In high school, Cheryl averaged nearly 37 points per game, and in one 1982 contest, she scored 105 points, setting a California high school record. She went on to play at the University of Southern California and helped spark a heated rivalry between USC and UCLA, where her brother Reggie was playing. USC fans taunted Reggie with chants of "Cher-yl, Cher-yl" whenever he got the ball. When she finished college, Cheryl decided against playing overseas, which was then the only professional opportunity available to female players. She briefly coached at USC before turning to sports commentating on television.

Playing overseas in Europe and Asia had become the only viable option for those graduating from college who wanted to continue playing ball. Much like the industrial teams, the leagues created in the 1980s were established by companies eager for publicity. International communities were also more willing to accept women's basketball as a viable, moneymaking venture, and the attraction of the American women who came to play brought out big crowds.

Teresa Edwards, who had played at the University of Georgia, joined a league in Japan and one in Italy after she graduated. It was financially lucrative, Edwards said, but a difficult existence. "There were lots of lonely nights and $1,000 phone bills," she told *Newsweek* magazine. Jennifer Azzi was a college star at Stanford, winning the Naismith and Wade awards her senior year as the best college player in the country. That year she led the Cardinals to the 1990 national championship. She had trouble finding a job overseas, and when she did, it was far from ideal. "In Italy the manager would drive by my house and make sure my lights were out at a certain time," she says. "In France, they had an idea that you should score twenty points a game. You score fifteen, and you're gone. And some people had trouble getting paid—it's cutthroat in a lot of places. But with no other place to play, what do you do?"

Back in the United States, the women's college game was going through difficult growing pains as athletic directors grappled with the problems created by having two national governing bodies—NCAA for men's sports and AIAW for women's sports. For one thing, the rules were extremely different. Coaches of women's sports were given wide latitude in recruiting by the AIAW, while coaches of men's sports were restricted by stringent, specific rules set down by the NCAA. The logical conclusion, many felt, was simply to move women's sports under the domain of the already powerful NCAA. "The AIAW had a lot of different little rules about recruiting, budgets, all kinds of things," says Betty Jaynes, then the women's coach at James Madison University in Virginia. "And some athletic directors hated that they couldn't get their arms around those coaches and that program." There also was a group of coaches and administrators who wanted to see the women's game follow the model set by the men. "It was a confusing time," Jaynes says. "A lot of the larger schools left the AIAW right away, and some of the smaller schools were left behind, standing with the soldiers in the trenches kind of thing." In 1982, postseason tournaments were held to crown both an AIAW and an NCAA national champion, with Rutgers taking the AIAW title and Louisiana Tech winning the NCAA trophy. It was the last game played under AIAW rules. The next year, colleges whose men's teams were NCAA sanctioned were required to switch their women's programs over as well. Under the NCAA umbrella, however, budgets were increased, and larger schools began to emerge as the superpowers of the sport.

Pat Summitt at Tennessee and Jody Conradt at Texas were two coaches at larger universities who realized early success in the NCAA league. Summitt had taken the UT job while she was rehabbing her injured knee, trying to get back into playing condition. As a player for the University of Tennessee-Martin, she had been strong, aggressive, and fierce on defense. She made her first national team in 1973 at the World University games in the Soviet Union and was so successful in regaining strength in her injured knee that she made the U.S. World Championship team in 1975 and the Olympic team in 1976. As a coach, an arena where she is better known, she led Tennessee to its first AIAW Final Four in 1976 and came within a few points of upsetting defending national champion Delta State. As an NCAA coach, she has become the most heralded of all women's coaches, guiding her Tennessee teams to national championships in 1987, 1989, 1991, 1996, 1997, and 1998. To say that Pat Summitt's presence contributed greatly to the surge of the sport in the late 1980s and 1990s is a mild understatement.

As the media began covering women's games, attendance did, in fact, grow. As the game quickened and became more physical, the media began writing more about who was playing the game, and public opinion began to change. The concept of women as athletes was no longer such a foreign or unusual one. Athleticism was in vogue, as evidenced by the aerobics craze of the 1980s—women and men alike were realizing the benefits of physical exertion. In the 1990s muscles and fitness became something to be admired. Strength no longer had to mean masculine; playing sports, being an athlete and a woman, was in. This mentality set the stage for the country to fall in love with a team that would change women's collegiate basketball forever.

Perhaps it was merely the timing. Perhaps it was the location—the University of Connecticut was close to Boston and New York, home cities of the ever powerful East Coast media, including ESPN, which showed great foresight by dramatically increasing the number of women's collegiate basketball games broadcast on its network. It was a sort of harmonic convergence, which made the UConn team a bona fide phenomenon during the 1994–95 season.

Nobody forecast the Lady Huskies' success. The program had never been especially strong, and the university hadn't seemed to care. Even as late as 1990, the women's basketball coaches shared an office with the track coaches. "When I answered the phone, I couldn't even say, 'Women's basketball,'" remembers assistant coach Chris Dailey. "I had to say, 'Connecticut,' and run down the hall and get the track coach when it was for him." The women's team had to share a locker room with the visiting baseball team, and games were sparsely attended.

In 1991, against odds and precedent, the UConn team advanced to the Final Four, and a sleeping-giant community was awakened. "People love to follow winners, and they said, 'Hey, we have a winner right here in our own backyard, and they went to the Final Four,'" Dailey says. The following year, the team moved its games to Gampel Arena, and word got around that the UConn women might have quite a team. Fans were intrigued by the past season's success, and they were curious about a new player on the squad who had been one of the most successful high school players in the country, Rebecca Lobo.

Lobo was born in Southwick, Massachusetts, and learned to play basketball in the backyard with her sister Rachel and her seven-foot brother, Jason. She told the *Boston Globe*, "Jason would beat us. He would intercept our passes because he had that reach. The only way to score against Jason is to take a hook shot." Lobo's height is one of her best assets—she was nearly six feet as a fourteen-year-old, and in high school she towered over most of the girls and boys in her classes. Every day after school, before homework or chores, she was in the driveway shooting basket after basket. "It took my mind away from a lot of things," she said. "I learned to work out problems on that driveway." At Southwick High School, she led her team to a 76–11 overall record and was, indeed, one of the most successful and high-profile players ever to enter college. Recruiters came out in droves. Coaches even attended Lobo's cross-country meets.

In the end, Lobo chose UConn despite its paltry existence, because it was close to home. "I think we got Rebecca on things other than what we had to offer here," says UConn head coach Geno Auriemma. "We didn't have much, but I think she liked the people and the situation." Lobo became UConn's all-time leading rebounder (1,268) and shot blocker (396) and won just about every award there was: Associated Press Female Athlete of the year, NCAA Woman of the Year, Naismith Award, Honda-Broderick Cup recipient, Academic and Athletic All-American, and the Women's Sports Foundation Team Sportswoman of the Year.

It was in Lobo's senior year, 1994, that UConn enjoyed the kind of success that changed the way the country viewed women's basketball. The team went undefeated in that 1994–95 season, upsetting number one–ranked Tennessee in a nationally televised regular-season game, which drew a record audience for a women's basketball game. The UConn team fed off of Lobo's magnetic personality and deft skills, which drew attention from all over the country. Lobo played with a love and passion for the game that was evident to anyone who watched. She was statuesque and pretty and played with a fierce aggressiveness never before seen in the women's game. And there was that amazing hook. People came out just to see her take and, more often than not, make that shot.

Lobo played that 1994 season as her mother, Ruth Ann, underwent chemotherapy for breast cancer. Rebecca feared she might lose her biggest fan, but, as she had with other worries when she was a child, she turned to the basketball court as a way of dealing with her mother's illness and the uncertainty of her future. Ruth Ann won her battle against cancer and was in the stands in Minneapolis when UConn met Tennessee again in 1995, this time in the national championship final. Hardly anyone believed that the Huskies could beat the Volunteers again. The first win, people thought, had been a fluke. Surely, with Tennessee star Nikki McCray, a feisty guard known for her defense, and Pat Summitt as the coach, UConn wasn't likely to win.

With nineteen thousand fans jammed into the Target Center and a record TV audience of 5.4 million, UConn and Lobo proved the pundits wrong. But the battle between the two teams was fierce. Lobo, Kara Wolters, and Jen Rizzotti were on the bench much of the first half because of foul trouble. Tennessee led by six at the break. But UConn rallied in the final minutes and won 70–64. In Connecticut between 3:45 and 6:00 P.M.—game time—two out of every three sets in use were tuned to the Huskies-Vols matchup, surpassing viewership even for the 1995 Super Bowl. And the day after the win, the *New York Times* ran a photo of the team on the front page. In Hartford, more than 100,000 people crowded the streets for a parade. "There were just people everywhere," says Rizzotti. "I had my hands out the whole time we were riding in that car, and I don't think I could have touched everyone. They all just wanted a little piece. I felt like every person in the state of Connecticut was there supporting us and just happy for what we did." Auriemma compares the game with the 1968 regular-season men's basketball matchup between UCLA and Houston. More than fifty thousand fans had crowded into the Astrodome to watch that game, which helped usher in a new era in men's college basketball. "Maybe, just maybe we did it for the women's game," he says. Perhaps they did.

A few months after UConn's dramatic win, dozens of talented young women were invited to Colorado Springs to try out for a national team that would travel the world for a year, in preparation for the Atlanta Olympics in 1996. That, in itself, was extraordinary, considering that in the past U.S. women's Olympic teams were assembled just six weeks before the Olympics— the players had barely had time to learn one another's names, much less develop a chemistry. But this time the U.S. women's Olympic team would be ready. The Olympic team was under the guidance of the NBA, which lent its marketing arm, and USA Basketball, which gave the women a $3 million budget. Each team member would be paid $50,000. The corporate sponsorship USA Basketball had gleaned from major companies that recognized the changing atmosphere surrounding the game was remarkable. Sears, State Farm, Tampax, and Champion jumped on board, as did Nike, which—for the first time ever—devoted a portion of its $35 million summer marketing campaign to women's basketball.

Thousands of young women longed to be part of the team. Thousands more, like Lieberman and Meyers, longed to be ten years younger. Players who have played and studied the game and its growth knew that this national team would be special. Sheryl Swoopes had starred for Texas Tech University, scoring 47 points in the 1994 national championship final, the most points ever scored in an NCAA championship game, and leading the Lady Rangers to the title. She was a hit with young girls all across America, so much so that Nike named a shoe for her—Air Swoopes—the first basketball shoe to carry the name of a woman. Swoopes had dozens of offers to play overseas and, in fact, played for a brief stint in Italy. But she longed to star in front of American crowds.

Lisa Leslie was another immensely popular player who was burning to make the team. At six-foot-five Leslie had been a standout player at USC and in high school, where she scored 101 points in a single game. She also had aspirations to be a model and to make a living on the court and on the runway. She knew making the U.S. team would only enhance both careers. Swoopes and Leslie were named to the team, as was Teresa Edwards and one of her former teammates at the University of Georgia, Katrina McClain. At the time the U.S. team was being formed, McClain had an offer of $300,000 to play in Hungary. One of her goals was to make enough money to retire from the game, and the Hungarian season would put her well within striking range. But McClain, too, had an idea that this U.S. team would be special. Nikki McCray, who had just graduated from Tennessee; Katy Steding and Jennifer Azzi from Stanford; Carla McGhee from Tennessee; and Ruthie Bolton from Auburn were named. One of the last players added was Lobo, who had parlayed her remarkable season with UConn into big endorsement deals with Spaulding and Reebok. But Lobo arrived at camp in Colorado Springs overweight and out of shape and surrounded by jealousy that her new fame had wrought. She would spend the next year fighting to prove that she belonged with this talented group of players because of her game rather than her name.

The U.S. coach was Tara VanDerveer, who had turned the women's team at Stanford into a perennial national contender. Under her guidance, the Cardinals had reached four Final Fours and won two national championships. VanDerveer was a tough, no-nonsense, conditioning-minded coach who had studied the game by watching Bobby Knight's teams while she was a student at Indiana. When VanDerveer was chosen to head up the U.S. team, the president of USA Basketball, C. M. Newton, told her: "This isn't about bronze. This isn't about silver. This is about gold." NBA commissioner David Stern told her the immediate future of women's basketball—and the new women's professional league he had been secretly planning—depended on the success of the U.S. team. If they didn't win the gold, all of the effort, money, and planning would be wasted. VanDerveer felt the pressure, and at times it spilled onto the court, where she ruled with a heavy hand. She was criticized for the harsh manner in which she treated her players. "Tara was an exceedingly driven coach," said Sara Corbett, who spent a year with the U.S. women's team and authored a book, *Venus to the Hoop*, about its quest for the gold medal. "She worked her players in moments, harder than they wanted to be worked and sometimes some of the players felt they weren't getting the playing time that they deserved. But it's important to remember that Tara probably had more pressure on her than anybody else."

VanDerveer took the team from China to Australia to Russia and around the United States. The players won fifty-two games in front of record crowds of fans who came out in droves to see these new American superstars. The players would sign autographs and pose for pictures for hours after games, talk with their young fans, and make numerous off-court public appearances. They were visible, and they were touchable, unlike the men's team players, who seemed to run from publicity and fans. Their effect at the grassroots level perhaps did more for the game of women's basketball than anything else in history. Suddenly, little girls saw that being a player was not only acceptable but also revered by the American public. These women were beautiful and feminine and tough as nails on the court.

Girls bought USA jerseys with "Leslie" and "Lobo" on the back. Team posters sold out in every city where the team appeared. "I knew we had really made it when I looked up in the stands at a high school game I was coaching," says Mariah Burton Nelson, a former coach and author, "and I saw a boy wearing a Swoopes jersey in the stands. A boy." By the time the group reached the Olympics in Atlanta, the stage was set for more than a mere tournament. The team's first press conference was jammed with reporters. Players were mobbed by fans, much as the men's Dream Team had been four years earlier in Barcelona. Charles Barkley, playing on the men's team in Atlanta, became an unofficial cheerleader, often leading cheers in the stands and performing to choruses of "YMCA." Other faithful included Magic Johnson, Scottie Pippen, Chelsea Clinton, and George Steinbrenner. The women had truly arrived, and Atlanta was indeed the Olympics of the woman athlete.

The U.S. team had eight games to win on the way to the gold medal. After beating Cuba and the Ukraine in the early rounds, the team was scheduled to play next in the Georgia Dome against Zaire. VanDerveer said she worried about the majesty of the large arena intimidating her players, because she expected only 6,000 or so fans. By game time, 31,000 fans had crammed into the arena, the largest crowd ever to watch a women's basketball game. "It was almost too much to absorb," she wrote in her book, *Shooting from the Outside.* "All those people, sitting row upon row as far as we could see, cheering for us, waving American flags, holding up signs that read, 'The REAL Dream Team.' We were absolutely shocked when we walked into that arena." Two nights later, a crowd of 33,952 showed up for the team's game against Australia. In the final, against Brazil, the U.S. women dominated the entire game and won 111–87, finishing their remarkable year-long season 60–0 with a gold medal. "This is a great day for women's basketball," Sheryl Swoopes said at the post-game press conference. "It doesn't get any better than that. I think we all were feeling it." "It's the greatest feeling in the world," said Dawn Staley. "I could stop playing basketball right now. That's how good it feels."

Because of their success and the outpouring of attention the U.S. team received, nobody had to go to Europe to play professional basketball and nobody had to stop playing—if she didn't want to. A women's professional league was to be launched in the United States.

The Associated Basketball League was formed by Gary Cavalli, who put together a team of Silicon Valley investors to launch a nine-team league that would play in the 1996–97 season. Anxious and excited about the prospects of a basketball future in the United States, nine members of the U.S. national team signed with the ABL, including Sylvia Crawley, Ruthie Bolton, Valerie Still, and Teresa Edwards. Within a month the NBA, which had lent its support to the 1994 national team as a trial run for a women's league, would launch its own women's league, with Commissioner David Stern spearheading the movement. Originally, the ABL thought it had a television deal with ESPN and a commitment from Nike, but with the NBA's announcement, ESPN turned down the ABL's proposal because it wanted to see how things would develop with the newer league. Instantly, the leagues were in conflict, but considering the U.S. national team's success and the numbers of fans who had flocked to the games, Stern decided to go ahead with the eight-team league even with the existence of the ABL, scheduling games to begin in June of 1997.

Stern and the WNBA hired Val Ackerman, a lawyer who was one of the first women to receive a basketball scholarship at the University of Virginia. Her job was to develop a model for the proposed league. She went about trying to sign the remaining U.S. national team players who were not signed by the ABL, landing Lisa Leslie, Rebecca Lobo, and Sheryl Swoopes, who originally had said she'd play with the ABL. "What you people have to understand," Sheryl told a packed press conference the day she signed with the WNBA, "is that when the ABL was first announced we were just so excited to have a league to play in. We didn't even know that the NBA was thinking of forming a league. The NBA had a lot to offer. This isn't personal. I don't think people should get mad with each other. To me, what this means is there is a lot of interest in women's basketball." "The ABL started just a few weeks after the Olympics, and I was exhausted," Lisa Leslie said, explaining her decision. "My mom made the decision for me." The WNBA was to have a team in her home city of Los Angeles.

The ABL averaged 3,536 fans per game its first season and garnered the corporate sponsorships of Nissan, Lady Foot Locker, and the Phoenix Insurance Group. The league lost close to $4 million that first season, but the outlook for its second season was good, with SportsChannel and Black Entertainment Television considering television packages. The WNBA, with its high-profile "We Got Next" campaign, spent $15 million in marketing that first season compared to the $1.5 million spent by the ABL. NBC, ESPN, and Lifetime television climbed on board with five-year commitments. Thirty-three games were televised nationally, and average attendance was just over 9,000 per game.

In 1998 Tina Thompson, formerly of USC, led the Houston Comets to the first WNBA Championship. She and coach Van Chancellor were helped immensely, however, by the return of Sheryl Swoopes, who took the court just weeks after giving birth to her son, Jordan. The WNBA added two expansion teams its second season, placing teams in Washington, D.C., with Nikki McCray, and in Detroit, where Nancy Lieberman became the general manager and head coach. In one of the more interesting moves of the 1998 off-season, Lieberman acquired thirty-eight-year-old Lynette Woodard, who left her job as a stockbroker on Wall Street to play in the WNBA's inaugural season with the Cleveland Rockers. Woodard hadn't played organized basketball for more than five years but wanted the chance to be a part of the professional league she never had the choice of joining out of college. She was a standout player for the University of Kansas and went on to become the first Kansas student ever to have a jersey number retired at the end of a college career. She made her biggest impact on the basketball world, however, in 1985, when she became the first woman to join the Harlem Globetrotters.

In 1998 the WNBA also got a huge marketing lift when league representatives discovered a player from Poland, Malgorzata Dydek, who surprised everyone at the pre-draft camp by measuring in at seven feet, two inches. The 7–21 Utah Starzz had the first pick in the draft that year and wasted no time in choosing Dydek, who became an instant celebrity because of her height. "She was listed at six-foot-six," said Utah Starzs head coach Denise Taylor. "I saw her next to some men close to that height and said, no way is she six-six."

The Columbus Quest, behind another aging veteran, thirty-six-year-old center Valerie Still, won the first two ABL championships in March of 1998. Still, who once starred for the University of Kentucky, scored twenty-five points and grabbed six rebounds in an 86–81 win in game five against the Long Beach Sting Rays to win the 1998 ABL title.

For its third season, the ABL also added two expansion teams, one in Nashville and one in Chicago, coached by former Bulls assistant Jim Cleamons, who had been fired a year earlier by the Dallas Mavericks. The league also scored a major coup in the league wars by placing eight players on the eleven-woman U.S. roster for the 1998 world championships, including ABL MVP Natalie Williams, who played basketball and volleyball for UCLA.

Though the fate of the two leagues is uncertain, most players are hoping for some sort of merger in the future. For now, however, they are thrilled with the competition and the existence of two leagues, and salaries are at an all-time high. The leagues are bolstered by the college players who are drawing major attention because of the success of the college programs. Media attention has skyrocketed in the late 1990s and record crowds are pouring into arenas across the country to see women's college games.

A controversy early in the 1998 season, which involved the UConn women's basketball team and a decision to allow its injured star, Nykesha Sales, to limp onto the court and score an uncontested basket to become the school's all-time leading scorer, brought dialogue regarding women's college ball to an all-time high. Many people marveled not so much at the act, but at the attention it received. For several weeks in February, Sales's basket was what America debated on radio and television talk shows, in newspapers, and at dinner tables. "If this was ten years ago and it happened," said ESPN's Dick Schaap, "nobody would have cared because nobody would have known."

To say that the 1997–98 college basketball season was filled with magic is to describe a year of phenomenal play by outstanding players before unprecedented crowds. The University of Tennessee stunned the country with its talent and dominance, winning its third straight national title by going 39–0. Many believe it was, perhaps, the greatest women's collegiate team to date. The Lady Vols took their game and their name to a level even higher than that of Lobo and UConn, and they did it by thrilling record crowds with breakaways, finger rolls, and no-look passes and at a pace so furious that opponents were left gasping for air by the end of the games. "I've never seen a team like this," said Rutgers coach Vivian Stringer, whose team was beaten by Tennessee 92–60 in the semifinals of the Mideast Regional. "It is the greatest group of athletes, depthwise, ever assembled."

That the magician was Pat Summitt was of no surprise to anyone. With her hard-driving ways on the court and mothering ways off it, Summitt maintained a level of quality at Tennessee unseen by any other program. Tough and gritty, she used her experience gleaned over twenty-four seasons not only to recruit top athletes, but also to mold them into a team. In 1997 she threw out the slow, pass-oriented game in favor of an up-tempo, fast-break style that played to the talents of her athletes.

Nobody was more talented on that squad than Chamique Holdsclaw, who dazzled the nation in a way nobody had ever seen, grabbing rebounds, making one-handed steals, and nailing jumper after jumper after jumper. In leading the best women's team ever assembled to its third straight title, Holdsclaw also established herself as perhaps the best woman ever to play the game. In the championship game against Louisiana Tech, she scored twenty-five points and grabbed ten rebounds. The finals of the NCAA tournament was won by the Lady Vols, who cruised to a 93–76 victory.

Holdsclaw was raised in Astoria, Queens, mainly by her grandmother. She had enormous feet as a twelve-year-old, was tall and skinny, and was determined to play basketball against the boys in her neighborhood. Her grandmother, June, recognized Chamique's talent early. "I knew she liked to play ball, and I encouraged her," she says. "She never liked ballet." "She is better than I ever was," says Nancy Lieberman-Cline. "She's better than Cheryl Miller was, Ann Meyers, Swoopes, all of them. This is Michael Jordan in braces and a ponytail."

Two months before she led the Vols to victory, Holdsclaw and her teammates were touring Jordan's office in Chicago when "his airness" suddenly appeared in the room. "Hey, what's up, 'Meek'?" he asked. She froze. "I was like, 'Michael Jordan knows my name,'" Holdsclaw says. "I was speechless, in awe." It turns out that Jordan was a bit in awe, too. Before the final, Jordan sent the Lady Vols a telegram that read: "Good luck in the tournament and your undefeated season. Michael."

By the end of the school year, the three-time All-American Holdsclaw was mobbed by agents wanting to represent her when she decides to play professional basketball. Experts predicted she'd become the first woman player with true bargaining power in endorsement offers as well as with the two professional leagues. Strangely, the attention Holdsclaw drew to herself and to the game was not considered unusual, merely a logical progression in the lightning-quick pace with which the game evolved during the 1990s. There was talk that perhaps she would leave college early for one of the professional leagues. There was talk that she would become the first million-dollar-a-year player. Nobody seemed surprised.

A June 1998 article in *The New York Times* reported that Holdsclaw and her coach, Summitt, attended a New York Liberty WNBA game. While Holdsclaw plans to complete her term at the University of Tennessee in 1999, Summitt says Holdsclaw would love to be in the WNBA, maybe even in New York. Summitt also admitted that she herself, the highest paid college women's coach, finds the idea of moving into the professional league very intriguing. "I never thought I'd see something like this," she said at the Liberty game. "I like this, I like this for me." Until she decides to cross over into the professional league, *if* she decides to, there is her new book, *Reaching for the Summitt*, to publicize, and her beloved assistants, returning players, and a new group of freshman who await her return to UT.

Around the country, in record numbers, little girls are piling into gyms, tugging on jerseys, and shooting basket after basket after basket. They don't have to dream of being Dr. J or Michael Jordan or Jerry West if they don't want to. They can be Rebecca Lobo or Sheryl Swoopes or Chamique Holdsclaw, even Pat Summitt.

There are those who think that women have reached the pinnacle in the game of basketball. Looking back over history, of games played on three courts with one dribble, of women playing in skirts and stockings with dyed hair, participating in beauty contests, and playing for hosiery companies, it is easy to reach that conclusion. The women's game has evolved from its modest beginnings where physical exertion was deemed inappropriate to a level so physically demanding that conditioning and strength training are required elements of a daily, year-round regimen for women who want to excel. It has gone from being a sport that women had to work odd jobs to play, to a sport that women are paid to play. The 1990s was a springboard for the women's game; how high it can go remains a debatable issue.

"We have only begun to scratch the surface," says Betty Jaynes, who founded the Women's Basketball Coaches Association. "Look at the numbers, the record numbers of young girls participating in basketball at the AAU level. With those kinds of numbers, we won't reach the pinnacle for a long, long time."

CONCLUSION:
A SEISMIC SHIFT
IN THE CULTURE
Lucy Danziger

One year ago I had the good fortune to launch a magazine called *Condé Nast Sports for Women* devoted to women who are active in sports and fitness. To me, it was only natural that women would flock to such a publication for a regular fix of inspirational stories and instructional information. I felt like I had a front row seat at the revolution. As a journalist, I was covering the greatest story of my era—a seismic shift in the culture, a new take on how women live, what their body image is all about, and what the long, involved definition of a modern woman will be as the twenty-first century begins.

During the development phase of the magazine, I heard over and over again that we were ahead of our time, that a sports magazine for active women would not necessarily be a hit. But then came the 1996 Olympics, dubbed the Women's Games because of the historic firsts set by female athletes, and the twenty-fifth anniversary of Title IX, the gender equity law that required schools and colleges to afford the same opportunities in sports to girls and boys. And astonishingly, in 1997, the same year as our launch, two basketball leagues for women debuted, the ABL and the WNBA, providing the opportunity for Americans to watch elite women play in major arenas around the country. The convergence of these events changed public perception of what women were ready to do, and what they wanted to read about. It was clearly the perfect time for a mainstream glossy magazine serving active women in all areas of their sports and fitness interests.

We made one miscalculation, however, and that was with the name of the magazine, *Sports for Women*. Having grown up defining myself as a jock, comfortable with all things sporty and committed to staying fit, I believed women would want their magazine to be called "sports" because of what it said about our changing point of view. Yet to the majority of magazine

buyers, sports still means the Big Four, the sports women have traditionally seen their husbands watch on television: football, baseball, hockey and
basketball. (Women are increasingly joining in as fans and now comprise 40
percent of all major league audiences.) We needed to change the name of
the magazine to reflect the fact that being active is a personal passion for
women, not an arm's-length, fan relationship. The word that brings to mind
participation is "fitness"; women feel most comfortable with that catchall to
describe their physical activities. So we bought the assets of a magazine called
Women's Sports & Fitness and created a winning combination with just a small
title change. Within one month of the switch to the new name, our circula-
tion story was a success and our magazine was off to a flying start.

The overwhelming reaction to the new *Women's Sports & Fitness* has
been uniquely enthusiastic, from an array of voices: women in their thirties
write in to tell us that they came to their passion for sports and fitness later
in life, and are now making up for lost time. Younger women, who have been
raised on a steady diet of team sports, tell us that our magazine is the first
one to "understand" them and their priorities. Outdoorswomen, fitness-
conscious women, and sports enthusiasts all look to the magazine as confirmation of their new lifestyle choices. "Finally!" is the word I have heard over
and over about this modern approach to the female reader as an able-bodied,
thinking woman. "Finally, a magazine devoted to strong, athletic women,"
who are confident and driven to challenge themselves.

Yet the magazine simply reflects the time in which we live, when women
want to be physically fit, strong, capable, and healthy and want to enjoy what
their bodies can do. At last count, the number of women and girls across the
country who participate in sports has risen to more than 40 million. They
are the real story of this generation—not the professionals, but all the women
who'll never appear in the sports pages, the ones who flock to the parks and
fields, gyms and mountains, courts and rivers to get into the action.

These women are setting goals, and not just the one that's measured
by the scale. They're concerned with being healthy and fit, but are also eager
to accomplish something and have fun. For them, being strong is the point,
and that doesn't just mean muscles. The new American woman no longer
asks if she can play—she shows up with the ball.

She may not wear a team jersey or do anything else in a conventional
way. She's secure enough to "own" sports and even remake them. This new
approach shows up first among the younger players and then finds its way
to the rest of us. We don't do sports the way men do, but that doesn't mean
we have to be self-effacing and sweet. And we no longer see sports as a
female ghetto. They can be single-sex or coed, an escape or a social out-
ing. What's important is that we are making sports whatever we want them
to be.

We don't "consume" sports the same way as our male counterparts do, but we ought to pay attention to the world of professional sports. What happens among talented sportswomen at the elite levels makes its way into the culture. It's our version of the trickle-down concept: When women get paid to play basketball in front of 17,000 spectators, the rest of us, contenders in our own world of sports, feel a little bit more legitimate and take our pursuits more seriously.

When I was interviewing editors and writers for our new magazine, I asked each person, "What sports do you do?" After a momentary squirm came the standard answer: "Oh, I'm not an athlete."

"But what do you enjoy?" I would press on. "Well, I play tennis, swim, just tried rock climbing at the wall in my gym, I grew up fishing, I ran the marathon last year with my boyfriend. . . ." was a typical response. I'd point out that she just named five sports, yet still did not consider herself an athlete. "Oh, well, I was never picked for the teams in school." It always came back to the dreaded choosing of sides. This seventh-grade ritual was universally cited by grown women as the defining moment for their sports identity (or lack of one).

I started to believe that one's athletic self-image was frozen in puberty: You were either a jock or a nerd, a gym-class cutter or a junior superstar. It took years, even decades, of modest sports successes for many women to change these self-portraits. And in most cases, the sports they eventually chose lay outside the traditional definition: in-line skating, Pilates, yoga, jogging, hiking, and other physically demanding disciplines never given legitimacy by "sports" coverage. Millions of women out there are working in individual ways to express their strength. To proclaim they aren't athletes is to say, "I am my own person, and I defy classification."

Most women don't want to be given a grade, a shot, a stat sheet. We just want to be active, healthy and, above all, enjoy ourselves. It's not the labels we give ourselves—jock, athlete, rookie, natural, couch potato—that matter, but the feeling of accomplishment, and how much we have to gain, out there, doing our thing.

So it's simple: women care only about their own personal activity level, what their own fitness challenge is, their own sports passion, and don't want to be bothered with details about the pros and the elite athletes, right? Not so, as one exciting news story we ran recently showed us.

In 1998, another Olympics came along, and we all rallied around a new team, the U.S. Women's Ice Hockey team, led by Cammie Granato, Karyn Bye, and A. J. Mleczko. Even before the gold medal was within reach, it was clear that teams like this, and stories like this, rarely happen more than once a decade. Olympic viewers were ready to make the same emotional investment we made watching the legendary 1980 U.S. men's hockey team, which won the gold medal against mighty Russia. This time it was the women's turn to warm our hearts, and Pulitzer prize winning author David Halberstam covered the story for *Women's Sports & Fitness*. At 7,000 words, it was a commitment to read, yet women from all around the country told me later how meaningful that story was to them. And I was thrilled. It wasn't the kind of piece that readers generally ask for. Yet nestled in between workout trends and other pertinent advice, it was the perfect dose of inspiration.

A few days after the closing ceremonies in Nagano, two stars of the U.S. women's ice hockey team swung into New York City for an appearance on the "Today Show" and wanted to know if they could stop by our offices. We were, of course, thrilled to see them. It was only fitting that we would want to congratulate them in person and feel the heft of their gold medals.

It's truly awesome to watch a team that has strived for greatness in relative obscurity achieve its ultimate goal. All of these women had played on boys' teams growing up, often following brothers onto the ice, and in some cases forced to hide their gender and sign up for teams under first initials or boy's names, or face the objections of coaches and other parents. All in all, thirteen medals were won by American athletes in Nagano, eight by women. Still, women's ice hockey was a focus of the Winter Games, and I felt like a proud parent, having rooted for these young women for months, as I watched them attain their dream. That is what the Olympics are all about: bursting through the barriers, outstripping expectations and finding new potential, new strength, and new levels of commitment. Watching these players, we were inspired and felt honored to be able to tell them so.

I'm always amazed at the changes I've gotten to witness—in my lifetime of playing sports, and in the short period I've worked on a magazine for active women. I tell people that mine will be the last generation that remembers a time when women didn't routinely participate in sports. I was twelve when Title IX passed, and shortly thereafter I attended a boarding school that had just gone coed. Because they wanted to offer the girls the same education the boys had enjoyed for over a hundred years, they instigated teams and sports programs that were not available to most women of my generation. So I got an advance preview of what Title IX would bring some twenty years later, and it was amazing what the girls could do out there. Growing up, my mother would tell me "We didn't have television when I was a girl." I can only imagine the look of incredulity on my daughter's face when I tell her, "Most girls didn't play sports when I was a girl." She won't believe it. She won't be able to imagine a time when girls and boys didn't do sports equally, and even together. The future is here, in the form of sports-crazed teenage girls. They will grow up to be active, physically confident women. They will be inspired by magazines like the one I helped create, and by historically significant books like this one.

NOTES

Introduction

Aronson, Sidney H. "The Sociology of the Bicycle." In *Sociology and Everyday Life*, edited by Marcello Truzzi. Englewood Cliffs, N.J.: Prentice-Hall, 1968.

Blue, Adrianne. *Grace Under Pressure*. London: Sidgwick & Jackson, 1987.

Cayleff, Susan E. *Babe: The Life and Legend of Babe Didrikson Zaharias*. Urbana: University of Illinois Press, 1995.

Delehanty, Hugh J. "The Blooming of Bicycling." *Women's Sports & Fitness*, August 1981.

Faludi, Susan. *Backlash: The Undeclared War Against American Women*. New York: Crown Publishers, 1991.

Festle, Mary Jo. *Playing Nice: Politics and Apologies in Women's Sports*. New York: Columbia University Press, 1996.

Green, Harvey. *Fit for America: Health, Fitness, Sport, and American Society*. New York: Pantheon Books, 1986.

Guttmann, Allen. *Women's Sports: A History*. New York: Columbia University Press, 1991.

Levine, Suzanne, and Harriet Lyons, eds. *The Decade of Women: A* Ms. *History of the Seventies in Words and Pictures*. New York: Paragon, 1980.

Lorde, Audre. *Sister Outsider: Essays and Speeches*. Freedom, Calif.: Crossing Press, 1984.

"The Revolutionary Bicycle," *The Literary Digest* 12 (July 20, 1895): 334, cited in Sidney H. Aronson, "The Sociology of the Bicycle," in *Sociology and Everyday Life*, edited by Marcello Truzzi. (Englewood Cliffs, N.J.: Prentice-Hall, 1968).

Twin, Stephanie. *Out of the Bleachers: Writings on Women and Sport*. Old Westbury, N.Y.: Feminist Press, 1979.

Willard, Francis. *How I Learned to Ride the Bicycle*. 1895. Excerpted in Stephanie Twin, *Out of the Bleachers: Writings on Women and Sport* (Old Westbury, N.Y.: Feminist Press, 1979).

Woolum, Janet. *Outstanding Women Athletes*. Phoenix: Oryx Press, 1992.

Track and Field

Biracree, Tom. *Wilma Rudolph: Champion Athlete*. Chelsea House, 1988. This quotes extensively from *Wilma* by Wilma Rudolph (with Martin Ralbovsky) (New York: New Amsterdam Library, 1977).

Cahn, Susan K. *Coming on Strong: Gender and Sexuality in Twentieth-Century Women's Sports*. New York: Free Press, 1994.

Cayleff, Susan E. *Babe: The Life and Legend of Babe Didrikson Zaharias*. Champaign, Ill.: University of Illinois Press, 1995.

Guttmann, Allen. *Women's Sports: A History*. New York: Columbia University Press, 1991.

Joyner-Kersee, Jackie, with Sonja Steptoe. *A Kind of Grace*. New York: Warner Books, 1997.

Leder, Jane. *Grace and Glory: A Century of Women in the Olympics*. Chicago: Triumph Books, 1996.

Phillips, Ellen. *The VIII Olympiad*. World Sport Research and Publications, 1996.

Pieroth, Doris Hinson. *Their Day in the Sun: Women of the 1932 Olympics*. Seattle: University of Washington Press, 1996.

Tricard, Louise Mead. *American Women's Track and Field: A History, 1895 through 1980*. Jefferson, N.C.: McFarland & Company, 1996.

Wallechinsky, David. *The Complete Book of the Summer Olympics*. Boston: Little, Brown, 1996.

Baseball/Softball

Berlage, Gai Ingham. *Women in Baseball: The Forgotten History*. Westport, Conn.: Praeger Publishers, 1994.

Gregorich, Barbara. *Women at Play*. New York: Harcourt Brace, 1993.

Johnson, Susan E. *When Women Played Hardball*. Seattle: Seal Press, 1994.

Thorn, John, and Pete Palmer, eds. *Total Baseball: The Ultimate Encyclopedia of Baseball*. 3rd ed. New York: HarperPerennial, 1993.

Tennis

Collins, Bud, and Zander Hollander, eds. *Bud Collins' Tennis Encyclopedia*. Detroit: Visible Ink Press, 1997.

Danzig, Allison, and Peter Schwed, eds. *The Fireside Book of Tennis*. New York: Simon & Schuster, 1972.

Engelmann, Larry. *The Goddess and the American Girl: The Story of Suzanne Lenglen and Helen Wills*. New York: Oxford University Press, 1988.

Lichtenstein, Grace. *A Long Way, Baby: Behind the Scenes in Women's Tennis*. New York: William Morrow & Co., 1974.

Lloyd, Chris Evert, with Neil Amdur. *Chrissie: My Own Story*. New York: Simon & Schuster, 1982.

Navratilova, Martina, with George Vecsey. *Martina*. New York: Knopf, 1985.

Seles, Monica, with Nancy Ann Richardson. *Monica: My Journey from Fear to Victory*. New York: HarperCollins, 1996.

Golf

Burnett, Jim. *Tee Times*. New York: Scribner, 1997.

Cayleff, Susan E. *Babe: The Life and Legend of Babe Didrikson Zaharias*. Champaign, Ill.: University of Illinois Press, 1995.

Golf, the Greatest Game: The USGA Celebrates Golf in America. New York: HarperCollins, 1994.

Hauser, Melanie. *Under the Lone Star Flagstick.* New York: Simon & Schuster, 1997.

Kahn, Liz. *The LPGA: The Unauthorized Version.* Group Fore Publications, 1996.

Macdonald, Robert S., and Herbert Warren Wind, eds. *The Greatest Women Golfers.* Trumbell, Conn.: Classics of Golf, 1993.

Boating

Guttmann, Allen. *Women's Sports: A History.* New York: Columbia University Press, 1991.

Huntington, Anna Seaton. *Making Waves: The Inside Story of Managing and Motivating the First Women's Team to Compete for the America's Cup.* Arlington, Tex.: Summit Publishing Group, 1996.

Lewis, Linda. *Water's Edge: Women Who Push the Limits in Rowing, Kayaking, and Canoeing.* Seattle: Seal Press, 1992.

The Olympic Factbook: A Spectator's Guide to the Summer Games. Detroit: Visible Ink Press, 1996.

Riley, Dawn, and Cynthia Flanagan. *Taking the Helm: One of America's Top Sailors Tells Her Story.* Boston: Little, Brown, 1995.

Skiing

Johnson, Anne Janette. *Great Women in Sports.* Detroit: Visible Ink Press, 1996.

Layden, Joe. *Women in Sports: The Complete Book on the World's Greatest Female Athletes.* Santa Monica, Calif.: General Publishing Group, 1997.

Markel, Robert; Susan Waggoner; and Marcella Smith. *The Women's Sports Encyclopedia: The Comprehensive Guide to Women's Sports, Women Athletes & Their Records.* New York: Henry Holt, 1997.

Sherrow, Victoria. *Encyclopedia of Women and Sports.* Santa Barbara, Calif.: ABC-CLIO, 1996.

Figure Skating

Brennan, Christine. *Inside Edge: A Revealing Journey into the Secret World of Figure Skating.* New York: Simon & Schuster, 1996.

———. *Edge of Glory: The Inside Story of the Quest for Figure Skating's Olympic Gold Medals.* New York: Simon & Schuster, 1998.

Costello, Emily. *Tara Lipinski: Triumph on Ice.* New York: Bantam Books, 1997.

Epstein, Edward. *Born to Skate: The Michelle Kwan Story.* New York: Ballentine Books, 1997.

Kwan, Michelle. *Michelle Kwan: Heart of a Champion.* New York: Scholastic Trade, 1997.

Sanford, William R. *Dorothy Hamill.* Parsippany, N.J.: Silver Burdett Ginn, 1993.

Smith, Beverly. *A Year in Figure Skating.* Toronto: McClelland & Stewart, 1996.

Swimming

Blossom, Laurel, ed. *Splash: Great Writing about Swimming.* Hopewell, N.J.: Ecco Press, 1996.

Friedman, Sally. *Swimming the Channel.* New York: Farrar, Strauss & Giroux, 1996.

Guttmann, Allen. *Women's Sports: A History.* New York: Columbia University Press, 1991.

Johnson, Anne Janette. *Great Women in Sports.* Detroit: Visible Ink Press, 1996.

Layden, Joe. *Women in Sports: The Complete Book on the World's Greatest Female Athletes.* Santa Monica, Calif.: General Publishing Group, 1997.

Pieroth, Doris Hinson. *Their Day in the Sun: Women of the 1932 Olympics.* Seattle: University of Washington Press, 1996.

Sherrow, Victoria. *Encyclopedia of Women and Sports.* Santa Barbara, Calif.: ABC-CLIO, 1996.

Sprawson, Charles. *Haunts of the Black Masseur: The Swimmer as Hero.* New York: Penguin, 1994.

Equestrian Events

Burke, Jackie. *Equal to the Challenge: Pioneering Women in Horse Sports.* New York: Howell Book House, 1997.

Newsum, Gillian. *Women & Horses.* New York: Howell Book House, 1988.

Smythe, Pat. *Jump for Joy.* New York: A. S. Barnes, 1955.

————. One Jump Ahead. New York: A. S. Barnes, 1957.

Steinkraus, William, ed. *The US Equestrian Team Book of Riding.* New York: Simon & Schuster, 1976.

Strassburger, John. *The Chronicle of the Horse.* Middleburg, Va.: Olympic Results issue, 1996.

Winants, Peter, ed. *American Gold: The Story of the Equestrian Sports of the 1984 Olympics.* Middleburg, Va.: Chronicle of the Horse, 1984.

Gymnastics

Greenberg, Stan. *The Guinness Books of Olympics Facts & Feats.* Guinness Superlatives Limited, 1983.

Greenspan, Bud. *100 Greatest Moments in Olympic History.* Santa Monica, Calif.: General Publishing Group, 1995.

Markel, Robert; Susan Waggoner; and Marcella Smith. *The Women's Sports Encyclopedia: The Comprehensive Guide to Women's Sports, Women Athletes & Their Records.* New York: Henry Holt, 1997.

Ryan, Joan. *Little Girls in Pretty Boxes: The Making and Breaking of Elite Gymnasts and Figure Skaters.* New York: Warner Books, 1995

Wallechinsky, David. *The Complete Book of the Olympics.* Boston: Little, Brown, 1991.

Soccer

Akers, Michelle, and Tim Nash. *Standing Fast: Battles of a Champion.* JTC Sports, 1997.

Lopez, Sue. *Women on the Ball.* Scarlet Press, 1997.

Macy, Sue. *Winning: A Photohistory of American Women in Sports.* New York: Scholastic Sports, 1996.

Murray, Bill. *The World's Game: A History of Soccer.* Champaign, Ill.: University of Illinois Press, 1996.

Hockey

Avery, Joanna, and Julie Stevens. *Too Many Men on the Ice.* Victoria, British Columbia: Polestar, 1997.

Cochrane, Jean; Abby Hoffman; and Pat Kincaid. *Women in Canadian Life: Sports.* Markham, Ontario: Fitzhenry & Whiteside, 1977.

Etue, Elizabeth, and Megan K. Williams. *On the Edge: Women Making Hockey History.* Toronto, Ontario: Second Story Feminist Press, 1996.

Laklan, Cari. *Golden Girls: True Stories of Olympic Women Stars.* McGraw-Hill, 1980.

Long, Wendy. *Celebrating Excellence: Canadian Women Athletes.* Victoria, British Columbia: Polestar, 1995.

McDonald, David. *For the Record: Canada's Greatest Women Athletes.* New York: John Wiley & Sons, 1981.

McFarlane, Brian. *Proud Past, Bright Future: One Hundred Years of Canadian Women's Hockey.* North York, Ontario: Stoddart, 1994.

McWhirter, Norris. *Guinness Book of Women's Sport Records.* New York: Sterling Publishing, 1979.

Stewart, Barbara. *She Shoots . . . She Scores! A Complete Guide to Girls' and Women's Hockey.* Toronto, Ontario: Doubleday Books, 1998.

Basketball

Blais, Madelaine. *In These Girls Hope Is a Muscle.* New York: Atlantic Monthly Press, 1995.

Corbett, Sara. *Venus to the Hoop: A Gold Medal Year in Women's Basketball.* New York: Doubleday, 1997.

Lieberman-Cline, Nancy, and Robin Roberts, with Kevin Warneke. *Basketball for Women.* Champaign, Ill.: Human Kinetics, 1996.

Lobo, Rebecca, and Ruth Ann Lobo. *The Home Team: Of Mothers, Daughters & American Champions.* New York: Kodansha International, 1996.

Markel, Robert; Susan Waggoner; and Marcella Smith. *The Women's Sports Encyclopedia: The Comprehensive Guide to Women's Sports, Women Athletes & Their Records.* New York: Henry Holt, 1997.

Shea, Jim. *Husky Mania: The Inside Story of the Rise of U Conn's Men's and Women's Basketball Teams.* New York: Villard Books, 1995.

Summitt, Pat, with Sally Jenkins. *Reach for the Summit: The Definite Dozen System for Succeeding at Whatever You Do.* New York: Bantam Doubleday Dell, 1998.

VanDerveer, Tara, with Joan Ryan. *Shooting from the Outside: How a Coach and Her Olympic Team Transformed Women's Basketball.* New York: Avon Books, 1997.

*A*BOUT THE AUTHORS

*M*ARIAH *B*URTON *N*ELSON, a former Stanford and professional basketball player, is a public speaker and the author of *Are We Winning Yet?* (Random House, 1991), *The Stronger Women Get, The More Men Love Football* (Avon, 1995), and *Embracing Victory, Life Lessons in Competition and Compassion* (Morrow, 1998). She lives in Arlington, Virginia.

*K*ATHLEEN *M*C*E*LROY is an editor at *The New York Times*. Born in Texas to a sports-loving mother and a sportswriter and journalism professor father, she has written about and edited sports for more than fifteen years. Her birth was even announced in *The Houston Post*'s sports section. She now lives in Forest Hills, Queens.

*A*MY ELLIS NUTT is a features writer at *The Star-Ledger* in Newark, New Jersey. Formerly a writer-reporter at *Sports Illustrated,* she covered everything from golf to sailing to the history of sports. She has won two national awards, one in column writing from the Women's Sports Foundation, and another for best magazine news story from the Golf Writers Association of America. In May, her first book, *A Good Swing is Hard to Find* coauthored with LPGA star Helen Alfredsson, was published by Doubleday. She lives in Bridgewater, New Jersey.

*G*RACE *L*ICHTENSTEIN, a former *New York Times* reporter and bureau chief and former Executive Editor of *World Tennis,* is the author of *A Long Way Baby, Behind the Scenes in Women's Pro Tennis,* as well as five other books. She has been a regular contributor on tennis and other subjects to such publications as *The New York Times Magazine, Vogue, Ms., Rolling Stone,* the *Los*

Angeles Times, and the *Washington Post.* A native New Yorker, she lives in Manhattan.

MELANIE HAUSER has been covering golf, the NFL, professional, amateur, and college sports on the national level in the southwest for twenty-three years. She spent twenty years in newspapers and now writes for *Golf World, Golf Digest, Sports Illustrated, Golf Magazine, The New York Times,* the *Washington Post,* the *Boston Globe, Business Week, Golf Journal,* and *Golf for Women.* She is a columnist for Golf Web. Her first book, *Under the Lone Star Flagstick,* was published in 1997 by Simon & Schuster. She lives in Houston, Texas.

ANNA SEATON HUNTINGTON is a contributing writer for *The New York Times, Glamour, Women's Sports & Fitness, Harper's Bazaar,* and *Human Resources.* She is the author of *Making Waves, The Inside Story of Managing and Motivating the First Women's Team to Compete for the America's Cup.* She sailed with the first all women's America's Cup team, America³, and was a two-time member of the U.S. Olympic rowing team in 1988 and 1992, winning a bronze in the women's pair in 1992. She lives in Albany, California.

JEAN WEISS, the former senior editor of *Women's Sports & Fitness* magazine, has skied since 1967. Though she enjoys Alpine, Nordic, and snowboarding, telemark is her favorite. She lives in Boulder, Colorado.

MICHELLE KAUFMAN, thirty-three, is a sportswriter for the *Miami Herald* and worked previously at the *Detroit Free Press* and *St. Petersburg Times.* Though she cannot land a triple axel (or a single axel, for that matter), she has been covering figure skating for nine years. She covered the winter and summer Olympics in 1992, 1994, 1996, and 1998. In between, she writes stories and columns about basketball, football, baseball, and soccer. She has won numerous writing awards from the Associated Press Sports Editors association. She lives in Miami, Florida.

KAREN KARBO is the author of two novels, *The Diamond Lane* and *Trespassers Welcome Here,* each of which was named a *New York Times* Notable Book of the Year. Her nonfiction has appeared in *Vogue, Esquire, Entertainment Weekly,* and *The New Republic.* Her story for *Outside* on the America's Cup All-Women's crew was anthologized in *The Best American Sports Writing of 1996.* She is a contributing editor at *Conde Nast Sports for Women* and recently coauthored, with Gabrielle Reece, *Big Girl in the Middle.* She lives in Portland, Oregon.

JACKIE BURKE is the author of two horse-related books, including *Equal to the Challenge, Pioneering Women in Horse Sports.* With a journalism degree from MTSU, she has written for such publications as the *Nashville Banner, The Review Appeal* (Tennessee), and a long list of horse, sailing, and general interest magazines. She is the mother of two daughters with steeplechase riders' licenses, and has held a license of her own for steeplechase training and horse show judging. She lives, writes, and rides in the Virginia Hunt Country.

JANE LEAVY, a novelist and sportswriter, is the author of *Squeeze Play,* and a contributor to many other collections, including *Diamonds Are a Girl's Best Friend, Best Sports Stories,* and *Child of Mine.* A former staff sportswriter at the *Washington Post,* she has written most recently for the *New York Times,* the *Washington Post,* and *Sports Illustrated.* She lives in Washington, D.C., with her husband and two children.

ELISE PETTUS has written for *The New York Times, New York* magazine, and *Conde Nast Sports for Women* on subjects ranging from surfers to research scientists. A graduate of Brown University and Columbia School of Journalism, lives in New York City.

BARBARA STEWART is a freelance writer living in Victoria, British Columbia. She is the author of two books on women in sports, including *She Shoots . . . She Scores! A Complete Guide to Women's Hockey,* and contributes to several Canadian publications, notably *Hockey Illustrated.* She is a regular contributor to CBC Radio's Basic Black and Inside Sports, and has worked in editorial at HarperCollins. She is currently researching women's history of Canada.

SHELLEY SMITH is a journalist with ESPN who won a sports Emmy in 1997 for a piece on Magic Johnson. She worked for *Sports Illustrated* as a writer for eight years covering super bowls, NHL, NBA, golf, and tennis, among other sports. She is the author of *Just Give Me the Damn Ball* with New York Jets player Keyshawn Johnson in 1997 and is currently writing *Games Girls Play,* with sports psychologist Caroline Silby. She lives in San Pedro, California.

LUCY DANZIGER is editor-in-chief of *Women's Sports & Fitness* magazine. She has been a writer and editor for magazines and newspapers for sixteen years, having written and edited for *The New York Times, Allure, Manhattan Inc., New York* magazine, and other mainstream publications. She graduated from Harvard University and now lives in New York City.

$\mathcal{P}$HOTO CREDITS

Skiing
Gretchen Fraser, 1947, AP Wide World Photos
Suzy Chaffee, 1977, AP Wide World Photos
Picabo Street, 1998, AP Photo/Diether Endlicher

Figure Skating
Sonja Henie, 1936, AP Wide World Photos
Peggy Fleming, 1968, AP Photo/file
Michelle Kwan, 1997, AP Photo/Andrew Vaughan

Swimming
Gertrude Ederle, 1926, Corbis-Bettman
Aquacade, 1939, Corbis-Bettman
Janet Evans, 1988/AP Wide World Photos

Equestrian Sports
Mrs. Fletcher Harper, Courtesy of Jennifer Youngman
Kathy Kusner, Courtesy of Kathy Kusner
Blythe Miller, Chip Miller, Courtesy of Douglas Lees

Gymnastics
Nadia Comaneci, 1976, Archive Photos
Mary Lou Retton, 1984, AP Wide World Photos
Kerri Strug, 1996, AP Wide World Photos

Soccer
Michelle Akers, Jon Hayt/Reuters
Members of the U.S. Olympic Soccer Team, 1996,
AP Photo/Michael Lipchitz
Mia Hamm, AP Photo/Chris O'Meara

Ice Hockey
Manon Rheume, AP Photo
Catherine Granato, AP Photo/Kevork Djansezian
Members of the U.S. Olympic Hockey Team, 1998, Corbis-Bettman

Basketball
Lambert/Archive Photos
Cheryl Miller, 1984, AP Wide World Photos
Rebecca Lobo, Lisa Leslie, Theresa Weatherspoon, 1997, AP Photo/
Emile Wansteker

GRATEFUL
ACKNOWLEDGMENTS . . .

. . . to all the women whose lives make up this book, and all the women who played before me, paving the way for the little girls who will play long after me.

. . . to the fifteen contributors who wrote these stories down: to Kathleen for her countless drafts, to Grace for her early commitment, to Jackie and Barbara for their late arrival, to Elise for defeating morning sickness, to Karen for balancing weddings and projects, to Amy and Jane for their friendship and conversation, to Anna for living it, to Mariah for studying it, to Melanie, Michelle, Shelley, and Jean for reporting it, and to Lucy for her magazine; to their spouses, children, and employers for leasing them to me.

. . . to all the people who were fundamental to the making of this book: to my father for moonlighting as publicity and marketing coordinator, to my mother for her editing and writing on the horse piece as well as her unfailing encouragement, to Susan for the time line, to Alice for the title, to Granny and G'ma for the cab money home, to Michael for taking me to see it live in Nagano, to Muriel and Michael for keeping me on schedule, to Charles and Patrick for their work on the cover, to Judy for pitching it, to Miwa for getting it out, to my bosses who saw that this idea had potential, to Sarah and Kevin for their work on the hockey piece, to Jill for her copyediting, to Sandy, Karen, Irby, Joan, Sid, and all those who gave me names and contacts to get me going, to Lisa for her piece, to Rebecca for the first outside read, to Diann for her two-minute messages, to George for the sushi, to Lauren for her cards and flowers, to Tina for her pep talks, to my roommates/teammates, past and present, who waited up and woke me up, sent clips and cards, and to my coaches of old, Inman, Turnbull, Russ, and Shepperd.

. . . to my coach, teammate, trainer, and cheerleader on the project, Anton.